For the three women who have taught me the truly important lessons in life:

My mother, Carol Joan McLeod (1937-1990), from whom I learned to love learning

My grandmother, Marjorie Pauline McLeod (1915-1996), from whom I learned to love the past

and

My wife, Mousumee Dutta, from whom I have learned to love humanity

NATURAL JUSTICE AND THE HIGH COURT OF AUSTRALIA

Natural Justice and the High Court of Australia

A study in common law constitutionalism

IAN HOLLOWAY
Professor and Dean of Law,
The University of Western Ontario
Barrister and Solicitor of the
Supreme Court of Nova Scotia

Ashgate

Published by
Ashgate Publishing Limited
Gower House
Croft Road
Aldershot
Hampshire GU11 3HR
England

Ashgate Publishing Company
131 Main Street
Burlington, VT 05401-5600 USA

Ashgate website: http://www.ashgate.com

British Library Cataloguing in Publication Data
Holloway, Ian
Natural justice and the High Court of Australia : a study in common law constitutionalism
1. Justice, Administration of - Australia 2. Common law - Australia 3. Constituational law - Australia
I.Title
342.9'4

Library of Congress Control Number: 2001098448

ISBN 0 7546 2218 5

Printed and bound by Athenaeum Press, Ltd.,
Gateshead, Tyne & Wear.

Contents

Preface

I once heard it said that the road to completion of a book is the most humbling of journeys, for it requires one to lay bare to all the world one's limitations and imperfections. In the course of writing this work, the truth of this statement has become more evident to me than in my vanity I might have cared to think. There are many people to whom I owe debts of gratitude – both intellectual and emotional – which must be acknowledged if I am to feel that my journey is really ended.

First, I would like to acknowledge the assistance of Professor John McMillan, my former colleague at the Australian National University. For the most part, this work was completed while I was employed full-time at the ANU. It has therefore been characterised by a series of fits and starts over a number of years. Had it not been for a combination of John's wisdom, kindness, graciousness, patience and encouragement, I would not be in the position of writing these acknowledgments today. John is a scholar and gentleman of the old school, and the academic world is a poorer place for not having more like him. If Australia is ever really to become the clever country, the academy will first have to adjust its priorities so as once more to cultivate people like him.

I also want to make reference to the assistance and support given me by several of my colleagues. I happen to have been blessed to work in a real community of scholars at the ANU, and I have no doubt that whatever quality there may be in this work owes all to the influence and example of my colleagues. My thanks go to all of my former colleagues, but I hope that I might be forgiven if I single out a few for particular mention: Robin Creyke (who was the very first person I met in Canberra, and with whom I came to enjoy a particularly happy teaching relationship in administrative law), Professor Leslie Zines (who so kindly took the time to initiate a recent migrant into the 'personality' of Australian public law), Fiona Wheeler (who always made time for my questions about the Constitution – and who I consider to be among the best public law scholars in Australia today), Adrienne Stone (who, with her appointment to the ANU in 1997, added a wonderful breath of life and energy to the public law area in Australia), Simon Bronitt (who has, for many years now, proven to be a bastion of friendship and support) and – not least of all – John Williams (now of the University of Adelaide, but a Doctor of Philosophy of the Australian National University, whose research has served as a tremendous inspiration for my own work).

I would like to make special mention of Peter Bayne. Peter has an unrivalled breadth of legal knowledge, and in my opinion there is no one who studies administrative law in Australia today who does not owe a special debt to Peter's scholarship. In my own case, while this project has changed shape considerably since the beginning, it still bears the marks of his scholarly influence, and I want publicly to express my thanks to him for all that he has done for me. I also want to acknowledge that my avenue of enquiry in this work was suggested by one of Peter's pieces in the *Australian Law Journal*, 'The Common Law Basis of Judicial Review'.

Much of the actual writing of this book was done while I was on sabbatical leave in the University of Cambridge. I would accordingly like to express my appreciation to Professor Sir David Williams QC (who encouraged me to apply for a visiting Scholarship, and who graciously acted as a host during my stay in England), Dr Gordon Johnson, the President of Wolfson College, and the Fellows of Wolfson College (for having made me feel so welcome during the term of my Scholarship), and Professor Kevin Gray and the members of the Faculty of Law (for having treated me so collegially as a member of Faculty during my stay). While speaking of my time in Cambridge, I want also to mention Mr Justice Bryan Beaumont, of the Federal Court of Australia. Mr Justice Beaumont was also on leave at Wolfson College during my time there, and I had the exceedingly pleasant and supportive experience of being befriended by both him and his wife, Jeanette.

I expect that more law graduates than we teachers would care to admit would say similar things, but my experience as an undergraduate student of administrative law was not a fulfilling one. I left the course with only a very hazy sense of the law, and an even more hazy sense of the role that judicial review played in the constitution. It was not until I started to work as an articled clerk that I began to actually understand the process – and constitutional significance – of judicial control of administrative action. I therefore would be remiss if I did not acknowledge the role played in my education by my three mentors, first as a clerk, then as a colleague, at the wonderful old Nova Scotian law firm of McInnes, Cooper and Robertson: Eric Durnford QC, Peter McLellan QC and Brian Johnston QC. In 1992-1993, I also had the privilege of serving as Law Clerk to the Honourable Julius Isaac, Chief Justice of the Federal Court of Canada. It was from Chief Justice Isaac that I first began really to appreciate the process of judicial review from a judicial perspective, something which has stood me in useful stead ever since. I hope that the Chief Justice might see a little bit of himself in this work.

I want as well to express my gratitude to Ms Nanette Love for all of her assistance in preparing the manuscript for publication, and to my research assistants, Ms Jennifer White and Ms Tracey Cronin, for their meticulous help in readying the project for its final form.

Finally, I want to express my deepest thanks of all to my wife, Mousumee Dutta. Had it not been for her love, care and support, this would not have happened.

> *I shall ever try to keep all untruths out*
> *from my thoughts, knowing that thou art*
> *that truth which has kindled the light of*
> *reason in my mind.*
>
> *I shall ever try to drive all evils away*
> *from my heart and keep my love in flower,*
> *knowing that thou hast thy seat in the*
> *inmost shrine of my heart.*
>
> *And it shall be my endeavour to reveal*
> *thee in my actions, knowing it is thy power*
> *gives me strength to act.*
>
> *R Tagore, 1912*

I have tried to describe the law as it stood in mid-1999, but I would note that a pair of recent judgments of the High Court suggest that the issues discussed remain live ones. Both *Re Refugee Review Tribunal; Ex parte Aala* (2000) 176 ALR 219 and *Re Minister for Immigration and Multicultural Affairs; Ex parte Miah* (2001) 179 ALR 237 confirm that the juridical basis for the imposition of a duty to observe nature justice remains unsettled. Moreover, though the cases were dealing with constitutional law in the formal sense, the judgments do not hint at any lessening of the doctrine's robustness in the Australian setting.

The University of Western Ontario
London
July, 2001

Table of Cases

B

D

G

H

I

M

Table of Legislation

Imperial

Commonwealth

New South Wales

Queensland

South Australia

Tasmania

Victoria

Western Australia

Northern Territory

Norfolk Island

English and United Kingdom

Ceylon

New Zealand

Trinidad and Tobago

Treaties and International Conventions

Introduction: Natural Justice and Theories of the State

Broadly speaking, administrative law concerns two themes: power and ambivalence.

Over the past century or so we have come to expect the state to play an active part in our day-to-day lives; to provide us with succour if we are sick, or poor, or unemployed. The problem, though, is that we have not surrendered the instinctive yearning for autonomy that had been groomed in our ancestors over the course of several centuries, and which had come to be entrenched in the form of liberal ideal. Thus the theme of ambivalence. We want the state to do things which we feel will make our lives better, but we are reluctant to cede to it the tools that it thinks it needs to do the job: the discretions to coerce and categorise, to lump us in with others, and to treat us as members of classes rather than as individuals.

The accompanying theme of power emerges when it comes to reconciling the push and pull that stems from our ambivalence. Central to every administrative law case is tension among the branches of government. Administrative law litigation has at its base a conflict over power – over whether the executive has the power under law to take a course of action which it has chosen and which one of us disputes.

But if the theme of ambivalence lies within us, the theme of power is rooted in the constitution. It is trite, but the modifying clause, 'under law', in the penultimate sentence is the critical one, for it means that the dynamics of dispute resolution in administrative law cases are legal, rather than political. The disputes themselves may be a consequence of political choice but, given our conception of the rule of law as enshrining the judge as the ultimate interpreter of law and legality, it is the nature of judicial predisposition – the inherited instincts, traditional beliefs and acquired convictions of the bench, to borrow Cardozo's words[1] – that in the end plays the determinative role in setting the parameters by which our ambivalence is to be reconciled. And, as Dicey reminded us,[2] the source of

---

[1] *The Nature of the Judicial Process* (1921), at 12.
[2] *The Law of the Constitution* (8th ed. 1915), at 191:

our evolving *corpus* of public law is the ordinary adjudicative work of the courts. It is because of this that judicial review of administrative action is properly conceived of as an exercise in constitutional adjudication.[3]

It was for that reason that in their book, *Law and Administration*,[4] Harlow and Rawlings began famously with the observation that underlying every theory of administrative law, there is a theory of the state.[5] T R S Allan was making the same point when he said that public law, rationally construed, is an exercise in political theory.[6] The concern of this work is with one aspect of Australian public law *cum* political theory: the doctrine of natural justice, or procedural fairness as it is sometimes referred to, as it has been developed over the decades by the High Court of Australia. Simply stated, the object is to examine the High Court's evolving holdings in natural justice cases and to explore the theories of the state which have been embodied in them.

The Hypothesis: Natural Justice and Foundational Law

Natural justice has been described as 'fair play in action',[7] and 'fairness writ large and juridically'.[8] But perhaps a more vivid way of putting it is to say, as Aronson and Dyer have, that along with the rest of administrative law, natural justice is concerned with the 'civilising' of government discretion.[9] Natural justice is, Aronson and Dyer have written, 'a principle of common sense and common decency'.[10] In this sense, natural justice might be seen as the quintessential Australian legal doctrine, for it is at

---

> We may say that the constitution is pervaded by the rule of law on the ground that the general principles of the constitution ... are with us the result of judicial decisions determining the rights of private persons in particular cases brought before the courts.

I should note that I shall refer in the main to the 8th ed. of *The Law of the Constitution*, for that is the last that Dicey edited himself. The 8th ed. has a lengthy introduction, and at pp xxxvii-xlviii, Dicey set out his refined thoughts on the perils of the growth of the administrative state. It accordingly contains Dicey's own last word on the place of administrative law in the common law system.

[3] See T R S Allan, 'The Common Law as Constitution: Fundamental Rights and First Principles', in C Saunders (ed), *Courts of Final Jurisdiction: The Mason Court in Australia* (1996) 146, at 148.

[4] (1984).

[5] At 1.

[6] *Supra*, n 3.

[7] Harman LJ, in *Ridge v Baldwin* [1963] 1 QB 539 (CA), at 578.

[8] Lord Morris, in *Furnell v Whangerei Schools Board* [1973] AC 660, at 679.

[9] M Aronson and B Dyer, *Judicial Review of Administrative Action* (1996), at 124.

[10] *Id*, at 385.

base a legal formula for the 'fair go'. One aspect of this work is to consider this – to examine the way in which natural justice has been employed by the High Court as a means of redressing governmental unfairness.

In this respect there are, as will be seen in the chapters which follow, three major natural justice issues which have emerged in the High Court in recent years: *why* natural justice can be said by the courts to apply, even in the face of parliamentary silence on the question (*ie*, the doctrinal basis of natural justice); *when* natural justice applies (*ie*, the range of interests protected by natural justice); and *to whom* natural justice extends (*ie*, the range of actors on whom the courts will impose natural justice obligations). Each of these issues will be examined in depth (in chapters seven, five and six, respectively), but my interest in the doctrine of natural justice runs also at a deeper level.

In my view, natural justice is a matter of interest precisely because judicial review is an exercise in constitutionalism. Administrative law doctrine is traditionally thought to be rooted in the Whiggish values of the Glorious Revolution. The doctrines of *ultra vires*, and of jurisdictional control generally, are premised on the twin foundations of the separation of powers and the sovereignty of parliament, both of which established themselves in our legal discourse as a result of the constitutional tumult of the seventeenth century. Yet a reading of today's cases makes it clear that the courts regularly act in such a way as to show that the doctrine of parliamentary sovereignty only goes so far. Quite apart from overt constitutional limitations on legislative power in Australia, the substance of the holdings in the recent natural justice cases in the High Court leads to the observation that the notion of legislative paramountcy has become partially fictionalised in this country, and that it is limited by vaguely-defined and subjectively-interpreted, yet clearly authoritative, notions of 'foundational' justice. This work is largely concerned with the exploration of this development – what one might describe as the transition from a *lex* to a *jus* of the doctrine of natural justice.

Therein, in my contention, lies the real academic fascination with the doctrine of natural justice. The cases which will be examined show that in recent years, the High Court has formulated the compass of natural justice in extremely broad terms. Briefly to foreshadow the analysis, the High Court has come to eschew the conventional understanding of the basis of judicial review – rooted, as has been said, in the twin foundations of the separation of powers and the supremacy of parliament. Instead, the Court has said that *the common law*, rather than assumptions or presumptions about parliamentary intent, is the basis for the imposition of the duty to observe natural justice.

To this extent, the High Court has been enunciating a doctrine of natural justice that retains an element of 'naturalness', and connection with its historical roots. But the cases demand the question: what theory of the constitution is implicit in such a view of natural justice? To state it in Harlow's and Rawlings's terms, which constitutional philosophy inheres in a view which enshrines the common law, rather than legislation, as the source of procedural rights against the state? The Court's holdings in the recent natural justice cases seem to signify a return to an older constitution; one in which the law, rather than sovereignty of the parliament, lies at the foundation of the constitutional order. But at the same time, the Court has explicitly denied the existence in Australia of the historical foundation by which such a constitution could exist. My argument is that a dissonance has come to characterise the High Court's public law discourse, which needs to be resolved if the rule of law is not to suffer damage.

A second argument which will be made is that notwithstanding the broad phrasing of the reach of natural justice, the High Court has largely failed to anchor the doctrine by reference to any legal or social purpose. We are said to have a purposive constitution, yet it is difficult to see what purpose the High Court sees the doctrine of natural justice performing, except in vague and shapeless terms. As will be seen in the chapters to follow, the trigger for the doctrine has come to be expressed so broadly that natural justice now exists in the High Court in an inchoate, reactive form. It is my contention that if it is to become a useful tool to protect individual interests in the new governmental and administrative environment, the Court must be more definite in explaining what objects the observance of procedural fairness is intended to serve.

The Plan of the Work

This book consists of eight chapters, in addition to this Introduction. The first chapter considers the idea of 'natural' justice. This includes a review of the doctrine's historical roots, as well as its place in the ancient constitution. Chapter one will also consider the impact on the early administrative law of the constitutional revolution which began in England in 1688. Among other things, my argument is that if it is considered more broadly as a revolution in thinking about government, the Glorious Revolution was not in fact completed until the latter part of the nineteenth century. The point will also be made that though it was English in genesis, the values inherent in the constitutional revolution were transmitted throughout the settled parts of the Empire, and came to form part of the legal fabric in the Australian colonies.

Chapters two through four deal with the actual evolution of natural justice through this century, up to the early 1970s. This was the period of maturation for administrative law, and the period during which it came to be acknowledged by common lawyers as a body of 'real' law. It was also a time of protracted political conflict between the judiciary and the executive about the nature of government and, more specifically, about the extent of the legal power of the executive to engage in collective enterprise and enforced wealth distribution. For the reasons discussed earlier, much of this conflict found itself channelled into the courts. The chief focus of these three chapters will be this conflict as it was manifested judicially, but an integral part of the discussion will involve a consideration of the academic debate that took place in the middle decades of the century about the role of the central government in the modern state. To anticipate the substance of the chapters, the picture which emerges is, among other things, one of an Australian doctrine of natural justice which was theoretically stunted when compared with its English counterpart.

The specific subject of chapter two is the emergence in the first half of this century of the 'planned state', and the challenges that that posed to the understandings and assumptions of the ancient constitution. It was during this period that hints of a divergence of view among judges about the place of the common law doctrine of natural justice came to be seen. Some judges – notably Griffith CJ in the Australian setting – continued to view natural justice in 'ancient' terms. Others, including Isaacs and Higgins JJ, indicated an awareness of the changes in the day-to-day workings of the constitution and began to enunciate a view of natural justice which attempted to reconcile common law values with a new style of governance in which considerable discretionary power was vested in the executive.

Chapter three deals with the post-War period – roughly from 1945 to the late 1950s. During this period, the divergence in judicial attitude continued, but now it manifested itself in national terms, in the form of a cleavage in approach between the High Court in this country and the House of Lords in England. Sir William Wade has described this period in England as the 'twilight' of natural justice.[11] It was a time during which the English courts seemed to renounce natural justice's ancient constitutional foundation, and to reduce common law procedural rights to a

[11] 'The Twilight of Natural Justice?' (1951) 67 *LQR* 103.

highly structured, yet effectively neutered, shell. In Australia, in contrast, natural justice reverted during much of this period to a distinctly *un*-structured form. The High Court's holdings in natural justice cases between the end of the Second World War and the latter part of the 1950s enunciated a doctrine that was, compared to its English counterpart, largely unconstrained by technicality. It was only at the very end of the 1950s, as the twilight period was coming to an end in England, that an Australian version of 'twilightism' came to appear.

Chapter four is concerned with natural justice in the 1960s and early 1970s – the era when natural justice began a renaissance which has continued unabated to this day. What characterised this revival in both Australia and England was a new willingness in the law to recognise things other than legal rights as being deserving of procedural protection. Chapter four will also set the scene for the second half of the book: chapters five through eight. There, I shift my attention to the present, to consider the recent developments in the Australian law of natural justice, as set out in the judgments of the High Court in the Barwick, Gibbs and Mason eras.

Chapter five deals with the idea of the 'legitimate expectation', whereby natural justice can be triggered to protect not just legal rights or entitlements, but also the *expectation* of entitlements. As will be seen, it is the legitimate expectation which has acted as the driving force behind the evolution of natural justice in Australia in the past twenty-five years. Chapter six examines the process by which the High Court has extended the reach of natural justice (and judicial review generally) to cover not just the administration *per se*, but also the Cabinet and the Crown – entities which, until relatively recently, were thought to be largely immune from the reach of judicially imposed procedural values.

Chapter seven looks at the process by which the High Court has in recent years renounced the need to rely on presumptions about legislative intent as the basis for judicial review and for the imposition of natural justice obligations. It is this feature, more than anything, which leads one to the observation that the High Court's holdings on natural justice have implicit in them the terms of an alternate, yet unarticulated, constitutional settlement. This, in turn, leads to chapter eight, where it will be argued that the theory of the state implicit in the High Court's recent holdings is an inconsistent one, which requires refinement if natural justice is to survive as a useful tool into the future.

It is appropriate to say at this stage that much of the discussion of Australian legal developments will consist of their juxtaposition against contemporary events in England. In this day and age, such an approach might otherwise be open to criticism, particularly given that comparatively little attention is devoted to the judgments of Australian courts other than the High Court. Nevertheless, the approach is defended in the present context on two bases. First, throughout much of the period with which this book is concerned Australia still considered itself very much a British country, and British legal and political thought had an important impact on Australian law and politics. As Geoffrey Sawer once noted, much of the inspiration to reform administrative law in Australia, especially with respect to first principles, has come from England.[12] The point is that it is impossible to understand the evolution of the High Court's vision of Australian public law without a good historical sense of the law as it evolved in England during the same period.

Secondly, it will be one of my arguments that the doctrine of natural justice has suffered in this country as a result of its under-theorisation as an element of constitutional law. To make such an argument, a comparator is needed. So while the focus of this thesis is on the evolution of the Australian version of the doctrine of natural justice, a good deal of the discussion necessarily will involve consideration of English developments.

A Word About Usage

As may have become evident already, I am using the expressions 'natural justice' and 'procedural fairness' more-or-less interchangeably. In fact, as will be discussed in chapter six, there was for a time in the 1970s a spirited debate about whether the two expressions represented different legal concepts. Moreover, there are some who think that the term natural justice ought not to be used any longer on the grounds that it is misleading. Lord Roskill, for instance, once said that the expression 'natural justice' is 'no doubt hallowed by time and much judicial repetition, but it is a phrase often widely misunderstood and therefore as often misused. The phrase perhaps might now be allowed to find a permanent resting place and be better replaced by speaking of a duty to act fairly.'[13]

There are others who acknowledge that the two expressions may be synonyms, but who say that procedural fairness should be the preferred expression because it is flexible and does not carry with it any of the emotive or legalistic baggage associated with the older term 'natural justice'. Sir Anthony Mason, for example, once said that 'the expression

[12] *Ombudsmen* (1964), at 23-24.

[13] *Council of Civil Service Unions v Minister for the Civil Service* (the '*GCHQ Case*') [1985] AC 374, at 414.

"procedural fairness" more aptly conveys the notion of a flexible obligation to adopt fair procedures which are appropriate and adapted to the circumstances of the particular case'.[14]

Sir Robert Megarry made this same point with characteristic humour, when he said: 'justice is far from being a "natural" concept – the closer one gets to a state of nature, the less justice does one find'.[15] Less jocularly, Ormrod LJ once said that 'the romantic word "natural"' served little purpose except to couch the proceedings with an air of nostalgia.[16] In my view, however, 'natural justice' is the more appropriate general term for the doctrine, at least in the Australian setting, precisely *because of* the ancient baggage. As has been suggested, and for reasons which will become apparent in the chapters to follow, I am of the opinion that the terms of the constitutional vision implicit in the recent natural justice cases embody an attempt to return to ancient constitutional understandings.[17]

Natural Justice or Judicial Review?

The reader will also note that parts of this work deal not with the law of natural justice strictly speaking, but with the law of judicial review more generally. Indeed, in some sections discussion shifts back and forth between the two almost reflexively. This is so for three reasons. First, many of the leading cases on natural justice are also leading cases on judicial review. Many of the cases discussed in chapter six, for example – concerning the application of a duty to observe natural justice on the Crown and Cabinet – fall within this class. Secondly, two of the cases which, for many years, were treated as leading authorities on natural justice (*Board of Education v Rice*[18] and *R v Electricity Commissioners, Ex parte London Electricity Joint Committee*[19]), in fact dealt with the question of

---

[14] *Kioa v West* (1985) 159 CLR 550, at 585. More pointedly, in *Local Government Board v Arlidge* [1915] AC 120, at 138, Lord Shaw said:

> In so far as the term 'natural justice' means that a result or process should be just, it is a harmless though it may be a high-sounding expression; in so far as it attempts to reflect the old *jus naturale* it is a confused and unwarranted transfer into the ethical sphere of a term employed for other distinctions; and, in so far as it is resorted to for other purposes, it is vacuous.

[15] *McInnes v Onslow-Fane* [1978] 1 WLR1520, at 1530.

[16] *Norwest Holst Ltd v Secretary of State for Trade* [1978] Ch 221, at 226.

[17] Moreover, it is an expression still found in Australian legislation. See, *eg*, the *Administrative Decisions (Judicial Review) Act 1977* (Cth), para 5(1)(a).

[18] [1911] AC 179.

[19] [1924] 1 KB 171. Both of these cases are discussed in chapter two.

reviewability, not natural justice *stricto sensu*. Thirdly, as will be seen in chapter six, one of the important questions to be examined with respect to the scope of natural justice is whether the existence of a duty of fairness necessarily implies that the courts must have jurisdiction to enforce it. There have been some in Australia, including Lionel Murphy, who have expressed the opinion that natural justice can exist as a parliamentary duty as well as a legal duty. But in the eyes of the majority of the Court, the question of the existence of a duty to observe the rules of natural justice necessarily presupposes the existence of a justiciable issue.

In sum, what follows is an attempt to contribute to the better understanding of the evolution of our system of public law in Australia.

1 The Idea of 'Natural' Justice

Antiquity is something that we tend to value highly in the common law. Radical reformers may decry it, but in the common law scheme of doing things, change is almost always justified, at least in part, by demonstrating that it enjoys the sanction of the past. This is because as a precedent-based system, the common law represents an inherently conservative scheme of social ordering. The yardstick against which the propriety of present conduct is measured is always the past – in the form of previously-decided cases.

To dwell for a moment on this point of first principle, the precedents that we apply in common law adjudication are evidence of the derivative nature of today's law. Precedent represents a connection with the law as it was understood by our grandparents, and by their grandparents before them. John Wisdom may have been correct in asserting that the process of reasoning in the common law resembles the legs of a chair, together supporting a premise, rather than the links in a chain leading logically to one.[1] But the commencement point for any systemic evaluation about the Australian legal system must be the observation that the legs which we use to construct *today's* chairs of legal reasoning are ones which are made from wood which grew in the English forests in the time of the Angevins and the Tudors.

Antiquity and Change in Public Law

This is as much the case with respect to reasoning in public law as in any other area of the common law. So it was, for example, that in *Commissioner of Police v Tanos*, a case from the 1950s dealing with proceedings under public morals legislation, Dixon CJ and Webb J thought it necessary to draw upon authority dating from the time of Queen Elizabeth I,[2] and to make note of the classical foundations of the idea of

---

[1] 'Gods', Chapter X, in *Philosophy and Psychoanalysis* (1964), at 157-158.

[2] (1958) 98 CLR 383, at 395 (referring to *Boswel's Case* (1583) 6 Co Rep 48b, 77 ER 326).

fairness in administrative decision-making.[3] It was likewise that the Kerr Committee – whose task was to lay out the framework for a 'new' Australian administrative law – felt it appropriate to premise its recommendation that a right to procedural fairness be enshrined on the basis that the doctrine of natural justice had existed in the common law for several centuries.[4]

Even in the case of an 'activist' judge, who claims to be making change to public law doctrine in order to bring it into line with present-day conditions, the change will invariably be justified by reference to public policy, underlying principles, foundational values, or some like thing. Dworkin once wrote of what he called 'background rights', which he described as 'rights that provide a justification for political decisions by society in the abstract'.[5] In a similar vein, Dawn Oliver has written recently of public law's 'underlying values'.[6] But expressions like these are in fact codes for something which lies deeper in a desire for change. Such references – to policy, principle, or values – are almost always metaphors for a desire to recapture a balance in the relationship between law, morals and society that was thought to exist at some time in the past. To put it another way, a judicial activist is spurred to want to effect change in order to right an imbalance, and 'imbalance' is a relative description – generally used in our legal discourse to relate the present to the past.[7] It is

---

[3] 'The older authorities even recur to the lines from Seneca's *Medea ... Quicunque aliquid statuerit, parte inaudita altera, Aequum licet statuerit, haud aequus fuerit.*' (98 CLR, at 395-396).

[4] *Report of the Commonwealth Administrative Review Committee* (1971), para 39.

[5] *Taking Rights Seriously* (1978), at 93.

[6] See 'The Underlying Values of Public and Private Law', in M Taggart (ed), *The Province of Administrative Law* (1997), at 217, 'Common Values in Public and Private Law and the Public/Private Divide' [1997] *Pub L* 630.

[7] Consider, for example, the holding of the High Court in *Mabo v Queensland (No 2)* (1992) 175 CLR 1. At the time, it was widely heralded as instigating a 'legal revolution' (see, *eg*, the essays in M A Stephenson and S Ratnapala (eds), *Mabo: A Judicial Revolution* (1993)). Moreover, much of the criticism of the decision was founded on the belief that the judges of the High Court were inappropriately using present-day social values to judge historical facts (see, *eg*, the comments of Sir Harry Gibbs, *id*, at xiii). But the reality of the judgments arguably shows quite the opposite. One way to interpret the case is to say that the majority judgments reflect a desire simply to bring today's Australian law into conformity with western European philosophical values which have been in existence for hundreds of years. When Brennan J spoke in his judgment of the 'expectations of the international community', and the 'contemporary values of the Australian people' (175 CLR, at 42), for instance, he was implicitly drawing upon the authority of fundamental Judeo-Christian values, in an attempt to shame the positive law of Australia into accepting

for this reason that any discussion of the present-day Australian law of natural justice must begin in the England of several centuries ago.

Natural Justice and the Ancient Constitution

It is sometimes thought that we are not aware of the exact origins of the modern doctrine of natural justice. In fact, this is a bit of an oversimplification, for we *can* point with reasonable precision to the earliest judicial references to the two traditionally-accepted limbs of natural justice today: *audi alteram partem*[8] and *nemo judex in causa sua*.[9] Moreover, we know that natural justice has its foundation in a concept of rather broader reach – the notion of 'natural law'.

Natural law was probably the original English constitution. The idea that there were some things that one simply did not do – even if one were King – unless one wished to be condemned to suffer eternal damnation, was the first limit on the power of government. In its very earliest form, natural law may have been no more enforceable at law than a constitutional convention is today, but as between a ruler and his conscience, the law of God undoubtedly had some controlling force.[10] But leaving aside for the moment the extent to which the spiritual constitution provided much day-to-day benefit for the King's subjects, the courts over time came to view themselves as seized, as the King's agents, with

---

modification. It was in a similar spirit that Deane and Gaudron JJ felt constrained in *Mabo* to justify their proposal for change in the law by noting that the case before them was an extraordinary one. They seem to have felt decidedly uneasy being cast in the revolutionary role. 'If this were any ordinary case', they said, 'the Court would not be justified in reopening the validity of fundamental propositions which have been endorsed by long-established authority and which have been accepted as a basis of the real property law of the country for more than one hundred and fifty years' (175 CLR, at 109).

[8] *Bagg's Case* (1615) 11 Co Rep 93b, 77 ER 1271, is typically cited as the case which establishes the proposition, but H H Marshall noted that there are also several references to it in the Yearbooks. See *Natural Justice* (1959), at 18. For more on *Bagg's Case* and its significance, see E G Henderson, *The Foundations of English Administrative Law* (1963), at 46 *ff.*

[9] *The Earl of Derby's Case* (1613) 12 Co Rep 114, 77 ER 1390 (though Marshall noted several references to it in the Yearbooks as well. See *id*, at 16).

[10] Remembering, of course, that in the past, people used actually to believe Scripture. As Harold Laski put it, '[t]he decline of the traditional religious faiths into a polite ceremonial expressing a creed upon which most people do not dream of acting has been remarkable' (*Where Do We Go From Here? An Essay in Interpretation* (1940), at 25).

jurisdiction to apply natural law. In the formative period of the common law, natural law was used as a stop-gap, when there was no earthly law to apply. It was in this vein that Yelverton CJ once said:

> We shall do in this case as the canonists and civilians do where a new case comes up concerning which they have no existing law; then they resort to the law of nature which is the ground of all laws, and according to what they consider to be the most beneficial to the common wealth they do, and so also we shall do. If we are to make a positive law on this point we ought to see what is most necessary for the common weal and make our law accordingly.[11]

The early references to natural law point to something which is often overlooked in our discussions of the modern-day version of natural justice. This is that the doctrine arose as a part of a European, rather than solely English, legal tradition.[12] Maine argued that (notwithstanding Coke's characterisation in *Calvin's Case*), the expression 'natural law' as invoked by the courts most often referred in fact to principles of Roman law, rather than to a Hobbesian-type of law of nature or to an Aristotelian-based 'law of reason'. The practice of identifying the Roman law with the law of nature, he said in his lectures on international law, was an old practice, and it was done as a means of allowing Roman legal principle to be quoted and used in a country in which its authority was not recognised.[13]

Nevertheless, as a rhetorical device, at a time when the various organs of state were jockeying for power, reference to natural law understandably could prove to be quite effective. It is not at all surprising therefore to learn that Coke made liberal use of it. In *Calvin's Case*, for instance, he said:

> [T]he law of nature is part of the law of England ... [T]he law of nature was before any judicial or municipal law ... [T]he law of nature is immutable. The law of nature is that which God at the time of the creation of the nature of man infused into his heart, for his preservation and direction; and this is *lex æterna*, the moral law, called also the law of nature.[14]

---

[11] (1468) YB 8 Edw IV 21 (quoted in Marshall, *supra* n 8, at 7).

[12] For more on the notion of a 'Western' legal tradition, see P Parkinson, *Tradition and Change in Australian Law* (1994), chapter 2, and R C van Caenagem, *An Historical Introduction to Western Constitutional Law* (1995).

[13] H Maine, *International Law* (1888), Lecture 1, at 20-21.

[14] (1608) 7 Co Rep 1a, at 12b, 77 ER 377, at 391-392.

In a like way, Lord Mansfield made use of the concept as part of his project to modernise the customary law merchant and incorporate it into the common law. In *Moses v Macferlan*, he said: 'In one word, the gist of this kind of action is that the defendant, upon the circumstances of the case, is obliged by the ties of natural justice and equity to refund the money.'[15]

The high point of natural law in the common law system was undoubtedly the assertion that it could trump statute law.[16] When read in context, the famous passage in *Dr Bonham's Case*, that courts could declare void Acts of Parliament which were 'against common right and reason',[17] amounts to such a claim. But even more pointed in this respect was the judgment in 1614, in *Day v Savadge*, that 'an Act of Parliament made against natural equity, as to make a man judge in his own cause, is void in itself'.[18] In a similar way, Holt CJ once said that '[i]f an Act of Parliament should ordain that the same person should be party and judge, or, which is the same thing, judge in his own cause, it would be a void Act of Parliament; for it is impossible that one should be judge and party'.[19]

The sheer baldness of assertions like these was not to be seen again in English law after the seventeenth century.[20] Yet, the sentiment, and the

---

[15] (1760) 2 Burr 1005, at 1012, 97 ER 676, at 681.

[16] On this question, generally, see Sir F Pollock, *A First Book of Jurisprudence* (1929), at 265-271.

[17] (1610) 8 Co Rep 113b, at 118a, 77 ER 646, at 652.

[18] (1614) Hob 85, at 87, 80 ER 235, at 237.

[19] *City of London v Wood* (1702) Mod 669, at 687, 88 ER 1592, at 1602. He continued: '[A]n Act of Parliament can do no wrong, though it may do several things that look pretty odd.'

[20] Though it is worthwhile to note that Blackstone actually referred to the principle in one part of the *Commentaries*. He said that the law of nature 'is binding over all the globe, in all countries, and at all times; no human laws are of any validity, if contrary to this' (I *Comm* 41). And as late as 1824, in *Forbes v Cochrane* 2 B & C 448, at 469-470, 107 ER 450, at 458-459, Best J suggested that in the case of slavery, natural law might still trump parliamentary law. After referring to two West Indian statutes which permitted the sale of slaves, he said:

> Both these statutes, however, were local in their application being confined to the West India Islands only. I do not, therefore, feel myself fettered by anything expressed in either of them ... If indeed there had been any express law commanding us to recognise those rights we might then have been called upon to consider the propriety of that which has been said by the great commentator upon the laws of this country: 'That if any human law should allow or injoin us to commit an offence against the divine law we are bound to transgress that human law' ... We have the authority of the civil law for saying that slavery is against the rights of nature.

confidence with which it was expressed, remain significant, for they provide evidence of the comparative antiquity of today's law. Simply put, any notion that 'activist' judges in the field of judicial review are a recent phenomenon is a false one. Moreover, the old cases also highlight the fact that the ancient law of judicial review is rooted in the constitution – in a mechanism for limiting the power of what we would now know as the legislative and executive branches of government.

At the same time, though, it should be recognised that the notion of natural law was somewhat different from the rather more limited doctrine of natural justice as we understand it today. Marshall claimed that it was not until the latter half of the last century that the bias and hearing rules came to be referred to together under the umbrella of natural justice.[21] In fact, there were references in positive law to what we would understand today to be the bias rule as early as the thirteenth century, in both *Magna Carta* and the *Provisions of Oxford*.[22] Whatever the case, the fact is that together or separately, both limbs of the doctrine became firmly entrenched as principles of constitutional adjudication (to use T R S Allan's characterisation[23]) during the seventeenth, eighteenth and early nineteenth centuries. In this respect, the judgments in *Day v Savadge* and its successors are important in that they provide among the earliest examples of the link between natural law (though it was described in *Day v Savadge* as 'natural equity') and the bias rule. The link was well-encapsulated by Holt CJ, when he said in *City of London v Wood*:

> It is against all laws that the same person should be party and judge in the same cause, for it is a manifest contradiction; for the party is he that is to complain to the judge and the judge is to hear the party; the party endeavours to have his will, the judge determines against the will of the party and has the

[21] He dated it to *Spackman v Plumstead Board of Works* (1885) 10 App Cas 229 (*supra* n 8, at 15-16).

[22] See, *eg*, the 1215 version of *Magna Carta*, arts 24 ('No sheriff, constable, coroner or other bailiff of ours shall hold pleas of our crown') and 40 ('To no one will we sell, to no one will we deny or delay right or justice'). Similarly, the *Provisions of Oxford* (1258) ordained that 'justices shall accept nothing unless it is a present of bread and wine and like things ... as have been customarily brought for the day to the tables of the chief men'.

[23] 'The Common Law as Constitution: Fundamental Rights and First Principles', in C Saunders (ed), *Courts of Final Jurisdiction: The Mason Court in Australia* (1996) 146, at 148.

> authority to enforce him to obey his sentence: and can any man act against his will or enforce himself to obey?[24]

The link between natural law and the other present-day element of natural justice – the 'hearing rule' – was explicitly made in 1723, in the famous case of *Dr Bentley*, in which Fortescue J is reported as having said that 'The laws of God and man both give [a] party an opportunity to make his defence, if he has any'.[25] In the latter part of the eighteenth century, Lord Kenyon CJ did much to add authority to the hearing rule. Indeed, it was through his judgment in *R v Gaskin* that we were bequeathed the Latin formulation of the hearing requirement. He spoke of 'one of the first principles of justice, *audi alteram partem*', which he described as of paramount importance: 'It is to be found at the head of our criminal law that every man ought to have an opportunity of being heard before he is condemned.'[26] Similarly, in *Harper v Carr*, he said that it was 'an essential rule in the administration of justice that no man shall be punished without being heard in his defence'.[27]

Natural Justice, Judicial Review, and the Establishment of Constitutional Government in Early Colonial New South Wales

Similar statements, and similar judicial sentiments, can be found in the early judgments of the colonial courts in New South Wales. Indeed, the New South Wales cases are of special interest in the present context for they provide further illustration of the way in which judicial review can be said to be a foundational element of the constitution, in terms of providing the basis for the establishment of the rule of law.

In part, the establishment of the rule of law in New South Wales stemmed from the fact that through the passage of the *New South Wales Act* in 1823, which marked the transition from military to civil rule in New South Wales, the Imperial government intended to set up a 'proper' legal

---

[24] 12 Mod, at 687, 88 ER, at 1602.

[25] *R v Chancellor of the University of Cambridge* (1723) 1 Str 557, at 567, 93 ER 698, at 704.

[26] (1799) 8 TR 209, at 210, 101 ER 1349, at 1350.

[27] (1797) 7 TR 271, at 275, 101 ER 970, at 972. In *R v Benn and Church* (1795) 6 TR 198, 101 ER 509, he made the point once more. It is, he said, 'an invariable maxim in our law that no man shall be punished before he has the opportunity of being heard'.

system in the colony. But, given the endemic corruption in New South Welsh political culture, simple legislative change would not alone have been enough. The critical element in the transformation of New South Wales from an *a*-constitutional to a *proto*-constitutional state was the preparedness of the colonial courts to engage in judicial review. In this regard, when the present Supreme Court of New South Wales was established (by the *New South Wales Act*) in 1824, it was formally vested with all the 'Jurisdiction and Authority' of the three English common law courts.[28] The colonial court thereby acquired the power to issue the prerogative writs of mandamus, certiorari, prohibition, *habeas corpus* and *quo warranto*.[29] This meant that a public law dynamic could develop in New South Wales in the same way that it had in England.[30]

In fact, it was through the use of prerogative writs in cases involving review of what we would today think of as administrative action that the law began, for the first time in an effective way, to impose legal control upon the institutions of power in the colony. From the very beginning of his tenure in 1824, Chief Justice Sir Francis Forbes[31] took it as being without question that he had the authority to assert a supervisory jurisdiction over the Executive. Any other view would have been anathema to the common law tradition of which Forbes was to prove himself an extremely jealous custodian. For example, in *R v Wentworth,*

---

[28] 4 Geo IV, c 96 ('the *New South Wales Act'*), s 2.

[29] On this generally, see J M Bennett, *A History of the Supreme Court of New South Wales* (1974), 178-182 and A C Castles, *An Australian Legal History* (1982), 185-188.

[30] On this point, I have argued elsewhere that it is incorrect to speak of a reception of English law in Australia. In my view, Australia did not receive English law, but it received – and this serves as the foundation-stone of today's Australian constitutionalism – English *legal culture* ('Sir Francis Forbes and the Earliest Australian Public Law Cases', unpublished paper, 1998).

[31] A few biographical words on Forbes might be of interest. Forbes had been born in Bermuda and, while he had been educated in England, nearly all of his professional practice had taken place in the colonies. Between 1810 and 1817, he served as the Attorney-General and King's Advocate of Bermuda. In 1817, he was appointed Chief Justice of Newfoundland, where he served until 1822. In that year, he went to England where he played a role in the drafting of the *New South Wales Act*. In 1823, he was appointed Chief Justice of New South Wales, in which office he served until 1837. He was knighted shortly after his retirement, and he died in Sydney in 1841. For more on his life, see C H Currey, *Sir Francis Forbes: the first Chief Justice of the Supreme Court of New South Wales* (1968).

Campbell and Dunn, one of the famous civil jury cases,[32] his Honour summed up his view, when he noted that 'every court has of necessity a power to compel [the Executive] to execute its process. This is a power necessarily incident to the creation of courts.'[33] This was a view that Forbes reiterated several times during his tenure as a judge. In one judgment, while he was still sitting in Newfoundland, he drew an express link between judicial review and constitutional principles. 'It is', he said, 'part of the constitutional law of the land that there must reside somewhere a supreme judicial authority to watch over the proceedings of all inferior tribunals, and to keep the scales of justice even and uniform.'[34]

It is notorious that in the period from the ascendancy of the ill-remembered New South Wales Corps in the 1790s up to 1823, corruption and bias among the magistrates was perhaps the chief concern with the administration of justice in the colony.[35] This being the case, among the most important of Forbes's early judgments were the ones concerning the notion of procedural fairness, and the standards of official conduct which would be expected of the magistracy. In the early period, there were at least three cases – now largely forgotten[36] – in which failures to observe natural justice figured importantly in the reasons for questioning the propriety of magisterial proceedings.

The first case of the trio was *R v Rossi, Principal Superintendent of Police*.[37] Rossi was accused of having attempted to induce a prosecutor to drop a case against an accused thief. The alleged thief was a young woman, and the suggestion was that Rossi had, for improper motives, tried to act as an informal mediator between her and the complainant. In the

---

[32] On the so-called 'civil jury cases', and their place in Australian legal history, see A C Castles, 'The Judiciary and Political Questions: The First Australian Experience, 1824-1825' (1973–76) 5 *Adel L Rev* 294.

[33] (1825) www.law.mq.edu.au/scnsw/html/r_v_wentworth__campbell_and_du.htm.

[34] *Clift v Holdsworth* (1819) 1 NLR 167, at 168.

[35] See, *eg*, B Kercher, *An Unruly Child: A History of Law in Australia* (1995), at 25-27.

[36] I should say a word about the reports of these early cases. The first published law reports in New South Wales were *Legge's Reports*, compiled in the 1890s, and in which the earliest reported case dates only from 1830. Apart from some scholarly consideration of a few celebrated cases, little is now known of the foundational years of the Australian court system. Bruce Kercher of Macquarie University has, however, recently completed the first stage of a large-scale project to publish on the Internet annotated copies of the extant records of the early workings of the Supreme Court of New South Wales. Through the Kercher project, lawyers and legal scholars are able to have access to many of the Court's early judgments that have effectively been lost to working law for a century and a half.

[37] (1826) www.law.mq.edu.au/scnsw/html/r_v_rossi__principal_superinte.htm.

end, Forbes found for Rossi, but in the course of his judgment, he made comments which foreshadowed by almost a century the famous comments of Lord Hewart CJ that justice must not only be done, but it must be seen to be done.[38] In one report of his reasons for judgment in the case, Forbes CJ is reported to have said: 'a Magistrate should never step aside from the simple line of Magisterial duty; he should not afford the world a shadow of suspicion; he should be free from taint, and pure as an angel, if possible.'[39]

Similarly, in *Ex parte Matthews*,[40] the second case, Forbes CJ held fatally flawed a judgment of an inferior tribunal which had been based upon a combination of unsworn evidence for one party and a refusal to hear evidence from the other. Forbes is reported as having said that '*audi alteram partem* is a maxim in the British Jurisprudence which [a decision-maker] is not at liberty to set aside'. In the same vein, in the third case, the *Newspaper Acts Opinion*,[41] he said: 'By the laws of England, founded in the law of nature, every man enjoys the right of being heard before be can be condemned either in his person or property.'

The Paradigm Natural Justice Cases

Yet, as has been noted, these early New South Welsh cases have been all but forgotten by the Australian legal system. Notwithstanding the historical significance of the Forbes judgments when considered in retrospect, the starting point for most discussions of the law of natural justice in Australia has been a series of decisions of the English courts dating from the middle part of the last century.[42] They form the paradigm

---

[38] '[J]ustice should not only be done, but should manifestly and undoubtedly be seen to be done': *R v Sussex Justices, Ex parte McCarthy* [1924] 1 KB 256, at 259.

[39] In another, he was reported as having put the point rather less poetically:

> I would say, taking all the circumstances of the case together, that most conscientiously I believe, the error of the Magistrate did not proceed from a corrupt motive, but from a mistaken feeling, though it certainly was of a reprehensible character. The motives and conduct of a Magistrate, should not only be correct, but above suspicion (*supra* n 37).

[40] (1827) www.law.mq.edu.au/scnsw/Cases1827-28/html/ex_parte_mathews__1827.htm.

[41] (1827) www.law.mq.edu.au/scnsw/Cases1827-28/html/newspaper_acts_opinion__1827.htm.

[42] This is apparently the case in England, as well. See, for example, *R v Bow Street Metropolitan Stipendiary Magistrate, Ex parte Pinochet Ugarte (No 2)* ('the *Pinochet*

from which later cases were patterned. An appreciation of them is, therefore, essential to any informed understanding of today's law.

The first of these 'paradigm' cases, *Capel v Child*,[43] involved the question of whether the Bishop of London was required to hear a parish priest whom the Bishop felt had been neglecting his duties. In holding that he was required to hear the vicar, Bayley B said that:

> it is considered an invariable maxim of law, that you cannot proceed against a party without his having the opportunity of being heard ... I know of no case in which you are to have a judicial proceeding, by which a man is to be deprived of any part of his property, without his having an opportunity of being heard.[44]

This view was reiterated with approval in another of the paradigm cases, *Wood v Woad*.[45] *Wood v Woad* considered the case of a member of a mutual insurance society who had been expelled under a term of the society's rules which gave the society's committee the power to do so in any case where it felt that a member's conduct was 'suspicious'.[46] The society's position was that it had an unfettered discretion in such matters, and that Wood (the expelled member) had agreed to this upon joining. Kelly CB acknowledged the text of the rules, but he said the committee was:

> bound in the exercise of their functions by the rule expressed in the maxim *audi alteram partem*, that no man shall be condemned to consequences resulting from alleged misconduct unheard and without having the opportunity of making his defence. This rule is not confined to the conduct of strictly legal tribunals, but is applicable to every tribunal or body of persons invested with authority to adjudicate upon matters involving civil consequences to individuals.[47]

The third paradigm case, *Dimes v Grand Junction Canal*,[48] concerned the bias rule, rather than the hearing rule. The case involved a decision in

---

Case') [2000] 1 AC 119, where the legal analysis focussed almost exclusively on Lord Campbell's judgment in *Dimes v Grand Junction Canal* (1852) 3 HLC 759, 10 ER 301.

43 (1832) 2 C & J 558, 149 ER 235.

44 2 C & J, at 579, 149 ER, at 244.

45 (1874) LR 9 Ex 190.

46 See LR 9 Ex, at 192.

47 LR 9 Ex, at 196.

48 (1852) 3 HLC 759, 10 ER 301.

equity by Lord Cottenham LC, in a suit between a public company and a property owner. The Vice-Chancellor had initially ruled in favour of the company and, on appeal, Lord Cottenham affirmed the ruling.[49] It then became known by the property owner that Lord Cottenham had a financial interest in the company. On further appeal, the House of Lords held that the Lord Chancellor's interest should have disqualified him from hearing the case. In his speech, Lord Campbell (the author of *The Lives of the Chancellors* and a future Lord Chancellor himself) said that the issue was not whether Lord Cottenham was biased in fact, but whether in the circumstances, there could be said to have been a fear or apprehension of bias. He said:

> No one can suppose that Lord Cottenham could be, in the remotest degree, influenced by the interest he had in this concern; but it is of the last importance that the maxim that no man is to be a judge in his own cause should be held sacred. And that is not confined to a cause in which he is a party, but applies to a cause in which he has an interest.[50]

Lord Campbell's speech displayed a concern not merely with systemic integrity of the judicial system itself, but also with the educational effect that judicial review can have on administrative decision-makers. 'It will', he said,

> have a most salutary influence on these tribunals when it is known that this high court of last resort, in a case in which the Lord Chancellor of England had an interest, considered that his decree was on that account a decree not according to law, and was set aside. This will be a lesson to all inferior tribunals to take care not only that in their decrees they are not influenced by their personal interest, but to avoid the appearance of labouring under such an influence.[51]

Probably most frequently-cited today of the paradigm cases, however, is *Cooper v Wandsworth Board of Works*,[52] decided eleven years after *Dimes*. Like *Capel v Child* and *Wood v Woad*, it concerned the reach of the hearing rule. Section 76 of the *Metropolis Local Management Act*

---

[49] For some of the early proceedings, see *Dimes v The Grand Junction Canal Company* (1846) 9 QB 469, 115 ER 1353.

[50] 3 HLC, at 793, 10 ER, at 315.

[51] *Ibid.*

[52] (1863) 14 CB(NS) 180, 143 ER 414.

1855 empowered the local authorities to demolish any house built without prior notice to the authorities. Cooper was found to have so constructed a house and an order was made by the local Board of Works to tear it down. All of the judges in the Common Pleas, though, held that Cooper was entitled to have the order set aside. Erle CJ said:

> [A]lthough the words of the statute, taken in their literal sense, without any qualification at all, would create a justification for the act which the District Board has done, the powers granted by the statute are subject to a qualification which has been repeatedly recognised, that no man is to be deprived of his property without an opportunity of being heard.[53]

Willes J said that he was:

> of the same opinion. I apprehend that a tribunal which is by law invested with power to affect the property of one of Her Majesty's subjects, is bound to give such subject an opportunity of being heard before it proceeds; and that that rule is of universal application, and founded upon the plainest principles of justice.[54]

But most famous of all is the judgment of Byles J, who said:

> [A] long course of decisions, beginning with *Dr Bentley's Case*, and ending with some very recent cases, establish that, although there are no positive words in a statute requiring that the party shall be heard, yet the justice of the common law will supply the omission of the legislature.[55]

From the Seventeenth Century to the Nineteenth: the changing context of public administration

The timing of these paradigm cases – particularly *Cooper v Wandsworth Board of Works*, with its *Dr Bonham's Case*-like enunciation of the relationship between the common law and legislation – is striking, for they were decided as England was in the midst of a profound change in the

[53] 14 CB(NS), at 187, 143 ER, at 417.
[54] 14 CB(NS), at 190, 143 ER, at 418. *Cf*, however, Willes J's views on the sanctity of legislative law as expressed in *Lee v Bude & Torrington Ry Company* (1871) LR 6 CP 582.
[55] 14 CB(NS), at 194, 143 ER, at 420. Keating J concurred (14 CB(NS), at 196, 143 ER, at 420).

nature of government and administration. Constitutional scholars date the advent of the parliamentary era to the Glorious Revolution of 1688, and the installation of William and Mary on the throne on 'terms'. From an administrative law perspective, though, this is only partly accurate. The more complete view is to say that the parliamentary era was the product of a sustained period of evolution in the philosophy and practice of government which began in 1688, but which did not reach its completion until the early years of the twentieth century. It is this factor which makes the paradigm natural justice cases, with their pre-Revolutionary manner of expression, seem so out of place.

There is a charming story, perhaps apocryphal, that one of the first things that Lord Palmerston, the Prime Minister, had to explain to the newly-acceded Queen Victoria in 1838 was what was meant by the expression 'bureaucracy'. As Sir Cecil Carr told the story, the Prime Minister was able to comfort the young Queen that she need not trouble herself overly about the term. 'Lord Palmerston', wrote Carr, 'felt able to assure the Queen that bureaucracy was a phenomenon exclusively continental.'[56] The fascinating aspect of the story seen from our standpoint today is that we know that just as his Lordship was speaking, the very basis of government in England and her colonies was undergoing a metamorphosis – and that British society was coming to embrace the idea of bureaucracy with considerable relish.

Insofar as Lord Palmerston was commenting on size, however, he was more or less accurate at the time of Victoria's accession. In 1838, the central government – what we know today as the bureaucracy – was very small. Paul Craig has noted, for instance, that in 1833, the Home Office had a staff of only twenty nine.[57] Furthermore, the impact of the government in London upon the lives of the citizenry, at least in a direct sense, was quite limited.[58] In Great Britain, the traditional approach to governance was very much one of Tory 'squireocracy': local responsibility and control, based on the remnants of feudalism and generations-old connections of families with the land. Responsibility for

---

[56] *Concerning English Administrative Law* (1941), at 1.

[57] *Administrative Law* (3rd ed, 1994), at 42.

[58] On this point, see generally, N Chester, *The English Administrative System, 1780-1870* (1981) and H Parris, *Constitutional Bureaucracy: The Development of British Central Administration Since the Eighteenth Century* (1969). See, also, J Willis, *The Parliamentary Powers of English Government Departments* (1933) and H W Arthurs, *Without the Law: Administrative Justice and Legal Pluralism in Nineteenth Century England* (1985).

local government lay, for the most part, with Justices of the Peace (who were often local squires) and other unpaid parish, borough and county officers.[59]

Sitting alongside the Justices of the Peace were a series of so-called 'Boards'. For those limited functions of state in which the Crown wanted to maintain a direct role, a specialist Board, whose members were appointed under royal authority, would be set up. The Board of Trade and Plantations (or 'Board of Trade', as it is known in shortened form) is perhaps the most familiar example of the old Board system, but at the height of the Board system, in the eighteenth century, a number of others existed.[60] Yet most of the central governmental work as was required tended to be (to use the modern expression) contracted out. As Patrick Atiyah once put it, '[i]t seemed ... natural to farm out the jobs that needed to be done to officials or institutions who could then raise the money needed to defray the cost of the services by charging for their use'.[61]

The point is that it is not inaccurate to argue that at least as it is understood in the modern sense, there was no real 'government' in those days. Not only was there no civil service to speak of, but the idea of a 'prime' minister, acting as *chef de cabinet*, was only beginning to take shape by the end of the eighteenth century.[62] This was the constitutional and governmental context in which the law of judicial review and the rules of natural justice were developed. As the apparatus of judicial control of the administration (*viz*, the prerogative writs) was developing, much of the actual administrative responsibility rested with Justices of the Peace – members of what we would today consider to be to the judicial branch of government. To put it another way, the *milieu* in which judicial control had to be exercised was generally one of like controlling like: Justices of the King's Bench controlling, under what Sir Edward Coke described as an irrevocable delegation from the Crown,[63] Justices of the Peace. This was the constitutional setting in which the very early administrative law took root.

---

[59] On this, see especially Chester, *supra* n 58, chapter 8.

[60] *Eg*, the Board of Woods, Forests and Land Revenues, the General Board of Health, the Board of Admiralty, *etc*.

[61] *The Rise and Fall of Freedom of Contract* (1979), at 19.

[62] On this, see *id*, at 17.

[63] The King 'hath committed all his power judiciall, some in one court, some in another ... the King hath wholly left matters according to his laws to his judges' (4 *Inst* 73).

There were a few exceptions to this,[64] but the observation to be made is that at the time when the early public law was at its most expansive, and in its most creative phase – when the register of prerogative writs was being compiled, so to speak – the people who required control were for the most part fellow, *albeit* inferior in the organisational scheme of things, members of the judiciary. So it was that the writs of certiorari and prohibition, the two remedies most commonly used when checking executive action (in the days before the use of the declaration became commonplace), came to be said to lay only against inferior judicial officers.[65] The fact that the courts would only issue the writs against judicial bodies, or their analogues, meant that the existence of a *legally enforceable* right to procedural fairness became inextricably wrapped up with the identity of the decision-maker. As will be discussed in the next two chapters, this came to lead in this century to a series of arcane decisions on the indicia of 'judicial' decision-making. From our perspective today, when we are for the most part free of concern about procedural intricacies, all of this seems not only highly restrictive, but quite off-point. But viewed according to the terms in which they were written, the two great prerogative writs made perfect sense in their scope.

The Constitutional Settlement and the Separation of Powers

After the scope of the prerogative writs became more-or-less settled, though, several things happened which contributed to a change in the dynamics of the relationship between the judiciary and the other arms of government. The first, of course, was the Glorious Revolution of 1688-1689. There is a good deal of exaggeration in the way in which the Glorious Revolution is spoken of. Parliamentarians view the passage of

---

[64] The story of the Sewer Commissioners, for instance, is an interesting illustration of a very early use of what we would today think of as an administrative tribunal, and of the extent to which the courts bridled at the notion that they could be excluded from their supervision. On the story of the Sewer Commissioners, see L L Jaffe and E G Henderson, 'Judicial Review and the Rule of Law: Historical Origins' (1956) 72 *LQR* 345 and I Holloway, 'A Sacred Right: Judicial Review of Administrative Action as a Cultural Phenomenon' (1993) 22 *Man L Rev* 28.

[65] For a summary of the old law, see *Halsbury's Laws of England* (1st ed. 1909), Vol 10: 'Crown Practice', paragraphs 310 (certiorari) and 299 (prohibition).

the *Bill of Rights*[66] as the moment of supreme triumph – as the culmination of the long, evolutionary project to restore the 'ancient rights of Englishmen'.[67] Likewise, Diceyists view the enshrinement twelve years later, in the *Act of Settlement*,[68] of the principle of judicial independence as the linchpin of the rule of law. Hyperbole aside, however, the structure of the Australian constitution, with its entrenched separation of powers and its provision for judicial tenure,[69] bears living witness to the abiding nature of the values which underlay the constitutional revolution which gave rise to them.

But a different way of looking the Glorious Revolution is to say that it resulted in – or, rather, that it gave rise to a dynamic which would result in – a hardening of the constitutional arteries. In the century and a half prior to 1688, the roles of what we would today call the three branches of government were in a state of tension and constant flux.[70] After 1689, the tension did not completely dissipate, but the existence of a written vision of the Revolutionary settlement in the form of the *Bill of Rights* and the *Act of Settlement* served to confine the various governmental actors within a broad late seventeenth century conception of the nature of governance. In the case of countries like Australia (and the United States), which did

---

[66] Arguably, the first modern example of revisionist history was the nineteenth century interpretation of the events of 1688-1689 as a manifestation of the English love of liberty. As John Willis wryly noted:

> Neither the economic nor the constitutional historian is equipped to tell the whole story of the Tudor and Stuart periods, but today many educated men, and lawyers in particular, are inclined to attribute to the commons, in their famous political manoeuvres against the king, a devotion to abstract concepts which is without parallel, certainly in modern politics, and to neglect the very real conflict of economic interest between the regulatory traditions of the aristocratic royalists and the free-trade aspirations of the middle-class parliamentarians.

'The Approaches to Administrative Law: The Judicial, the Conceptual, and the Functional' (1935) 1 *UTLJ* 53, at 54. For illustrations of what he describes as the 'vulgar' Whig interpretation of the Glorious Revolution, see M Loughlin, *Public Law and Political Theory* (1992), chapters 1 and 2.

[67] Blackstone, for example, described constitutional evolution in England as 'a gradual restoration of that ancient constitution whereof our Saxon forefathers had been unjustly deprived, partly by the policy and partly by the force, of the Norman' (IV *Comm* 413). See also M Loughlin, *Id*, at 4-7, 13-17.

[68] 12 & 13 Will III, c 2.

[69] The Constitution, s 72.

[70] Consider that falling within this period were the Reformation, the struggle leading up to the accession of Elizabeth I, the union of the Crowns under the Stuarts, the Civil War, and the Restoration.

not merely enact the revolutionary vision, but rather which constitutionalised it in a formal way, the imperative to confinement in role has been even more stark.

Front and centre among the revolutionary values, of course, was the felt need to divide and separate governmental power. It has for some time been fashionable to point out that formal constitutional text notwithstanding, a strict separation of powers has never been a part of our constitutional inheritance, and that Montesquieu was guilty of a gross misunderstanding of the way in which things actually worked in England.[71] Nevertheless, it is clear that the Glorious Revolution enshrined a vision of *functional* separation, especially between the judiciary and the political branches, within the British model of government.[72] Coupled with the limitations that had been written into the use of the writs of certiorari and prohibition, namely that they only lay against judicial officials, this proved to be the foundation-stone for a problem which the courts three centuries later would still find tremendously perplexing. The question was a plain one: when actors who were clearly not judicial in character began exercising power that had formerly been exercised by justices of the peace, was judicial review to follow?

Enlightenment Values and the 'Science of Legislation'

Of equal importance in considering the place of natural justice for present purposes is the Enlightenment. Accompanying the Glorious Revolution in time, and infusing it in philosophical respects, the intellectual renaissance

---

[71] Oliver Wendell Holmes Jr, for example, wrote of Montesquieu: '[T]he England of the threefold division of power into legislative, executive and judicial was a fiction invented by him' (*The Common Law* (1881), at 263). In a similar vein, Maitland once wrote:

> It is curious that some political theorists should have seen their favourite ideal, a complete separation of administration from judicature, realised in England – in England of all places in the world, where the two have for ages been inextricably blended. The mistake comes of looking just at the surface and showy parts of the constitution.

(quoted in Sir H Shawcross, 'The State and the Law' (1948) 11 *Mod L Rev* 1, at 2). See also J Finkelman, 'Separation of Powers: A Study in Administrative law' (1935) 1 *UTLJ* 313.

[72] See, *eg*, F A Hayek, *Law, Legislation and Liberty* (1973), vol 1, at 128:

> Although it is true that the actual constitution of Britain then did not conform to that principle, there can be no question that it did then govern political opinion in England and had gradually been gaining acceptance in the great debates of the preceding century.

which we know as the Enlightenment has played an overarching role in shaping the course of the evolution of the doctrine of natural justice. If from the Glorious Revolution came a rationalisation of the constitution, from the Enlightenment came a move to rationalise the system of governance more generally. If Aronson and Dyer are correct in saying that administrative law is concerned with the civilising of government,[73] then the Enlightenment was concerned with the *rationalising* of government. This took many forms: Blackstone's *Commentaries*,[74] for example, represented the product of a generational instinct to conceptualise the common law as a single *corpus*, and to bring order and rational coherence to what had thus far been little more than a disparate accumulation of judicial rulings.

Similarly, the substantive law of contract, tort and property all underwent dramatic reform during and after the Enlightenment.[75] Benthamism and Beccarianism[76] were both outgrowths of the Enlightenment. And from a legal process point of view, the great procedural reforms of the early to mid-nineteenth century which culminated in the passage of the two *Judicature Acts* in 1873 and 1875, were reflective of the same tendency – as were the moves to 'professionalise' the judicial work of the House of Lords and the Privy Council.[77] Simply stated, the advent of the modern era brought about an amendment to the terms of the Whiggish conception of the social contract. Dicey discussed this in his work *Law and Public Opinion in the Nineteenth Century*.[78] He dated the naissance of the change to the

[73] *Judicial Review of Administrative Action* (1996) at 124.

[74] *Commentaries on the Laws of England* 4 vols (1765-1770).

[75] On legal theory and law reform generally during this period, see D Lieberman, *The Province of Legislation Determined: Legal Theory in Eighteenth Century Britain* (1989).

[76] The Marchese de Beccaria (1738-1794) was the author of *Dei Delitti e della Pene* ('*On Crimes and Punishment*'), which represents one of the earliest attempts to study the criminal law in a systematic way. Among other things, Beccaria was an early advocate of social and legal reform to prevent crime, rather than the use of the majesty of the law simply to punish it. He is said to have been an important influence on Bentham. See H L A Hart, 'Bentham and Beccaria', in *Essays on Bentham* (1982), at 40, and C Phillipson, *Three Criminal Law Reformers: Beccaria, Bentham, Romilly* (1923).

[77] On this, see R Stevens, *Law and Politics: The House of Lords as a Judicial Body, 1800-1976* (1979), chapters 2-5, and L Blom-Cooper and G Drewry, *Final Appeal: A Study of the House of Lords in its Judicial Capacity* (1972), 23-43.

[78] (1905; 2nd ed, 1914).

publication of John Stuart Mill's *Political Economy*,[79] and Mills's attempt to marry economic concerns with concerns of social welfare, but in his view in the modern era, 'an alteration becomes perceptible in the intellectual and moral atmosphere of England'.[80]

All of these things – including the Glorious Revolution itself (at least as it came to be cast in Whig mythology) – can be seen as part of a broader trend to apply the scientific method to social life. We laugh today at some of the excesses of Victorian-era social mores, but to the Georgians and Victorians themselves, their era was all about progress.[81] 'Progress' denoted rationalism and logic generally, but applied to governance, it meant two things: professionalism and expertise. It is in this vein that Martin Loughlin has written about the emergence of a 'science of legislation' in the late eighteenth century. He described the project as one of 'social, political and legal thought, the object of which was to draw connections between such facets of social character as property, opinion, manners and justice ...'[82]

According to Loughlin, this new legal science was rooted in the Scottish Enlightenment, particularly in the work of Adam Smith and John Millar, a Professor of Law in the University of Glasgow. Its aim was to create a model for mapping social dynamism, and to tailor to it (for the work built on Montesquieu's admonition that there had to be a 'fit' between society and law) a model of the legislative process which would enshrine progress as the paramount legal and constitutional aim. As Loughlin put it, the objective of the legal scientists 'was to formulate criteria for evaluating the laws and institutions of society and which could then be used to guide government on the use of the legislative power'.[83] It was in *this* sense that the Enlightenment posed a challenge to the old public law – to adapt principles which had developed under pre-Revolutionary thinking about the constitution to a different way of thinking about government and its place in the constitutional order.

---

[79] *Principles of Political Economy With Some of Their Applications to Social Philosophy* (1848).

[80] *Law and Public Opinion in England*, *supra* n 78, at 245.

[81] For an interesting, and thought-provoking, reassessment of Victorian society and Victorian notions of progress, see G Himmelfarb, *The De-Moralization of Society: From Victorian Virtues to Modern Values* (1994). See also M Valverde, *The Age of Light, Soap, and Water: Moral Reform in English Canada, 1885-1925* (1991), especially chapters 3 and 7.

[82] *Supra* n 66, at 4.

[83] *Ibid.*

The Franchise, Social Strain and Administrative Power

For the reasons just discussed, it is wrong to think that social welfare is exclusively a twentieth century concern. Indeed, ancient feudalism represented a not ineffective (if offensive to our sensibilities today) means of providing a crude 'safety net'.[84] And despised as they may be as a consequence of Dickens' fiction, the old Poor Laws were actually aimed at reducing the level of poverty in society. But it is true to say that a *centrally-administered* system of social welfare provision is of comparatively recent creation. In large measure, it stemmed from the onset of the Industrial Revolution, which came to place the old, localised system of administration in England under an intolerable strain, particularly in London, the Midlands and the north.

During the first half of the nineteenth century, for example, the population of Birmingham increased by over three hundred per cent, and those of Manchester and Liverpool by over four hundred per cent.[85] Clearly, a system of social welfare provision which relied on generalists and volunteers could not cope with this. The result both in the big cities and in the country was anarchic. J A G Griffith once described the impetus for the introduction of bureaucracy in England in characteristically provocative terms, when he said that '[a]rguments about the nature of epidemics gave way to the beginnings of bacteriology and did more to shape the British constitution than the activities of Lord John Russell or Lord Palmerston'.[86] Even Dicey was moved by the extent of poverty and social dislocation, and saw therein the seeds of governmental transformation. He said of the first half of the nineteenth century:

> The time was out of joint. The misery and discontent of city artisans and village labourers were past dispute ... The wages earned by labourers in the

[84] As an aside, S F C Milsom once made the interesting observation that it is easier for an administrative lawyer today to appreciate the concept of land ownership under Feudalism than it would have been for legal historians like Maitland, writing in the last century:

> We can see the language and ideas of our own property law being rendered inappropriate by governmental powers of the same juristic nature as those once exercised by lords. You are less of an owner when you cannot effectively realise your property without planning permission, for example, in the same way as you had not quite become owner so long as you needed your lord's licence to alienate.

'F W Maitland', in *Studies in the History of the Common Law* (1985) 261, at 275.

[85] W R Cornish and G de N Clark, *Law and Society in England 1750-1950* (1989), at 322.

[86] 'Administrative Law and the Judges', Pritt Memorial Lecture, 1978, at 5.

> country were miserably low. The horrors connected with factory life were patent. Widespread was the discontent of the whole body of wage-earners ... There was rick-burning by labourers in the country, there were acts of violence by trade unionists in the towns. The demand for [reform] was the sign of a social condition which portended revolution.[87]

Coinciding with the industrial revolution in time was a move towards parliamentary reform. With the passage of the Great Reform Bill in 1832[88] (the year of Bentham's death, incidentally) people began not only to take a greater interest in the working of parliament, but also to make greater demands of it. To put it in today's language, with the broadening of the franchise, parliament began to be 'relevant' to ordinary people in a way that it had not hitherto been. One should not overstate the effect of the 1832 Reform Bill, for even after its passage less than five per cent of the population could vote.[89] But 1832 marked the first time that places like Birmingham, Sheffield and Leeds – places which had experienced the most serious social dislocation as a result of the industrial revolution – received parliamentary representation.[90]

Furthermore, the early decades of the nineteenth century were also the time of Benthamism, and of Bentham's *dicta* on the importance of uniformity of administration throughout the country. As Carr has noted, implicit in Bentham's writing was the view that uniform administration depended upon a large increase in the activity of the central government.[91] So the reformed British Parliament began to pass, with increasing rapidity as the century went on, a series of statutes which attempted to frame some sort of national response to the huge shifts in demography, and to their attendant problems.[92] As Carr described it, '[t]he new Parliament, impulsive, rather undisciplined, and very serious, knew that the country

---

[87] *Law and Public Opinion in England*, *supra* n 78, at 211-212.
[88] *Representation of the People Act 1832*.
[89] Craig, *supra* n 57, at 54.
[90] See M Gilbert, *The Dent Atlas of British History* (2nd ed. 1993), at 84.
[91] *Supra* n 56, at 9.
[92] These included acts with short titles which are suggestive of the mind-set that parliament was bringing to the problem: the *Factory Act 1833*, the *Poor Law Amendment Act 1834*, the *Municipal Corporations Act 1835*, the *Railway Regulation Act 1840*, the *Towns Improvement Clauses Act 1847*, the *Public Health Act 1848*, the *Nuisances Removal and Disease Prevention Act 1848*, the *Metropolis Local Management Act 1855* and the *Local Government Act 1858*. For a more complete listing, see Arthurs, *supra* n 58, bibliography.

expected it to experiment and to risk the impact of State interference upon individual liberties'.[93] He continued:

> A series of non-party royal commissions and committees explored social conditions; their conclusions shocked public opinion and revealed the gap in the local administration of those times between efficient government in some places and scandalous neglect in too many others. Parliament, fortified by the reports and recommendations of these exploratory bodies, gave a smooth passage to several controversial Bills which were in no way the product of the governmental machine. And so Britain got a quick and quiet revolution in the laws of factories, poor relief, municipal corporations, prisons and presently public health ...[94]

This legislation frankly puts the lie to the notion that the nineteenth century was a period of *laissez faire*. Indeed, it shows that it is quite mistaken to label the nineteenth century as the high point of 'classic liberalism' – or at least that it is mistaken to equate classic liberalism with *laissez faire*, as many of us do. To be sure, people held dear the institution of private property, for it was private property which was the engine for the creation of private wealth. But at the same time, it was the property-owning class, as much as the radical reformers, who drove the move to bureaucratise. As Atiyah put it:

> The new industrial middle classes of England brought with them some very insistent desires and demands, and it was their gradual success in achieving these which in the end largely destroyed the individualist society and the free market economy which had brought them power and prosperity. They wanted law and order in the streets; they wanted an end to filth and slums and insanitary houses; they wanted regularity in life, in business, in the payment of debts and the observance of contracts; they wanted greater decency and refinement in life, an end to barbarities and cruelties, to the slave trade, to the pillory and public executions, to public drunkenness, to the employment of children as chimney sweeps and women in coal mines.[95]

---

[93] *Supra* n 56, at 3.

[94] *Ibid*. He concluded with a suggestion of a lesson for a world in crisis:

> This reinforcement of the governmental process by a concentration of the intelligence of men of independent mind, not always attached either to Parliament or to political parties, is an object lesson to which our eyes turn in these no less stimulating times.

[95] *Supra* n 61, at 231.

Importantly, though, while the new legislation sought to provide a national response to the challenges of the industrial era, it retained for the most part a model of local responsibility and local administration. It is true that a common feature of this post-Reform Bill legislation was the replacement of the generalist Justices of the Peace with 'task-specific' administrative bodies. But only in a minor way did the nineteenth century legislation involve the national government in the direct administration or regulation of local affairs. The Benthamite view of the importance of centralisation was largely limited to the appointment of national inspectorates.[96] This meant that in England, even after the local government reforms, public administration remained the province of a myriad of different entities, which varied dramatically in resources, ability and integrity.[97] As Atiyah has noted, the growth of government during the nineteenth century was no more the result of a national plan than was the Industrial Revolution in the century which preceded it.[98] England, he wrote, 'stumbled into the modern administrative state without design, and even contrary to the inclinations of most Englishmen.'[99]

It is also important to appreciate that the nineteenth century attempts at introducing an effective bureaucracy pre-dated the national income tax. Most taxes were levied by local authorities as rates. So whatever governmental interference there was with rights in private property tended to occur at the local level. The point to be taken from all of this is that given that the Queen's judges in London had a well-established tradition of exercising control over local authorities, it is not surprising that even in the mid-nineteenth century, the courts might not have seen as manifestly apparent a conflict between the ancient constitutional values (such as were expressed in *Cooper v Wandsworth Board of Works* and the other paradigm cases) and the newer philosophy of government.

Law and Administrative Government in Colonial Australia

This English exegesis is necessary for, as noted, the English case law from the nineteenth century is still considered elemental in Australia. But while

---

[96] *Eg*, the Poor Law Commissioners.

[97] Chester, for example, noted that as late as 1870, responsibility for local administration in England and Wales was shared by 65 county units and 97 quarter sessions boroughs, 224 municipal borough councils and no less than 637 boards of health! (*supra* n 58, at 347).

[98] *Supra* n 61, at 224.

[99] *Id*, at 236.

in Australia, the pressures of progress were largely the same as in England during the nineteenth century, the administrative situation was really quite different. As Paul Finn has put it, in England the forces driving the evolution of public administration were centripetal, and led 'piecemeal but inexorably to an accretion of power to the central government'.[100] In Australia, in contrast, the forces were *centrifugal*: 'In shaping the administrative system, the potent central authorities controlled (and often retarded) the devolution of power to local and regional units.'[101] 'Their augmented responsibilities', he continued, 'particularly in developmental activity, exaggerated their pre-eminence in the colonial scheme of things'.[102]

In the nineteenth century, neither Australia nor New Zealand had the tradition of local government that the English had. On the contrary, from the very beginnings of the settlement of Australasia, the central government had exercised the lion's share of control and direction. All administrative initiatives accordingly came within the purview of central authority. As Pember Reeves, one of the leading Australasian liberals of the late nineteenth century, described it:

> Before 1890, the State was already the great landlord, the chief employer of labour, was virtually the sole owner of the land transport, as well as of the telegraphs and telephones. It undertook the business of land registration and transfer, and in one colony, New Zealand, had established a large life insurance office, and a public trust office ... In addition to railway-making, the governments were spending millions on roads, bridges, harbour works, and water-supply. They had always taken the completest powers of inspection over flocks and herds, and in the eighties were beginning to inspect factories in the interests of women and children workers.[103]

Necessarily, therefore, there was less of the *ad hoc*-ery in colonial Australia that Atiyah has written of in the English context. This is not to say that the colonial governments were not inept or corrupt (for every student of Australian colonial history knows just how deeply both ineptitude and corruption came to be entrenched in governmental practice

[100] *Law and Government in Colonial Australia* (1987), at 2.
[101] *Id*, at 2-3.
[102] *Id*, at 3.
[103] *State Experiments in Australia and New Zealand* (1902), vol. 1, at 50.

in the early years after settlement[104]). But in terms of actual systemic *design*, there was an integrity in government in Australia that was lacking in the Mother Country at the time.

Sir Frederic Eggleston, the great modern Australian liberal thinker,[105] suggested that a related difference between Australia and Great Britain was that in Australia, there was not the same instinctive distrust of governmental involvement in private affairs. This was because an Australian *grundnorm* was one of state intrusion upon what in England would have been considered the private. 'In the smaller communities of Australia', Eggleston wrote in the 1930s, 'thrown from the beginning upon the State for development of their untouched resources, there has been little feeling against State action, and no resistance to its constant use for all sorts of purposes.'[106]

In this regard, a feature of governance from the beginning in Australia was the prevalence of the Board system, at a time when, in England, Boards had largely fallen into disuse. As Finn noted of New South Wales, between 1856 and 1900, more than fifty acts of parliament were passed to set up or re-constitute statutory bodies.[107] Given that the proliferation of the boards coincided with the introduction of responsible government in the colonies,[108] Finn has argued, the notion of ministerial responsibility – on which Dicey had set so much store – did not develop here in the same way that it did in Great Britain.[109] Stephen J once suggested that the practical consequence of this was that even after the adoption of responsible government in the 1850s, the Australian colonial Governors exercised a degree of real governing power that was not possessed by Queen Victoria in the United Kingdom.[110]

Another difference that is significant for present purposes is that Crown liability legislation (which, among other things, rendered the

---

[104] See, *eg*, B Kercher, *Debt, Seduction and Other Disasters* (1996) and L A Whitfield, *Founders of the Law in Australia* (1969).

[105] See, *infra*, chapter 2.

[106] *State Socialism in Victoria* (1932), at 11.

[107] *Supra* n 100, at 58.

[108] In New South Wales, representative government was introduced in 1842 by virtue of the *Australian Constitutions Act (No 1)* (13 & 14 Vict, c 59). Responsible government was provided for by the *New South Wales Constitution Statute 1855* (18 & 19 Vict, c 54). See, generally, Castles, *supra* n 29 (chapter 8), Kercher, *supra* n 35 (chapter 7) and A C V Melbourne, *Early Constitutional Development in Australia* (2nd ed, 1963).

[109] *Supra* n 100, at 13-14.

[110] *FAI Insurances v Winneke* (1982) 151 CLR 342, at 354-355. See also G Sawer, "Councils, Ministers and Cabinets in Australia" [1956] *Pub Law* 110.

Boards liable to suit) was introduced much earlier in Australia than in Britain.[111] And this, of course, built on the so-called 'repugnancy' clauses that had been a feature of the various colonial constitutions since the 1820s.[112] By these, the colonial courts had been vested with jurisdiction to determine whether locally-enacted legalisation was repugnant to the law of England and, consequently, unconstitutional.[113] So from the very early days, the Australian courts became accustomed to pronouncing on the *vires* of colonial legislation.[114] Together, these things: the retardation of the development of local government in the English style and the existence of legislation which permitted governments to be sued, suggest that the parallel between the conditions in which the nineteenth century English law of natural justice developed, and the conditions in which public law had to operate in Australia was not an exact one.

The Paradigm Cases Reconsidered

In light of this, some question is thrown on the appropriateness of reliance upon the paradigm cases as leading authority. As has been suggested, the striking thing about the paradigm cases when they are read in context is their tone, which is in many ways reminiscent of the seventeenth century and before. The cases (particularly *Cooper v Wandsworth Board of Works*, with its reference to the common law 'supplying the omission of the legislature') seem to have taken little account of the shifting context of government in which they were decided. To return to the Harlow and Rawlings point,[115] the theory of the state implicit in the paradigm cases was one in which rights in individual autonomy preceded governmental interests in collective efficiency. Taking them in the English *milieu*, there

---

[111] (1853) 16 Vict, No 6 (SA), (1857) 20 Vict, No 15 (NSW), (1857) 21 Vict, No 29 (Vic), (1859) 23 Vict No 1 (Tas), (1866) 29 Vict, No 23 (Qld). In Great Britain, equivalent legislation was not introduced until 1947 (*Crown Proceedings Act 1947*). See, also, Finn, *supra* n 100 (chapter 6), Kercher, *supra* n 35, at 100-101.

[112] See Castles, *supra* n 29.

[113] See, *eg*, the *New South Wales Act* (4 Geo IV, c 96), s 29.

[114] The high point of this, of course, was the work of Boothby J in the 1860s, who effectively rendered South Australia lawless. Among other things, he held that the South Australian constitution was unconstitutional. It was Boothby's excess that led to the passage of the *Colonial Laws Validity Act 1965*. For more on this remarkable man and his legacy, see Kercher, *supra* n 35, at 97-102.

[115] See *supra* Introduction, at 2.

is little or no acknowledgment – overt or otherwise – of the changes in government, and in approaches to administration, that were taking place. Taking them in the Australian setting, their dissonance is even more stark.

Nevertheless, in a practical way, this gulf of understanding between law and government may not have been especially problematic when, in England, the executive still did not involve itself much in the day-to-day administration of local affairs. Nor, possibly, was it a great concern in Australia in the days when recourse to the superior courts was logistically difficult for anyone who did not live in Sydney, Melbourne or Adelaide. Accordingly, in the nineteenth century in both Australia and England, the opportunity for conflict over the supervision of local administration was relatively narrow. But, as will be seen in the next two chapters, in the twentieth century, as the central executive began to wish to play a significant role in local affairs, the constitutional clash was to come into the open.

2 Judicial Review in the Planned State[1]

There is a tendency to think that ours is the first generation whose system of public law has had to wrestle with the problem of the co-existence of the administrative decision-maker and the court of law. The truth is, however, that ours is at least the fifth or sixth generation of twentieth century administrative lawyer which has had to grapple with the problems that follow from what one might loosely call 'administrative adjudication', and the judicial reaction thereto. In fact, the major conceptual difficulties facing administrative law in Australia today are all direct lineal descendants of a series of jurisprudential doubts that began to trouble minds in the latter years of the nineteenth century and the early years of the twentieth regarding the basis by which inexpert, irresponsible (in the political sense) judges could, or *should*, exercise supervision over 'expert' decision-makers. The story of natural justice in the common law for the first sixty-odd years of the twentieth century was the story of these doubts, and of the struggle between the competing claims of bureaucratic expertness and judicial fairness.

The Twentieth Century Phases of Natural Justice

The historian Eugen Weber once admonished the scholar to remember that history cannot be seen as a linear progression.[2] Nevertheless, the evolution of natural justice in this century can be seen broadly in four phases. The first of the phases ran roughly between 1911, with the judgment of the House of Lords in *Board of Education v Rice*,[3] and 1929, with the publication by Lord Hewart, the Lord Chief Justice, of his polemical attack on executive discretion, *The New Despotism*. The second ran

[1] This title is adapted from W Friedmann, *The Planned State and the Rule of Law* (1948).

[2] 'History is not a linear progression, but rather like a meandering river' (televised lecture entitled 'The Western Culture', 3 May 1992).

[3] [1911] AC 179.

roughly from 1929, with the appointment in the United Kingdom of the Committee on Ministers' Powers,[4] as a reaction to Lord Hewart's book, to the end of the Second World War, when the House of Lords and Privy Council began to deliver a series of judgments which seemed severely to cut back the doctrine's scope to a weakened, emaciated form.

The third phase ran from the end of the War to the 1960s. In England, the end of the third phase would be dated at 1963, with the judgment of the House of Lords in *Ridge v Baldwin*.[5] In Australia, it dates from 1968, when the High Court delivered its judgment in *Banks v Transport Regulation Board*.[6] As hinted at in the Introduction, there was something of a divergence in approaches to natural justice in Australia and England during this period, but in both countries, the doctrine came to suffer from the effects of non-theorisation, which seemed to render it in danger of becoming moribund. The final broad phase began in the 1960s and to date has not stopped. To borrow the words of Bernard Schwartz, there has been since the 1960s a 'judicial revolution' with respect to the doctrine of natural justice.[7] For reasons which will be discussed in chapter four, it might actually be more accurate to describe it instead as a judicial renaissance, but whichever term is used, in the past thirty years the retrenching attitude has been all but forgotten in an era of seemingly boundless judicial self-confidence.

It is the first two phases which will be the subject of this chapter. As foreshadowed at the end of the last chapter, the picture that will emerge is one of considerable tension between law and politics, and between rival visions as to the place of common law values in the modern state. Briefly stated, the first phase represented an intellectual commitment on the part of substantial segments of the higher judiciary to 'softening', or 'thinning' the requirements of natural justice when applied to the work of the bureaucracy. This reflected a view, shared with the political branches of government, of the problems associated with a move to larger, more centralised, bureaucracy. In some ways, it was the most jurisprudentially sophisticated of the four phases – in the sense that it was during this period

---

[4] Commonly known as 'the Donoughmore Committee', after its first chairman, the Earl of Donoughmore. Sometimes also known as 'the Scott Committee', after its second chairman, Sir Leslie Scott (later Scott LJ).

[5] [1964] AC 40.

[6] 119 CLR 222.

[7] B Schwartz, *Lions Over the Throne: The Judicial Revolution in English Administrative Law* (1987), at 11.

that the judiciary displayed its most sophisticated level of sensitivity to the problems facing government.

The second phase, in contrast, represented a sharp judicial reaction to perceived abuses of power on the part of the executive, and a corresponding wave of criticism of the judiciary on the part of academic lawyers. If the first phase was the most sophisticated, then the second phase was certainly the most *complicated* in the doctrine's history, for the applicability of natural justice came to be determined according to a series of semantic distinctions about the nature of the decision-making process. And in the English context, it was this second phase that gave rise to the first outpouring of real administrative law scholarship – much of which, it should be noted, was hostile to the imposition of common law values on the administration.

The Twentieth Century and the Collective State

Sitting alongside the theoretical tensions stemming from the Enlightenment and the Glorious Revolution that were discussed in chapter one, there were certain factors which made the twentieth century the scene for concerted conflict over the reach of judicial review in a way that its predecessor had not been.[8] As discussed in chapter one, while there had been a dramatic shift in the nature of governance in England during the nineteenth century, which became more tangible after the passage of the first *Representation of the People Act* in 1832, the fulcrum of administration remained at the local level throughout the century. So the dynamics of the relationship between the judiciary and the central executive did not change appreciably before the 1900s. In the twentieth century, however, the focus of administrative effort shifted discernibly to the centre, with the result that judicial views of fairness and political views of necessity were brought into direct clash.

One of the causes of this, of course, was the fact that more often in that century than at any other time since the demise of feudalism as a working system, society had been mobilised *en masse* in the interests of the state. It was the century of both total war and cold war, and of citizen armies. It was also the century of Great Depression, long-term

[8] These factors were discussed by W Friedmann, in an article published in 1951 in the *Canadian Bar Review*: 'Judges, Politics and the Law', 29 *Can Bar Rev* 811.

recession, and jobless recovery. The existence of a succession of perceived national crises – which stretched in a near un-broken line from about 1903[9] to the mid-1960s[10] – served to give the state a much greater claim on the private lives of the citizenry than it had previously had.

A second, and related, factor was the explosion in population that took place in the late nineteenth and twentieth centuries. In the first chapter, the effect of population growth on government in the mid-nineteenth century was discussed, but the rate of growth in fact increased as the century went on. Cornish and Clark have noted, for example, that the population of England and Wales almost doubled between 1871 and 1941.[11] A similar pattern in population growth could be seen in Australia. In 1871, the total population of Australia (excluding Aboriginal peoples) was a little over 1.6 million. By 1921, it had increased more than three hundred per cent.[12]

This was accompanied by a trend towards urbanisation that began with the Industrial Revolution, but which accelerated into the early years of the twentieth century. In 1871, there were thirty-seven cities and towns in England with a population of 50,000 or more. By 1901, this increased to seventy-five, and by 1931, it had reached one hundred and thirteen.[13] In Australia, it is well-known that the vast majority of the population has always lived in a thin belt stretching along the eastern and southern coasts. But in the fifty year period between 1871-1921, the proportion of workers employed in primary industries in Australia dropped from forty-four per

---

[9] With the publication of Erskine Childers' novel *The Riddle of the Sands*, which raised a popular fear in Great Britain and the Empire of German imperial expansionism. For Australian purposes, one special significance of this book is that it led to the repatriation of much of the Royal Navy to home waters. In August–September 1908, the so-called American 'Great White Fleet' visited Australia. In some respects, this marked the first step in the shifting of Australia's national security posture from a British to an American orientation.

[10] The 1960s are chosen here because viewed with the hindsight that the passage of thirty-odd years gives, they seem to represent a sea change in the attitudes of people in the Western world to authority.

[11] They note that in the decade 1871-1881, it increased from 22.8 million to 26 million. By 1901, it was 32.6 million. Despite the losses of the First World War, by 1921, it had grown to 37.9 million. In 1941, it was 41.7 million. See W R Cornish and G de N Clark, *Law and Society in England 1750-1950* (1989), at 74, n 95.

[12] G T McPhee, 'The Urbanisation of the Australian Population', in P D Phillips and G L Wood (eds), *The Peopling of Australia* (1928), at 170.

[13] Cornish and Clark, *supra* n 11.

cent to just under twenty-six per cent.[14] By 1927, no less than sixty-two percent of the non-Aboriginal Australian population was living in urban areas.[15] Simply put, in the twentieth century people were living in much closer contact with one another than in the past. So even if it had been true at some point in the past that man could be an island, this became quite impossible after he forsook the bush or the pasture for the city.

What is also interesting in the Australian context, apart from the simple increase in numbers of people living in towns and cities, is the demographic make-up of the urban population. For unlike Great Britain, Australia was throughout much of the nineteenth century still a sparsely-populated, non-industrialised settler nation. In the 1850s, there had been a massive influx of immigrants into the Australian colonies, accompanying the Gold Rush. But as the alluvial gold supplies petered out, many of the unskilled members of the mining population made their way to the cities, especially Melbourne. At the same time, technological improvements in the agriculture industry reduced the need for unskilled labour. So not only was the urban population on the rise, but much of the increase was taking the form of unskilled, poorly-educated working men.

Partnered to this was the fact that for much of the period in question, Australia had a relatively young population. The immigrants attracted by the Gold Rush tended to be young, and of family-raising age. Likewise, the assisted passage programmes which existed prior to the First World War were aimed at encouraging migration by young adults and parents with children.[16] When taken with the Australian culture of government which was discussed in chapter one, the inevitable offshoot of such a great population shift was a growth in the role of government in private life: both as planner of public works, and as arbiter of disputes over competing claims on public wealth.

A third cause for the expansion of government in this century is related to, and in a metaphysical sense underlies, the first two. As Friedmann described it, there was in the modern era 'an evolution of social philosophy'.[17] Dicey described this alteration as the 'growth of collectivism', and he attributed it to a combination of moral

---

[14] McPhee, *supra* n 12, at 167.

[15] *Ibid.*

[16] W D Borrie, *The European Peopling of Australasia: A Demographic History 1788–1988* (1994), at 181.

[17] 'Judges, Politics and the Law', *supra* n 8, at 822.

philanthropism[18] and perceived commercial necessity.[19] The result was a decided push towards executive-empowering legislation (which, of course, Dicey thought anti-constitutional[20]), and away from the emphasis on local regulation that had been the feature of welfare provision up to and including the last century.

A fourth factor, which stemmed from the Victorian and Edwardian obsessions with progress, was an extreme faith in science, and growth of a 'cult' of expertise. This was touched upon in the last chapter, but throughout the latter half of the last century and the first half of this one, it was an article of faith that the non-partisan application of scientific expertise could remedy most of society's ills. As part of this broad project, the then-new field of political 'science' (the name itself being a significant one) began to propound a new vision of government, in which the state assumed an active role as provider – a vision of, as some put it, a 'public service' state. William Robson, one of the leading English administrative law scholars of the middle part of the century, was making this point when he paraphrased Maine, and said that in the twentieth century, 'we are moving from contract to public administration.'[21]

One aspect of this shift in thought which is of special interest for present purposes was the foundation of the London School of Economics and Political Science by Sidney and Beatrice Webb in 1895. Unlike the ancient universities in England, the LSE was dedicated to the 'the impartial scientific study of society'.[22] As Lord Beveridge, who served as Director between 1919-1937, once wrote, the aim of the college was 'treating economics, politics and social sciences primarily as sciences based on observation and analysis of facts, rather than analysis of concepts'.[23] As a part of this endeavour, Beveridge placed great emphasis on the study of law, and among his accomplishments were the creation of

---

[18] *Law and Public Opinion in the Nineteenth Century* (2nd ed. 1914), at lxi:

> In truth a somewhat curious phenomenon is amply explained by the combination of an intellectual weakness with a moral virtue, each of which is discernible in the Englishman of today.

[19] *Id*, at 247.

[20] See *The Law of the Constitution* (8th ed. 1915), at 198.

[21] *Public Administration Today* (1948), at 3 (quoted in M Loughlin, *Public Law and Political Theory* (1992), at 201).

[22] The Rt Hon Lord Beveridge, *Power and Influence* (1953), at 168.

[23] *Id*, at 175.

the first full-time chair of law in the University of London[24] and the foundation of a law journal – tellingly entitled the *Modern Law Review*.[25] During Beveridge's tenure, the LSE became the centre for the 'scientific' study of public law in the modern state,[26] and the influence of its scholars on administrative law will be returned to shortly.

Positive Liberty, the Planned State and the 'New Legislation'

Inherent in the shifts in social feeling – which Dicey deplored and the London School of Economics applauded – was a burgeoning desire for what Isaiah Berlin would come to describe as "positive liberty".[27] This is the notion that if it is to have any substantive meaning, freedom must amount to more than the absence of external restraint. It must also include the ability actually to fulfil one's desires. 'The "positive" sense of the word "liberty" derives from the wish on the part of the individual to be his own master', wrote Berlin:[28]

> I wish my life and decisions to depend on myself, not on external forces of whatever kind ... I wish to be a subject, not an object; to be moved by reasons, by conscious purposes, which are my own, not by causes which affect me, as it were, from the outside.[29]

The yearning for positive liberty is another offspring of the Enlightenment. It stems from the idea that 'the essence of man is that they are autonomous beings'.[30] It is a craving for positive liberty that lies at the heart of much of today's talk about 'empowerment'. Proponents of empowerment often gloss over the fact that the realisation of positive liberty must involve considerable coercion – including a forced redistribution of opportunity-providing resources (to wit, property). But leaving aside the metaphysical question (that Berlin wrestled with) of

---

[24] Whose occupant was Edward Jenks, who had formerly been Professor of Law in the University of Melbourne.
[25] Founded in 1937.
[26] On this, see also Loughlin, *supra* n 21, at 174-176.
[27] 'Two Concepts of Liberty', inaugural lecture as the Chichele Professor of Social and Political Theory, Oxford, 1957 (reprinted in *Four Essays on Liberty* (1969), 131 *ff*).
[28] *Id*, at 131.
[29] *Ibid*.
[30] *Id*, at 136.

whether this renders the notion a self-negating proposition,[31] it is clear that a clamour for positive liberty involved a change in the ideal of governance.

Until comparatively recently our legal history was the story of the deliberate exclusion of the state from the sphere of private activity. From *Magna Carta* onwards, the story of the common law was the story of the evolution of 'negative liberty', in Berlin's terminology – of liberty in the sense of being liberated from governmental interference. 'Liberty', as our passports say, meant the freedom to go about one's affairs without let or hindrance. Under this conception of liberty, the expectations of the state are very limited. At the risk of oversimplification, one expects the state to do very little: to provide an army to protect from without and a police force to protect from within, and a series of law courts in which to resolve private disputes in a peaceful manner. Apart from that, one wants just to be left alone. But as Dicey and others noted, in the nineteenth century this began to change. People began to expect the state to do a great deal, indeed. Rather than leaving them alone, people expected the state to play an active part in their day-to-day lives. They expected it to do things to make our society better; more just. In a word, people expected the state to help shape society.

Together, these shifts drove governments to increase their levels of activity, and their consequent output. For the purposes of administrative law, the critical factor was that while the state was quite willing to accede to demands to make society better, it demanded a *quid pro quo*. It demanded the ability to coerce the citizenry and to categorise it. As part of this, the nature of legislation began to change. The 'new' legislation vested significant amounts of discretionary power in the Executive, including broad delegated law-making power. To cope with the new pressures and new demands, governments demanded the power to plan and to regulate, rather than merely to react:

> The planned state is today an irrevocable reality in modern society, far more than party controversies would admit. Every modern state exercises a multitude of supervisory regulating and managing activities which no modern government, whatever its complexion, could afford to drop. The notion of a

[31] As his biographer described Berlin's thesis, 'it might be necessary to increase taxation on the incomes of the few in order to bring greater social justice to the many, but it was a perversion of language to pretend that no one's liberty would suffer as a result' (M Ignatieff, *Isaiah Berlin: A Life* (1998), at 228).

> government which concerns itself with military defence, foreign affairs, police and legal justice, is now a thing of the past.[32]

Australia as a 'New' State

The circumstances of Australia's establishment as a federated common-wealth showed that these concerns were also apparent there. Indeed, in some respects, the concerns about state planning were perhaps even more pronounced in Australia than in England. The Australian experience with centrally-administered boards during the colonial period has already been mentioned[33] but, arguably, the federation movement itself was partly reflective of a feeling that in the modern polity, planned efficiency was more important than old-fashioned notions of individual negative liberty. As Geoffrey Sawer once noted, the allocation of powers in section 51 of the Constitution suggests that one of the new Commonwealth's main purposes was to provide 'the convenience of a number of codes and Australia-wide administrative agencies relevant to the conduct of commerce and industry'.[34]

Whatever the case, in an essay published in 1933, W G K Duncan wrote that 'the whole conception of government, and governmental functions, has changed during the course of this century'.[35] 'The state', he continued,

> can no longer be conceived as a policeman 'keeping the ring' and enforcing a few Marquess of Queensberry prohibitions. The state must now assume an active and positive role in the regulation of the whole social process. In particular, it has been forced to undertake an elaborate network of 'social

---

[32] Friedmann, 'The Planned State and the Rule of Law', *supra* n 1, at 5.

[33] See chapter 1.

[34] *Australian Federal Politics and Law 1901-1929* (1956), at 323.

[35] 'Modern Constitutions', in G V Portus (ed) *Studies in the Australian Constitution* (1933), at 10. See, also, W P M Kennedy, 'Aspects of Administrative Law in Canada' (1934), 46 *Jurid Rev* 203, at 207:

> [There is a] growing conviction in Canada, that the development of new industries, natural resources, colonisation, transportation, communications, due to the vastness of the country, and the unremunerative character of these enterprises and undertakings in their early stages, imposes an obligation on the governments to aid and to supervise.

services' in order to mitigate the consequences of economic and social inequality.[36]

In an article written two years after federation, Harrison Moore alluded to some of the practical implications of the demands of modern government for a country in Australia's position, as well as the impact of the demands on the old constitutional order:

> The statute book abounds with instances not merely of new functions of administration cast upon old or new authorities, but with powers of a very far reaching kind. This is largely due to a change in the working of our constitutional forces. During the nineteenth century, the preparation of legislation has come to be one of the principal duties of the Government, and it takes its modern form from the fact that it is no longer devised by a body distinct from and jealous of the Executive, but expresses to a very great extent the views of the Executive as to the public needs. Thus we have in an ever increasing degree the delegation of a power of supplementary legislation to the Government ...[37]

In fact, in the years following federation, the new Commonwealth governments – of all political stripes – embarked upon a programme of regulation with considerable vigour. This was particularly the case with its adoption of a significant degree of regulation, enforced by arbitration, in the labour market. Insofar as the hallmark of the modern approach to legislation included, as Moore suggested, the delegation of law-making power to the executive, it is interesting to note that in the first twenty-seven years after federation, the Commonwealth government alone proclaimed no less than three thousand six hundred pages of regulations![38]

The Moore and Duncan pieces are in fact merely part of a rich body of Australasian scholarship on the new style of governance, or 'progressivism', as it is often referred to.[39] This included work by W Jethro Brown,[40] Alfred

---

[36] *Ibid.*

[37] 'The Enforcement of Administrative Law' (1903) 1 *Comm L Rev* 13, at 14.

[38] K H Bailey, 'Administrative Legislation in the Commonwealth' (1930) 4 *ALJ* 7, at 9. See also his evidence before the Senate Select Committee on Standing Committees, 1929-1930, at 18-19.

[39] See G Davison, 'Progressivism', entry in Davison *et al* (eds), *The Oxford Companion to Australian History* (1998), at 529.

[40] See, *eg*, 'The Hare System in Tasmania' (1899) 15 *LQR* 51, *The New Democracy: A Political Study* (1899), *The Austinian Theory of Law* (1906), *The Underlying Principles of Modern Legislation* (1912), *The Prevention and Control of Monopolies* (1914), 'The

Deakin,[41] W Pember Reeves,[42] H B Higgins[43] and, in a slightly later period, Sir Frederic Eggleston.[44] Deakin, of course, was one of the framers of the Australian Constitution and the second Prime Minister of the Commonwealth. Higgins was another framer of the Constitution, an Attorney-General, President of the Commonwealth Arbitration Court and a Justice of the High Court. Brown and Reeves were professors – Reeves subsequently to become a Director of the LSE, and Brown, President of the South Australian Industrial Court. Eggleston was variously a senior public servant, a state cabinet minister, a diplomat, and a founder of the Australian National University.

Read today, much of this scholarship rings of a usually charming chauvinism, which is probably rooted in a sense of pride and confidence at a young society seeming to have accomplished so much.[45] Some of the writing also displayed a faith in scientific progress that in many respects went beyond charming innocence – eugenics and the desirability of maintaining a racially pure population stock formed an integral limb of much of the pre-First World War work, for instance.[46] So, too, did some of the work have an air of proto-fascism about it.[47] But it is clear that it was

---

Separation of Powers in British Jurisdictions' (1921) 31 *Yale LJ* 24. See, generally, on Brown's work, O M Roe, 'Jethro Brown: The First Teacher of Law and History in the University of Tasmania' (1977) 5 *U Tas L Rev* 209 and O M Roe, *Nine Australian Progressives* (1984).

[41] Unlike the others, Deakin did not commit his views to published form, as such. But there can be no doubt either as to the substance of his views or to the effect that they had on the young Commonwealth. See his book *The Federal Story* (published posthumously, 1944). See, also, his 'secret' correspondence on behalf of the London *Morning Post*, a selection of which was published under the title *Federated Australia* (J A La Nauze ed, 1968). For more on his political views generally, see W Murdoch, *Alfred Deakin: A Sketch* (1923) and J A La Nauze, *Alfred Deakin: A Biography* (1965).

[42] See *State Experiments in Australia and New Zealand* (1902). On Reeves, see K Sinclair, *W P Reeves, New Zealand Fabian* (1965).

[43] See *A New Province for Law and Order* (1922). See also J Rickard, *H B Higgins, The Rebel as Judge* (1984).

[44] See *State Socialism in Victoria* (1932), *Search For a Social Philosophy* (1941), *Reflections of an Australian Liberal* (1953), 'A Theory of Social Integration' (unpublished MS at author's death). See also W Osmond, *Frederic Eggleston: An Intellectual in Australian Politics* (1985).

[45] Eggleston, for instance, wrote that '[i]n the Australian Commonwealth ... there is a political and social system which more nearly approaches the idea of a social laboratory than any other community in the world' (*State Socialism in Victoria*, at 5).

[46] See, *eg*, Reeves, *supra* n 42, at xxv-xxviii, 100; Roe, *supra* n 40, at 229.

[47] In *The Underlying Principles of Modern Legislation*, for instance, Jethro Brown wrote:

all rooted in a desire, as Jethro Brown's biographer has put it, 'to endow liberalism with stronger elements of social sympathy and recognition of human and historical complexity'.[48] Eggleston described Australian progressivism as 'constructive liberalism'.[49] It was, he said, rooted in 'the liberalism of Lloyd George and not that of Gladstone'.[50] The Australian constructive liberal, he continued, 'believes that the scope of human action can be enlarged by social re-organisation and cooperation, provided that the machinery created does not smother individual initiative and diminish personal responsibility'.[51]

Jethro Brown's work is of special interest in this respect, for it offers the most juridically complete vision of the new society that was being striven for. In his 1912 book, *The Underlying Principles of Modern Legislation*, he set forth a comprehensive argument for a new approach to law-making and parliamentary governance. *Underlying Principles* is a rambling work full of spiritual and poetic metaphor, which even now is infectiously exciting to read. But if one stands back from its prose, what emerges from the pages is a clear vision of government based not on spirituality, but rather on a linear rationality, and a scientific quest for the improvement of humankind. In his own words, Brown's was a project of 're-birth'.[52] First of all, he said, the old notion of legal sovereignty had to be re-defined, to accord with modern understanding. 'The older theory of sovereignty', he claimed, 'has become increasingly untenable:'

> Loyalty to rulers is felt, not as loyalty to persons, but as loyalty to the State for which those rulers act. The making of laws by the legislature and their interpretation by the courts, as well as all the administrative actions of government, are effected by individuals who possess no inherent authority but

---

A community where each individual desires to promote the common good, and where this desire exercises a controlling influence over his will, is a much higher and more efficient type of social union than a community where popular decisions represent a mere coincidence of a multitude of particular wills, each of which is bent upon some private gain ... By the proclamation and reiteration of such ideals, the world of sordid actualities has been transformed in the past and will be transformed in the future (at 146-147).

[48] Roe, *supra* n 40.

[49] *Reflections of an Australian Liberal*, at 1.

[50] *Ibid.*

[51] *Id*, at 6.

[52] *Supra* n 40, at 107-110.

> derive their right to exercise their functions, mediately or immediately, from the community of which they, like the humblest citizen are a part.[53]

Importantly for present purposes, Brown discounted the importance of individual autonomy in the progressive state. The object of those in political power, he argued, was to determine what he described as the 'social will'. But this was not the same thing as governing according to opinion poll. Social will was not to be equated with 'actual will', which Brown thought could be corrupted by several factors, including the population's ignorance of what was in its own best interests.[54] In Brown's conception, the social will – which amounted to a 'true unity of will'[55] – could only be determined by legislators once they had become conscious of the community of interest, which might well differ from the community's actual will.[56]

In return, the citizen had to seek to become conscious of his dependence upon the collective: 'The more the citizen reflects upon his daily life, the more he will realise how completely dependent he is, in living that life, upon the support of the State of which he is a member.'[57] And once the legislature had determined the social will, Brown thought that it was justified in acting for the benefit of citizens, even where the citizenry preferred to be left alone: '[T]he liberty of an individual may be promoted by restrictions that the State imposes upon him in his own interests.'[58]

In this regard, the Australian version of the programme for the new state was similar to that of English progressives like T H Green, L T Hobhouse (who was the first professor of Sociology at the LSE) and the Webbs.[59] Yet, Australian progressivism differed in some important respects

---

[53] *Id*, at 132. *Cf* Mason CJ, in *Australian Capital Television v The Commonwealth* (1992) 177 CLR 106, at 137:

> The very concept of representative government and representative democracy signifies government by the people through their representatives. Translated into constitutional terms, it denotes that the sovereign power which resides in the people is exercised on their behalf by their representatives.

See also *infra* chapter 6.

[54] Reeves *id*, at 143-148.

[55] *Id*, at 144.

[56] *Id*, at 153.

[57] *Id*, at 125.

[58] *Id*, at 63.

[59] See, *eg*, Green, *Essays, Moral, Political and Literary* (1898), *Lectures on the Principles of Political Obligation* (1921), and J R Rodman (ed), *The Political Theory of T H Green* (1964); Hobhouse, *Democracy and Reaction* (1904), *Liberalism* (1911), *The Elements of Social Justice* (1922); S Webb, *Socialism in England* (1890), S & B Webb, *Industrial*

from English progressivism. For one thing, Australia had no real landed aristocracy. Nor did it have hereditary lower classes. So while, as in Great Britain, there was a significant degree of tension between wage-earning labour and those who employed it, in Australia the conflict tended to be grounded more strongly in simple economics, rather than in political class theory.

There was also a certain pragmatism in Australian progressivism, which allowed it to forsake some of the doctrinal purity deemed integral by English progressives. Pember Reeves, for example, once described Australian progressivism as an 'ill-defined blend of Radicalism, Socialism, and Trade Unionism'.[60] Accordingly, he said, 'it is of more use to examine what the Progressives have done than to try to define what they believe'.[61] Jethro Brown described his own work as 'scientific, not political'.[62] He contrasted it with that of J A Hobson, one of the leading English liberal theorists, who, he said, had a 'militant purpose'.[63] It was in this same vein that Mr Justice Higgins said of the Court of Conciliation and Arbitration – which was one of the Australian progressives' chief accomplishments[64] – that it had 'nothing to do with' with abstract theory. Rather, it saw its duty as 'to shape its conclusions on the solid anvil of existing industrial facts'.[65] The 'new' Australian legislation, therefore, enjoyed the freedom of being able to deal with each piece of proposed legislation on its own merits, and without having to consider whether it fitted with some overall programme of 'social reconstruction'.[66]

The point to be taken from this is that the legal and political contexts in which the superior courts both in Australia and Great Britain faced the new century was one which was really quite different from the contexts in which

---

Democracy (1914), *The Problems of Modern Industry* (1902), *A Constitution for the Socialist Commonwealth of Great Britain* (1920).

[60] *Supra* n 42, at 91.

[61] *Ibid.*

[62] *The Underlying Principles of Modern Legislation*, *supra* n 40, at vii.

[63] *Id*, at 167.

[64] See Sawer, *supra* n 34, at 40.

[65] *Supra* n 43, at 37. Interestingly, though he was to sit on it for twenty-two years, Higgins was initially opposed to the creation of the High Court. He was of the view that constitutional interpretation could best be carried out by the state courts and the Judicial Committee of the Privy Council. See Commonwealth of Australia, *Parliamentary Debates*, House of Representatives, 9 June 1903, at 632-635.

[66] *Ibid.* Probably the best analysis of the issue-by-issue nature of the 'new' Australian legislation during this period can be found in Geoffrey Sawer's books *Australian Federal Politics and Law 1901-1929* (1956) and *1929-1949* (1963).

the doctrines of judicial control of administration, including the doctrine of natural justice, initially developed. Whereas in the old days, the courts felt more-or-less comfortable in applying the doctrine of natural justice in a manner unencumbered by technicality – as seen, for example, in the paradigm cases of *Wood v Woad* and *Cooper v Wandsworth Board of Works* – by the early twentieth century, some judges would come to feel themselves on a less secure footing. Judges now found themselves having to balance their instinctive concern for common law values and the fairness of individual treatment, with evidence of a political will to accord primacy to the demands of collective efficiency.

A Doctrine in Transition

A neat illustration of the theoretical tensions involved in attempting to balance the progressive project with common law assumptions, and of the path that natural justice was to take from the older, more fluid, form it occupied in the nineteenth century and before, to the more restrictive conception that came to characterise it in parts of the twentieth century can be seen in the different judgments in the now usually-overlooked 1912 judgment of the High Court in *Municipal Council of Sydney v Harris*.[67]

Considered in light of the authorities considered in the last chapter, *Municipal Council of Sydney v Harris* is not at all exceptional in its result. Griffith CJ and Barton and Isaacs JJ concurred in holding that someone whose substantive rights in real property were to be interfered with by the executive had a procedural right to a hearing before this could take place. But what is striking about the case is that there were three different approaches to the question of why natural justice applied. Griffith CJ's was very much a judgment cast in the old, 'paradigm' tradition, in which natural justice would be held applicable as a matter of common law reflex to protect private property rights. Barton J's view was similar, but he tempered his approach with an acknowledgment that modern legislation sometimes demanded that common law rights be curtailed in the name of the collective good. The judgment of Isaacs J, in contrast, revealed an awareness of the changing legislative landscape, and a willingness to take account of governmental context in determining whether traditional natural justice rights were to be accorded.

[67] 14 CLR 1.

Harris involved a set of stables in Sydney, owned by Sir Matthew Harris, a prominent municipal politician.[68] Section 84 of the *Sydney Corporation Act 1902* (NSW) gave the City Surveyor the authority to issue condemnation notices against buildings and to require their repair at the owner's expense. If an owner of a condemned building proved to be recalcitrant, the Act provided that the City Council could direct the Surveyor to carry out the work himself, with the expenses to be borne by the owner. Such an order was made against Harris's stables. But rather than carrying out the work, Harris disputed the accuracy of the Surveyor's conclusions, and his solicitor wrote to the City Council requesting a hearing to '[furnish] evidence to show that the stables in question are not in a ruinous state as alleged in the said notice'.[69] The Council refused the request and issued a direction to the City Surveyor to carry out the repair work at Harris's expense. Harris then obtained a writ of mandamus from the Supreme Court, directing the Council to hear him.[70] The City, in turn, appealed to the High Court.

As has been said, Griffith CJ's judgment echoed the tone of the nineteenth century paradigm cases. He stated simply:

> The general rule of law is that a person so circumstanced – that is, who is liable to be called upon by some public authority to incur a heavy burden or loss – is entitled to be heard and to have the opportunity of giving reasons why such an order should not be made and enforced against him.[71]

The Chief Justice then referred to *Cooper v Wandsworth Board of Works* and other nineteenth century cases[72] as authority for the proposition that it did not matter that the City Council was not a court. He said:

> [The obligation to observe natural justice] is not confined ... to strictly judicial proceedings, but applies to any case in which a person or public body is invested with authority to decide. Whenever a public body is

[68] Harris (1841-1917) sat on the Sydney Municipal Council between 1883-1900, and served as mayor between 1898-1900. From 1894-1901, he also represented Sydney-Denison on the Legislative Assembly.

[69] 14 CLR, at 2.

[70] *Ex parte Sir Matthew Harris* (1911) 11 SR (NSW) 524.

[71] 14 CLR, at 5.

[72] Including *Wood v Woad* (1874) LR 9 Ex 190 and *Hopkins v Smethwick Local Board of Health* (1890) 24 QBD 712. Griffith CJ also referred to *Lapointe v L'Association de Bienfaissance et de Retraite la Police de Montreal* [1906] AC 535.

> entrusted with power to decide whether a person shall suffer pecuniary loss the principle applies.[73]

In fact, all three judges made liberal reference to *Cooper v Wandsworth Board of Works* and its nineteenth century sisters. Barton J, for example, said: 'That the right to be heard is not confined to cases where the proceeding is strictly judicial is shown in the case of *Cooper v Wandsworth Board of Works*.'[74] He said that on the basis of the Common Pleas' decision in *Cooper*, 'the principle [of *audi alteram partem*] therefore applies to this class of case unless it can be gathered from the terms of the statute that the legislature intended it to be exercised without giving the owner an opportunity of being heard'.[75] But where a statute is silent on the matter of a hearing right, he said, 'the courts will not assume that the legislature intended to prohibit it, unless such intention can be gathered from the statute by clear implication'.[76]

Isaacs J also cited *Cooper v Wandsworth Board of Works*,[77] but he took a different view of the legal context. Unlike the Chief Justice and Barton J, he attributed the obligation to accord natural justice (and, implicitly, the right to engage in judicial review for procedural unfairness) to a presumption of the intent of the legislature. This represented a discernible move away from the 'natural' sense of the doctrine's basis, as had been expressed in the paradigm cases:

> [I]f the requirement of a direction by the Council concerns primarily and ultimately the property and mutual obligations of others, it is plain on ordinary principles of construction that the persons affected must have some opportunity to be heard in their own defence.[78]

The differences in approach to the question of the *source* of natural justice obligations between the three judges in *Harris* will be returned to in chapter seven. But notwithstanding differences as to the ultimate source of the duty, as to result the Court was *ad idem*: in circumstances like these, where a public body was to deprive an owner of the full

---

[73] 14 CLR, at 7-8. See also *Meyers v Casey* (1913) 17 CLR 90, at 104 and 145-146, where Barton ACJ and Powers J used similar language.

[74] 14 CLR, at 9-10.

[75] 14 CLR, at 10-11.

[76] 14 CLR, at 11.

[77] 14 CLR, at 15.

[78] 14 CLR, at 14.

enjoyment of his property, there was an obligation to provide some sort of a hearing. Of the three, though, only Isaacs J ventured to offer a view as to exactly what sort of a hearing was required:

> No formalities are necessary here. All that is required is a full and fair opportunity of putting the case before Council ...
>
> The proper method of procedure depends, of course, largely on the nature, constitution and ordinary course of practice of the body to whom the power is entrusted. All that must be taken to be held in view by the legislature when creating the power and the connoted duty, and to be part of the implication. Natural justice looks only to substance, not to form. If form is necessary that must be founded on other considerations than natural justice.[79]

It is also significant, and perhaps not surprising, that of the three members of the High Court, it was Isaacs J who expressed himself in 'new' terms. Sir Owen Dixon once described Sir Samuel Griffith as a 'legal mind of the Austinian age, representing the thoughts and learning of a period which had gone'.[80] Geoffrey Sawer described him as 'right of centre' in his approach to collectivist legislation.[81] Isaacs J, in contrast, once said that he thought it was 'the duty of the Judiciary to recognise the development of the nation and to apply established principles to the new positions which the nation in its progress from time to time assumes'.[82] Otherwise, he said, '[t]he judicial organ would otherwise separate itself from the progressive life of the community and act as a clog upon the legislative and executive departments rather than as an interpreter'.[83]

The first of the 'thinning' cases, which symbolised the beginning of the first of natural justice's twentieth century phases, was the decision of the House of Lords the year before *Harris*, in *Board of Education v Rice*.[84] *Rice* was a judgment of the House of Lords in the pre-World War I period of Liberal reform ascendancy. H H Asquith had become Prime Minister in 1908, and together with Viscount Haldane, David Lloyd George and the

---

[79] 14 CLR, at 15-16.

[80] 'Address upon the occasion of retiring from the office of Chief Justice of the High Court of Australia', in *Jesting Pilate* (1965) 255, at 258.

[81] *Supra* n 34, at 55, n 129.

[82] *Commonwealth v Colonial Combing, Spinning & Weaving Co Ltd* (1922) 31 CLR 421, at 438-439.

[83] *Ibid.*

[84] [1911] AC 179.

young Winston Churchill in his cabinet, he embarked on a concentrated programme of reform, much of which involved the expansion of the executive powers of the central government. As all know, this soon led to a constitutional clash with the Lords (in their political capacity) of monumental proportions, but in his speech in *Rice* – which Robert Stevens described as 'gently chiding'[85] – the Liberal Lord Chancellor Loreburn gave a clear indication of the judicial attitude towards social legislation that the Asquith government wished to foster.[86]

The issue in *Board of Education v Rice* was whether mandamus would issue against the Board of Education, to require it to determine whether a local school authority was avoiding its duty under the *Education Act 1902* to maintain the efficiency of its schools, by permitting lower salaries to be paid to teachers in church-associated schools (the 'voluntary schools') than in state-run ones. For reasons which are not clear from the report of the case, but which presumably reflect the political sensitivity of the matters in issue (Cozens-Hardy MR, for example, said that the passage of the *Education Act* had 'effected a revolution'[87]), the Board of Education declined to rule on the issues placed before it by the voluntary schools. The voluntary schools succeeded in obtaining a writ of mandamus against the Board from the Divisional Court,[88] which was affirmed by the Court of Appeal.[89] The Board then appealed to the House of Lords.

The actual issue for decision in *Rice*, therefore, was not whether natural justice applied. It was accepted that some sort of a duty of fairness was incumbent on the Board. Rather, the question was whether mandamus would issue against the Board of Education, requiring it to make a decision. But in the course of discussing whether the prerogative remedy of mandamus would issue against an entity like the Board, Lord Loreburn LC delivered what came for several decades to be one of the most commonly quoted judgments in English administrative law. He began by discussing the changed context of the determination of 'questions' by the executive government, which had come about as a result of the increased involvement of the state in private life:

---

[85] R Stevens, *Law and Politics: The House of Lords as a Judicial Body, 1800-1976* (1979), at 178.

[86] Though it should be noted that the controversy in *Rice* actually involved a piece of legislation passed by the preceding Conservative administration.

[87] [1910] 2 KB, at 172.

[88] [1909] 2 KB 1045.

[89] [1910] 2 KB 165 (*sub nom R v Board of Education*).

> Comparatively recent statutes have extended, if they have not originated, the practice of imposing upon departments or officers of State the duty of deciding or determining questions of various kinds. In the present instance, as in many others, what comes for determination is sometimes a matter to be settled by discretion, involving no law. It will, I suppose, usually be of an administrative kind; but sometimes it will involve matter [*sic*] of law as well as matter of fact, or even depend upon matter of law alone.[90]

Having done this, his Lordship noted the actual procedural obligation that arose in the circumstances – what was incumbent upon these new types of decision-makers in order for them to satisfy the demands of procedural fairness. It is interesting to note how similar it was to what Isaacs J had said in *Municipal Council of Sydney v Harris*:[91]

> In such cases the Board of Education will have to ascertain the law and also to ascertain the facts. I need not add that in doing either they must act in good faith and fairly listen to both sides, for that is a duty lying upon everyone who decides anything. But I do not think they are bound to treat such a question as though it were a trial. They have no power to administer an oath, and need not examine witnesses. They can obtain information in any way they think best, always giving a fair opportunity to those who are parties in the controversy for correcting or contradicting any relevant statement prejudicial to their view.[92]

---

[90] [1911] AC, at 182.

[91] In light of the fact that *Board of Education v Rice* preceded *Harris*, it is interesting to note that *Rice* was not referred to by any of the judges in the High Court. This seems to have been a not uncommon phenomenon in Australian administrative law – which perhaps should lead to a re-evaluation of the commonly-held assumption that until very recently a 'cultural cringe' monopolised the Australian judicial mind. There have been at least four instances where the High Court did not consider recent decisions of the House of Lords in important administrative law cases. Apart from this one, they were *Metropolitan Meat Board v Finlayson* (1916) 22 CLR 340 (failing to consider *Local Government Board v Arlidge* [1915] AC 120. See *infra*), *Testro Brothers Pty Ltd v Tait* (1963) 109 CLR 353 (failing to consider *Ridge v Baldwin* [1964] AC 40. See *infra* chapter 4), and *Craig v South Australia* (1995) 184 CLR 163 (failing to consider *R v Hull University Visitor, Ex parte Page* [1993] AC 682).

[92] [1911] AC, at 182. On this in an Australian context, see also *Randall v Northcote Corporation* (1910) 11 CLR 100, at 105-106, in which Griffith CJ held that while natural justice *per se* did not attach to the proceedings of a town council, the councillors nevertheless had a general duty to make decisions in accordance with 'the rule of reason and justice, not according to private opinion', and must not be 'arbitrary, vague and fanciful, but legal and regular' (quoting Lord Halsbury, in *Sharp v Wakefield* [1891] AC 173, at 179).

All of this was, strictly speaking, *obiter dicta*.[93] But Lord Loreburn's speech in *Board of Education v Rice* nevertheless came to have an important effect in later years in shaping the scope of the obligation to observe natural justice. It did so in two different ways – which in some respects sit in opposition to one another. First, by saying that the duty lay upon 'every one who decides anything' – in other words, by describing in broad terms the circumstances in which the duty was present – he was providing ammunition for those who were in favour of continued judicial involvement in the review of the work of the executive.[94]

At the same time, by making the same point that Isaacs J had made in *Municipal Council of Sydney v Harris*, namely that natural justice ought not to be viewed as a synonym for the judicial process, he was overtly injecting a note of 'thinness' into the doctrine. When taken with their Lordships' actual holding on the matters in issue – that when it heard the dispute, it would be permissible for the Board to countenance discriminatory treatment of the church schools, provided only that their efficiency was not impaired, which was something for the Board to decide[95] – this added fuel to the fire of those who *opposed* judicial involvement in the administrative process. For anti-judicial reviewists, this proved to be the lever with which the procedural impositions of natural justice could be pared back. Indeed, in a way, the subsequent story of natural justice can be described as a fight between the two competing visions inherent in Lord Loreburn's speech.

The Liberal reformist line of deference to the executive was made even more plain, three years later, in the House of Lords' judgment in

---

[93] Moreover, it was a point which the respondent voluntary schools were not called upon to argue.

[94] See, *eg*, Dicey's note, 'The Development of Administrative Law in England' (1915) 31 *LQR* 148. This piece is sometimes taken as an admission by Dicey that he had been wrong in denying that a *droit administratif* was alien to English legal culture, but it is instructive to remember that in the very first paragraph, he asserted a robust claim for judicial control of the executive. He said that the principle arising from *Board of Education v Rice* was that 'any power conferred upon a Government department by statute must be exercised in strict conformity with the terms of the statute, and that any action by such department which is not so exercised should be treated by a court of law as invalid'.

[95] On the issue of whether discrimination between schools was permissible, his Lordship said:

> I do not find anything ... in the statute itself which prohibits the local authority from doing for some schools more than it does for others, even if the circumstances are indistinguishable ([1911] AC, at 183).

Local Government Board v Arlidge.[96] *Arlidge* was heard by what we would today describe as a stacked bench.[97] Viscount Haldane LC is said deliberately to have chosen a panel of Law Lords (himself,[98] Shaw,[99] Moulton[100] and Parmoor[101]) who had all been active Liberal politicians. He wanted to ensure that the government's reformist programme received a sympathetic hearing.[102] And in this respect, he succeeded. The speeches in *Arlidge*, particularly those of Lords Haldane and Shaw, took the 'thinning' aspect of Lord Loreburn's speech in *Rice* much further. As Stevens put it, the decision in *Arlidge* 'removed any serious threat that the courts might exercise even procedural due process over departments of the central government'.[103]

Local Government Board v Arlidge involved a statutory scheme not dissimilar to that in issue in *Sydney Corporation v Harris*. The *Housing and Town Planning Act 1909* conferred upon local authorities the power to make closing orders in respect of any dwellings which they found to be unfit for human habitation. Arlidge was the owner of a house which had been made the subject of a closing order. He appealed the order to the Local Government Board. A public hearing was duly held by an inspector on behalf of the Board, at which Arlidge and his solicitor were in attendance, and at which Arlidge gave evidence. When the Local Government Board upheld the closing order, Arlidge applied for a writ of certiorari, on the basis, *inter alia*, that he had been denied natural justice. He argued that he was entitled to know the identities of the actual decision-makers within the Board and to appear in person before the Board before it made a determination in his case.

---

[96] [1915] AC 120, rev'g [1914] 1 KB 160 (CA), rev'g [1913] 1 KB 463.
[97] Stevens, *supra* n 85, at 198.
[98] MP 1885-1911, LC 1912-15. Lord Haldane was in his day widely credited with having great skill at, and faith in, the science of public administration. See Sir J Anderson, *Administrative Technique in the Public Service* (1949).
[99] MP 1892-1909.
[100] MP 1885-1886, 1894-1895, 1890-1906.
[101] Conservative MP 1895-1914, but thereafter he voted as a Liberal in the House of Lords. Parmoor was, some may be interested to note, the father of Sir Stafford Cripps, and the brother in law of Beatrice Webb.
[102] He is also alleged to have done the same in *Nocton v Lord Ashburton* [1915] 1 Ch 274 (Prof W R Cornish to author, 30 October 1998).
[103] *Supra* n 85, at 192.

Arlidge had lost at first instance,[104] but had succeeded on appeal.[105] In his judgment in the Court of Appeal, Hamilton LJ[106] said '[b]y all means let the appellant and the Local Authority too, if it wishes see and address the judge, it is all in his day's work'.[107] He also suggested that the decision-making process could benefit from more openness: 'Time spent in removing a grievance or in avoiding the sense of it', he said, 'is time well spent, and the Board's officials will, like good judges, amplify their jurisdiction by rooting it in the public confidence.'[108] In the House of Lords, however, Viscount Haldane LC began with an admonishment about paying attention to the different juridical context involved in the new types of case. While there was no doubt in his mind that the matter before the Local Government Board was one affecting property rights, this alone was not enough to dispose of the issue – at least not in 1914. For the reality, his Lordship said, was that the nature of parliamentary goals had changed with the onset of the modern age. At one time, the preservation of individual liberty may have been the paramount concern of legislation. But parliament now considered 'higher interests than those of the individual'.[109] Accordingly, it was 'dangerous for judges to lay much stress on what a hundred years ago would have been a presumption considerably stronger than it is today'.[110] As will be seen, statements like this about 'the new legislation' came to play a highly significant role in clipping natural justice's wings during the twilight phase.

---

[104] [1913] 1 KB 463.

[105] [1914] 1 KB 160.

[106] Later Lord Sumner.

[107] [1914] 1 KB, at 203-204.

[108] *Ibid*. The full passage reads as follows:

> [I]f it was our function to advise the Local Government Board as to its procedure generally, or to criticise the procedure actually adopted as such, I should for my part suggest that the more open the procedure is the better. By all means let both the appellant and the Local Authority see the inspector's reports; a discreet and careful officer is not likely to offend, and if, in spite of discretion and care, he is harassed by actions for libel he may well be defended and indemnified by his Department. By all means let the appellant, and the Local Authority too, if it wishes, see and address the judge, it is all in his day's work. By all means let the appellant have the last word and as many of them in reason as he likes. Time spent in removing a grievance or in avoiding the sense of it, is time well spent, and the Board's officials will, like good judges, amplify their jurisdiction by rooting it in the public confidence.

[109] [1915] AC, at 130.

[110] [1915] AC, at 130-131.

In Lord Haldane's view, natural justice *was* required to be observed by the Local Government Board, but this did not include the trappings of the ordinary judicial process. 'The decision must be come to in the spirit and with the sense of responsibility of a tribunal whose duty it is to mete out justice', he said,[111] but 'what [the] procedure is to be in detail must depend upon the nature of the tribunal'.[112] In this case, he noted that the Local Government Board was an entity charged with 'executive functions' which were required to be carried out 'in the interests of the community'.[113] This negated any obligation on the part of the Board to provide an opportunity for people to appear before it in person. And since the Board was represented in Parliament by a responsible minister, there was no requirement to identify individual decision-makers.

So, too, did Lord Parmoor hold that the requirements of natural justice (which he called 'substantial justice'[114]) had been satisfied in the circumstances,[115] as did Lord Moulton.[116] Lord Shaw of Dunfermline (who had also sat on *Board of Education v Rice*) was strongest of all, though, in his denunciation of the notion that Arlidge had any more procedural rights than he had already been given. He described Arlidge's claim that he had a right to know the identity of the actual decision-maker as a 'grotesque demand to individualise the department for private purposes'.[117]

With respect to the question of natural justice and the Board more generally, Lord Shaw allowed that 'when a central administrative board deals with an appeal from a local authority it must do its best to act justly, and to reach just ends by just means.'[118] But he rejected completely the suggestion that the proceedings of the Board could be likened in any significant respect to those of a judicial tribunal. The curial model could in some cases provide a guide to administrative tribunals, but 'that the judiciary should presume to impose its own methods on administrative or executive officers is a usurpation. And the assumption that the methods of natural justice are *ex necessitate* those of Courts of justice is wholly unfounded.'[119]

---

[111] [1915] AC, at 132.
[112] *Ibid.*
[113] *Ibid.*
[114] [1915] AC, at 140.
[115] [1915] AC, at 142.
[116] [1915] AC, at 146-147.
[117] [1915] AC, at 136.
[118] [1915] AC, at 138.
[119] *Ibid.*

He then dealt the mortal blow – and sounded the clarion call for those at both ends of the political spectrum who were concerned about the intersection of the judicial process and the bureaucracy:

> In so far as the term 'natural justice' means that a result or process should be just, it is a harmless though it may be a high-sounding expression; in so far as it attempts to reflect the old *jus naturale* it is a confused and unwarranted transfer into the ethical sphere of a term employed for other distinctions; and, in so far as it is resorted to for other purposes, it is vacuous.[120]

In these respects, *Local Government Board v Arlidge* is possibly of more jurisprudential interest than *Board of Education v Rice*.[121] Lord Loreburn's speech in *Rice* has tended to be more frequently quoted than Lord Shaw's in *Arlidge*, but the explicit doctrinal relaxation in Lord Shaw's formulation of the obligations associated with the doctrine of procedural fairness, together with the sheer forcefulness of his language, served to stake out the boundaries of the conflict that would dog the doctrine for forty years.

The High Court and the New Legislation

An Australian bedfellow of *Local Government Board v Arlidge*, but which in fact went even further in thinning out the obligations of procedural fairness in governmental decision-making processes, was the judgment in 1916 (a year after *Arlidge*) in *Metropolitan Meat Board v Finlayson*.[122] It is interesting to see how, in *Finlayson's Case*, the 'legislature-centric' view of the duty to observe natural justice which had been hinted at in the judgment of Isaacs J in *Municipal Council of Sydney v Harris* was further developed.

Metropolitan Meat Industry Board v Finlayson involved the interpretation of the *Meat Industry Act 1915* (NSW). The Act made it an offence to operate private abattoirs in the Sydney metropolitan area, except with permission of the Metropolitan Meat Industry Board, which

---

[120] *Ibid*.

[121] For other examples of this 'thinning' of the requirements of natural justice in action by their Lordships, see *De Verteuil v Knaggs* [1918] AC 557 (PC, Trin) and *Wilson v Esquimalt and Nanaimo Railway Company* [1922] AC 202 (PC, Can).

[122] (1916) 22 CLR 340 (rev'g *Ex parte Finlayson* (1916) 16 SR(NSW) 591).

was established by the Act to oversee the meat industry. Finlayson was the owner and operator of a private abattoir. When he applied to the Board for permission to continue to operate his meat-slaughtering business, he was refused. When asked the reasons why, the Board replied simply that it 'was not prepared to supply the particulars requested'.[123] Finlayson applied to court for a writ of mandamus, complaining that he had been denied a fair hearing. *Finlayson* was in fact a test case – there were a series of appeals on the same point pending before the Court.[124]

The parliamentary debates on the Bill make it clear that the intent of the legislature was to create a scheme to oversee the operation of the slaughtering industry in Sydney, as a means of accomplishing several 'new' legislative goals, including pollution abatement, improving the quality of meat on the market, and responding to concerns about cruelty to animals.[125] Nevertheless, what strikes one about *Finlayson* is just how deferential the judges of the High Court[126] were when faced with this example of new (or, as Isaacs J called it, 'novel'[127]) legislation which dealt with something other than a formal property right in the strict legal sense. This was in sharp contrast not only to the approach that had been taken by Griffith CJ in *Harris* just a few years earlier, but also to the way in which the Full Court of the Supreme Court of New South Wales had viewed Finlayson's position.

In the Supreme Court, all three judges held that the rules of natural justice were applicable – on the basis of an application of *Local Government Board v Arlidge*. Pring J, for example, quoted extensively from the speeches, and said that in their light, the Board had failed in its duty to Finlayson and his colleagues: 'The applicant's right of property was at stake. Nevertheless, he was not informed by the Board what reason they had for destroying that property.'[128] The High Court, in contrast, saw this as a simple case in which absolute discretion had been given to the Metropolitan Meat Industry Board, which displaced completely any procedural or other obligations to private abattoir operators. And while

---

[123] The facts of the case are summarised in the judgment of the Full Court of the Supreme Court of New South Wales, 16 SR(NSW), at 597-598.

[124] See 22 CLR, at 344.

[125] See the second reading speech of the Hon G Black, Colonial Secretary, New South Wales *Parliamentary Debates*, Legislative Assembly, 16 November 1915, at 3545-3548.

[126] Griffiths CJ, Barton, Isaacs and Rich JJ.

[127] 22 CLR, at 345.

[128] 16 SR(NSW), at 601.

Cooper v Wandsworth Board of Works, *Harris*, *Rice* and *Arlidge* were all referred to by counsel in argument, none of these authorities were referred to in the judgments. Griffith CJ, for example, simply said: 'These words are plain enough. On their face they mean that the business of slaughtering cattle in the metropolitan district is to be a government monopoly, except in so far as the Board may consent to its being carried on by private persons.'[129]

Finlayson's Case can possibly be explained as one of wartime exigency. But it shows how, when faced with (to use Isaacs J's expression) a novel legislative provision, the Court could be moved to adopt a standoff-ish attitude towards the doctrine of natural justice, even where common law rights and freedoms (here, the freedom to carry on business[130]) were being infringed. But what of the case where the Court was faced with the infringement of interests which fell short of property or common law rights? Taken on its face, Lord Loreburn's speech in *Rice* would suggest that a duty of fairness would attach to 'everyone who decides anything'. But what if this conflicted with a statutory provision which seemed to vest the government with the right to make decisions without any hearing? This was the question posed by *Gillen v Laffer*.

Gillen v Laffer[131] involved the interpretation of the South Australian *Crown Lands Acts 1915-1919* and *Discharged Soldiers Settlement Acts 1917-1919*. Under the latter Acts, provision was made for the sale of unalienated Crown lands to returned men, the purchase price being paid by long-term instalments. The agreements of purchase and sale contained a standard clause whereby in the event of default, the agreement would be rescinded and title would automatically re-vest in the Crown. The agreements also contained a clause which provided that if, within the first ten years from the date of sale, the Minister was 'satisfied on such evidence as he deem[ed] sufficient' that the returned soldier was not capable of properly managing the land, then the Minister could rescind the agreement.[132]

Gillen was a returned soldier, who had purchased a parcel of land through this scheme. But he had defaulted, and was thought by the government to have thereby indicated an unfitness to properly manage the

---

[129] 22 CLR, at 343.
[130] On this as a common law right, see *R v Barnsley Metropolitan Borough Council, Ex parte Hook* [1976] 1 WLR 1052.
[131] (1925) 37 CLR 210 (rev'g [1924] SASR 514).
[132] See 37 CLR, at 212.

land. The issue for the courts was whether, before re-taking possession, the Crown had to provide Gillen with a hearing of any sort. Today, there would be little doubt that Gillen would have a right to be accorded natural justice.[133] In 1925, though, the issue was not so straightforward.

As one might have expected, some judges in the High Court saw *Gillen v Laffer* as a *Cooper v Wandsworth Board of Works* sort of case, in which property rights were at stake, and in which, *ipso facto*, natural justice applied. Knox CJ, for example, tracked the language used by Griffith CJ in *Harris*. He said: 'I think the case is one in which the maxim *audi alteram partem* applies ... The Minister is a person invested by law with authority to adjudicate upon a matter with civil consequences to an individual.'[134] Similarly, Rich J said that '[t]he nature of the thing done – deprivation of property – implies a judicial act', and hence, an obligation to observe the rules of natural justice.[135] Higgins J, however (with whom the Privy Council agreed on further appeal[136]), saw the case differently. This was not, in his view, the type of case in which the law was being called upon to defend ordinary rights in property.

To Higgins J, this was an archetypal 'new legislation' case, in which interests other than the rights of a fee-holding citizen and the state *inter se* were involved:

> The imagination must grasp the concrete position. The power [to rescind sales] is confined to the first ten years, as years of probation; the contract is one in which the chief object of the vendor is to benefit the purchaser, because the purchaser is a man who served in the Great War; the facts of which the Minister is to be satisfied involve issues of such a character as might lead to endless debate; and the Minister, as administrator, is under a duty to other returned soldiers to see that the first holder is not blocking them without advantage to himself, and under a duty to the State to see that its generosity be not wasted.[137]

---

[133] See *infra* chapter 5 (though also *cf 'Sydney' Training Depot Snapper Island Ltd v Minister for Sport, Recreation and Tourism* (1987) 14 ALD 464).

[134] 37 CLR, at 220 (quoting, without reference, Kelly CB in *Wood v Woad* (1874) LR 9 Ex 190, at 196).

[135] 37 CLR, at 229. On this question of defining an act as judicial, and hence reviewable, by reference to its effect, see also Rich J's views in *R v Commonwealth Rent Controller, Ex Parte National Mutual Life Association* (1947) 75 CLR 361, at 373 (discussed *infra* chapter 3).

[136] [1927] AC 886 (*sub nom Laffer v Gillen*).

[137] 37 CLR, at 225-226.

So rather than being a property case, this was in his opinion one of 'mere contractual relation'.[138] In 1925, natural justice rights were bound up in the notion of 'judicial' or 'quasi-judicial' decision-making.[139] Accordingly, he said that 'nothing is further from the intendment of this clause than a judicial or quasi-judicial inquiry'.[140] As noted, the Privy Council agreed with Higgins J.[141] Their Lordships – who, significantly, included both Lords Haldane and Shaw – said that it was 'obvious that the authorities contemplated that amongst the more or less experimental cases there would be a certain number of failures'[142] and that parliament had 'intended to put into the hands of the responsible minister means whereby such cases might be readily dealt with, and, if necessary, a fresh start made'.[143]

Two years after its judgment in *Gillen v Laffer*, the High Court was again called upon to determine the extent to which natural justice attached to 'novel' relations between the state and the citizen. The issue in *Boucaut Bay Co Ltd v The Commonwealth*[144] was whether a Minister had to provide a hearing to someone before rescinding their contract to provide a coastal shipping service in the Northern Territory. The contract contained a 'state of mind' provision respecting termination: if the Minister was of the view that the agreement was not properly being carried out by the contractor, he could rescind it with a month's notice. Speaking for a unanimous Court,[145] Isaacs ACJ said that whether a hearing was required depended upon a contextual interpretation both of the contractual provision and of the Minister's decision-making resources. This was, of course, quite different from the Griffith view that natural justice applied 'whenever a public body [was] entrusted with power to decide whether a person shall suffer pecuniary loss'.[146]

As to the process of interpreting the contract, Isaacs ACJ said: '[I]n interpreting [the termination] clause, the surrounding circumstances have to be considered. The services contracted for had to be performed in a part of the Commonwealth remote from the Seat of Government, sparsely

[138] 37 CLR, at 227.
[139] See *infra*.
[140] 37 CLR, at 225.
[141] See [1927] AC, at 896.
[142] [1927] AC, at 895.
[143] *Ibid*.
[144] (1927) 40 CLR 98.
[145] Isaacs ACJ, Gavan Duffy, Powers and Rich JJ.
[146] *Municipal Council of Sydney v Harris*, 14 CLR, at 5.

settled and with poor means of communication, and with not improbable necessity for emergent action.'[147] As to the latter factor, he continued: 'The Minister ... would be dependent in most cases on departmental officers. He would call for inquiries and they would send him their reports. He could be trusted to act impartially and honourably ...'[148]

Again, this sort of contextual sensitivity reads very differently from the absolutist tones seen in the paradigm cases. To reiterate, this first phase in the twentieth century evolution of natural justice showed a development of a comparatively sophisticated view amongst some judges of the place of common law principles *vis-à-vis* new legislative goals. Particularly notable in this respect in the Australian context were the judgments of Isaacs and Higgins JJ. But with the onset of the second phase in the latter part of the 1920s, this sort of curial sensitivity seemed to fade from view.

The Confusion of a Doctrine: the *Electricity Commissioners* formulation

In fact, it was an English case, wrestling with this same problem of how to view non-proprietary interests for judicial review purposes, that served to hasten the end of the first phase. This was the decision of the Court of Appeal in 1924, in *R v Electricity Commissioners, Ex parte London Electricity Joint Committee.*[149] Leaving aside for a moment the actual holding, the *Electricity Commissioners* case came to stand for the proposition[150] that in order for writs of certiorari or prohibition to issue against an executive decision-maker – in other words, in order for there to be a *legally enforceable* obligation to observe the rules of natural justice – the decision-maker not only had to have power to affect a citizen's legal rights, but he or she also had to have a 'superadded' duty to act judicially. This was a highly significant development, for not only did it cut directly against the grain of the nineteenth century case-law, but it seemed to amount to a refutation of the formulation offered by Lord Loreburn in

---

[147] 40 CLR, at 105.

[148] *Ibid.* See also on this point his judgment in *Moreau v Federal Commissioner of Taxation* (1926) 39 CLR 65, in which he expressed faith in the fairness and impartiality of the upper ranks in the Public Service.

[149] [1924] 1 KB 171.

[150] See, *eg*, W Friedmann, *Principles of Australian Administrative Law* (1950), at 82.

Board of Education v Rice that 'anyone who decided anything' had an obligation to be fair (however thin this obligation may have been in the circumstances) in the course of so doing.[151]

R v Electricity Commissioners was in many ways the paradigm case to emerge from the new legislation. The *Electricity (Supply) Act 1919* created a body known as the Electricity Commissioners. The intention, as set out in sub-section 1(1) of the Act, was to establish a professional tribunal to 'promote, regulate, and supervise the supply of electricity' within the United Kingdom. In the event that the Electricity Commissioners were of the view that the supply of electricity in any district was in need of improvement, they could, following public consultation with those concerned, devise a scheme for the creation of an entity known as a 'joint electricity authority' with some power to take over the assets and liabilities of the pre-existing providers of electricity within the district.

A controversy arose over the provision of electricity to Greater London. In the process of the Electricity Commissioners' consultation over the establishment of a joint electricity authority for London, a disagreement arose between the London County Council and the private companies that had hitherto been providing electricity to London. The LCC was insistent that there be only one joint electricity authority for Greater London, whereas the companies were equally insistent that there be at least two.[152] The Electricity Commissioners' chosen solution was to attempt a compromise of sorts by creating a single London and Home Counties Joint Electricity Authority, but then requiring in its scheme that the Joint Authority delegate most of its effective authority to two sub-committees. The Joint Electricity Authority sought a writ of prohibition against the Electricity Commissioners, to prevent them from proceeding further with the scheme. The Commissioners, in response, argued that

---

[151] A curious thing about this case – as with *Rice* – was that the actual holding ought to have suggested something quite different. In fact, were anyone today who was unfamiliar with its legacy closely to parse *Electricity Commissioners*, they would almost certainly come to a very different conclusion about what propositions the case stands for. We see it as a limitation on judicial review, but its contemporaries saw it differently. John Willis, for instance, described *Electricity Commissioners* as an 'enlargement of the powers of the court' ('Three Approaches to Administrative Law', *infra* n 200, at 63).

[152] The facts are set out at [1924] 1 KB, at 172-180. One wonders whether the fact that eight pages were devoted by the editors of the *Law Reports* to the facts, itself speaks to the novelty of the dispute.

since they were not a judicial body, and that since theirs was not a judicial proceeding, the prerogative writ of prohibition should not be issued.

The Court of Appeal found that the proposed order was *ultra vires*, on the basis that the Commissioners did not have the power to require a delegation, and prohibition was issued. All three Lords Justices spoke, but Atkin LJ's judgment has become known as the leading one. 'It is to be noted', he said,

> that [the prerogative writs of certiorari and prohibition] deal with questions of excessive jurisdiction, and doubtless in their origin dealt almost exclusively with the jurisdiction of what is described in ordinary parlance as a Court of Justice. But the operation of the writs has extended to control the proceedings of bodies which do not claim to be, and would not be recognised as, Courts of Justice. Wherever any body of persons having legal authority to determine questions affecting the rights of subjects, and having the duty to act judicially, act in excess of their legal authority they are subject to the controlling jurisdiction of the King's Bench Division exercised in these writs.[153]

The problem was in Atkin LJ's use of the conjunction 'and', in formulating the circumstances in which the prerogative writs would lie: 'any body of persons having legal authority to determine questions affecting the rights of subjects, *and* having the duty to act judicially'. In later cases, it came to be taken as a requirement that before an obligation to observe natural justice could exist, a double threshold had to be met. Gone were the easy formulations of Lord Loreburn in *Board of Education v Rice* and Griffith CJ in *Municipal Council of Sydney v Harris* that natural justice was required of 'anyone who decides anything',[154] or that it applied in 'any case in which a person is invested with authority to decide'.[155] Now, not only did the decision-maker have to have the power to affect rights, but there also had to be some external indication that the decision-maker was to behave in a judge-like fashion when exercising this power. In *R v Legislative Committee of the Church Assembly, Ex parte Haynes-Smith*, decided a few years later, Lord Hewart CJ discussed the *Electricity Commissioners* decision. 'In order that a body may satisfy the required test', Lord Hewart said:

[153] [1924] 1 KB, at 205.
[154] [1911] AC, at 182.
[155] 14 CLR, at 7.

> it is not enough that it should have legal authority to determine questions affecting the rights of subjects; there must be superadded to that characteristic the further characteristic that the body has the duty to act judicially.[156]

His Lordship continued:

> The duty to act judicially is an ingredient which, if the test is to be satisfied, must be present. As these writs in the earlier days were issued only to bodies which without any harshness of construction could be called, and naturally would be called Courts, so also to-day these writs do not issue except to bodies which act or are under the duty to act in a judicial capacity.[157]

In other words, it came to be assumed that in order for the obligation to observe procedural fairness to be triggered, the decision-maker not only had to have the power to call upon a citizen to bear a burden or loss,[158] but his decision-making process also had to resemble that of a court. In the case before Lord Hewart, for example, neither the National Assembly of the Church of England nor its Legislative Committee were found to be amenable to the writ of prohibition, on the basis that they were engaged in the business of drafting of Church legislation for adoption by Parliament.[159]

On the surface, this sort of construction seems indicative of the same sort of sensitivity to the changed context of government as the cases discussed in the previous section. But when it is read with other cases, Lord Hewart's judgment seems really quite odd: in *R v Electricity Commissioners*, the preparation of an Order in Council which was to become incorporated in an enactment was deemed to be sufficiently judicial to be amenable to prohibition. But in Lord Hewart's case, just four years later, which purported to apply the very same legal principles to the very same type of activity – the drafting of legislation which would be adopted by parliament – prohibition would not lie because there was found to be no duty to act judicially. The difference in result between the two can easily be explained on grounds of judicial disinclination to involve itself in the business of internal church disputes. But as a matter of

---

[156] [1928] 1 KB 411, at 415 (holding that the writs of certiorari and prohibition would not issue to stop implementation of a new Prayer Book).

[157] *Ibid.*

[158] *Municipal Council of Sydney Corporation v Harris* 14 CLR , at 5 (*per* Griffith CJ).

[159] By virtue of the *Church of England Assembly (Powers) Act 1919*.

application of enunciated principle, the line between the two cases seems a blurry one.[160]

In fact, to apply literally Atkin LJ's test to *Electricity Commissioners* itself, one ought to have concluded that the prerogative writs would not lie. One searches the facts of the case in vain for anything other than their authority to affect the property rights of the electricity companies that would have indicated that parliament intended that the Commissioners had a duty to act judicially. Certainly, in his own judgment, Atkin LJ referred merely to their confiscatory power.[161] For his part, Bankes LJ also noted that the Commissioners were required to conduct local hearings before formulating any scheme,[162] but with respect, one cannot imagine that this alone gave their work a judicial character. Were this the case, then every Royal Commissioner would be held to be acting judicially, which was not the law in 1923.[163]

Moreover, a double-threshold test like that proffered by Lord Hewart is circular. Judges have *always* (or at least since the doctrine assumed its present form) had an obligation to accord natural justice.[164] So to say that someone must observe natural justice if they have an obligation to behave like a judge, especially in a jurisdiction like England with no constitutionally-mandated separation of powers, is at once both to state the obvious and to beg the question. Moreover, to place the emphasis on the formal constitution of a decision-maker rather than upon their power to interfere with the liberty of the citizen is to run the risk of denying procedural protection when it is needed most.

Lord Hewart and *The New Despotism*

The student of administrative law today does not know whether to pity or ridicule Lord Hewart. Certainly, in his own time, the latter rather than the former tended to be more common. But whatever one's views, it is clear

---

160 And contrast Lord Hewart's views in the *Church Assembly* case with his decision in *R v Postmaster-General* [1928] 1 KB 291, where he held that the giving by a doctor of a medical certificate *was* a judicial act, in respect of which certiorari would issue.

161 [1924] 1 KB, at 207.

162 [1924] 1 KB, at 198.

163 See *Commonwealth Sugar Refineries v Attorney-General* (1912) 15 CLR 182, var'd [1914] AC 237 (*sub nom Attorney-General (Commonwealth) v Commonwealth Sugar Refineries Ltd*).

164 See *Cameron v Cole* (1943) 68 CLR 571, at 589 (*per* Rich J).

that there are few more quixotic figures in modern legal history. As noted at the beginning of this chapter, it was the publication in 1929 of his book, *The New Despotism*, that ushered in the second of natural justice's twentieth century phases. Evaluating his role in the evolution of administrative law is not, though, altogether a straightforward matter. As Solicitor-General during the latter part of the First World War, for instance, he successfully argued the Crown's case in the infamous *Zadig* case concerning executive discretion.[165] As Attorney-General, he played a key role in both the preparation and passage of emergency powers legislation, which had a significant limiting impact on personal liberties.[166] Indeed, his skills as a government advocate in the House of Commons were such as to cause Lloyd George to delay his appointment to the bench in order to retain his services in the House of Commons.[167] In fact, no less than ten of the thirty statutes that he was later to criticise so vehemently were passed whilst he was Attorney-General.[168] But overshadowing all else that he did, and nowadays constituting practically the only thing he is remembered for,[169] was the publishing of *The New Despotism*.

---

[165] *R v Halliday, ex p Zadig* [1917] AC 260 (holding that under the Defence Regulations, the King in Council could suspend Habeas Corpus for people deemed to be of hostile origin). The case was in many ways a precursor of *Liversidge v Anderson* [1942] AC 206. For an Australian equivalent, see *Lloyd v Wallach* (1915) 20 CLR 299.

[166] Some have also argued that Lord Hewart was responsible for the delay in introducing Crown liability legislation in Great Britain. See Sir C T Carr, *Concerning English Administrative Law* (1940), at 24-25.

[167] Under English practice of the time, as Attorney-General, he had a *de facto* claim on the Chief Justiceship when Lord Reading CJ was appointed Viceroy of India in 1921. Lloyd George would not permit Hewart to be taken away from the Commons, however, so as a stop-gap, Lawrence J was appointed Lord Chief Justice on the implicit – though constitutionally quite inappropriate – understanding that at a time of Lloyd George's choosing, he would resign in favour of Hewart. See Jackson, *The Chief*, *infra* n 168, at 126-145.

[168] See J M Jacobs, *The Republican Crown: Lawyers and the Making of the State in Twentieth Century Britain* (1996), at 140. For further criticism of Hewart, including criticism of his performance as a judge, see R Stevens, *The Independence of the Judiciary: The View From the Lord Chancellor's Office* (1993), at 29-33. For a rather more sympathetic picture, see R Jackson, *The Chief: The Biography of Gordon Hewart, Lord Chief Justice of England* (1959).

[169] It was Lord Hewart who said, in *R v Sussex Justices, Ex parte McCarthy* [1924] 1 KB 256, at 258, that 'justice should not only be done, but should manifestly and undoubtedly be seen to be done'. But though the line is famous, that Lord Hewart was the utterer is generally not so well-remembered.

It is difficult for us today to conceive of the magnitude of the storm caused by this book. Perhaps the best analogy would be to imagine Sir Ronald Wilson offering his views on Aboriginal genocide in a published work while still a sitting justice of the High Court who was about to hear *Wik*, or to imagine Sir William Deane offering his views on reconciliation in commercially published form whilst awaiting the hearing in *Mabo v Queensland (No 2)*. When viewed in hindsight, it really does seem an extraordinary thing: that the Lord Chief Justice of England – the senior professional judge in the Kingdom – would write a book in which he accused the government of engaging in a conspiracy to subvert peoples' rights. Yet that is exactly what happened.

In fact, Lord Hewart was not the first member of the English judicial establishment to express alarm over the extent of law-making power that had been vested in the Executive. As early as 1911, Lord Cozens-Hardy, the Master of the Rolls, delivered a public speech in which he said that 'in recent years it has been the habit of parliament to delegate very great powers to government departments', which he described as a 'very bad system and one attended by great danger'.[170] But Lord Hewart's voice was by far the best-heard.

Briefly stated, the thesis of *The New Despotism* was that through the large-scale use of delegated law-making provisions, parliament was, unconstitutionally, ceding sovereignty to the executive. The result was to produce 'a despotic power which at one and the same time places Government departments above the Sovereignty of Parliament and beyond the jurisdiction of the Courts'.[171] In a later essay, he described it as 'bureaucratic tyranny'.[172] *The New Despotism* was really a reaction against the growth of the administrative state, and so it probably ought not to have caused surprise – but for the identity of the author. Picking up on Dicey's reference to the French *droit administratif*, Lord Hewart spoke scornfully of administrative law as 'profoundly repugnant' to English notions, and as something 'which, upon analysis, prove[s] to be nothing more than administrative lawlessness'.[173]

---

170 'Encroachment of the Executive: The Master of the Rolls on a Modern Danger', *The Times*, 4 May 1911 (quoted in *The New Despotism*, at 144-145).

171 (1929), at 14.

172 'The Mischief of Bureaucracy', in *Not Without Prejudice* (1937) 92, at 98.

173 *Supra* n 171, at 13. It should not be thought, though, that Lord Hewart was completely without a sense of humour. Contrasting the Glorious Revolution with the 'new' legislative environment, he said:

There is more than a little irony in the fact that Lord Hewart was moved to write this book. As has been noted, he was the one who was responsible for transforming Atkin LJ's formulation of when the prerogative writs of certiorari and prohibition would lie into a firm requirement that there be a 'superadded' duty to act judicially. He was also the president of the Divisional Court in *R v Electricity Commissioners* which had held that the prerogative writs would not lie in the circumstances, and which had been overruled by the Court of Appeal of which Atkin LJ was a member.[174] And, above all else, he was a former Cabinet member who had himself sponsored the very sort of legislation of which he now complained.[175] Moreover, there is some evidence that Hewart came later to regret writing the book, and using the intemperate language that he did to describe the civil service.[176]

Nevertheless, though some of his critics denied it at the time,[177] Lord Hewart's book struck a responsive chord among many people in England and throughout the Empire.[178] In a debate on an industrial regulation bill, for example, Lord Banbury spoke of the 'vicious principle' of 'giv[ing] power to a government department to usurp the functions of parliament'.[179]

> The old despotism, which was defeated, offered Parliament a challenge. The new despotism, which is not yet defeated, gives Parliament an anaesthetic (*Id*, at 17).

And he told the wonderful story of:

> a distinguished Anglo-Indian civilian, who, returning home on leave after a prolonged absence, passed the Houses of Parliament on his way from Victoria to Charing Cross. 'What place is that?' he asked. 'That, sir,' was the answer, 'is Parliament – the Houses of Parliament.' 'Really,' he exclaimed, though his exclamation was in fact slightly different, 'does that rubbish still go on?' (*Id*, at 14-15)

[174] See [1924] 1 KB, at 180.

[175] Not surprisingly, this irked his critics in Whitehall more than anything else. See, Jackson, *supra* n 148, at 216.

[176] *Ibid.*

[177] See, *eg*, F Frankfurter, 'Foreword: Courts and Administrative Law – The Experience of English Housing Legislation' (1936) 49 *Harv L Rev* 426.

[178] See, *eg*, the review of *The New Despotism* at (1930) 1 *Can Bar Rev* 77.

[179] His Lordship said:

> This bill perpetuates a vicious principle which unfortunately has grown much in the last few years. It gives power to a government department to usurp the functions of parliament and to pass what they call regulations which have the effect of an act of parliament and which deal with His Majesty's subjects; in fact, this does what in days gone by caused a king to lose his head.

Parliamentary Debates, House of Lords, 14 February 1929, at 932-933 (on the Factory and Work Shop (Cotton Cloth Factories) Bill). While this was actually before the formal

In a similar vein, the Oxford historian (and sometime MP) Sir John Marriot wrote an essay entitled 'Law and Liberty', in which he argued that 'the prevailing and increasing disposition on the part of the British parliament to confer upon the Executive quasi-judicial and quasi-legislative functions is wholly misplaced and ought to be resisted'.[180] Oxford Professor of Jurisprudence (and University of Sydney graduate) Sir C K Allen was moved to publish a series of his essays which touched upon like themes under the title *Bureaucracy Triumphant*.[181]

Some other judges were inspired to join in Hewart's act of insurrection. Scrutton LJ once spoke patronisingly in a judgment of 'an all-wise civil service'.[182] Sir William Mulock, the Chief Justice of Ontario, delivered a public address in which he spoke of 'the ever-increasing practice' of 'depriving our people of the protection of the law and of the Courts, by vesting in autocratic bodies the power to arbitrarily deal with matters affecting our liberties and rights'.[183] In Sir William's view, administrative decision-makers were 'reviv[ing] the Star Chamber method of conducting their proceedings behind closed doors'.[184]

In Australia, Professor Kenneth Bailey wrote that the tendency to broad delegation 'has excited considerable apprehension in Great Britain and it is salutary that the subject should be attracting a good deal of

---

publication of *The New Despotism*, Lord Banbury made specific reference to 'a very great note or warning' that Lord Hewart had given (*ibid*).

[180] *The Fortnightly Review*, July 1928.

[181] (1931).

[182] *R v Minister of Labour, Ex parte National Trade Defence Association* [1932] 1 KB 1, at 11.

[183] 'Address of the Chief Justice of Ontario' (1934) 12 *Can Bar Rev* 32, at 38. For other Hewart-inspired examples of this same sentiment, see J W de B Farris, 'Justice of the Courts' (1938) 16 *Can Bar Rev* 509; W Johnson, 'The Lawyer and Administrative Boards' (1943) 3 *R du B* 233; W Johnson, 'The Rule of Law Under an Expanding Bureaucracy' (1944) 22 *Can Bar Rev* 380.

[184] *Ibid*. In terms of intemperateness of language, Sir William seems to have done his best to match Lord Hewart phrase for phrase. Consider Sir William's description of the process of administrative adjudication:

> The presiding officer is not required to know anything of the law which he is to administer; free, of his own will to hear the case in public or private, in the presence or absence of the parties; with or without evidence; with or without the assistance of lawyers to prevent perjury; free to disregard the evidence and the law and to give the final decision without any reasons therefor, and not appealable to any court. Is that the position to which anyone with British blood in his veins should quietly submit? (*Id*, at 39).

attention in Australia, too'.[185] Sir Frederic Eggleston expressed the view that Australian 'state socialism', as he described it, had 'extended to even greater lengths than the paternalism of the eighteenth century in Great Britain'.[186] He continued by saying that while 'State action is looked on with favour by all the advanced parties in Great Britain to secure their aims, most thinking people are convinced that the inefficiencies of State action are responsible for many of our acute problems, and are looking for ways of limiting it'.[187] Even Jethro Brown was moved to express alarm at more or less the same time: 'In Australia', he wrote, 'there has been a recent tendency to substitute administrative "discretion" for the judicial process ... Encroachments upon the Rule of Law open the way to irremediable abuses.'[188]

The Academic Backlash

On the other hand, some commentary on Lord Hewart's work, especially that emanating from the academy, was scathing in the extreme. Felix Frankfurter, for instance, wrote:

> Nothing better illustrates the elder Huxley's observation regarding the frequent survival of a theory long after its brains have been knocked out, than that the Lord Chief Justice of England should treat Dicey as gospel, and regard as constitutional spoilations those inroads upon the Rule of Law which Maitland had already noticed fifty years before.[189]

---

[185] 'Administrative Legislation in the Commonwealth', *supra* n 38, at 10.

[186] *State Socialism in Victoria* (1932), at 11.

[187] *Ibid.*

[188] 'The Separation of Powers in British Jurisdictions', *supra* n 40.

[189] *Supra* n 177, at 426-427. Frankfurter, as many will know, was one of the intellectual architects of the legal aspects of President Roosevelt's New Deal, and was to be appointed to the Supreme Court by Roosevelt in 1939. One of the central tenets of Frankfurter's jurisprudence was that the courts ought as much as possible to defer to the expertise of departmental civil servants:

> Legislative policies, under modern circumstances and in their different fields of operation must ... be given concreteness and adaptation through administrative agencies. Considerable areas of discretion must inevitably ... be committed to these agencies and, like all organisms, they must in part evolve their own procedure ('Foreword' (1938) 47 *Yale L J* 1, at 5).

John Willis described Lord Hewart as having 'descend[ed] from Olympus' in order to proffer his message of alarm.[190] He commented sarcastically that it 'would be out of place to criticise *The New Despotism* as a work of legal scholarship'.[191] Another commentator suggested that the book consisted of 'extravagant rhetoric' with 'a core of truth'.[192] He said that it amounted to 'a brilliant piece of journalistic propaganda, with the lights and shadows so skilfully heightened that the reader may easily fail to discover what the essential problems involved are'.[193] Sir Ivor Jennings attacked the sort of people who would share Hewart's views as people who 'wanted nothing which interfered with profits, even if profits involved child labour, wholesale factory accidents, the pollution of rivers, of the air, and of the water-supply, jerry-built houses, low wages, and other incidents of nineteenth-century industrialism'.[194]

In this same vein, William Robson wrote of C K Allen that he represented 'in a more refined and scholarly manner, the school of thought of which Lord Hewart was the crudest and most undiscriminating exponent'.[195] Some of the academic rivalry at play might be evident in the fact that Robson (of the LSE) later said that Allen's work 'typified the Oxford outlook of the day'.[196] For its part, the British government was so concerned about the book's impact that even before it was published, the Lord Chancellor convened the Committee on Ministers' Powers – the Donoughmore Committee – with a brief to 'consider the powers exercised by or under the direction of ... Ministers of the Crown', and to 'report what

---

[190] *The Parliamentary Powers of English Government Departments* (1933), at 3.
[191] *Ibid.*
[192] 'Book Review: *The New Despotism*' (1930) 1 *Pol Q* 125, at 127. He also wrote that 'The spectacle of the Lord Chief Justice of England attacking with passion the *bona fides* of the civil service is not a pleasant one' (*Id*, at 131).
[193] *Id*, at 125. The author was apparently of sufficient standing that he chose to remain anonymous. Authorship of the piece is attributed to 'XYZ'.
[194] Jennings, *The Law and the Constitution* (1933), at 309-310.
[195] W Robson, *Justice and Administrative Law* (2nd ed. 1947), at 367. It is, though, appropriate to note that some gentleness did survive the debate. In 1935, for instance, Sir Ivor Jennings published a piece entitled 'In Praise of Dicey' (13 *Pub Admin* 123). And even Harold Laski was moved to say that it was Dicey 'who captivated me most': 'I didn't always agree and I sometimes doubted accuracy, but I never stopped admiring' (quoted in R A Cosgrove, *The Rule of Law: Albert Venn Dicey, Victorian Jurist* (1980), at 112-113).
[196] 'Justice and Administrative Law Reconsidered' [1979] *Cur Leg Prob* 107.

safeguards are necessary to secure the constitutional principles of the sovereignty of Parliament and the supremacy of the Law'.[197]

What makes *The New Despotism* so important today is not its thesis. The clearly exaggerated hyperbole in which it was written makes it amusing to look at in a kind of voyeuristically arrogant way. But from an academic point of view, the book is significant in the way it served as a lightning rod for competing visions of administrative law. Among the leading academic critics of the Hewart view of administrative law (or administrative law*lessness*, to his characterisation), four in particular stand out: Sir Ivor Jennings,[198] William Robson,[199] John Willis[200] and D M Gordon.[201] Jennings and Robson both taught at the LSE, Willis (though English by birth and education) taught at Dalhousie Law School in Nova Scotia and later at the University of Toronto,[202] and Gordon was a solicitor in private practice in British Columbia.[203] In the years surrounding the

---

[197] *Report of the Committee on Ministers' Powers*, Cmnd 4060, April 1932, at 1. For a present-day English assessment of the Report, see Stevens, *supra* n 168, and Jacobs, *supra* n 168.

[198] See, *eg*, 'Courts and Administrative Law – The Experience of English Housing Legislation', *supra* n 177, *The Law and the Constitution* (1st ed. 1933), *Principles of Local Government Law* (1st ed. 1931).

[199] *Justice and Administrative Law* (1st ed. 1928, 2nd ed. 1947), 'The Report of the Committee on Ministers' Powers' (1932) 3 *Pol Q* 351. For something of a retrospective view, see his 'Justice and Administrative Law Reconsidered', *supra* n 196.

[200] *The Parliamentary Powers of English Government Departments* (1934), 'Three Approaches to Administrative Law' (1935) 1 *UTLJ* 53, 'Administrative Law and the *British North America Act*' (1939) 53 *Harv L Rev* 251. In a notice of the inaugural issue of the *University of Toronto Law Journal*, published in the *Law Quarterly Review* in 1935, Professor Goodhart said that Willis's piece, 'Three Approaches to Administrative Law', 'shows that a sound, realistic approach [to the question of executive power] is preferable to the more prejudiced views of certain other writers' (51 *LQR*, at 288). A thinly veiled reference to Lord Hewart, one assumes?

[201] 'Relation of Facts to Jurisdiction' (1929) 45 *LQR* 459, 'Observance of Law as a Condition of Jurisdiction' (1931) 47 *LQR* 386; 557, 'Administrative Tribunals and the Courts' (1933) 49 *LQR* 94; 419.

[202] An interesting and moving obituary of Willis by a former student was published in the Toronto *Globe and Mail*, 3 July 1997. I myself was lectured by him as a law student in the early 1980s, and I remember thinking that the passion with which he spoke seemed a rare thing in law school.

[203] In some ways, Gordon was the most interesting of the group. He received his legal education through working in a law office, and he spent his life in private practice. Despite this, over a period spanning nearly fifty years, he published eighty-one major pieces. For more on his life and work, see K Roach, 'The Administrative Law Scholarship of D M Gordon' (1989) 34 *McGill LJ* 1.

publication of *The New Despotism*, each wrote significant critical pieces in response to Lord Hewart's work and the Diceyan view of the rule of law upon which Lord Hewart had built.[204] Today, this Anglo-Canadian scholarship offer us a valuable insight into the mind of the Great Depression-era administrative lawyer.[205]

In considering the nature of the 'administrative law mind', it is interesting to reflect on the significance of the timing of both the book and the response. *The New Despotism* was published in November, 1929 – just a few days after the crash of the American stock market and before the full extent of global depression had hit Great Britain. The responses to Lord Hewart all came out during the 1930s, at the height of the economic crisis. When Hewart was writing his book, it was still possible for someone – even an intelligent, reform-minded person like Hewart[206] – to feel that the executive had gone too far in its involvement in the private sphere, and that a properly operating Parliament could still exert scrutiny over governmental affairs. A year or so later, only a *naïf* could hold such a view. And by 1931, with a coalition 'National' government in power in Britain, attitudes like Lord Hewart's must have seemed even more silly and antediluvian. Perhaps that explains the bitterness on both sides: when Hewart wrote, he did so in a climate of relative prosperity. When his critics responded, they did so in a climate of economic, social and political desperation.[207] To borrow a description once offered in an only slightly

---

[204] Robson, for example, published the first edition of *Justice and Administrative Law* in 1928, before *The New Despotism*.

[205] Other examples of important Canadian writing on administrative law during this period include N Tennant, 'Administrative Finality' (1928) 6 *Can Bar Rev* 497, J Finkelman, 'Separation of Powers: A Study in Administrative Law' (1930) 1 *UTLJ* 313, and W P M Kennedy, 'Aspects of Administrative Law in Canada' (1934) 46 *Jurid Rev* 203. See also F R Scott, 'Administrative Law: 1923-1947' (1948) 26 *Can Bar Rev* 268. For other references to contemporary English writing, see Loughlin, *supra* n 21, and J Jowell, 'The Rule of Law Today', in J Jowell and D Oliver (eds), *The Changing Constitution* (3rd ed. 1994). Another interesting book published at the beginning of this period is F J Port, *Administrative Law* (1929). Even though it pre-dated *The New Despotism*, Port adopted a comparative approach, which reads as an interesting counterbalance to Hewart.

[206] Hewart, for example, was one of the campaigners for women's rights in Parliament. See his essay 'Peeresses and Parliament', in *Essays and Observations* (1930), 278.

[207] In a remarkable little book entitled *Government in Transition* (1934), Lord Eustace Percy, a Conservative MP, made this point in terms which provide some idea of just how bleak the times must have seemed to those in positions of political authority:

> Five-year plans, whatever their worth, can only be drawn up by those who have themselves the responsibilities and the powers of government. But it is not useless – at least one hopes not – to seek to express in words the almost inarticulate feeling that

different context, the sharpness of the reaction to Hewart and the ideology he symbolised represented 'the huddling together of frightened people, uncertain of their way in a chaotic world'.[208]

What linked the academic critics (for on detail, there were differences among them – Robson, for example, was in favour of establishing a form of general administrative appeals tribunal[209]) was an alarm at the extent to which the courts, in the guise of their supervisory jurisdiction, had the power to subvert the new legislation. In his book *Justice and Administrative Law*, Robson argued that it was the 'narrowest type of legalism' to suggest that non-curial tribunals 'must necessarily and inevitably be arbitrary, incompetent, unsatisfactory, injurious to the freedom of the citizen and to the welfare of society'.[210] In this respect, the Anglo-Canadian scholarship was very much cast in the 'cult of the expert' mould. As John Willis once asked,

> were the courts competent to control the administration of statutes, in the pith and substance of which the [bureaucracy] was more thoroughly trained, and of whose social philosophy it had a deeper understanding than a divisional court which is an aggregation of three judges casually meeting on Monday morning?[211]

Robson said that 'executive justice', as he described it, was 'a feature of the governmental order likely to grow extensively during the present century', because it is 'inherently connected with modern social evolution'.[212] But a bloody-minded judge, the Anglo-Canadian scholars thought, could, through the crafty use of the prerogative writs, thwart the clearly-indicated intention of parliament that the executive be given lee-way to get on with its work. And the doctrinal tool that they viewed with most alarm in this regard was the separation of powers.[213]

---

seems to be in all men's minds at the present day – a sense of the powerlessness of any programme, based either upon existing political faiths or upon present immediate necessities, to prepare the world for a wholly new era in its history (at 3).

[208] R St G Stubbs, 'Lord Bennett' (1951) 29 *Can Bar Rev* 631, at 653.

[209] See 'Justice and Administrative Law Reconsidered', *supra* n 196. See also 'The Report of the Committee on Ministers' Powers' (1932) 3 *Pol Q* 346.

[210] 2nd ed. *supra* n 195, at xv.

[211] 'Three Approaches to Administrative Law', *supra* n 200, at 73-74.

[212] *Justice and Administrative Law* (2nd ed. 1947), at xvi.

[213] See, *eg*, Finkelman, *supra* n 205.

The use of the separation of powers either to invalidate administrative actions as being *ultra vires*, or to impose additional procedural requirements on the decision-making process through the doctrine of natural justice, could neuter the efficient application of state power upon which the planned, efficient, public-service state so depended. As Sir Ivor Jennings once put it, 'social reform is useless if it is not rapid'.[214] It was for this reason that even the *Electricity Commissioners* formulation and the 'thin' Haldane/Isaacs' view of the actual requirements of natural justice, which may to us seem quite restrictive, caused considerable consternation among the proponents of the public service state. It was in this frame of mind that Willis could describe the holding in *Electricity Commissioners* as 'an enlargement of the powers of the court', something which he viewed with great concern.[215]

The *Housing Act* Cases and the Perfidiousness of Semantics

As said, the essence of the academic concern was with the competence of judges to undertake judicial review of decisions made by 'experts' under the new legislation. This anger was most often expressed in terms of criticism of the formal approach that the courts had adopted to judicial review. This had involved the practice of classifying the actions of the executive according to categories which corresponded to the separation of powers – the 'conceptual approach', as John Willis called it.[216]

The focal point for the real legal conflict between the two visions of administrative law in England up to the end of the Second World War came in a series of cases involving an attempt by the state to provide housing for the poor, by requiring that slums be torn down and that unused land be given over to housing development. In these cases, which are collectively often referred to as the '*Housing Act* cases', the courts almost invariably found the decision-making process to be one in which natural justice was required.[217] The *Housing Act* cases are useful because they

[214] 'Courts and Administrative Law', *supra* n 177, at 447.

[215] 'Three Approaches to Administrative Law, supra n 200, at 63.

[216] *Id*, at 69-75.

[217] See, *eg*, *R v Housing Appeal Tribunal* [1920] 3 KB 334, *R v Minister of Health, Ex parte Davis* [1929] 1 KB 619 (CA), *R v Minister of Health, Ex parte Yaffe* [1931] AC 494, *Errington et al v Minister of Health* [1935] 1 KB 249 (CA), *Frost v Minister of Health* [1935] 1 KB 294, *Offer v Minister of Health* [1936] 1 KB 40, *Stafford v Minister for Health*

placed all of the key issues on the table: new legislation aimed at rectifying serious social problems, but which interfered with common law property rights, in a situation in which there was a profound political difference of view as to what the interests of justice required in the circumstances. In other areas, in which real property interests were not involved, the courts seemed prepared to take a rather more open-ended view of the executive's authority.[218]

The complete story of the *Housing Act* cases is an involved one, and its details are not central to present purposes.[219] The end result of the cases is that the courts adopted an approach to the *Housing Act* (and like legislation) which involved dividing decision-making processes into three.[220] In the course of exercising his jurisdiction to give approvals to housing plans, the Minister could, before objections were lodged, inform himself as he saw fit without regard to natural justice. Once objections had been lodged, however, a litigation-like '*lis*' was said to exist, which obliged the Minister to provide natural justice rights to the objectors – and which significantly, forbad him from discussing the project with local authorities in the absence of the objectors. Once the objections had been dealt with, the decision became administrative, and natural justice rights no longer existed.[221]

One can easily empathise with the view taken by the Anglo-Canadian scholars of this sort of semanticism, and it has long been fashionable to

---

[1946] KB 621, *Miller v Minister for Health* [1946] KB 626, *Price v Minister for Health* [1947] 1 All ER 47, *Summers v Minister for Health* [1947] 1 All ER 184, *B Johnson and Co (Builders) Ltd v Minister of Health* [1947] 2 All ER 395. See, also, Jennings, 'Courts and Administrative Law – The Experience of English Housing Legislation', *supra* n 177.

[218] Not surprisingly, but interestingly in light of the recent Australian developments (discussed in chapter 5), among the least encumbered areas of executive activity in England was the deportation of 'undesirables'. This was seen to be an area of untrammelled executive discretion. See, *eg*, *Ex Parte Venicoff* [1920] 3 KB 72. See also the first edition of *de Smith* (1959), at 118. This was the case in Australia, too. See *R v MacFarlane, Ex parte O'Flanagan and O'Kelly* ('the *Irish Envoys Case*') (1923) 32 CLR 518.

[219] Though for a thorough analysis of these cases from an Australian perspective, see N A Manetta, 'The Implication of the Principle *Audi Alteram Partem* in Administrative Law' (unpublished PhD thesis, University of Cambridge, 1991).

[220] For a summary of this, see *Johnson and Co v Minister of Health* [1947] 2 All ER 395 (CA).

[221] See, on this point, Jennings, 'Courts and Administrative Law – The Experience of English Housing Legislation', *supra* n 177. See also S A de Smith, 'The Limits of Judicial Review: Statutory Discretions and the Doctrine of *Ultra Vires*' (1948) 11 *Mod L Rev* 306, at 312-314.

decry the *Housing Act* cases as an illustration of legal formalism gone awry. Sir Anthony Mason once referred to the sorts of distinctions made in the cases as 'abstract complexities' which (mercifully) 'have been banished from the stage or at least relegated to the wings'.[222] As J A G Griffith, the present-day ideological counterpart of the Anglo-Canadian scholars,[223] has said, 'on any local authority scheme of any magnitude, central or regional civil servants of the Department concerned are or should be involved continuously from the early stages of planning'.[224] The approach taken in the *Housing Act* cases, he argued, provided clear evidence that '[t]he courts have failed to understand the administrative system'.[225]

Yet, Griffith was wrong not to recognise that to a certain extent, the courts had little choice in the matter. The reality was that would-be suitors were seeking to invoke their jurisdiction and, as discussed in chapter one, the remedies they had at hand – the prerogative writs – for the most part limited them to supervising judicial functions. In other words, the courts were driven by systemic limitation to engage in a classification process. To do otherwise would have amounted to a surrender of jurisdiction to the executive branch which, arguably, would have been unconstitutional.[226] Moreover, there *was* at some point a distinction in kind to be made between types of decision-making. Even the legal realist Roscoe Pound argued that not to recognise this was to run the risk of facilitating abuse of discretion within the public service.[227]

---

[222] *FAI Insurances v Winneke* (1982) 151 CLR 342, at 360.

[223] And Professor of Law at the LSE. For more on Griffith's views on administrative law, see Loughlin, *supra* n 21, at 197-201.

[224] Griffith, 'Administrative Law and the Judges', Pritt Memorial Lecture (1978), at 11-12.

[225] *Ibid.*

[226] See, eg, *Bank of New South Wales v Commonwealth* ('the *Bank Nationalisation Case*') (1948) 76 CLR 1, at 362-365 (*per* Dixon J), *R v Coldham, Ex parte Australian Workers' Union* (1983) 153 CLR 415 and *O'Toole v Charles David* (1991) 171 CLR 232. See also Sir A Mason, 'The Importance of Judicial Review of Administrative Action as a Safeguard of Human Rights' (1994) 1 *AJHR* 1 and R Creyke, 'Restricting Judicial Review' (1997) 15 *AIAL Forum* 22.

[227] *Administrative Law: Its Growth, Procedure and Significance* (1942), at 59-60:

> There are those today who tell us that, at least so far as administrative agencies are concerned, [decision-making] functions cannot be distinguished. It is true that no rigid, analytical distribution among distinct functionaries is expedient, even if it were possible. But the methods appropriate to exercise of the several functions are distinct and must be so under any but an autocratic policy. When we are told by a leading advocate of administrative absolutism that 'little or no assistance is to be derived

The key to understanding the *Housing Act* cases is to remember that formerly, the courts in England had given the notion of 'judicial function' an expansive interpretation when property rights were at issue. The decisions in *Wood v Woad*[228] and *Cooper v Wandsworth Board of Works*[229] represent illustrations of this: when the state was purporting to divest someone of the full enjoyment of their property rights, natural justice applied. It was the effect of the proposed executive action – a deprivation of property – that served as the trigger for the classification. Property-depriving acts were *deemed* to be judicial in nature. As Rich J had said in *Gillen v Laffer*, '[t]he nature of the thing done – deprivation of property – implies a judicial act.'[230] But, as the provisions in issue in cases like *Finlayson* (and *Gillen v Laffer*) illustrated, in much of the new legislation parliament was seeking to vest the executive government with greater discretionary power to interfere with private interests, including conventionally-understood liberties. In order to execute the functions of the planned state, the executive government required a freer hand to interfere with private property. This was the point implicitly acknowledged by Higgins J in *Gillen v Laffer*, when he said that 'nothing is further from the intendment of this clause than a judicial or quasi-judicial inquiry'.[231] Considerable freedom of manoeuvre on the part of the executive was a *sine qua non* for an efficient public service.

Faced with these parliamentary signals, yet being institutionally unwilling to countenance a complete abdication of their sense of responsibility to the individual (as Lord Denning put it[232]), the courts attempted to develop indicia for determining when it would be appropriate for intervention.[233] This is what took place through the *Housing Act* cases. 'Ministerial' activity usually referred to activity that was seen as non-

from an analysis of the distinction between administrative and judicial functions', what is really meant is that from his postulate the separation of powers ... cannot be maintained. An absolute parliament having succeeded to the Stuart attempt to set up an absolute monarchy, an absolute administrative hierarchy is the next step.

228 (1874) LR 9 Ex 190. These cases are discussed in chapter 1.

229 (1863) 14 CB(NS) 180, 143 ER 414.

230 37 CLR, at 229.

231 37 CLR, at 225.

232 In an essay written in 1951 called 'The Spirit of the British Constitution', Denning LJ (as he then was) spoke of 'a sense of the supreme importance of the individual and a refusal to allow his personality to be submerged in an omnipotent state' (29 *Can Bar Rev* 1180, at 1182).

233 For more on this, see Gordon, 'Administrative Tribunals and the Courts', *supra* n 201.

discretionary. For example, the execution of a warrant was deemed to be a ministerial action. For obvious reasons, judicial intervention here was seen as inappropriate. At the other end of the classificatory spectrum sat 'administrative' decision-making. This referred to activity that was entirely policy-based, and in which the executive official was vested with the maximum discretion.[234] Judicial intervention here was also seen as inappropriate. 'Judicial' activity – the only activity which was in theory amenable to the prerogative writs of certiorari and prohibition – lay somewhere in the middle. According to most definitions, it involved the determination of rights and liabilities, on the basis of the ascertained facts and the application to them of pre-determined standards (*ie*, principles of 'law').

It will be readily apparent that there were significant problems with a classification scheme of this nature, and that the Anglo-Canadian scholars had a point to their criticism. Most obviously, few, if any, of the courses of governmental activity can be divided neatly like this. To attempt to adopt a multi-functional classification approach is conceptually artificial and in most cases also not practicable.[235] Moreover, to attempt to adopt one can give rise to serious issues of systemic injustice. A Canadian judge once said that what underlay criticism of the 'functional' approach was the:

> realisation that the classification of statutory functions as judicial, quasi-judicial or administrative is often very difficult, to say the least, and to endow some with procedural protection while denying others any at all would work injustice when the results of statutory decisions raise the same serious consequences for those adversely affected, regardless of the classification of the function in question.[236]

---

[234] An interesting Australian example of this can be seen in *Moses v Parker* [1891] AC 245, which held that a Tasmanian statute which referred property disputes to a judge of the Supreme Court, with the direction that he be guided only by equity and good conscience, did not involve the exercise of judicial power. See also *Fielding v Thomas* [1896] AC 600 (PC, NS) (though *cf* the comments of Isaacs J, in *British Imperial Oil Co v Federal Commissioner of Taxation* (1925) 35 CLR 422, at 438-439).

[235] On this point, see the judgment of Lord Greene MR, in *Johnson & Co v Minister of Health* [1947] 2 All ER 395 (CA).

[236] *Nicholson v Haldimand-Norfolk Regional Board of Commissioners of Police* [1979] 1 SCR 311, at 325 (*per* Laskin CJ).

It was for this reason that the Donoughmore Committee, which acknowledged the necessity for executive discretion in the modern era,[237] favoured the use of an additional expression, which from time to time one saw in the *Law Reports*: 'quasi-judicial'.[238] Quasi-judicial decisions were ones which embodied the fact-finding and law-applying elements of the judicial function, but which did not involve the determination of rights.[239] In the Committee's view, quasi-judicial decisions were to be reviewable in the courts, and therefore attracted the obligation to accord natural justice. But it was as clear as it was with the original tri-partite classification system that the lines – in this case between 'quasi-judicial' decisions (which were to be reviewable) and 'administrative' decisions (which were not) – would become blurred. The problem was not in the labels; it was in the very process of classification itself.[240]

In point of fact, however, this 'problem' of linguistic shading was a mask for a much broader concern amongst those in favour of the public service state, including the Anglo-Canadian scholars. This was the concern about judicial temperament. It is trite that given our conception of the rule of law, it would always fall to a judge ultimately to decide whether a given decision was ministerial, judicial, quasi-judicial or administrative. In principle, classification was supposed to be an exercise in statutory interpretation. The decision as to reviewability was something which was determined through the process of interpreting the legislation which vested the executive with its decision-making authority. It was for this reason that much of the literature in the post-Hewart years was

---

[237] The Committee described the practice of delegation of discretionary authority to the Executive as 'inevitable'. It said that it was:

> a natural reflection of changes in our ideas of Government, which had resulted from changes in political, social and economic ideas, and of changes in the circumstances of our time which have resulted from scientific discoveries.

(*Report of the Committee on Ministers' Powers*, Cmnd 4060, 1932, at 5.)

[238] On quasi-judicial powers generally, see H W R Wade, 'Quasi-judicial and its Background' (1949) 10 *Camb LJ* 216. For a very early example of the expression's use in Australia, see *R v Arndel* (1906) 3 CLR 557, at 571-572.

[239] *Supra* n 237, at 73-75. D M Gordon summed up the Committee's view as amounting to nothing more precise than that quasi-judicial decisions were ones which were 'not exactly judicial'('Administrative Tribunals and the Courts', *supra* n 201, at 95).

[240] For examples of the contemporary criticism of the Committee's recommendation on this point, see Jennings, *The Law and the Constitution*, *supra* n 194 (3rd ed, 1943), Appendix 1, and Robson, *Justice and Administrative Law*, *supra* n 195 (2nd ed, 1947), at 401-403.

concerned with statutory interpretation.[241] But, as Sir Otto Kahn Freund put it so aptly, 'the power to interpret is the power to destroy'.[242] When the common law courts approached the interpretation of 'new' legislation, they did so from a perspective of instinctive distrust of untrammelled discretion, and a concern for the maintenance of private property rights.

In this respect, the Anglo-Canadian scholars were correct in their alarm. For common law judges, the 'normal' type of decision-making process was the judicial one, in which individual interests were given the maximum safeguard. Nor did many of the judges have the background knowledge to engage in the sorts of purposive interpretation that the new legislation required. As John Willis once said, '[t]o the construction of a real-property statute the judge brings ready-made philosophy which has evolved by age-long decisions upon real property; but he has no such aid on questions of public law'.[243] So judges tended to view the process of conceptual classification as one of adding or subtracting processes from the judicial model. As D M Gordon described it, while the courts never acknowledged the failings of the system of functional classification, they 'to some extent atoned for their failure by ignoring the only definitions they have been able to formulate'.[244]

The Myopia of the Anglo-Canadian Scholarship

Yet, viewed from the hindsight of more than sixty years, the failings of the Anglo-Canadian scholarship can be seen to have been two-fold. First, in their spirited defence of administrative discretion on the basis of superior expertise, they were sometimes just as guilty of hyperbole as Lord Hewart. As Roscoe Pound said in 1937, '[t]hose who urge administrative absolutism and preach the psychological impossibility of an objective judicial process, and the futility of systems of law, make great claims just now to an exclusive touch with reality. But this is an old habit of

---

[241] See, *eg*, J A Corry, 'Administrative Law and the Interpretation of Statutes' (1935) 1 *UTLJ* 286, J Willis, 'Statute Interpretation in a Nutshell' (1938) 16 *Can Bar Rev* 1, M Amos, 'The Interpretation of Statutes' (1934) 5 *Camb LJ* 163 and W Friedmann, 'The Interpretation of Statutes in Modern British Law' (1950) 3 *Vand L Rev* 544.

[242] 'The Impact of Constitutions on Labour Law' (1976) 35 *Camb LJ* 240, at 244 (paraphrasing Marshall CJ in *McCulloch v Maryland* (1819) 17 US (4 Wheat) 316).

[243] 'Three Approaches to Administrative Law', *supra* n 200, at 59-60.

[244] 'Administrative Tribunals and the Courts', *supra* n 201, at 105.

jurists.'[245] The fact is that there was a grain of truth in what Lord Hewart had had to say. The reality of government's limitations inevitability gave rise to a potential for executive injustice.

This was something on which G W Keeton, who was, more than most, sympathetic to the ideals of the new legislation, was moved to comment. It was, he said, 'idle to deny that the existing safeguards of private right in administrative tribunals are inadequate, and that increasingly wide delegations of power at times give officials a dangerous immunity from control'.[246] The Anglo-Canadian scholars tended to gloss over this. In the eyes of many – including people 'on the inside' – it was simply a nonsense to speak of a government of experts. Sir John Anderson (the Anderson of *Liversidge v Anderson*), for example, recalled that when he began in the public service, he 'received no instruction and no training of any kind'.[247]

If anything, this observation was more acute in Australia where, until the middle years of the twentieth century, the normal pattern of recruitment to the Public Service was to take in either boys at the age of 14 or returned men from the Armed Services.[248] Very few public servants had matriculated from secondary school, and almost none had university degrees. As early as 1920, Harrison Moore spoke critically of the Australian Public Service recruitment practices in light of the new demands that were being placed on government: '[T]he system is based on a conception of public administration as a clerical service under a political head, a conception which becomes more inadequate every year as the

---

[245] 'Fashions in Juristic Theory', Presidential Address to the Holdsworth Club, University of Birmingham, at 15.

[246] 'The Twilight of the Common Law', in *The Nineteenth Century and After* (April, 1949) 230, at 231. One of the notorious examples of this injustice, to which Keeton made special reference, was *Blackpool Corporation v Locker* [1948] 1 KB 349 (CA), in which a municipal council first confiscated a home and its contents without lawful authority, and then refused for six months to respond to a request by the dispossessed homeowner to reveal the source of the legal power on which it was purporting to rely.

[247] *Supra* n 98, at 6. It is also telling of the Civil Service's own lack of progressive instincts that at the Exchequer, for example, officials went on using Latin well into modern times, except where they were specifically required by statute to use English (E Cohen, *The Growth of the British Civil Service 1780-1939* (1965), at 37, 50). And, until after the First World War, the Head of the Treasury was opposed to the introduction of the telephone, on the grounds that it would impair the handwriting of civil servants (E O'Halpin, *Head of the Civil Service: A Study of Warren Fisher* (1989), at 30).

[248] L F Crisp, *Australian National Government* (4th ed. 1978), at 437.

functions of administration extend.'[249] W K Hancock was more direct when he wrote in 1930 that 'Democratic sentiment applauds the sound argument that every office boy should have a chance to become a manager and perverts it into a practical rule that no one shall become a manager who has not been an office boy'.[250]

Moreover, much of the new legislation seemed cobbled together and hastily-written. Sir Frederick Pollock once asserted that 'contentious Bills dealing with administrative government often emerge from Committee disfigured by obscure and ill-drawn compromises between the views of opposed parties'.[251] Such views were sometimes heard on both sides of politics. Sir Lyndon Macassey, a prominent member of the British Labour Party, for example, once complained that 'Government Bills are forced through parliament under the pressure of the government whips; there is little time for discussion of their provisions either in the House or Committee'.[252] Lord Greene later made the same point from the perspective of the judge sitting on judicial review, though in slightly less forgiving terms:

> The technique of legislation, the parliamentary procedure by which legislation of this character is carried through without the necessity of critical examination, the ignorance of the legislators on what are often highly technical subjects, their tendency to concentrate their attention in debate on matters likely to excite the interest of the public or the press ... all these factors working together result in ill-digested legislation which is then thrown at the heads of judges, who have to do with it the best that they can.[253]

But, despite all of this, and notwithstanding the myopia of the Anglo-Canadian scholars, the years to come were to see the sort of curial stubbornness represented in the *Housing Act* cases give way in England to

---

[249] Quoted *id*, at 437-438.

[250] *Australia* (1st ed.), at 142.

[251] 'Note' (1915) 31 *LQR* 153.

[252] 'Law-making by Government Departments' (1923) 5 *J Comp Leg and Int'l Law* 73, at 77-78. He continued:

> [L]egislation is passed in the most general terms and left to some Government Department to apply as it thinks fit under machinery or rules made by it; the Cabinet is therefore in a position through its member at the head of a Government Department to embark on a particular policy which has never in any detail been discussed in parliament or communicated to the public (*ibid*).

[253] 'Law and Progress', the 13th Haldane Memorial Lecture (1944), at 12.

a form of capitulation. They were also to see the beginning of a definite cleavage in Australian and English approaches to natural justice. The focus of the next chapter will be to explore both of these developments, and to consider their portent for the decades to follow.

3 The Twilight of Natural Justice?

Judges may be politically irresponsible, but they are seldom politically unaware. Lord Mansfield is famous for having said that political consequences ought not to form part of the judicial reasoning process,[1] but in an area like administrative law, political considerations can seldom be far from the surface. The cases discussed in the last chapter make this plain. In the early part of this century – during what I have described as natural justice's first phase – some judges were overt in their acknowledgment of the changed political context in which public law litigation was being conducted. In the second phase, after the tumult which followed publication of *The New Despotism*, there came to be in England an ostensible retreat to legal formalism in judicial review cases. That is what was implicit in the *Housing Act* cases. But this was no less an indication of political awareness. As the Anglo-Canadian scholars pointed out, it was through the manipulative use of legal formalism that common law judges were able to blunt the administrative will.

Following the Second World War, however, developments in English public law began to give rise to a concern that the courts had finally capitulated to the Anglo-Canadian scholars, and that natural justice had entered its 'twilight' phase.[2] As Wade and Forsyth described it, '[t]he courts showed signs of losing confidence in their constitutional function and they hesitated to develop new rules in step with the mass of new regulatory legislation'.[3] de Smith put it a bit more wryly when he wrote that by the 1950s, 'valedictory addresses to the *audi alteram partem* rule in English administrative law were becoming almost commonplace'.[4]

---

[1] 'The constitution does not allow reasons of State to influence our judgments; God forbid it should! We must not regard political consequences; how formidable soever they might be: if rebellion was the certain consequences, we are bound to say *Fiat justitia, ruat coelum*' (*R v Wilkes* (1770) 4 Burr 2527, at 2561-2562, 98 ER 327, at 346-347).

[2] H W R Wade, 'The Twilight of Natural Justice?' (1951) 67 *LQR* 103.

[3] Sir W Wade and C Forsyth, *Administrative Law* (7th ed. 1994), at 17.

[4] *Judicial Review of Administrative Action* (2nd ed. 1968), at 154.

Broadly speaking, there were two factors which contributed to this third, twilight phase in England. The first was the sheer magnitude of electoral support for Labour shown in the general election of 1945. This, coupled with the popularity of the programme of social reform set out in the *Beveridge Report* of 1944,[5] could not help but make it clear to the judges that an obstructionist approach to administrative law was out of touch with the public mood. Secondly, and equally importantly, judges began to realise that notwithstanding the flaws associated with the Anglo-Canadian scholars' arguments,[6] there were some significant practical limitations in the ability of the common law to grapple adequately with the sorts of issues in dispute in administrative law cases.

In the Australian context, though, the legal reaction to the post-War era was rather more ambivalent. On one hand, there were a series of cases, which will be discussed shortly, in which Sir Owen Dixon attempted to introduce into Australian law a doctrine of deference to administrative expertise. But there was here nothing like the political jolt that the election of the Atlee government caused in England. So Dixon CJ's efforts notwithstanding, the doctrine of natural justice in Australia continued to be stated broadly by the High Court throughout the late 1940s and 1950s. In fact, as will be seen in chapter four, the Australian 'twilight' period did not begin until after the English one had effectively ended. The result of this was that during this third phase, there came to be seen a discernible schism between English and Australian approaches to natural justice.

The Twilight Phase of Natural Justice in England

Three cases can be used to illustrate the state of the English common law inheritance at the end of the 1950s. The first is the decision of the House of Lords in *Franklin v Minister of Town and Country Planning* – the so-called *Stevenage Case*.[7] In this case, the House of Lords seemed to adopt an approach to the doctrine of natural justice which was the complete inverse of the *Electricity Commissioners* approach, and which had the effect of dramatically limiting the doctrine's reach. Specifically, their Lordships used the existence of a statutory decision-making procedure to

---

[5] *Full Employment in a Free Society* (1944). The Beveridge Report, which was translated into eleven languages (including Hebrew and Serbo-Croat!) served as the blueprint for much of the Atlee government's programme. Lord Beveridge's autobiography was published in 1953, under the title *Power and Influence*.

[6] See, *supra* chapter 2.

[7] [1948] AC 87.

negate the obligation to observe natural justice. Rather than using it as proof of the superaddition – to establish the fact that there existed in the decision-maker a duty to act judicially – the Lords in this case used it to show that there was no such duty.

Franklin v Minister of Town and Country Planning arose out of a plan to build a 'new town' after the Second World War. The new towns' legislation[8] was part of Britain's post-War reconstruction programme. The new towns were intended both to provide homes for people who had been bombed out, and to act as a showcase for the Labour Government's agenda of post-war central planning. The case was, therefore, one of central political import.

One of the ideas in the post-War programme was to build a series of 'garden towns' away from large population centres, in order to avoid urban sprawl.[9] Stevenage was a small town north of London, in Hertfordshire, set amidst farmlands, which had been identified as the candidate for the first of the new garden towns. None of the landowners had indicated a firm desire to sell their land, however. Accordingly, in 1946, just before the New Towns Bill received second reading in the House of Commons, the Minister of Town and Country Planning visited Stevenage to meet with the landowners, purportedly to discuss their concerns. But by this time, the actual plans for the Stevenage new town were fairly well developed. So in the course of the meeting, the Minister suggested that it would be futile for the property owners to resist the new town idea.[10] The owners sought to quash the draft Order in Council declaring Stevenage to be a new town on the basis that it had been actuated by bias. In the King's Bench Division, they had succeeded, but the Court of Appeal had held that no bias had been made out.[11]

---

[8] The *New Towns Act 1946*.

[9] On the subject of the 'new towns' generally, see M Clapson, *Invincible Green Suburbs, Brave New Towns: Social Change and Urban Dispersal in Postwar England* (1998) and M Aldridge, *The British New Towns: A Programme Without a Policy* (1979).

[10] Although 'harangue' might be a more accurate description than 'suggest'. The following is an excerpt from the transcript of the Minister's talk with the residents:

> I want to carry out a daring exercise in town planning (*Jeers*). It is no good your jeering: it is going to be done (*Applause and boos; cries of 'Dictator'*) ... The project will go forward. It will do so more smoothly and more successfully with your help and cooperation. Stevenage will in a short time become world famous (*Laughter*) ... [W]e have a duty to perform and I am not going to be deterred from that duty. While I will consult as far as possible all the local authorities, at the end, if people are fractious and unreasonable, I shall have to carry out my duty (*Cry of 'Gestapo!'*) ([1948] AC, at 90-91).

[11] (1947) 176 LT 312 (CA).

Rather than affirming the decision of the Court of Appeal, the House of Lords took the opportunity to correct the law, and to hold that the question of possible bias was irrelevant because, in the circumstances, the Minister did not have a duty to act judicially.[12] Speaking for all their Lordships,[13] Lord Thankerton said that the Minister's only obligation was to comply with the statutory procedure, which required him to consider all objections raised to a new town scheme (which, the Minister testified in an affidavit, he had done). In light of the statutory procedure, the common law rules of natural justice were not applicable in the circumstances.

The second of the English 'twilight' cases (and formally more significant, since it was binding on Australian courts), was actually not English at all. It was the decision of the Judicial Committee of the Privy Council in 1951, in *Nakkuda Ali v Jayaratne*.[14] In this case, the Privy Council was determining whether a writ of certiorari should issue against the Ceylonese Controller of Textiles for having unlawfully cancelled Nakkuda Ali's licence to engage in business as a fabric merchant in Colombo.

In revoking the licence, the Controller of Textiles was purporting to act under the authority of the wartime Defence (Control of Textiles) Regulations 1945, which empowered him to order a revocation where he 'had reasonable grounds to believe that any dealer is unfit to be allowed to continue as a dealer'. The cancellation took place following an exchange of correspondence between Nakkuda Ali and the Controller. The allegation was that Nakkuda Ali had fraudulently falsified his books, so as to be able to unlawfully claim credit from the bank. It is apparent from the record[15] that Nakkuda Ali had known for some time that he was under suspicion, and before the cancellation took place, he had actually been invited to make written submissions on the allegations (the substance of which were fully known to him), which he did through his proctors. It was only after having considered Nakkuda Ali's submissions, that the Controller determined that he was unfit, and cancelled the licence accordingly.

Nakkuda Ali's argument was that he had been denied natural justice by not having been permitted to see the affidavits on file with the Controller, which had presumably been used to counter his own letter of explanation.[16] But to get to this stage of the case, he first had to show that

---

[12] [1948] AC, at 102.
[13] Lords Thankerton, Porter, Uthwatt, du Parcq and Normand.
[14] [1951] AC 66.
[15] See [1951] AC, at 68-69.
[16] [1951] AC, at 70.

the Controller was amenable to the writ of certiorari – *ie*, that he was engaged in quasi-judicial decision-making, and that he had the power to affect Nakkuda Ali's rights.[17] It was on this point that Nakkuda Ali fell down. He argued that the inclusion of the requirement that the belief of unfitness be 'reasonable' in the regulations imported an obligation on the part of the Controller to act judicially. This placed the Privy Council on the horns of a dilemma. On one hand, it was anxious to distance itself from the highly-criticised and disreputed judgment of the House of Lords in *Liversidge v Anderson*.[18] But on the other, it was concerned (since it was effectively deciding a question of English law[19]) not unnecessarily to deviate from the principles espoused by the Court of Appeal in *Electricity Commissioners*, and which had since become well-entrenched in the case law.

One cannot help but wonder what the Privy Council's position might have been had the alleged violation of Nakkuda Ali's procedural rights been more egregious, but in the end, their Lordships found that the Controller of Textiles did *not* have a superadded duty to act judicially, and hence that the remedy of certiorari was not available to quash any departure from the obligation to observe natural justice.[20] In reaching this conclusion, the Board pointed to the fact that the statutory regime did not lay down any procedure at all according to which the Controller was to exercise his power. Nor did the regulations provide for a right of appeal, or anything else which might have suggested that the Controller was to engage in judicial-like deliberations when determining a licence. It is this latter point that makes *Nakkuda Ali v Jayaratne* difficult to square with the holding in *Franklin v Minister of Town and Country Planning*. There, the claim for a right to natural justice failed because there was a statement of legislative intent with respect to the decision-making process. Here, it failed because there was *not* one.

---

[17] On the basis of the *Electricity Commissioners* formulation.

[18] [1942] AC 206 (holding that regulation 18B of the UK Defence (General) Regulations 1939, which provided that the Home Secretary could make detention orders if he had 'reasonable cause to believe any person to be of hostile association or origins', merely required the existence of a subjective belief on the part of the Home Secretary. Though the holding itself is now largely forgotten, Lord Atkin's stinging dissent has come to represent a classic statement of the ideals of administrative law). On the Regulation and its implementation, see the two very interesting pieces by A W B Simpson: 'Rhetoric, Reality and Regulation 18B' [1988] *Denning LJ* 123, and 'The Judges and the Vigilant State' [1989] *Denning LJ* 145.

[19] The Privy Council stated that the law of Ceylon on this point was the same as the law of England ([1951] AC, at 75).

[20] [1951] AC, at 78.

The third of the twilight cases was the decision of the English Divisional Court in *R v Metropolitan Police Commissioner, Ex parte Parker.*[21] In fact, while not formally binding upon Australian authorities in the way that *Nakkuda Ali v Jayaratne* was, *Parker* is, for reasons which will become apparent in the next chapter, of perhaps equal interest in its actual holding.

Parker was a licensed taxi-cab driver in London of many years standing. In the course of his career as a driver, Parker had had several encounters with the law. As the evidence in the proceeding showed,[22] he had been convicted on several occasions of traffic offences whilst driving his taxi. As a result, prior to this litigation, he had incurred two suspensions: one in 1947 and another in 1951. In October of 1952, Parker was alleged to have allowed his taxi to be used for the purpose of allowing prostitutes to engage in their trade. Thereupon, the Commissioner of the Metropolitan Police summoned Parker to a hearing before the Taxi Licensing Committee, where he was given the chance to hear the evidence of the two police constables who had made the allegations against him. Parker was given a chance to speak on his own behalf after having heard the evidence against him, but he was refused the opportunity to call his own alibi witness. At the conclusion of the hearing, the decision was taken to revoke his licence, which was later confirmed in writing. Not surprisingly, Parker applied for a writ of certiorari to quash the revocation on the basis that by having been denied the right to call his own witness, he had been denied natural justice.

The revocation had been carried out under the authority of paragraph 30 of the London Cab Order 1934, which, like the textile regulation in *Nakkuda Ali*, contained a 'state of mind' provision. It gave the Commissioner the right to revoke a taxi licence if he was 'satisfied, by reason of any circumstances arising or coming to his knowledge ... that the licensee is not a fit person to hold such a licence'. Like the Privy Council two years beforehand (though it is worthwhile to note that *Nakkuda Ali* was cited neither in argument nor judgment in *Parker*), the Divisional Court[23] found that in exercising his discretionary powers, the Commissioner of Police was not acting in a judicial capacity.[24] In his judgment, Lord Goddard CJ said that it was:

---

[21] [1953] 1 WLR 1150.

[22] See [1953] 1 WLR, at 1150-1151.

[23] Lord Goddard CJ, Parker and Donovan JJ concurring.

[24] For earlier illustrations of Lord Goddard's mindset with respect to the reviewability of an exercise of discretionary power by officials, see *R v Brighton Rent Tribunal* [1950] 2 KB

> impossible to find on the wording of the order under which the Commissioner acted that he was either in the position of a judge or of a quasi-judge; exactly what a quasi-judge is nobody has ever attempted to define, but I suppose it is a person who has to decide on evidence and come to a conclusion on facts.[25]

The continuing importance of procedural intricacy then showed its head: in order for the writ of certiorari to issue, there had to be something to quash. 'One thing that weighs with me', his Lordship said,

> is that in considering whether a tribunal is a judicial tribunal or a quasi-judicial tribunal, one would expect to find that the tribunal had to make an order or something in the nature of an order, because otherwise there is nothing to be brought up and quashed in this court.[26]

In this case, he concluded, there was no order:

> The motion is to bring up an order of the Commissioner. There is nothing here to show that there ever was an order. It was simply a decision of the Commissioner that by reason of facts coming to his knowledge, he was satisfied that the licensee was not a fit person to hold the licence, and that is all.[27]

The most striking part of the judgment, however, was Lord Goddard's discussion of the legal rights pertaining to a licence. In a word, there were none:

> [T]he very fact that a licence is granted to a person would seem to imply that the person granting the licence can also revoke it. The licence is nothing but a permission, and if one man gives permission to do something it is natural that the person who gives the permission will be able to withdraw the

---

410, and *Dormer v Newcastle-upon-Tyne* [1940] 2 KB 204. See also *Ex parte Fry* [1954] 1 WLR 730.

[25] [1953] 1 WLR, at 1155.

[26] *Ibid.*

[27] *Ibid.* With respect to his Lordship, this was rather a specious argument. As has been noted, paragraph 30 of the London Cab Order provided that a cab-driver's licence was 'liable to revocation or suspension by the Commissioner' if the requisite state of mind could be shown to have existed. But the mere formation of the state of mind did not equate with revocation. Even after the necessary frame of disposition was formed, the licence was merely *liable* to be revoked. There was still required to be a command; a direction, that the revocation take place. It was this that could have been removed into the Divisional Court. In this case, the letter confirming the revocation would, if it did not have the status of an order itself, have been evidence of the order.

> permission. As a rule, where a licence is granted, the licensor does not have to state why he withdraws the permission.[28]

The Twilight of the Common Law?

Now, in all three of the twilight cases, it is difficult to gainsay the substantive result. In *Stevenage*, their Lordships were concerned with the provision of housing for dispossessed people. Nakkuda Ali knew perfectly well what the allegation against him was, and he had been given a full opportunity to meet the case for revocation. Likewise, the cab driver Parker had been given an oral hearing, and had even been allowed to place on the record the evidence that his alibi witness would have given.[29] Moreover, one cannot help but think that the outcome in *Parker* was motivated at least in part by a judicial perception of relative equities – not least of all in light of the fact that Lord Goddard was presiding.[30]

But there is another way of looking at the cases, too. That is to consider them within the political context of their time – the aftermath of the Second World War. As seen in the last chapter, before the War, the courts in England were faced with a barrage of criticism from the Anglo-Canadian scholars, but this only resulted in judicial craftiness in a semantic disguise – as evidenced by the *Housing Act* cases. During the War, however, the private rights that were associated with public law understandably came to be interpreted in a limited fashion. One can consider the administrative law decisions of the House of Lords during the period: *Liversidge v Anderson*,[31] *Greene v Secretary of State for Home Affairs*,[32] *Duncan v Cammell, Laird and Company*[33] and *Barnard v*

---

[28] [1953] 1 WLR, at 1154. His Lordship was expressing quite a different view on the licence point than had Scrutton LJ in *R v London County Council, Ex parte Entertainment Protection Association* [1931] 2 KB 215. On the other hand, a not dissimilar conclusion had been reached by the Supreme Court of New South Wales in *Ex parte McCarthy, Re Milk Board* (1934) 35 SR(NSW) 48. See also some of the comments made by the High Court in *Metropolitan Meat Board v Finlayson* (1916) 22 CLR 340 (discussed in chapter 2). On the legal status of a licence, see also *Thomas v Sorrell* (1673) Vaugh 330, 124 ER 1098, and W N Hohfeld, 'Some Fundamental Conceptions as Applied to Judicial Reasoning' (1913) 23 *Yale LJ* 16 (discussed in chapter 4).

[29] Its substance is referred to in the judgment of Donovan J [1953] 1 WLR, at 1157-1158.

[30] In the *Oxford Companion to Law*, for instance, Lord Goddard is described as a 'strong, stern judge with little faith in lenient treatment of criminals [who] frequently increased sentences in frivolous appeals'.

[31] [1942] AC 206.

[32] [1942] AC 284 (holding, like *R v Halliday, Ex parte Zadig* [1917] AC 260 in the First World War, that Habeas Corpus rights had been suspended by wartime regulations).

Gorman.[34] Each of these cases displayed a highly deferential attitude towards the Executive. And immediately at the end of the War, the Labour government was elected, with its large-scale programme of nationalisation and central planning. Aneurin Bevan made clear the new government's attitude towards judicial review when he said in the debate on the National Health Service Bill that Labour would allow no 'judicial sabotage of Socialist legislation'.[35] Sir Hartley Shawcross, the Labour Attorney-General,[36] was slightly more elegant in phrasing when he said that 'Parliament has felt that there are good reasons for taking the administration of certain classes of legislation more and more outside the province of the ordinary courts and placing them in the hands of expert tribunals'.[37]

Moreover, by the late 1940s, the Appellate Committee of the House of Lords had come to be dominated by Labour appointees. The Labour Lord Chancellor, Viscount Jowitt, was for obvious reasons not one to engage in sabotage himself, and it is significant that of the combined number of seven law lords who heard *Franklin* and *Nakkuda Ali*, six (Thankerton,[38] Uthwatt, du Parcq and Normand in *Franklin*, Oaksey and Radcliffe in *Nakkuda Ali*) were Labour appointees. Only Lord Porter was appointed by a non-Labour prime minister (Chamberlain, in 1938). And while in his early years, Porter showed some antipathy towards 'statism' (he had, for example, dissented in the Lord Haw Haw appeal in 1945[39]), the evidence is that became significantly more 'statist' as he got older.[40]

In an amusing passage, J A Griffith once said that the twilight-era cases provide an illustration of the judges 'lean[ing] over backwards to the point of falling off the bench.'[41] But Griffith's anti-judicial embroidery aside, it is clear that the post-War period in England was one of a definite

---

33 [1942] AC 624 (upholding the right of Crown privilege with respect to documents sought to be produced in litigation).

34 [1941] AC 378 (holding that Customs officials could not normally be liable for false imprisonment or malicious prosecution).

35 *Parliamentary Debates*, House of Commons, 23 July 1946, at 1983.

36 And, as an aside, the Chief British Prosecutor at the Nuremburg War Crimes Trials.

37 'The State and the Law' (1948) 11 *Mod L Rev* 1, at 5.

38 Though it should be noted that Lord Thankerton was appointed by the Ramsay MacDonald government in 1929.

39 *Joyce v Director of Public Prosecutions* [1946] AC 347.

40 See, *eg*, Porter, 'English Practice and Procedure – More Particularly in Criminal Matters' [1949] *Cur Leg Prob* 13. He also seems to have become somewhat anti-academic. In a debate in the Lords over the Defamation Bill 1952, he said of legal scholars: 'If it were not for the mercy of God, they might be judges themselves' (*Parliamentary Debates*, House of Lords, 15 July 1952, at 1109).

41 'Administrative Law and the Judges', Pritt Memorial Lecture (1978), at 13.

shift in judicial temperament *vis-à-vis* the executive. In a piece written in 1948, Stanley de Smith wrote that '[t]he courts, acknowledging the supremacy of Parliament are now loath to accept the argument that it is their function to require the Executive to observe standards of fairness which the Legislature has not thought fit to impose expressly upon it'.[42] Stevens has described this as the period of 'substantive formalism' in the British judiciary, in which faced first with an extended period of extreme national peril, and then with a government which enjoyed a huge electoral mandate for social and economic reform, the bench developed a pronounced disinclination to wish to interfere with the work of the executive.[43]

In this regard, there were several instances during this period of judges making extra-judicial statements which reflected a real sense of capitulation and loss of confidence on the part of the common law. Lord Greene, for instance, said that 'the judiciary is not concerned with policy. It is not for the judiciary to decide what is in the public interest.'[44] More revealingly, perhaps, Lord Parker said that 'in modern Britain, where no agreement exists on the ends of Society and the means of achieving those ends, it would be disastrous if the courts did not eschew the temptation to pass judgment on an issue of policy. Judicial preservation may alone dictate restraint ...'[45] This was patently different in tone from Lord Hewart, his predecessor but two in the office of Lord Chief Justice.

The expression of attitudes such as this caused some people seriously to argue that the common law had ceased to have a constructive role to play in public law. In an essay written in 1949, which, perhaps because it was published in a non-legal periodical, received considerable prominence in intellectual circles, Professor Keeton offered a very pessimistic view of the future of the common law as an instrument of constitutionalism. He suggested that 'ordinary courts have exhausted their usefulness in the era of rapid change through which we are passing.'[46] But this view did not stop at the academy. In 1956, Mr Justice Devlin (as he then was) said much the same thing: 'The common law has now, I think, no longer the

---

[42] 'The Limits of Judicial Review: Statutory Discretions and the Doctrine of *Ultra Vires*' (1948) 11 *Mod L Rev* 306, at 323.

[43] See Stevens, *Law and Politics: The House of Lords as a Judicial Body, 1800-1976* (1979), chapters 10-11.

[44] 'Law and Progress', 13th Haldane Memorial Lecture (1944), at 11.

[45] 'Recent Developments in the Supervisory Powers of the Courts Over Inferior Tribunals' (1959), at 27-28 (quoted in *de Smith* (5th ed,1995), at 7).

[46] 'The Twilight of the Common Law', *The Nineteenth Century and After* (April, 1949) 230, at 231. For a more conventional legal academic expression of his views, see 'Natural Justice in English Law' [1955] *Cur Leg Prob* 24.

strength to provide any satisfactory solution to the problem of keeping the executive, with all the powers which under modern conditions are needed for the efficient conduct of the realm, under proper control.'[47] This was a view echoed by many senior civil servants, who argued that there had been such a profound change in the nature of government since the Great Depression, that the old assumptions about the doctrine of separation of powers as a means of constitutional control no longer fit with reality.[48]

Pragmatism and the Law in the Australian Planned State

While there was simply nothing like the same level of litigation in Australia that there was in England, either before or after the War, the dynamics of public law litigation not surprisingly bore many of the same characteristics as in England. But in order to fully appreciate the position of the High Court in Australia during this same period, it is first necessary to go back to the inter-War years, to examine in more detail the relationship that came to develop between the Court, the Parliament and the Commonwealth Executive.

In an article published in the *Canadian Bar Review* in 1937, Mr Justice Evatt offered a fairly broad view of the judicial role in overseeing the procedure of administrative decision-makers, which, notwithstanding his Labor Party and progressive credentials, bore some resemblance to the sorts of attitudes displayed by English judges of the time.[49] Evatt J also had occasion to express his views about the place in administrative law of the curial model of decision-making. In his opinion, it was integral to the proper functioning of an administrative system:

> The interposition of an independent tribunal operates as a continuing guarantee ... By such means administrative action is controlled by open investigation before a judicial officer. The importance of a public hearing is universally recognised.[50]

Yet there were also differences between the situations in Australia and England. For one thing, from the First World War up to the early

---

[47] 'Public Policy and the Executive' [1956] *Cur Leg Prob* 1, at 14.

[48] See, *eg*, Sir O Franks, *Central Planning and Control in War and Peace* (1947) and H R G Greaves, *The Civil Service in the Changing State* (1947).

[49] 'The Judiciary and Administrative Law in Australia' 15 *Can Bar Rev* 247. See also J D Holmes, 'An Australian View of the Hours of Labour Case' (1937) 15 *Can Bar Rev* 495.

[50] *Fletcher v Nott* (1938) 60 CLR 55, at 80. See also *R v War Pensions Entitlement Appeal Tribunal, Ex parte Bott* (1933) 50 CLR 228, especially at 252-253.

beginning of the 1930s, there was in Australia a critical mass on the High Court which, as evidenced by cases like *Metropolitan Meat Board v Finlayson*, *Gillen v Laffer* and *Boucaut Bay v The Commonwealth*, which were discussed in chapter two, seemed to have accepted the philosophical premises of the new (or 'novel') legislation – at least where non-traditional, non-proprietary rights were involved. This included not only Justices Isaacs and Higgins, but also Mr Justice Evatt.[51] Speaking extrajudicially, for example, Evatt J once said that 'under existing economic and social conditions, decisions of an administrative character have to be made so frequently and speedily, and very often involve such questions of law and expediency, that the ordinary courts of law could not be expected to deal with them'.[52]

This was reminiscent both of Sir Ivor Jennings' assertion that 'social reform is useless if it is not rapid'[53] and the tenor of the speeches in *Board of Education v Rice* and *Local Government Board v Arlidge*, which were discussed in chapter two. But in England, in the years following the pre-1914 'thinning' cases, litigation over the new legislation tended to end in the Divisional Court and the Court of Appeal, where, as the *Housing Act* cases showed, the judges were less philosophically attuned to evolved theories of government. In the contemporary Australian setting, in contrast, appellate work on basic questions of judicial review still could make its way to the High Court. There, the judges often did a very credible job at ascertaining, and paying due faith to, the implicit preferences of parliament. When, for example, Sir Isaac Isaacs said in *Boucaut Bay Co v The Commonwealth* that 'the surrounding circumstances have to be looked at', and that the surrounding circumstances in the case before him included an appreciation of the environment in which the coastal shipping contract was to be carried out,[54] he was engaging in as sophisticated an approach to interpretation as one could hope to see today.

Likewise, when Higgins J spoke in *Gillen v Laffer* of the Minister's obligations to the collective welfare of the returned veterans as well as to the interests of individual land-owners,[55] he was displaying a sensitivity to the aims of the new legislation. And in *Shell Company of Australia v*

[51] Who sat in the Court 1930-1940. On Evatt's view of administrative law, see P Bayne, 'Mr Justice Evatt's Theory of Administrative Law: Adjusting State Regulation to the Liberal Theory of the Individual and the State' (1991) 9 *Law in Context* 1. See also L Zines, 'Mr Justice Evatt and the Constitution' (1969) 3 *Fed L Rev* 153.

[52] 'The Judiciary and Administrative Law in Australia' *supra* n 49, at 252.

[53] 'Courts and Administrative Law – The Experience of English Housing Legislation' (1936) 49 *Harv L Rev* 426, at 447 (discussed in chapter 2).

[54] (1927) 40 CLR 98, at 105.

[55] (1925) 37 CLR 210, at 225-226.

Federal Commissioner of Taxation, when the High Court (and the Privy Council on appeal) held that the taxation authorities were not exercising the judicial power of the Commonwealth,[56] they were attempting to render workable the Commonwealth system of national tax collection, without which the welfare state could never have existed. Whatever may be said about their English contemporaries, when the Australian cases are considered closely, it seems quite wrong to assert that the judges of Australian High Court in this period were unthinking slaves to formalism.

At the same time, by the time of the onset of the Great Depression in Australia, the Commonwealth parliament had to a degree come to accept that its ability to joust with the courts over judicial review was inhibited by section 75(v) of the Constitution, which gave the High Court an original jurisdiction to issue injunctions and writs of prohibition and mandamus.[57] In this respect, the fight over the basic premise of judicial review of administrative action had taken place a generation earlier in Australia than in the United Kingdom (chiefly concerning the effectiveness of privative clauses in the Commonwealth *Conciliation and Arbitration Act 1904*[58]). It was in a spirit of acknowledged defeat that as Commonwealth Attorney-General, Billy Hughes described the interplay between parliament and the High Court as a 'miserable battledore and shuttlecock business ... We throw the High Court an amending Act, and they hurl back its shattered remains. Then, spurred on by the demon of eternal hope, we pass another; again it is thrown back ...'[59]

Furthermore, the party political situation in Australia was different from England. In England, for much of the period from 1905-1935, what today would be broadly known as left-of-centre governments (Liberal, Labour or coalition) were in power. In Australia, in contrast, throughout the inter-war period, anti-Labor governments were in power for all but

56 [1931] AC 275. See also *British Imperial Oil Co v Federal Commissioner of Taxation* (1926) 38 CLR 153.

57 See *Bank of New South Wales v Commonwealth* ('the *Bank Nationalisation Case*') (1948) 76 CLR 1, at 362-365.

58 See *R v Commonwealth Court of Conciliation and Arbitration, Ex parte Whybrow & Co* (1910) 11 CLR 1, *R v Commonwealth Court of Conciliation and Arbitration, Ex parte Gulf Steamship Co Ltd* (1912) 15 CLR 586 and *Ince Brothers v Federated Clothing and Allied Trades Union* (1924) 34 CLR 457.

59 Australia, *Parliamentary Debates*, House of Representatives, 13 November 1914, at 652. For the complete story of the fortunes of privative clauses in the High Court (including more of Billy Hughes's views), see M Aronson and B Dyer, *Judicial Review of Administrative Action*, at 962-966.

three years.[60] For the period during which the controversy over *Electricity Commissioners* and the *Housing Act* was first brewing, the Commonwealth government was led by S M Bruce (in coalition with Earle Page). One of the kinder things said by Manning Clark about Bruce was that he 'believed in efficient government, in a businessmen's government'.[61] As Brian Galligan has described it, the Bruce-Page government was a conservative-leaning coalition 'that favoured private enterprise and a contraction of state intervention in the economy and industrial relations'.[62] Leslie Zines has noted that Bruce's chief concern was economic development – 'men, money and markets' – rather than social engineering.[63] The Bruce-Page government was followed, of course, by the onset of the Great Depression which, if anything, had more drastic effects in Australia than in Great Britain.[64] The combination of all of these factors led to a possibly less dogmatic view of the relationship between the legislative and executive branches among parliamentarians. As has been noted, *The New Despotism* struck a responsive chord among some in Australia,[65] but the sorts of high-blown rhetoric that accompanied Lord Hewart's book in England did not feature so commonly here.

Moreover, the desire for efficiency, of which Manning Clark wrote, gave rise to a sympathy even amongst conservative politicians in Australia for delegation of decision-making power to the executive. There was, it is true, repeated litigation in the High Court over the constitutionality of delegated legislation,[66] but this was more a mask for a deeper-running dispute over the power and place of trade unions in Australian society than a dispute over the power to regulate *per se*. For the most part, the period between the World Wars in Australia was characterised by what Geoffrey Sawer described as 'a curious dissociation between politics and constitutional law'.[67] Even Robert Menzies was moved to say in the 1930s that 'legislation by Parliament should deal with principles and fundamental rules, and the details of administration should be left to the Executive: I

---

[60] The governments were Hughes (1915-1923; anti-Labor after 1917), Bruce (1923-1929), Lyons (1932-1939), Page (1939), Menzies (1939). Scullin, the only Labor prime minister, was in power 1929-1932.
[61] *A History of Australia*, Vol VI (1987), at 260.
[62] *Politics of the High Court* (1987), at 103.
[63] 'Social Conflict and Constitutional Interpretation' (1996) 22 *Mon U L Rev* 195, at 196.
[64] See, generally, C B Schedvin, *Australia and the Great Depression* (1970).
[65] See chapter 2.
[66] See *Huddart Parker & Co Pty Ltd v Commonwealth* (1931) 44 CLR 492 and *Victorian Stevedoring Co and General Contracting Ltd v Dignan* ('*Dignan's Case*') (1931) 46 CLR 73.
[67] *Australian Federal Politics and Law 1901-1929* (1956), at 329.

have no great fear of executive legislation provided those principles are observed.'[68] Professor Bailey reported that the practical manifestation of attitudes like this was that 'wherever Parliament could reasonably hand over the work of implementing an Act, it was done. There [was] almost no exception to that rule.'[69]

It is also worthwhile to note that there did not seem to be in Australia the same scholarly negative attitude towards the judiciary and judicial review as in England and in Canada. This may have had something to do with the greater Australian willingness to shy away from ideological purity in debating law reform that was discussed in chapter two. It probably also had something to do with the fact that there simply were not very many full-time legal academics in Australia at the time. Whatever the cause, the written debate over judicial review was in some respects carried out in less ideologically polarised terms in Australia than in either England or Canada. It was for this reason that, as noted in chapter two, there was in Australia some scholarly sympathy for Lord Hewart's views.

Sir Federic Eggleston's acknowledgment of unease over the extent to which discretionary power was being vested in the executive has already been referred to.[70] In a similar vein, in an article published in 1935, the same year as John Willis's piece 'Three Approaches to Administrative Law',[71] C I Menhennitt took rather a different view from the Anglo-Canadian scholars. In the piece, entitled 'Administrative Tribunals in Victoria',[72] Menhennitt spoke, like Willis, Jennings, and the other Anglo-Canadian scholars, of the 'increasing control and direction of economic life' that the Great Depression had demanded of government.[73] But he concluded in a much different tone from them:

> As the policy of planned social and economic life is developed, every precaution should be taken to ensure that individual rights are interfered with only in accordance with the intention of the legislature, and only after every possible opportunity has been given to the individual to show cause why his rights should be left undisturbed.[74]

---

[68] Senate Select Committee on Standing Committees 1929-1930, *Evidence* at 13 (quoted in L F Crisp, *Australian National Government* (4th ed., 1978), at 419).
[69] Senate Select Committee on Standing Committees 1929-1930, *Evidence* at 18-19 (quoted in Crisp, *id*, at 418).
[70] In chapter 2.
[71] 1 *UTLJ* 53.
[72] 1 *Res Jud* 28.
[73] *Ibid.*
[74] *Id*, at 37.

Similarly, in 1936, Edward Sykes wrote a review of Jennings' *The Law and the Constitution* which is quite pointed in its criticism of the anti-judicial review thesis. 'Dr Jennings does not', Sykes wrote, 'really seriously deal with the underlying implication in Dicey's work that under the British system the dominant principle is that the rights of the individual should be secured.'[75] He took direct issue with the excessive ideological nature of the Anglo-Canadian scholarship:

> Dr Jennings is as much influenced by the idea of the 'public service' state concerned with the promotion of its subjects' material welfare as is Dicey by the idea of the 'public order' state, the functions of which are merely to defend the country and prevent disorder and crime. If the 'rule of law' be a political maxim used to bolster up a concept of the State which is now obsolete, one may retort that Dr Jennings' refutation of the doctrine of the 'rule of law' looks like a political maxim used to strengthen another concept of the State which has not yet arrived.[76]

Because of all these features, some Australian commentators suggested that a greater synergy existed (though of course they did not use this word to describe it) between the courts and the political branches of government in Australia than elsewhere in the common law world. In an article published in 1931, for example, E A Beecroft wrote:

> The rapid growth of [administrative] tribunals has brought with it, in some instances, the possibility of arbitrary administrative action without judicial review; yet in Australia the right of judicial review has, in respect of most of these tribunals, been carefully preserved, and no such serious protest against 'executive justice' has occurred as in Great Britain ...[77]

He continued:

> That is a good sign, because, under the conditions of modern life, what Mr Justice Higgins once referred to as 'the interdependence of the arms of government' will increase rather than decrease. Unless the new tribunals have the protection of the judiciary, administration will be seriously hampered and the ordinary courts will be overburdened with unnecessary litigation.[78]

---

[75] 1 *Res Jud* 56, at 58.
[76] *Ibid.*
[77] E A Beecroft 'Courts of Specialized Jurisdiction in Australia' (1931) 79 *U Penn L Rev* 1021, at 1050-1051.
[78] *Ibid.*

Yet this synergy was plainly a pragmatic, working one, rather than a synergy of constitutional theory. It was not dissimilar to the pragmatism which underlay the thinking about delegation of legislative power like that of Robert Menzies, quoted earlier.[79] As Beecroft put it:

> [Australian judges] more readily than the American judges, have abandoned, or at least learned to qualify, the cherished doctrine which they derived from Montesquieu and Blackstone, perhaps because that doctrine, in its purest form, was never so deeply fixed in their minds. They show little anxiety nowadays when a new instrument of government cannot be fitted precisely into one of the three traditional categories.

This latter passage is an illuminating one. If the problem with judicial review (including the imposition of natural justice requirements) in England during the middle decades of the century was one of sematic over-complication, the problem in Australia was arguably the converse: under-theorisation. This was to become apparent in the post-War years, as natural justice in England was entering its twilight period.

The High Court's Gloaming Shots

A review of the three High Court cases dealing with the entitlement to natural justice decided during the years which coincided with the twilight phase in England shows that here, the doctrine was stated in terms that were significantly less complicated than in England. Importantly, though, the three cases also represented a visible shift away from the comparatively sophisticated attempts to 'work with' the new legislation that was seen in the 'teens and 1920s, in the judgments and writings of Barton, Isaacs, Higgins and Evatt JJ.

The first of the cases, *R v Commonwealth Rent Controller, Ex parte National Mutual Life Association*,[80] arose in 1947 under wartime National Security regulations.[81] Some members of the Court purported to apply the *Electricity Commissioners* test, but others apparently felt it unnecessary to do so. The case involved the question of whether the Commonwealth Rent Controller, who had made a determination of the fair rent for certain premises, was obliged to have provided a hearing before making his determination.

---

[79] See *supra* n 68, and accompanying text.
[80] 75 CLR 361.
[81] The National Security (Landlord and Tenant) Regulations.

Regulation 23 specifically conferred upon the Rent Controller the right to determine fair rents of his own motion. Nevertheless, in their joint judgment, Latham CJ and Dixon J[82] held that since under the legislation the Rent Controller was also given the power to summon witnesses and to take evidence under oath, it could be inferred that he was under a duty to act judicially. For Rich J, the matter was much more straightforward. In his view, the legislation empowered the Rent Controller 'to determine the rights and liabilities of parties *and therefore* he is bound to act judicially.'[83] He did not refer to *Electricity Commissioners*. Instead, he approached this case in much the same way that Griffith CJ had approached *Municipal Council of Sydney v Harris* – holding that the action in question was deemed to be judicial in character simply by reason of the fact that it interfered with property rights. This was, of course, the same approach that he had taken in *Gillen v Laffer*, thirty years before, when he said that '[t]he nature of the thing done – deprivation of property – implies a judicial act'.[84] Starke J did cite *Electricity Commissioners*, but he said simply that the Rent Controller had authority 'to determine questions affecting the rights of subjects' (namely to determine the rents to be paid by them).[85] Like Rich J, it was for this reason that he held that the Rent Controller had a duty to act judicially.

Eight years later, in *Delta Properties Pty Ltd v Brisbane City Council*,[86] the Court held that before a local council could issue an order forbidding development of a piece of privately owned property, it had to provide the owner with the opportunity to convince the council otherwise. In this case, Ordinances made under the *City of Brisbane Acts 1924-1954* (Qld) forbad the construction of buildings on land which, in the opinion of the City Council, was not capable of being drained. The Council refused a building licence to Delta Properties Pty Ltd after receiving expert advice from its Engineer that the land in question would not drain. Nevertheless, the High Court held, there had to be an opportunity for Delta Properties to present its case. The Full Court[87] said:

> The situation which the section creates is that a prejudicial effect upon the rights of individuals with respect to property will occur whenever the council, in the exercise of its judgment, decides that land is, by reason of its

---

82 Williams J concurring (75 CLR, at 377).
83 75 CLR, at 373 (emphasis added).
84 37 CLR, at 229. See chapter 2.
85 75 CLR, at 376.
86 (1955) 95 CLR 11.
87 Dixon CJ, Webb, Fullagar, Kitto and Taylor JJ.

> situation, incapable of being drained ... In such a situation the law insists, according to long-established doctrine, that the step which will have that prejudicial effect ... requires for its efficacy the prior observance of the fundamental principles of natural justice.[88]

Interestingly, in holding that the obligation to observe natural justice was triggered, there was no reference at all in the judgment to *Electricity Commissioners* or to the element of superaddition. As had been the case in Rich J's judgment in the *Commonwealth Rent Controller* case, it was the mere fact that Delta Properties was being denied the full enjoyment of its property rights that triggered the 'long-established doctrine'.

A similar approach was taken in the third case from the same era, *Commissioner of Police v Tanos*.[89] *Tanos* involved a declaration that a restaurant owned by a Mr and Mrs Tanos was a disorderly house, on the basis that it sold alcohol without a licence. The *Disorderly Houses Act 1943* (NSW) gave a judge of the Supreme Court the right to make such a declaration *ex parte*, upon an appropriate affidavit being filed by a senior Police officer. Regulations made under the Act gave the judge discretion, if he thought it appropriate, to direct that a hearing be held prior to any declaration being made.

In *Tanos*, the High Court held that notwithstanding the structure of the governing Act, which made the *ex parte* proceeding the norm, hearings ought ordinarily to have been conducted. The judgment was reminiscent in this respect of *R v Housing Appeal Tribunal*, one of the very early *Housing Act* cases.[90] In their joint judgment, Dixon CJ and Webb J said that it was a 'deep-rooted principle of the law that before any one can be punished or prejudiced in his person or property by any judicial or quasi-judicial proceeding he must be afforded an adequate opportunity of being heard'.[91]

Now in one sense, this holding is unremarkable – after all, the declaration in question had been made by a judge, so it was hardly arguable that the proceeding was not judicial. But in another way, the decision was quite singular.[92] As has been noted, the parliamentary

---

[88] 95 CLR, at 18.

[89] (1958) 98 CLR 383.

[90] [1920] 3 KB 334.

[91] 98 CLR, at 395 (Taylor J concurring. See 98 CLR, at 397).

[92] In an amusing way, *Tanos* also says a great deal about the way in which Australian social mores have changed in the past forty years. The record suggested that the restaurant in question may well have formerly deserved its unsavoury reputation. But Mrs Tanos, who co-owned the restaurant with her husband, testified that she had taken steps to clean up the establishment's image. As Dixon CJ and Webb J put it:

direction was that applications for a declaration that a given set of premises was a disorderly house were to be made *ex parte*. The right to a hearing only arose because the regulations made it an option to be exercised at the judge's discretion. Yet, the Court concluded that the effect of the regulation was to limit the judge's discretion to do anything other than require a hearing *inter partes*. In effect, the holding was that a right to natural justice could be created not only by parliament, but also by the executive, through its own conduct.[93]

An Australian Twilight?

So at mid-century, there seemed to be a cleavage between English and Australian approaches to natural justice. In England, the doctrine had become infected by semantics and jargon. Ideas had given over to linguistics, with the result that natural justice was thought to have become a moribund doctrine. In Australia, in contrast, throughout the post-War period, the High Court's enunciation of natural justice had a nineteenth century air about it. There had been hints in the 1920s that the High Court seemed poised to adopt an overtly contextual approach to the relationship of procedural fairness and the 'new' legislation. But the late 1940s and 50s cases indicated a reversion to an older approach, whereby the existence of a duty to observe natural justice was thought to be a function of the effect of a given decision upon an individual, and derived from a 'deep-rooted principle of the law',[94] rather than something which depended upon the ascertainment of the scope of parliament's wishes.

As will be seen in later chapters, this was to prove to be a highly significant factor in determining the compass of natural justice in Australia in decades to come. But for a time, it seemed as though the twilight had

---

> The old customers were insistent on wine with their food, a fact of which the Tanos couple say they were unaware when they bought the business, but by means of Lebanese coffee, carefully brewed tea and a few soft drinks, coupled with the refurnishing of the room and the laying of some strips of carpet, the patronage of a much more desirable class of customer was obtained, a class which would not demand wine with their food (98 CLR, at 388-389).

[93] *Cf Attorney-General of Hong Kong v Ng Yuen Shiu* [1983] 2 AC 629, at 633 (*per* Lord Fraser of Tullybelton):

> Where an administrator takes the view that he can exercise his discretionary power only by obtaining information from the person affected by the exercise of such discretionary power he is conceding that a full investigation of facts is necessary ... The administrator is thereby acknowledging the duty to act fairly in the procedure selected and adopted for that purpose.

[94] *Tanos*, 98 CLR, at 395.

descended upon Australia, as well. Paradoxically, this took place as the English twilight was coming to a close, but in two cases: one dating from 1959, and the other from 1963, various judges of the High Court voiced an Australian version of the same sort of defeatist attitude that had been seen in the English judges.

The first of these cases, *Namatjira v Raabe*,[95] concerned an appeal against a conviction for supplying alcohol to an Aborigine, contrary to the Northern Territory *Licencing Ordinance*.[96] The *Licencing Ordinance* made it an offence to supply liquor to a person who was a ward of the state within the meaning of the Territorial *Welfare Ordinance*. Notwithstanding its short title, the *Welfare Ordinance* was intended to vest the Northern Territory government with broad *parens* authority to deal with the private affairs of the Aboriginal people. It did this by first defining the category of 'ward' broadly, but then by including a wide exclusionary clause. As the High Court noted, 'with the exception of what may be called transient aliens and a few others the exclusion [covered] everybody but Aboriginals'.[97] Indeed, the record showed that more than fifteen thousand people in the Northern Territory had been declared wards at the same time.[98]

Namatjira v Raabe was an interesting case in the sense that the denial of natural justice was a step removed, so to speak, from the person invoking it. The appellant's argument was that the Aborigine to whom he had sold liquor had been denied a hearing before being declared a ward. The declaration of wardship, therefore, was void, so one of the elements of the offence could not be made out. The High Court rejected this argument, however, and held that in the circumstances, a hearing prior to declaration of wardship was not required.

Speaking for a unanimous bench,[99] Dixon CJ acknowledged that ordinarily, one would assume that a hearing would be required in such an instance.[100] But given the particular circumstances of the legislation, he said, a contrary conclusion was warranted. The Court offered three reasons for this holding. First, the *Welfare Ordinance* provided for an appeal *de novo* on a declaration of wardship to a judge. This obviated the need for

---

[95] (1959) 100 CLR 664.
[96] *Licencing Ordinance 1939-1957* (NT), s 141.
[97] 100 CLR, at 667.
[98] *Ibid.*
[99] Dixon CJ, McTiernan, Fullagar, Kitto and Windeyer JJ.
[100] 100 CLR, at 668.

natural justice rights at first instance.[101] Secondly, the original decision-making power was vested in the Territorial Administrator, who was the head of government.[102] 'One would not expect to find', the Court said, 'if it was intended that each individual case were to be inquired into and the particular circumstances of the case ascertained, that such a duty or function would be committed to the head of a government.'[103] Finally, the *Welfare Ordinance* succeeded prior legislation under which Aborigines had what amounted to wardship status, so it was reasonable to assume that the same presumption was to apply under the new legislation.[104]

A number of things strike one about the judgment in *Namatjira v Raabe*, particularly when it is contrasted with the English twilight cases and with what I have described as the High Court's 'gloaming shots' of the late 40s and early-to-mid 50s.[105] The first is that unlike the Privy Council in *Nakkuda Ali v Jayaratne*, the High Court did not feel it necessary to discuss the decision in *Electricity Commissioners* or the question of superaddition. In this sense, *Namatjira v Raabe* was in step with the gloaming shots. But unlike them, it reads as a judgment which attempts to appreciate the context of regulatory legislation – which is quite different from the impression that one gets from, say, *Delta Properties Pty Ltd v Brisbane City Council*, where the Court had said that the mere fact of interference with rights in real property was sufficient to trigger natural justice. This seeming inconsistency is in fact emblematic of the approach to administrative law urged by Sir Owen Dixon.

Sir Owen Dixon and the Policy of Deference to Administrative Expertise

By any measure, Sir Owen Dixon occupies a magnificent place in the story of the Australian legal system. Colin Howard once said that Dixon's was 'by far the greatest single judicial influence on the interpretation of the

---

[101] Though it ought to be noted that the Court acknowledged that in order for the appeal right to provide any protection, one had to have access to the legal system in a practical sense. See 100 CLR, at 670.

[102] On the legal status of the Administrator of the Northern Territory, see *R v Toohey, Ex parte Northern Land Council* (1981) 151 CLR 170 (discussed in chapter 6).

[103] 100 CLR, at 669.

[104] See *ibid.*

[105] Considered from the perspective of the present day, of course, the thing which is most striking about the judgment is the extent to which the position of the Aboriginal people as lacking full legal capacity was accepted without comment by the High Court. It is unimaginable that such a decision could be rendered today.

Australian constitution'.[106] At his retirement from the bench in 1964, Sir Robert Menzies said that he had heard 'at least two Lord Chancellors give it as their opinion that your Honour was the greatest judicial lawyer in the English-speaking world', and that this view had been confirmed 'by the most brilliant and celebrated occupant of the Supreme Court Bench at Washington'.[107] As to the latter comment, Dean Acheson, the United States Secretary of State, is reputed to have said that had it been possible, Dixon would have been appointed to the US Supreme Court following his time as Australian minister in Washington.[108]

In part, Dixon's celebration was possible because he was a lawyer's judge, and because he sat at a time when the High Court and its members did not occupy the sort of position in the public consciousness that they do today. The self-described key to Dixon's judicial method was, of course, the oft-referred to 'strict and complete legalism'.[109] There was no other safe guide to judgment than this, he said. And central to Dixon's conception of legalism was his quest for underlying legal principle through rigorous employment of the doctrine of *stare decisis*. In his famous lecture, 'Concerning Judicial Method', he explained this. He said that the nineteenth century would probably come to be regarded as 'the classical period of English law':

> It was a period of legal rationalisation. The search for principle was a marked characteristic of many judges. Principles were not only used, they developed. There was a steady, if intuitive, attempt to develop the law as a science. But this was not done by an abandonment of the high technique and strict logic of the common law. It was done by an apt and felicitous use of that very technique and, under the name of reasoning, of that strict logic which it seems fashionable now to expel from the system.[110]

Yet despite this – and despite his reputation as a judicial polymath – Dixon's role in the development of Australian administrative law is something of an ambiguous one. The creed of strict and complete legalism was less apparently applied by Sir Owen in administrative law than it may have been in other areas, and it is not altogether clear that his legacy has

---

[106] Quoted by Sir Ninian Stephen, in *Sir Owen Dixon: A Celebration* (1986), at 22.
[107] 'Retirement of the Chief Justice' (1964) 110 CLR, at vii.
[108] Stephen, *supra* n 106, at 21.
[109] 'Swearing in of Sir Owen Dixon as Chief Justice' (1952) 85 CLR, at xiv. See also Sir D Dawson and M Nicholls, 'Sir Owen Dixon and Judicial Method' (1986) 15 *Melb U L Rev* 543 and Sir Harry Gibbs's remarks on Dixon's 'legalism' at Gibbs's retirement (162 CLR, at vii).
[110] In *Jesting Pilate* (1965), at 157.

been a completely helpful one. Indeed, in some respects, Dixon's administrative law work was actually to an extent inconsistent and, for reasons which will become apparent in chapter seven, this may well have contributed to some of the doctrinal uncertainty facing the system today.

In a pair of cases decided in the late 1940s, Dixon J enunciated an approach to judicial review which in some respects bore a similarity to the view proffered by the Anglo-Canadian scholars. The first of the cases was *R v Hickman, Ex parte Fox and Clinton*, decided within a week of the Japanese surrender in 1945.[111] The case involved the question of the extent of the jurisdiction of 'Local Reference Boards', set up under the Coal Mining Industry Employment Regulations. In his judgment, Dixon J (as he then was) suggested that a decision of a tribunal should not be overturned provided that 'its decision is a *bona fide* attempt to exercise its powers, that it relates to the subject matter of the legislation, and that it is reasonably capable of reference to the power given to the body'.[112]

Implicit in this holding was a view about the relative expertise of 'generalist' common law judges and 'expert' bureaucrats. It is reminiscent of the Anglo-Canadian scholars' view that the bureaucracy was more attuned to the problems of modern administration 'than a divisional court which is an aggregation of three judges casually meeting on Monday morning'.[113] In a like spirit, in *Water Conservation and Irrigation Commission (NSW) v Browning*,[114] decided two years later, Dixon J indicated that he was prepared to defer to the substantive views of a government commission, even when those views were offensive. In *Browning*, the New South Wales Water Conservation and Irrigation Commission had declined to approve the transfer of a lease to a farm because the prospective transferee was not of Australian origins.[115] Notwithstanding this, Dixon J said:

> The grounds of suitability, desirability and advantage are matters for the Commission's judgment. If the Commission considers divisions arising from race or from hostile affiliation undesirable, what is there in the statute to

---

[111] 70 CLR 598.

[112] 70 CLR, at 615. See also Gibbs J's comments to a similar effect in *Buck v Bavone* (1976) 135 CLR 110, at 119.

[113] J Willis, 'Three Approaches to Administrative Law', *supra* n 71, at 73-74.

[114] (1947) 74 CLR 492.

[115] The transferee was a naturalised British subject, born in Italy. The Commission's reasons for refusal were (i) that as someone of 'enemy origin', he was not desirable: lands were sought to be retained for returning *Australian* soldiers, (ii) Italians were not good farmers under irrigation methods and, (iii) it was undesirable to have more Italians living in the area in question (see 74 CLR, at 503).

> show that it is a consideration wholly outside the Commission's province? ... There may be much reason to doubt the validity of the reasoning by which the opinions of the Commission have been reached. But that is not for us.[116]

The reason for this, he explained, had to do with respect for parliament's judgment about functional expertise. 'The Commission', he said, was 'an administrative body entrusted with a full discretion.'[117] He continued: 'The Commission is responsible for the successful development of irrigation areas as well as for superintending and controlling them. The width and variety of its powers are enough to show that matters of policy are by no means withheld from the Commission.'[118]

Sir Owen's views on the separation of powers have been subjected to a vigorous criticism, partly on the basis that they relied upon a process of functional classification[119] – which, as chapter two showed, can, at the margins, be a highly arcane exercise. Yet, it is difficult to escape the conclusion that in a constitutional regime like Australia's, where the separation of powers is formally entrenched, what John Willis termed (derisively) 'functionalism' must underlie any doctrine of deference. So in Dixon's case, functionalism did not present any problems of principle – on the contrary, it represented a logical extension of legalism.

Some have suggested that Dixon's approach in *Hickman* and *Browning* stemmed from his time in the United States in 1942-1944, when he became close to Felix Frankfurter, whose attitude towards Lord Hewart was noted in chapter two. Whether or not this is true, judgments like these lead one to the conclusion that whatever else may have been his contribution to Australian law, Sir Owen Dixon's legacy to administrative law is something of an indeterminate one. Given the deferential tone in cases like *Hickman*, *Browning* and *Namatjira*, it seems a paradox that Dixon was *also* the author of the very loosely-stated judgments in the three gloaming cases: *R v Commonwealth Rent Controller, Delta Properties Pty Ltd v Brisbane City Council*, and *Commissioner of Police v Tanos*. In *Tanos*, it will be recalled, Dixon CJ joined with Webb J in saying that – notwithstanding evidence of parliamentary intent to the contrary – it was a 'deep-rooted principle of the law that before any one can be punished or prejudiced in his person or property by any judicial or quasi-judicial

---

[116] 74 CLR, at 506.
[117] 74 CLR, at 504.
[118] 74 CLR, at 505.
[119] See, F Wheeler, 'The Separation of Federal Judicial Power: A Purposive Analysis' (unpublished PhD Thesis, ANU, 1999), chapters 4 and 5.

proceeding he must be afforded an adequate opportunity of being heard'.[120] Apart from the fact that the three gloaming cases dealt with rights in land, it is difficult to reconcile this with a principled approach to deferentialism.

Testro Bros Pty Ltd v Tait

Leaving Sir Owen Dixon's legacy aside for the moment, the most outstanding example of 'twilight-ism' in Australian public law was seen in the 1963 decision of the High Court in *Testro Bros Pty Ltd v Tait*.[121] In it, the Court avowedly adopted the sort of emaciating analysis engaged in by the Privy Council in *Nakkuda Ali v Jayaratne* and by Lord Goddard in *Parker*.

The Testro brothers were principals in a series of companies engaged in speculative building projects. The litigation involved the appointment of Tait as an inspector under the Victorian *Companies Act 1961*, to carry out a special investigation into the affairs of the companies with a view to seeing whether they should be wound up, or whether prosecutions should be instituted against the Testros. Section 173 of the *Companies Act* conferred upon company inspectors the power to compel witnesses and to take examination on oath. After he had been so summoned, R C Testro, one of the brothers, requested leave to appear by counsel, which was granted. Counsel then requested the right to put questions to Testro following his examination by Tait. Counsel also requested that as the representative of the companies, he be permitted to be present throughout the taking of evidence and that he have the right to cross-examine all witnesses. He further requested to be informed of all allegations against the companies which might arise during the investigation.

Tait's position was that while he would have been prepared to have allowed counsel to appear for Testro personally during his examination, he would not agree to the requests made by counsel on behalf of the companies. Thereupon, both Testro and Testro Bros Pty Ltd applied to the Supreme Court of Victoria for a writ of prohibition to stop Tait from proceeding further, or alternatively for a writ of mandamus directing him to accede to the requests. The basis of the Testro case was that Tait was obliged to observe natural justice because through the issuance of his report, he had a power to affect their reputation and, hence, their pecuniary

---

[120] 98 CLR, at 395.
[121] 109 CLR, at 353.

interests.[122] O'Bryan J refused the applications, however, relying on the decision of the Full Court of the Supreme Court of Victoria in a similar case decided the year beforehand, *R v Coppel, Ex parte Viney Industries*.[123]

In *Viney Industries*, the Supreme Court of Victoria had held that an Inspector under the *Companies Act* was not required to act judicially, and hence was not obliged to accord natural justice.[124] The Full Court reviewed the existing authorities, including *R v Electricity Commissioners*, *R v Legislative Committee of the Church Assembly*[125] and *Nakkuda Ali v Jayaratne*. It concluded that a Company Inspector was not required to observe the rules of natural justice for two reasons. First, it held that there was no superadded obligation on his part to act judicially. Reviewing the provisions of the *Companies Act* in issue, it found, as the Privy Council had found in *Nakkuda Ali*, that there was nothing in the Act which would suggest that parliament had intended that the Inspector carry out his investigation in a judge-like fashion.[126]

The Court in *Viney Industries* also stated that having regard to 'broader considerations as to the object, purpose and scope of the investigation', as well as 'the nature of the report which it is contemplated will be produced as the result thereof', it was not of the view that the Inspector had the power to interfere with a company's legal rights.[127] In the Full Court's view, a report could either lead to the institution of a prosecution by the Attorney-General for violation of the *Companies Act*, or to an application to wind the company up. In either case, any actual interference with the firm's legal rights would come from the Court, not from the Inspector's report.[128] As the High Court put it in *Testro Bros v Tait*, the conclusion in *Viney Industries* was that an Inspector's report could not of its own force prejudicially affect the rights of a company.[129] It is equally clear from the judgment in *Viney Industries*, though, that one of the things which weighed heavily upon the Court was a fear of rendering

---

[122] 109 CLR, at 355.

[123] [1962] VR 630.

[124] This was also the position arrived at in two other cases, not cited by O'Bryan J in *Testro Bros Ltd v Tait*: *O'Connor v Waldron* [1935] AC 76 (PC, Can) and *St John v Fraser* [1935] 3 DLR 465 (SCC).

[125] [1928] 1 KB 411. See chapter 2.

[126] [1962] VR, at 638.

[127] [1962] VR, at 639.

[128] *Ibid.*

[129] 109 CLR, at 363.

the inspection process unworkable, were a requirement to observe natural justice to be imposed.[130]

In the High Court in *Testro Bros v Tait*, Testro Bros argued that an amendment to the *Companies Act* subsequent to the *Viney Industries* case had changed the complexion of the Inspector's power.[131] The amendment in question was sub-section 171(10) of the Act, which provided that an Inspector's report was 'admissible in any legal proceeding as evidence of the opinion *and of the facts upon which his opinion is based* of the inspector in relation to any matter contained in the report'.[132] In the version in issue in *Viney Industries*,[133] Inspectors' reports were only admissible as evidence of the opinion of the inspector. There was no reference to their admissibility as evidence of fact. In the view of Testro Bros, this was sufficient to vest Tait with the power, should he arrive at adverse conclusions about them, to adversely affect their rights.

Unfortunately for the Testros, the majority of the High Court took a different view. In a joint judgment, McTiernan, Taylor and Owen JJ held that notwithstanding the legislative amendment, one could not say that an Inspector appointed under the Act had a duty to act judicially. Starting from the premise that the interpretation given to the Act by the Victorian Full Court in *Viney Industries* – that the *Companies Act* did not disclose an intent that Inspectors had an obligation to act judicially – was correct, their Honours said that there was nothing in the new sub-section 171(10) or elsewhere which 'justifie[d] the conclusion that the Legislature intended to make such a fundamental change as is suggested in the character of an investigation'.[134] But having said this, they proceeded to dash cold water on any thoughts of aggrandisement that Tait may have been feeling as a result of his immunity. While it was true, they said, that sub-section 171(10) made reports evidence of fact, it was, the Court stressed, *prima facie* evidence only.[135] 'We should add', they continued, '... that we are of the opinion that the report of an inspector has no evidentiary value at all

[130] See, especially [1962] VR, at 638, line 28 *ff*. It is also worthwhile to note that the Court was heavily influenced by the decision of the Court of Appeal in *Re Grosvenor and West-End Railway Terminus Hotel Co* (1897) 76 LT 337, which held that an Inspector acting under the British *Companies Act 1862* was not under an obligation to act judicially.

[131] As an aside, it is fascinating to note that counsel for Tait was none other than E G Coppel QC – the respondent in *Viney Industries*!

[132] Emphasis added.

[133] *Companies Act 1958* (Vic), sub-s 146(9).

[134] 109 CLR, at 364.

[135] *Ibid*.

except where the fact of his opinion is a relevant issue in any particular proceedings.'[136]

Kitto and Menzies JJ both dissented. In Kitto J's view, the amendments *did* give the Inspector's report new significance: 'the report itself prejudices the rights by placing them in a new jeopardy'.[137] Likewise, Menzies J noted that an adverse report was 'an incontrovertible finding against the company which must be accepted by the Court upon a petition for winding up as establishing a ground for making an order'.[138] In his view, this was the critical distinction between this case and its predecessor:

> [A]s soon as findings or opinions are given legal consequences and are made the foundation in law for further proceedings in relation to the company, then the position changes and well-established principles require that the enquiry be subject to the control of the law to prevent departures from the basic principles of justice which are commonly described as natural justice.[139]

Testro Bros v Tait stands, with cases like *Nakkuda Ali v Jayaratne* and *R v Metropolitan Police Commissioner, Ex parte Parker*, as a testament to a way of thinking that was increasingly to concern observers – both academic and judicial – as the 1960s went on. *Parker* was perhaps the most overt in this respect, but in each of the cases, the way in which the court described the obligation to observe natural justice illustrated that the common law had become detached from the realities of the workaday constitution. These cases *did* seem to be proof of the views expressed by Professor Keeton and Mr Justice Devlin that the common law was no longer able to provide the citizen with protection against an unfair Leviathan.[140]

In the English context, the deficiency stemmed from a combination of doctrinal complexity and judicial brow-beatedness. In Australia, the English way of thinking clearly had had an impact – the judgments in *Testro Bros v Tait* make this plain. But the course of natural justice was different here during the period and the root cause of natural justice's malaise may have had a slightly different gloss. The 'gloaming shots' discussed earlier in this chapter showed that in the right circumstances, the doctrine of natural justice could still be stated robustly by the High Court.

---

[136] *Ibid.* Note, though, that the High Court was later to repudiate this point, in *Ainsworth v Criminal Justice Commission* (1992) 175 CLR 564. See chapter 5.

[137] 109 CLR, at 368.

[138] 109 CLR, at 375.

[139] 109 CLR, at 373.

[140] See *supra* nn 46 and 47, and accompanying text.

But the lack of evolved theorisation of the doctrine after the 1920s left the doctrine in a highly weakened state in terms of its compass.

This was illustrated by the holdings in *Testro Bros v Tait* and *Namatjira v Raabe*. The gloaming cases all dealt with real property interests (if not 'rights' *stricto sensu*). But with respect to other types of interests, the High Court's judgments suggest that Australian public law did not seem able or willing to take account of interests which, while not according exactly with traditional common law notions of proprietary dominion, might also be deserving of protection from arbitrary interference by the executive. The common law's achievement in the fourth phase was to bridge this gap, and to provide procedural protection for non-proprietary interests. The means by which this was accomplished will be the focus of the next chapter.

4 The New Property

On 10 May 1968, the High Court delivered its judgment in *Banks v Transport Regulation Board (Victoria)*.[1] Viewed from the standpoint of today, when we are concerned with such weighty substantive issues as the very foundations of our system of property ownership and the basis for our system of constitutional government, the anniversary does not seem like one much worth noting. Indeed, the only thing which strikes one when reading *Banks* today is its seeming unsingularity. In fact, the sole thing which might provoke the casual reader from a review of the case report is that the litigation actually made it to the High Court. As for the holding – frankly, the law as expounded by the Court in *Banks* seems to the current generation of administrative lawyers trite in the extreme.

Simply put, *Banks v Transport Regulation Board* involved the question of whether the Victorian Transport Regulation Board was entitled to revoke, on the basis of non-compliance with its conditions, the licence of a taxi-cab driver without first putting the specific allegations of non-compliance to him, and without giving him a chance to refute them. In holding that such a revocation was unlawful – that Banks had in the circumstances been denied natural justice – the High Court was mirroring a position on natural justice taken by the House of Lords nearly four years beforehand in *Ridge v Baldwin*.[2] Yet in doing so, the Court was heralding a renaissance for Australian administrative law.

For one thing, in its judgment in *Banks*, the Court effectively overruled one of its own decisions of just a few years standing,[3] at a time when such things were not so common. But even more significantly, the Court in *Banks* came expressly, if only indirectly, to embrace a change in thinking about the relationship between the citizen, the state, and public wealth that had been brewing in the common law world for some time. The aim of this chapter is to explore the jurisprudential line which led to *Banks*, and to place the judgments in the case in a broader legal and social

---

[1] 119 CLR 222.

[2] [1964] AC 40.

[3] *Testro Bros Ltd v Tait* (1963) 109 CLR 353.

context. The contention is that *Banks* and its context represents what the American Professor Bruce Ackerman would call a 'constitutional moment'.[4] In short, the argument is that when it is viewed in the context of the accepted assumptions of Anglo-Australian administrative law at mid-century, *Banks v Transport Regulation Board* stands out as a decision which heralded a much greater round of change than it is given credit for today.

The New Property

In April of 1964, Professor Charles Reich of Yale Law School published an article entitled 'The New Property'.[5] It was one of a series of pieces that he wrote in the 1960s in which he explored the more jurisprudentially troubling side of the welfare state (or the 'public interest state', as he termed it).[6] But it is wrong to think of Reich's work as reactionary in a negative, condemning sense. On the contrary, he regarded the use of the administrative apparatus as an instrument of wealth distribution as a good thing. His concern had rather to do with the way in which the law – which he viewed in a Hobbesian fashion as the shield for the citizen against the potentially soul-less power of the state – had allowed itself to fall out of step with reality of government; and had thereby allowed to become perilously close to irrelevant. In Reich's view, the problem was that the new role for the executive state as guarantor of what Sir Isaiah Berlin described as 'positive liberties'[7] had not been accompanied by an assumption of new responsibility by the judicial branch.

In this sense, 'The New Property' and its companion pieces represented an important response to the sort of administrative legal scholarship that had emanated in Reich's own country from the New Deal,[8]

---

[4] See *Reconstructing American Law* (1984).

[5] 73 *Yale LJ* 733.

[6] *Ibid*. See, also, 'Individual Rights and Social Welfare: The Emerging Legal Issues' (1965) 74 *Yale L J* 1245 and 'Law of the Planned Society' (1967) 75 *Yale LJ* 1227.

[7] 'Two Concepts of Liberty', in *Four Essays on Liberty* (Oxford, 1969), 131 *ff*. See chapter 2, 63-65.

[8] See, *eg*, the *locus classicus* of Depression-era American administrative law writing, *The Administrative Process* (1st ed. 1938), by James Landis. See generally on the advent of modern American administrative law scholarship: M Shapiro, *Who Guards the Guardians* (1988), chapter 2, J L Mashaw, *Due Process in the Administrative State* (1989), chapter 1, and P H Schuck (ed), *Foundations of Administrative Law* (1994), chapters 1, 3.

and in the British Commonwealth from the Anglo-Canadian scholars. As was illustrated by the twilight cases, this was in large measure a function of the fact that the courts had, consciously or not, adopted the distinction between legally-enforceable 'rights' and un-enforceable 'privileges' or 'licences' that Hohfeld had described in his famous article.[9] In the Hohfeldian analysis, only the former could command any correlative duty – for present purposes, any correlative duty on the part of the decision-maker to accord natural justice. This was precisely the premise on which Lord Goddard CJ had proceeded in *R v Metropolitan Police Commissioner, Ex parte Parker*.[10] In Reich's opinion, such a viewpoint could no longer stand. Or, at least, it could no longer serve as the foundation upon which procedural rights *vis-à-vis* the administration could be based.

In Reich's view, without an effective means for the law to check executive power, the public interest state would give rise to what he called a 'new feudalism'.[11] This is because American (and, by extension, Anglo-Australian) society retained the notion of individual dominion at the cornerstone of its conception of free humanity. Without the security of social tenure conferred by property rights, or an equivalent thereto, humankind could easily find itself at the mercy of a new feudal despot:

> The institution called property guards the troubled boundary between individual man and the state. It is not the only guardian; many other institutions, laws and practices serve as well. But in a society that chiefly values material well-being, the power to control a particular portion of that well-being is the very foundation of individuality.[12]

Similarly:

> Property is a legal institution the essence of which is the creation and protection of certain private rights in wealth of any kind. One of these functions is to draw a boundary between public and private power ... Thus, property performs the function of maintaining independence, dignity and

---

[9] 'Some Fundamental Legal Conceptions as Applied in Judicial Reasoning' (1913) 23 *Yale LJ* 16.

[10] [1953] 1 WLR 1150. See chapter 3.

[11] *Supra* n 5, at 768.

[12] *Id*, at 734.

> pluralism in society by creating zones within which the majority has to yield to the owner.[13]

In stating this, he noted, it is important to remember that property is a creature of law – and, hence, the responsibility of the law-givers to safeguard:

> Wealth or value is created by culture and by society; it is culture that makes a diamond valuable and a pebble worthless. Property, on the other hand, is the creation of law. A man who has property has certain legal rights with respect to an item of wealth; property represents a relationship between wealth and its 'owners'.[14]

The problem, as Reich saw it, was that under a traditional analysis, '[g]overnment largess [*sic*] is plainly "wealth", but it is not necessarily "property"'.[15] Simply put, when *choses* of value were not owned by their holders, but instead held upon a conditional and revocable grant from the state, the effect was to recreate the medieval relationship of feudalism. The extent of state involvement in modern life is what gave rise to the sinister aspect of welfare-ism: 'the doctrine that the wealth that flows from government is held by its recipients conditionally, subject to confiscation in the interest of the paramount state'.[16] To put it more pointedly, Reich's concern was that when peoples' livelihood has come to depend upon the active patronage of government, for the law to fail to appropriate to itself a role in the regulation of the patronage – for the law to treat the government's activity with respect to wealth distribution as non-justiciable 'largesse' rather than a new form of justiciable entitlement, in other words – was to undermine the very foundations upon which our vision of a free society was built.

The solution, therefore, was for the law to update the way in which it viewed the relationship between the citizen and the government; for it to recognise a 'new property':

> There can be no retreat from the public interest state. It is the inevitable outgrowth of an interdependent world. An effort to return to an earlier economic order would merely transfer power to giant private governments

---

[13] *Id*, at 771.
[14] *Id*, at 739.
[15] *Ibid*.
[16] *Id*, at 768.

> which would not rule in the public interest, but in their own interest. If individualism and pluralism are to be preserved, this must be done not by marching backwards, but by building these values into today's society. If public and private are now blurred, it will be necessary to draw a new zone of privacy. If private property can no longer perform its protective functions, it will be necessary to establish institutions to carry on the work that private property once did but can no longer do.[17]

Reich's view eventually came to be given a judicial voice in his own country in two decisions of the Supreme Court of the United States in the early 1970s, *Goldberg v Kelly*[18] and *Board of Regents of State Colleges v Roth*.[19] Though speaking in dissent in *Roth*, Marshall J adopted an almost rapturous application of Reich's ideas in the context of natural justice – or what the Americans refer to as 'procedural due process':

> Employment is one of the greatest, if not the greatest, benefits that governments offer in modern-day life. When something as valuable as the opportunity to work is at stake, the government may not reward some citizens and not others without demonstrating that its actions are fair and equitable. And it is procedural due process that is our fundamental guarantee of fairness, our protection against arbitrary, capricious and unreasonable government action.[20]

In many ways, Reich's work still reads remarkably freshly even now.[21] His discussion of the blurring between public and private could easily come from the pen of many of today's feminist scholars. And his conclusion that one could not turn the clock back – that to do so would merely be to transfer power to giant private 'governments' – rings very familiar to anyone interested in the debate over the merits of privatisation and economic rationalism.

But the real genius of Reich's scholarship from an administrative law perspective was that it captured so well the challenge to which the system had to rise if it was to survive as anything more than a relic of a

---

[17] *Id*, at 778.
[18] 397 US 254 (1970).
[19] 408 US 564 (1972).
[20] 408 US, at 589.
[21] Though for a partially critical retrospective view of Reich's writing, see R Rabin, 'Reflections on the New Property' (1990) *USF L Rev* 273. For an Australian perspective on the piece, see R Sackville, 'Property, Rights and Social Security' (1978) 2 *UNSW L J* 246.

pre-Diceyan age of local government. At the time that Reich was writing, not just natural justice but the whole of administrative law was in the doldrums. So much so that in the first edition of his classic work, published in 1959, de Smith felt confident in predicting that '[j]udicial self-restraint has won a decisive victory over judicial activism in a field where the contest might well have been an even one'.[22] The challenge of the 1960s, the beginning of the post-modern evolution towards rights consciousness, was to re-assert an active place for the judiciary, without undermining the benefits that collectivist legislation was intended to provide.

Administrative Expertise or Bureaucratic Tyranny?

Part of the impetus for the revival in natural justice's fortunes was the intellectual debate about notions of freedom and liberty which arose in the context of the pessimism over the state of the so-called 'free world' during the Cold War. What John Willis had termed the 'public service' state, whose watchwords were efficiency and expertise, had not fulfilled the promise that it had seemed to hold during the Great Depression. The Second World War had been over for some time, the Cold War was in full swing, and some people felt a chafing at what they perceived to be bureaucratic stuffiness and authoritarian tendencies within the public service.

Among the leading participants in this debate were F A Hayek[23] and Michael Oakeshott,[24] but to public lawyers, probably the best-known participant in the debate was Sir Isaiah Berlin, whose inaugural Oxford lectures, 'Two Concepts of Liberty', have already been referred to.[25] In

---

[22] At 18.

[23] See, *eg*, *The Road to Serfdom* (1944), *Individualism and Economic Order* (1948), *The Constitution of Liberty* (1960) and *Law, Legislation and Liberty* (1973-1979).

[24] See, *eg*, *On Human Conduct* (1975), *Hobbes on Civil Association* (1975), 'The Rule of Law', in *On History and Other Essays* (1983). As an aside, Oakeshott was Harold Laski's successor as Professor of Politics at the LSE. One former student has said that his appointment was made 'to the dismay and even horror of the socialists at the LSE and elsewhere' (N Podhoretz, 'A Dissent on Isaiah Berlin', *Commentary Online*, February 1999, www.commentarymagazine.com).

[25] See chapter 2. It is worthwhile to note that as with the Anglo-Canadian scholars, there were significant differences amongst these men. Oakeshott, for example, once introduced Berlin at a public lecture by describing him as 'a very Paganini of ideas' (Podhoretz, *ibid*).

1950, Berlin published a long essay, entitled 'Political Ideas in the Twentieth Century'.[26] In this essay, Berlin attacked the subversion of individual liberty that was inherent in communism. But 'Political Ideas in the Twentieth Century' amounted to much more than a simple critique of Soviet Marxism. It also amounted to a condemnation of much Western academic thought. As his biographer described Berlin's thesis:

> Both Soviet Marxism and post-war Western social democracy were prey to the same twentieth-century rationalist illusion: that, with sufficient social engineering, human evils could be abolished and individuals happily assimilated into a seamless social consensus. To be sure, Soviet Marxism was more ruthless in its contempt for democracy and human rights. But Western liberals could not remain complacent. The human desire to be relieved of the benefit of choice might lead the West to hand the dilemmas of public and private life over to experts, politicians, psychotherapists and others 'engineers of human souls.'[27]

It will be readily apparent that Berlin's criticism extended not only to the theme of the Anglo-Canadian administrative law scholars of the 1930s, but also to much of the writing of the Australian progressives earlier in the century. When Jethro Brown wrote, for example, that the object of modern government was to implement the 'social will', but cautioned that that was not to be equated with 'actual will', which could be corrupted by several factors including the population's ignorance of what was in its own best interests,[28] he was advocating the same sort of surrender of liberty that Berlin warned of. Yet the concern was compounded, in Berlin's view, by the fact that the 'public service state' was in fact not served by experts, but by what he termed 'engineers of human souls'.[29]

This latter concern was illustrated in a practical way by a series of cases which exposed particularly egregious instances of arrogance on the part of public servants towards the interests of private individuals. As early as 1948, in *Blackpool Corporation v Locker*,[30] concern had been raised about the heavy-handedness of municipal officials who first

---

On the difference in thought between Oakeshott and Hayek, see also M Loughlin, *Public Law and Political Theory* (1992), chapter 5.

[26] *Foreign Affairs*, Spring, 1950.

[27] M Ignatieff, *Isaiah Berlin: A Life* (1998), at 198.

[28] *The Underlying Principles of Modern Legislation* (1912), at 143-148 (discussed in chapter 2).

[29] Quoted *supra* n 27.

[30] [1948] 1 KB 349.

confiscated a private home and its contents without lawful authority, and then attempted to obstruct the legal process by refusing for six months to respond to a request from the dispossessed homeowner to reveal the source of the legal power on which it was purporting to rely.

This was followed in England by the infamous Crichel Down case, where the Ministry of Agriculture neglected to provide the former owner of expropriated land with the right to re-purchase it after the land was no longer required by the Air Ministry, which had caused its expropriation. The Minister of Agriculture had announced a policy of return of such lands to former owners, but civil servants in the Ministry had ideas about setting up a model farm, which they pursued despite the Minister's announcement. In the end, the Minister was forced to resign on the basis that he had lost control over the administration of policy in his department and a commission of enquiry was set up to look into the affair.[31] As Geoffrey Sawer put it, the enquiry's report 'sets out an incredible story of incompetence, muddle, folly and misjudgment'.[32] While finding no evidence of illegality in the government's action, the enquiry attributed much of the problem to a particular civil servant who was, as the enquiry described him, 'a man accustomed to having his own way and strongly resenting anyone questioning anything that he had done or querying any decision that he had come to or advice he had given'.[33]

Similar attitudes were seen in two notorious cases in Australia. The first was the Mudge case.[34] Mrs Mudge was the widow of a farmer whose land had been resumed by the Victorian government. The question arose as to the appropriate level of compensation to be paid.[35] The government took the position that it had an absolute discretion to determine the amount of compensation, that it was not required to offer any reason for its determination, and that its determinations were not subject to judicial review. The Supreme Court of Victoria held that determinations were reviewable, and it directed the government to re-consider the matter. But the government effectively refused to act on the Court's order, and in a subsequent application, Smith J said of the public servant chiefly concerned:

---

[31] On the Crichel Down affair, see R D Brown, *The Battle of Crichel Down* (1955). See also 'Administrative Tribunals', *Current Affairs Bulletin* 24 April 1967, at 166.

[32] *Ombudsmen* (1964), at 21.

[33] 'Report of the Public Inquiry Ordered by the Minister of Agriculture into the Disposal of Land at Crichel Down (Cmd 9176, 1954).

[34] See *Mudge v Attorney-General (Victoria)* [1960] VR 43.

[35] Under the *North-West Mallee Settlement Areas Act 1948* (Vic)

> He is, as he made plain by his demeanour and evidence upon his examination, a man who regards any investigation, let alone criticism, of his actions as an affront. When the mandatory order of 18 December 1959 was made he quickly took action aimed at either maintaining the Department's stand that no compensation should be paid or limiting the compensation to as small a sum as possible.[36]

In a similar spirit is the story of the Ansett case. Ansett was a wealthy man with political connections who exerted pressure on the Victorian government to acquire property to build a reservoir in a way that best suited Ansett but which seriously inconvenienced other property owners. As in the Crichel Down case, the government was forced by the weight of public opinion to conduct an enquiry. While (again, as in the Crichel Down affair) no illegality was found to have taken place, there was 'insensitivity to public opinion and to the feeling of the other persons affected, and an assumption by the [public service] that it was for authority to decide what was in the public interest and to go ahead accordingly'.[37]

Episodes like these lent credence not only to the sorts of concerns that had been expressed by Lord Hewart a generation or so earlier, but also to the spectre of bureaucratic malevolence raised by thinkers like Berlin, Hayek and Oakeshott. In such a setting, it can hardly be a surprise that the judicial instinct to act as a 'sovereign guarantor' of civil rights (as Sir William Mulock, the Chief Justice of Ontario, once put it[38]) not unnaturally began to revive itself.

A Doctrine Reborn

The first signs of a return to a more simply-defined conception of the doctrine of natural justice could be seen at the beginning of the 1960s. In *University of Ceylon v Fernando*,[39] the Privy Council did not quite adopt an expansive approach to natural justice, but it is significant that in defining the obligation to accord procedural fairness, their Lordships did not rely on *Nakkuda Ali* or *Electricity Commissioners*. Instead, they

---

[36] Quoted in Sawer, *supra* n 32, at 36. See also Victoria, *Parliamentary Debates*, Legislative Assembly, 17 April 1963, at 2865.
[37] Sawer, *id*, at 37.
[38] 'Address' (1934) 12 *Can Bar Rev* 35, at 38.
[39] [1960] 1 WLR 223.

reverted to the broad formulation of Lord Loreburn in *Board of Education v Rice*, to the effect that 'every one who decides anything' has a 'duty to act in good faith, and to listen fairly to both sides'.[40] The use of *Rice* as the definer of the reach of the doctrine was also evident two years later, in *Kanda v Government of Malaya*.[41] Speaking through Lord Denning, the Privy Council said: 'No one who has lost a case will believe he has been fairly treated if the other side had had access to the judge without his knowing.'[42]

Yet it is as much a commonplace as anything else in the common law that a new lease on life was given to the doctrine of natural justice by the decision of the House of Lords in 1963, in *Ridge v Baldwin*.[43] For in that case, their Lordships expressly adopted the sort of 'new property' characterisation which underlay Reich's thesis, and of which Marshall J of the US Supreme Court was later to speak so ebulliently in *Board of Regents v Roth*. Simply stated, it is *Ridge v Baldwin* that now symbolises the modernisation of natural justice in the Anglo-Australian world.

Beyond its substantive effect, *Ridge v Baldwin* offers an interesting study in common law method. It was decided before the *Practice Statement* of 1966, in which the House of Lords held that it could depart from its own previous decisions.[44] The previous decision in issue in *Ridge v Baldwin*, of course, was *Nakkuda Ali v Jayaratne*. As a judgment of the Privy Council, it was not, strictly speaking, binding on the Lords (in the way that it was on the Australian courts), but in the pre-*Practice Statement* era, it was not the norm for the House of Lords to depart from Privy Council decisions.[45] Yet even though in substance *Ridge v Baldwin* represented a new departure for natural justice in the form of an embracement of the new property ideas, if it is considered in *methodical*

---

[40] [1911] AC 179, at 182, quoted [1960] 1 WLR, at 231-232.

[41] [1962] AC 322.

[42] [1962] AC, at 337-338. In *R v Watson, Ex parte Armstrong* (1976) 136 CLR 248, at 263. Barwick CJ Gibbs, Stephen and Mason JJ said:

> It is of fundamental importance that the public should have confidence in the administration of justice. If fair-minded people reasonably apprehend or suspect that the tribunal has prejudged the case, they cannot have confidence in the decision. To repeat the words of Lord Denning MR which have already been cited, 'Justice must be rooted in confidence: and confidence is destroyed when right-minded people go away thinking: The judge was biased'.

[43] [1964] AC 40.

[44] [1966] 1 WLR 1234.

[45] Moreover, as has been noted, the Privy Council in *Nakkuda Ali* said that it was deciding a question of English as well as Ceylonese law.

terms the case is very much one in the old style; one in which the adoption of new principle was clothed in the language of distinguishment, and justified by a call on the authority of antiquity.

Ridge v Baldwin involved the dismissal of the Chief Constable of Brighton – Ridge. Along with several colleagues in the Brighton Police, both senior and junior, Ridge had been charged with conspiracy to obstruct the course of justice.[46] At trial, some of the policemen were convicted, but Ridge was acquitted. In the course of sentencing, however, the trial judge offered some highly critical remarks about Ridge's unfitness for leadership, and the poor example that he had set amongst his men. Subsequently, Ridge was charged with another offence of taking a bribe, but of that, too, he was acquitted.[47] Nevertheless, acting on the basis of the original trial judge's remarks, the local Watch Committee which, under the *Municipal Corporations Act 1882*, was the local police authority, resolved to sack Ridge from his post.

After learning of this, Ridge's solicitor requested an audience with the Watch Committee. This was granted, but the solicitor was not informed of the specific reasons upon which the decision to sack Ridge was based. Ridge then sought a declaration that his dismissal was contrary to natural justice. He also caused it to be made clear that he was not seeking reinstatement, but rather was looking for the restoration of his pension rights, which had been forfeited as a result of the dismissal. This is important, for it shows that it would have been open for the Lords to have taken a much narrower view of the case, and to have treated it as one in which 'old' property rights were in issue. In fact, the Watch Committee eventually settled the case, agreeing to pay Ridge arrears of salary and an annuity, as well as his costs.[48] Nevertheless, their Lordships took the opportunity to restate, and broaden, the law.

Ridge had lost at both levels prior to the House of Lords. At first instance, Streatfield J had held that natural justice was required in the circumstances, but that it had been accorded. The Court of Appeal,[49] however, held that the Watch Committee was acting administratively,

---

[46] For more on the facts of the case, see A W Bradley, 'A Failure of Justice and Defect of Police: A Commentary on *Ridge v Baldwin*' [1964] *Camb L J* 83 and A L Goodhart, '*Ridge v Baldwin*: Administration and Natural Justice' (1964) 80 *LQR* 105.

[47] After the Crown led no evidence. See [1964] AC, at 44-45.

[48] See Bradley, *supra* n 46, at 84.

[49] Holroyd Pearce, Harman and Davies LJJ.

rather than judicially, and hence that natural justice was not required.[50] The case in the House of Lords involved four separate issues, but the question which occupied most of the time of their Lordships (and the only important question for present purposes) was whether the Watch Committee was obliged to observe natural justice in the course of determining whether to dismiss Ridge. In the view of counsel for the Committee, in light of the twilight cases the answer was 'plain as a pikestaff'.[51] But, with the exception of Lord Evershed, all of their Lordships took rather a different view from counsel.

In Lord Morris's opinion, the fact that Ridge was being dismissed on the basis of unfitness was sufficient to turn the action of the Committee into a judicial action: 'before it could be decided that there had been neglect of duty, it would be a prerequisite that the question should be considered in a judicial spirit'.[52] In Lord Hodson's view, it was the consequence of the Committee's action that made natural justice necessary: 'the deprivation of a pension without a hearing is on the face of it a denial of natural justice ...'[53] For his part, Lord Devlin rather testily attributed the problem to the attempt by the legislation to oust the jurisdiction of the courts over dismissals.[54] Lord Evershed dissented, but even he would have been willing to extend the obligation to observe natural justice to administrative activity. Natural justice should be required, his Lordship said, 'in cases where the body concerned can properly be described as administrative – so long as it can be said, in Sir Frederick Pollock's language, that the invocation is required in order to conform to the ultimate principle of fitness with regard to the nature of man as a rational and social being'.[55]

The speech which has come to be viewed as the classic, however, was Lord Reid's. For it was he who, through his skilful manipulation of precedent, managed to render *Nakkuda Ali* and the other twilight cases effectively lifeless. Lord Reid noted that in holding that natural justice was not applicable, the Court of Appeal had not gone back any further in its review of authority than 1911, and the decision in *Board of Education v Rice*. This was problematic in his Lordship's view, because it had meant

---

[50] [1963] 1 QB 539.
[51] Quoted by Lord Hodson, [1964] AC, at 128.
[52] [1964] AC, at 121.
[53] [1964] AC, at 133.
[54] [1964] AC, at 140.
[55] [1964] AC, at 86.

that the Lords Justices were only looking at cases dealing with the 'new' legislation. They had, he noted, overlooked the long line of cases going back to 1615,[56] in which natural justice was held to apply to dismissal from employment. Lord Reid then proceeded to work his way methodically through these cases.[57] His conclusion was that the law on the point was clear: except in the case of service at pleasure, or in the case of contractual terms to the contrary, no person can be dismissed from employment without a hearing.

The mistake that the Court of Appeal had made, in Lord Reid's view, was to attempt to apply a 'one size fits all' approach to discretionary legislation. 'It appears', he said,

> that one reason why the authorities on natural justice have been found difficult to reconcile is that insufficient attention has been paid to the great difference between various kinds of cases in which it has been sought to apply the principle.[58]

This portion of Lord Reid's judgment is interesting, for it inverted a point on which the Anglo-Canadian scholars of the 1930s had placed great importance. As was discussed in chapter two, part of their refutation of Lord Hewart was to note that the conferral of broad discretion on the executive was as old as the hills. Therefore, they argued, Lord Hewart, and Dicey before him, were wrong to claim either that the rights of parliament or the ancient liberties of the subject were being usurped by the new legislation.

This argument had a three-fold purpose: to defuse some of the alarm raised by *The New Despotism*, to draw upon the authority of antiquity, and to show that by reading down the 'new' legislation, it was the *courts* who were usurping the rights of the executive. But in Lord Reid's speech, the Anglo-Canadian scholars were hoist with their own petard. Lord Reid took the point made by the Anglo-Canadians – that the conferral of discretionary power upon the executive was not purely the creation of the twentieth century state – and used it to justify judicial intervention. He was able to point to old cases, in which natural justice was held to attach to the decision-making processes of what we would today think of as administrative entities. By doing this, his Lordship was able to free the

[56] *Bagg's Case* 11 Co Rep 93b, 77 ER 1271.
[57] [1964] AC, at 66-71.
[58] [1964] AC, at 65.

law from the constraints which the politics of the first half of the twentieth century had placed on natural justice.

Lord Reid also deconstructed the *Electricity Commissioners* requirement of superaddition of a duty to act judicially. In his view, Atkin LJ's judgment had been misunderstood, most notably by Lord Hewart in the *Church Assembly* case.[59] What had been forgotten was the fact that certiorari had actually lain against the Electricity Commissioners, a 'new' body if ever there were one. And, he noted, neither Atkin LJ nor any of the other Lords Justices in *Electricity Commissioners* had based their judgment on the existence of a superadded duty.

Rather, what had happened was that Atkin LJ had 'inferred the judicial character of the duty from the nature of the duty itself'.[60] In Lord Reid's view, if this were permissible in a polycentric decision-making process such as was in issue in *Electricity Commissioners*, then it could hardly be held not to apply in a simple dismissal case like Chief Constable Ridge's.[61]

So it was that the House of Lords managed to get around the serious restrictions presented by the twilight cases. But in so far as Lord Reid was correct in suggesting that *Electricity Commissioners* had been given its life as a result of misunderstanding, the same thing can arguably be said about *Ridge v Baldwin* itself.[62] As Lord Reid plainly noted, the reason that the twentieth century cases could be circumvented was that *Ridge v Baldwin* was a case of a much older class. It was, moreover, a single instance, without polycentric features. Yet, *Ridge v Baldwin* has come to be understood to have heralded an unrestricted approach to natural justice generally.

Perhaps the point with both *Ridge v Baldwin* and *Electricity Commissioners*, as with the twilight cases, is that their force is not so much in their exact holding, but rather in where they stand in the evolution of public law's view of the executive. If the twilight cases were in part a function of the post-War reconstruction and the Labour government, then perhaps *Ridge v Baldwin* can partly be explained by the fact that it followed the Suez crisis and coincided in time with the Beatles. After the

---

[59] For a discussion of these cases, see chapter 2.

[60] [1964] AC, at 76.

[61] *Ibid.*

[62] For a very spirited criticism of the approach taken by the House of Lords in *Ridge v Baldwin*, particularly that taken by Lord Reid, see N A Manetta, 'The Implication of the Principle *Audi Alteram Partem* in Administrative Law' (unpublished PhD thesis, University of Cambridge, 1991).

Second World War, the law may have been faced with an overwhelming judgement of the electorate that a programme of large-scale bureaucratisation was to begin. But by the 1960s, there was not only an emerging distrust of authority among many sectors of society, but there was also (as the Crichel Down, Ansett and *Mudge* cases illustrated) a certain weariness of bureaucratic officiousness.

Yet, for all that it accomplished in stretching the reach of natural justice, *Ridge v Baldwin* largely left unanswered the question of exactly when the obligation to accord natural justice was triggered. If the old *Electricity Commissioners* requirement of superaddition was to be scrapped, what was to replace it? It was to this that their Lordships (in the guise of the Judicial Committee of the Privy Council) returned in early 1967, in *Durayappah v Fernando*.[63] In this case, the Ceylonese Minister of Local Government had dissolved the Jaffna Municipal Council. The question was whether natural justice applied to such a decision – whether the Minister was obliged to hear the Council before he determined to wind it up.

The Minister's power to dissolve was set out in a provision of the Municipal Councils' Ordinance which gave him the right to act '[i]f at any time ... it appears to him that a municipal council is not competent to perform'.[64] There had been a number of complaints made to the Minister that the Jaffna Council was misbehaving. The substance of the complaints is not apparent from the *Law Reports*, but, as Lord Upjohn put it, '[t]here is no doubt that this Council went through troublous times'.[65] He noted that in the two and a half years since the Council had been elected, it had gone through no less than four mayors.

The Minister therefore dispatched a representative to Jaffna to investigate and to make a report. The instructions to the investigator contained a specific note of the urgency with which the Minister wanted to deal with the case. Upon receiving the investigator's report, the Minister immediately dissolved the Council, and the Governor-General appointed special commissioners to carry out the Council's duties. Several members of the Council applied to court for writs of certiorari and *quo warranto* to

---

[63] [1967] 2 AC 337. For a view of the importance of this case as seen through contemporary Australian eyes, see G Nettheim, 'The Privy Council, Natural Justice and Certiorari' (1967) 2 *Fed L Rev* 215.

[64] Sub-s 277(1).

[65] [1967] 2 AC, at 347.

quash the Minister's order and to cancel the appointments of the special commissioners.

The Supreme Court of Ceylon held that natural justice did not apply to the Minister's decision to dissolve the Council. It did so on the basis that the reference in the Municipal Councils' Ordinance to it 'appear[ing] to the Minister' that a case of incompetence existed, displaced any duty to act judicially.[66] The Privy Council disagreed with this, and found that in the circumstances natural justice was required because as a result of the dissolution, the Jaffna Council had been deprived of its property. This brought the case squarely within the bounds of *Cooper v Wandsworth Board of Works*.[67] But in the course of their judgment, the Privy Council also took the opportunity to flesh out the doctrine of natural justice as it had emerged from *Ridge v Baldwin*. Specifically, their Lordships sought to outline the factors which would replace the old *Electricity Commissioners* requirement of superaddition as the trigger. Unfortunately, the judgment is written in a way which does not lend itself easily to the extraction of a clear *ratio decidendi*. Nevertheless, whether natural justice was required was said to depend upon a consideration of three factors:

> In their Lordships' opinion there are three matters which must always be borne in mind when considering whether [the doctrine of natural justice is applicable] or not. These three matters are: first, what is the nature of the property, the office held, status enjoyed or services to be performed by the complainant of injustice. Secondly, in what circumstances or upon what occasions is the person claiming to be entitled to exercise the measure of control entitled to intervene. Thirdly, when a right to intervene is proved, what sanction in fact is the latter entitled to impose upon the other.[68]

For reasons which will become apparent in chapter seven, it is problematic that in *Durayappah v Fernando*, the Judicial Committee did not really speak to natural justice's juridical basis – if the duty of fairness was not to be inferred as a result of some sort of legislative command, what was it to be? On what basis were these '*Durayappah* factors' chosen as the relevant ones? Moreover, as will be seen in the next chapter, the new triggering test set out in *Durayappah v Fernando* was not in fact

---

[66] See [1967] 2 AC, at 348.

[67] (1863) 14 CB(NS) 180, 143 ER 414. Their Lordships also said that they were guided by *Capel v Child* (1832) 2 C & J 558, 149 ER 235.

[68] [1967] 2 AC, at 349.

applied for very long in Australia.[69] But leaving these issues aside for the moment, it is interesting to see just how loosely their Lordships expressed the trigger for the doctrine, as compared not only with cases like *Franklin v Minister of Town and Country Planning* and *Nakkuda Ali v Jayaratne*, but also with *Ridge v Baldwin* itself.

Further, it is apparent that each of the factors to be considered permitted considerable scope for the imposition of judicial values. Inevitably, this meant that the lens through which executive decision-making processes were to be viewed was a curial one. So even if decision-makers were not to be surrogate members of the bench in a procedural sense, it was clear that their processes could not offend judicial sensibilities if they were to survive. With the judgment in *Durayappah v Fernando*, it seemed that the 'public service state' vision of the Anglo-Canadian scholars was receding even further into the horizon.

Towards a Recognition of the New Property in Australia

One of the most fascinating aspects of the common law method is the process by which some cases become leading cases while others are forgotten. Someone once said that in order for a case to become an instant landmark, what is required is notoriety – either of the parties or of the judge. Maybe the problem in 1963 was that there was no Newscorp to spread the news in Australia of the allegations that had been made against Chief Constable Ridge. Maybe it was that there were no Dennings, Goddards or Atkins involved in the hearing of *Ridge v Baldwin*. Whatever the case, *Testro Bros v Tait*, the high-water mark of the Australian twilight period was actually decided *after Ridge v Baldwin*. The only reference in the case to *Ridge v Baldwin*[70] is found in the dissent of Kitto J. In discussing what sort of dispositive power amounted in law to a power to affect rights, his Honour referred twice (but only in passing) to Lord Reid's speech.[71] None of the other judges referred to the case at all.

---

[69] For a discussion of their use (and modification) in Australia, see J McMillan, 'Developments Under the ADJR Act: Grounds of Review' (1991) 20 *Fed L Rev* 50, at 71-74. See also Aronson and Dyer, *Judicial Review of Administrative Action* (1996), at 399-400.

[70] Apart, that is, from the singularly un-enlightening statement in the summary of argument that counsel for Testro Bros 'also referred to *Ridge v Baldwin*' (109 CLR, at 358).

[71] 109 CLR, at 369, 370.

That *Ridge v Baldwin* was not addressed in any real way by the High Court in *Testro Bros v Tait* seems really quite extraordinary to us, given the fame that has come subsequently to attend to it – and especially to Lord Reid's speech. Wade and Forsyth describe *Ridge v Baldwin* as 'an important landmark',[72] and devote more space to it and its aftermath than to any other case in their treatise. The current editors of *de Smith* say that it 'gave a powerful impetus to the emergent trend' of judicial activism which, as of 1995, 'shows little sign yet of diminishing'.[73] But as far as the High Court of Australia was concerned in 1963, it was apparently seen as not worthy of any special attention.[74] It was not for five years – until 1968, in its decision in *Banks v Transport Regulation Board* – that the High Court came around to adopting the new approach to natural justice.

Banks is an interesting case, in that it deals with the very same question that was in issue in *R v Commissioner of Metropolitan Police, Ex parte Parker*,[75] namely the nature of the rights of a taxi-cab driver in his licence. This question – the question of the 'licence-as-property' that Lord Goddard had rejected so directly – had a unique significance in *Banks*. This is because one of the threshold issues which faced the High Court was whether Banks had an appeal to the Court as of right in respect of his loss. This turned upon whether in his writ of summons, he was raising a question concerning property or a civil right in excess of $3000.00.[76]

Attacking the issue just as directly as had Lord Goddard (as one would only expect him to have done), Barwick CJ made plain his disagreement with Lord Goddard's opinion:

---

[72] *Administrative Law* (7th ed, 1994), at 510.

[73] de Smith, Woolf and Jowell, *Judicial Review of Administrative Action* (5th ed. 1995), at 397.

[74] Though in fairness to all involved, it can sometimes be difficult to pick a winner. Writing shortly after the decision, Benjafield and Whitmore, for example, said that it was 'doubtful' that *Ridge v Baldwin* would ever stand for the proposition that 'an obligation [to observe natural justice] will be implied whenever there is a power to affect rights or impose obligations' ('The House of Lords and Natural Justice' (1963) 37 *ALJ* 140, at 143). Writing in 1966, they said that it was 'difficult to assess the precise effect of *Ridge's Case*' (*Australian Administrative Law* (3rd ed.), at 152). Another Australian writer said in 1967 that it was 'to be regretted that the approach of Lord Reid in *Ridge v Baldwin* has to date received such a lukewarm reception from the judiciary' (M Cullity, 'Book Review' 2 *Fed L Rev* 306, at 307). And an English commentator wrote shortly after the decision that '[a] lasting structure of administrative law can hardly be built on such a brittle foundation' (Bradley, *supra* n 46, at 83).

[75] [1953] 1 WLR 1150. See chapter 3.

[76] *Judiciary Act 1903* (Cth), cl 35(1)(a)(ii).

> I do not find the description of the licence which found favour with the Lord Chief Justice appropriate to a statutory licence to which a fit and proper person has a right and which relates to such an occupation as that of a cab driver. I do not think such a licence can be equated to the mere grant of a permission by a private person in respect of his own property.[77]

Having stated this, his Honour then expressed 'entire agreement' with Lord Reid's speech in *Ridge v Baldwin*.[78] And as for *Nakkuda Ali*, he neatly dismissed it both on the basis of Lord Reid's criticism of it not representing an accurate statement of the law, and on the basis that it pertained to wartime exigencies and therefore ought not to be applied to the circumstances of peacetime civil life. On the question of the Transport Regulation Board having a duty to act judicially, the Chief Justice said that in his view, 'the nature of the power and the circumstances of its exercise' were the source of the obligation.[79] This was, of course, redolent of the view taken by the Full Court of the High Court in *Delta Properties Pty Ltd v Brisbane City Council*,[80] and by Rich J in *Gillen v Laffer*.[81]

Barwick CJ referred as well to the obligation that the legislation placed on the Board to provide reasons for a revocation (which had not been the case in *Parker*), but he said that this merely reinforced the conclusion that he had drawn from the nature of the power itself.[82] As will be discussed below, this was a critically important point. The rest of the Court concurred with Barwick CJ. Significantly, the bench also included McTiernan, Owen and Taylor JJ – the three judges who had formed the majority in *Testro Bros v Tait*.

At the outset of this chapter, it was suggested that to today's reader, the only thing which strikes one about *Banks* is its unsingularity. But read in its historical context, the judgment represents a significant advance for the High Court in two respects. First, the case went a long way – further than even *Ridge v Baldwin*, in fact – in breaking the argument of circularity created by the *Electricity Commissioners* analytical formulation that the obligation to observe natural justice depended upon a power to affect rights *and* a superadded duty to act judicially. In Barwick CJ's

---

77 119 CLR, at 231.
78 119 CLR, at 233.
79 119 CLR, at 234.
80 (1955) 95 CLR 11, at 18. See chapter 3.
81 (1925) 37 CLR 210, at 229: 'The nature of the thing done – deprivation of property – implies a judicial act.' See also Lord Hodson in *Ridge v Baldwin* [1964] AC, at 133.
82 119 CLR, at 234.

view, the former was the source of the latter. It was the sheer enormity of the power (in this case, the power to deprive someone of their livelihood) that made procedural safeguards so imperative.

Secondly, in its holding, the Court came expressly to embrace the concept of the new property. Through its decision, it did exactly what Reich had urged the law to do: it acknowledged that the old ways of viewing the nature of proprietary interests were insufficient to protect civil rights in the era of the public service state. When the Chief Justice said that the taxi-cab licence amounted to a property interest within the meaning of the *Judiciary Act*, he was implicitly asserting a right within the courts to supervise the work of the executive with respect to new property interests. This was something that the Australian courts had not yet done in the modern era.

Locating the New Property Cases in History's Stream

In this respect, if we place *Banks* in its time frame – if, to paraphrase the American historian Carl Schorske,[83] we locate the case in history's stream – we can see that it represents a reconfirmation of the basic liberal premises of our society. The theory of the state that underlay its holding was one in which the interests of the individual were not to be readily sacrificed to the interests of collective efficiency. It was in this sense that it was suggested at the beginning of this chapter that the decision in *Banks* represented a constitutional moment.

Banks was also a judgment which preserved within the unwritten terms of the constitution a significant role for the judicial branch as protector of the (comparatively) powerless citizen against the state as Leviathan. In both of these respects, the judgment represents an explicit rejection of the underlying philosophy of the Anglo-Canadian scholarship, which tended to place a heavy premium upon the importance of 'expertise', and which favoured the vesting in the Executive of extensive, non-judicially reviewable, discretion.

It is no surprise that it was not until the relative economic prosperity of the 1960s that the courts felt confident to assertively restate liberalism as a basic social principle as was done in *Banks* and *Ridge v Baldwin*. For

[83] In *Thinking With History: Explorations in the Passage to Modernism* (1998), Schorske wrote: '[I]f we locate ourselves in history's stream, we can begin to look at ourselves ... as conditioned by the historical present as it defines itself out of – or against – the past.'

the reasons discussed in the last chapter, conditions after the Second World War gave rise, especially in England, to a pessimism about the future of the judicial role in administrative law. There had been some important and (as time would show) far-reaching decisions in administrative law cases, to be sure – notably *Wednesbury*[84] and *Northumberland Compensation Appeal Tribunal*[85] – but the accepted doctrine remained such that Lord Hewart could have just as happily railed against the state of the law in 1959 as he had in 1929. It was for that reason that de Smith could write at the end of the 1950s of the 'decisive victory' of 'judicial self-restraint'.[86]

Consider, though, what was to come within the next few years. In Australia, Sir Own Dixon – the steadfast proponent of 'strict legalism' – was to retire in 1964. In his place as Chief Justice was appointed Sir Garfield Barwick – a conservative, but (to use his own style[87]) a *radical* conservative; an unrepentant judicial activist.

Similarly, in England, Lord Denning was to be appointed Master of the Rolls in 1962. In the House of Lords, the passing of the old guard was characterised by the retirement of the arch-formalist Lord Simonds in 1962.[88] To the *de facto* chair of the Appellate Committee came Lord Reid, a Scottish judge without the same deferential instinct towards precedent as an English judge.[89] Consider, too, the line of decisions that was to follow: *Ridge v Baldwin*,[90] *Padfield v Minister of Agriculture*,[91] *Anisminic*,[92] and *Conway v Rimmer*[93] were all decided within a few years of one another. In

[84] *Associated Provincial Picture Houses v Wednesbury Corporation* [1948] 1 KB 223 (defining the concept of 'unreasonableness' in administrative law).

[85] *R v Northumberland Compensation Appeal Tribunal, ex parte Shaw* [1952] 1 KB 338 (reviving certiorari as a remedy to quash decisions which reveal an error of law on the face of the record).

[86] See *supra* n 22.

[87] Sir Garfield's autobiography was entitled *A Radical Tory: Garfield Barwick's Reflections and Recollections* (1995).

[88] In fact, there was a significant turn-over of membership of the Appellate Committee in this period. Apart from Lord Simonds, retiring Law Lords included Lords Morton (1959), Cohen (1960), Somervell (1960), Tucker (1961), Keith (1961), Jenkins (1963), Radcliffe (1964) and Devlin (1964).

[89] See, *eg*, his speech 'The Judge as Law Maker' (1972) 12 *JSPTL* 22, at 23-25.

[90] [1964] AC 40.

[91] [1968] AC 997.

[92] *Anisminic Ltd v Foreign Compensation Commission* [1969] 2 AC 147.

[93] [1968] AC 910.

administrative law terms, the 1960s really were, as Bernard Schwartz claimed, tantamount to a 'judicial revolution'.[94]

Lord Denning and the Broadening of Protected Rights

In this respect, no discussion of natural justice in the 1960s and 70s could be complete without some discussion of the work of Lord Denning. For, as with so many of our present-day 'balance-seeking' legal doctrines, Lord Denning played a significant role in actually spreading the reach of the newly-revived doctrine of procedural fairness.

For present purposes, Lord Denning's contribution to the evolution of natural justice came in two complementary forms. First, through cases like *Nagle v Fielden*[95] and *R v Barnsley Metropolitan Borough Council, Ex parte Hook*,[96] he drew an overt link between natural justice and the private rights to 'personhood'.[97] Secondly, it was Lord Denning who was responsible for introducing the notion of 'legitimate expectations' into our law. Through a series of three cases, which formed an integral part of his general project to reform the law to protect the interests of the weak from the predations of the strong, Lord Denning developed a new means of implying the existence of a duty on the part of a decision-maker to accord natural justice. In his view, when the state acted in such a way as to create an expectation that it would behave in a certain fashion, and it purported to (as Lord Denning was to put it) go back on its word, he felt that the courts had the power to require the state to accord procedural fairness, even if a legal right in the strict sense was not being affected by the state's capriciousness.

In *Schmidt v Secretary of State for Home Affairs*,[98] the first of these 'legitimate expectation' cases, his Lordship made it plain that he viewed Lord Reid's speech in *Ridge v Baldwin* as the signal for his new departure:

---

[94] B Schwartz, *Lions Over the Throne: The Judicial Revolution in English Administrative Law* (1987), at 11.

[95] [1966] 2 QB 633.

[96] [1976] 1 WLR 1052.

[97] See also *Lee v The Showmen's* Guild [1952] 2 QB 329, at 343 and *Enderby Town Football Club Ltd v Football Association Ltd* [1971] Ch 591. See further *Faramus v Film Artistes' Association* [1964] AC 925, at 947 (*per* Lord Pearce), and the remarks of Megarry V-C in *McInnes v Onslow-Fane* [1978] 1 WLR 1520, at 1528-1529. Also see R Baldwin and D Horne, 'Expectations in a Joyless Landscape' (1986) 49 *Mod L Rev* 685.

[98] [1969] 2 Ch 149.

> The speeches in *Ridge v Baldwin* show that an administrative body may, in a proper case, be bound to give a person who is affected by their decision an opportunity of making representations. It all depends on whether he has some right or interest, or, I would add, *some legitimate expectation*, of which it would not be fair to deprive him without hearing what he has to say.[99]

Schmidt v Secretary of State for Home Affairs involved a group of non-British students at a Church of Scientology college near Brighton, whose student visas in Great Britain were not renewed. The decision not to renew the visas came after the Minister of Health announced that the British government viewed Scientology as a harmful 'pseudo-philosophical cult', and that the government no longer recognised the college as a valid educational institution for the purpose of granting student visas. The Scientologists claimed that the decision not to re-new the visas was *ultra vires*. But a subsidiary argument made by them was that they had a right to a hearing before the renewal could be refused.[100]

The Scientologists lost on both counts, but Lord Denning made it clear that if, instead of refusing a renewal, the Home Secretary had attempted to revoke a valid visa, a legally-cognisable legitimate expectation would have existed: 'If his permit is revoked *before* the time limit expires, he ought, I think, to be given an opportunity of making representations: for he would have a legitimate expectation of being allowed to stay for the permitted time.'[101]

Lord Denning subsequently used this same principle as the foundation of his dissenting judgment in *Breen v Amalgamated*

---

[99] [1969] 2 Ch, at 170 (emphasis added).

[100] They were represented by Quintin Hogg QC, later Lord Hailsham LC. He framed his argument in the following way:

> Things must not go on which offend that general sense of fairness of ordinary men. Here the defendant applied a general rule, which he had made up his mind about before announcing his decision in the case. The same general principle applies to seeking permission to enter, refusing to extend the period of conditional entry and deportation. The administrative officer must not act capriciously ([1969] 2 Ch, at 163).

[101] [1969] 2 Ch, at 171 (original emphasis). It should be noted that while neither of the other members of the Court, Russell and Widgery LJJ, concurred on this point, Widgery LJ said, after referring to the licencing cases,

> I fully accept that [there may be natural justice issues] in cases where renewal is something which can reasonably be expected by the possessor of a licence and where the facts are such that a refusal of renewal is tantamount to the withdrawal of a right which the applicant legitimately expected to hold ([1969] 2 Ch, at 173).

Engineering Union,[102] a case in which an elected union steward's formal appointment had been blocked by the Union executive on the basis of reasons that were demonstrably false (and *prima facie* defamatory). Holding that in the circumstances, Breen had a right to a hearing, he said:

> Seeing that he had been elected to this office by a democratic process, he had, I think, a legitimate expectation that he would be approved by the district committee, unless there were good reasons against him. If they had something against him, they ought to tell him and to give him a chance of answering it before turning him down ... Who are [the union executive] to say nay to him and his fellow workers without good reason and without hearing what he has to say?[103]

The 'gut instinct' view of legitimate expectations seen in these two judgments, based on elementary notions of common fairness, came shortly thereafter to be intertwined with another view, based more closely on the doctrine of equitable estoppel. This modified form of legitimate expectation emerged from Lord Denning's judgment in the third case, *R v Liverpool Corporation, Ex parte Taxi Fleet* ('the *Liverpool Taxis Case*').[104] *Liverpool Taxis* involved a concern by Liverpool taxi drivers that unlicensed private hire cars were unfairly stealing their business.

In response to this, the Corporation of Liverpool decided to sponsor a Bill, which would have regulated the private cars in the same way that the public taxicab fleet was regulated. As a *quid pro quo*, however, the Corporation proposed to increase the number of available taxi licences. It assured the taxi drivers, though, that this would not take place until the sponsored legislation came into force. But the Corporation came to break its word. As Lord Denning put it so tellingly, 'without a word to the taxicab owners or their association',[105] the assurance was rescinded and a decision was taken to increase the number of taxi licences forthwith.

Predictably, Lord Denning reacted to this in a negative way. He held that while it was not open to the Corporation to fetter its discretion, neither was it open to it to go back on its undertaking:

---

[102] [1971] 2 QB 175.

[103] [1971] 2 QB, at 191. See also *R v Barnsley Metropolitan Borough Council, Ex parte Hook* [1976] 1 WLR 1052, at 1058.

[104] [1972] 2 QB 299.

[105] [1972] 2 QB, at 307.

> That principle [*ie,* the principle concerning fettering] does not mean that a corporation can give an undertaking and break it as they please. So long as the performance of the undertaking is compatible with their public duty, they must honour it ... At any rate they ought not to depart from it except after the most serious consideration and hearing what the other party has to say: and then only if they are satisfied that the overriding public interest requires it. The public interest may be better served by honouring their undertaking than by breaking it.[106]

Now, it is easy to criticise these cases. For example, insofar as *Liverpool Taxis* was intended to draw an analogy with equitable estoppel (though, to be fair, Lord Denning did not draw such an analogy himself), the major flaw is that the Liverpool taxi drivers had not worsened their situation in reliance upon the Corporation's undertaking. The critical element of detrimental reliance, upon which estoppel has always been founded,[107] was missing. And for their part, the legitimate expectation portions of Lord Denning's judgments in both *Schmidt* and *Breen* are open to charges of simple result-orientedness. In neither case did his Lordship offer any authority for his holding. Nevertheless, these three cases have together come to be taken as the foundation-stones of the modern doctrine of natural justice. Their legacy in Australia will be the subject of chapter five.

The Legislative Enshrinement of Common Law Values

It should not be thought, though, that the revival of interest in procedural fairness was accomplished solely as a result of a collective change of spirit among the judiciary. In the last chapter, it was noted that Geoffrey Sawer argued that in the 1920s and 1930s in Australia, there was a 'curious dissociation' between politics and public law.[108] This was no longer the case in the 1960s. In fact, there were indications that governments throughout the British Commonwealth had begun to realise that the interests of the public

---

[106] [1972] 2 QB, at 308 (applying his own previous decisions in *Robertson v Minister of Pensions* [1949] 1 KB 227 and *Lever Finance Ltd v Westminster (City) London Borough Council* [1971] 1 QB 222).

[107] See, eg, *Waltons Stores (Interstate) Pty Ltd v Maher* (1988) 164 CLR 387, and the authorities discussed therein.

[108] *Australian Federal Politics and Law 1901-1929* (1956), at 329.

would have to be paid greater attention if there were not to be serious political repercussions.

In this respect, an important, if today often-overlooked, episode in the debate over reform of administrative law was the third Commonwealth and Empire Law Conference, held in Sydney in August, 1965.[109] The conference drew together many of the important people in the law from around the Commonwealth, and from our vantage-point, the papers delivered offer a fascinating insight into the state of conventional thinking about administrative law in the mid-1960s.

There were four sessions of the Conference which were devoted to public law topics, two of which have a special interest for present purposes: 'The Place of the Administrative Tribunal in 1965' and 'The Proper Scope of Judicial Review'. On the first topic, it is interesting to note that all of the speakers – including a judge, a solicitor-general, a practising QC and a legal academic – were agreed not only that administrative adjudication had become a permanent feature of government, but that it was a desirable thing. The gloomy spectre of 'Hewart-ism' was gone. Mr Justice Else-Mitchell of the Supreme Court of New South Wales, for example, said that 'modern government requires many matters to be entrusted to some form of administrative determination by bodies other than the established courts', and that this was not to be deplored.[110]

Similarly, Donald Cormie QC, the dean of the Alberta Bar, said that Canada 'manages to obtain remarkably good government through a great proliferation of tribunals ...'[111] But at the same time, it was apparent that for the most part, the lawyers continued to think about the work of tribunals in common law terms. The Solicitor-General of New Zealand, for instance, said that the administrative tribunal 'undoubtedly has its place in the judicial system'.[112] Cormie QC expressed the view that not only was the bulk of adjudication taking place in the tribunals, but so was most 'judicial experimentation'.[113] Implicit in this way of speaking about tribunals, of course, was the assumption that the common law values, and common law rules of fairness ought presumptively to govern tribunal proceedings. Mr

---

[109] For some other thoughts on the significance of the conference, see L Curtis, 'The Vision Splendid: A Time for Re-appraisal', in R Creyke and J McMillan (eds), *The Kerr Vision of Australian Administrative Law – At the Twenty-Five Year Mark* (1998) 36, at 37-39. See also the Administrative Review Council, *First Annual Report* (1977), at 1.

[110] *Proceedings*, at 65.

[111] *Id*, at 83.

[112] H R C Wild QC, *id*, at 76.

[113] *Id*, at 88.

Justice Else-Mitchell said that '[f]rom a procedural point of view it is difficult to envisage any other special requirement which should be imposed on administrative tribunals ... which would not be equally ensured by an observance of the rules of natural justice ...'[114] The legislative initiatives that were to follow from the (re)association of law and politics were to embody these same implicit assumptions.

The first government to move to reform administrative law by statutory means was the Eden government in Britain. As noted, the Crichel Down affair had led to the resignation of the Minister of Agriculture in 1954. It also led the next year to the appointment of a Committee on Administrative Tribunals and Enquiries, chaired by Sir Oliver Franks. The Franks Committee's brief was to consider the constitution and operation of tribunals and governmental enquiries, and to make recommendations concerning, *inter alia*, 'the constitution and working of tribunals other than the ordinary courts of law'.[115]

Interestingly, the Franks Committee's membership was not monopolised by legal profession. Consequently, as Professor Wade once noted, it was 'not concerned with the law ... It was really a mobilisation of opinion among all sorts of people concerned with public affairs to see what were the real causes of the undercurrent of complaint about tribunals.'[116] Not surprisingly, therefore, the Committee's recommendations tended away from the doctrinal or abstract. Nevertheless, they for the most part embodied traditional common law assumptions and values. The Committee noted that the system of tribunals had become an integral – and essential – part of the British administrative state.[117] But it felt that the pedantic, yet *ad hoc*, way in which some tribunals had carried out their business had given rise to a reasonable feeling of discontent.[118] As a general proposition, the Committee recommended that tribunal and enquiry proceedings ought to be governed by three principles: openness, fairness and impartiality.

Importantly, the Franks Committee also recommended that some sort of appeal ought to lay from every administrative decision on the basis that it would both improve the quality of administrative decision-making and increase public confidence in the administrative system:

---

[114] *Id*, at 71.

[115] See, 1957 Cmd 218, paragraph 59.

[116] H W R Wade, *Towards Administrative Justice* (1963), at 70.

[117] See generally B Schwartz and H W R Wade, *Legal Control of Government: Administrative Law in Britain and the United States* (1972), at 151-153.

[118] See Wade, *Towards Administrative Justice*, *supra* n 116, at 70-71.

> The existence of a right of appeal is salutary and makes for right adjudication. Provision for appeal is also important if decisions are to show reasonable consistency. Finally, the system of adjudication can hardly fail to appear fair to the applicant if he knows that he will normally be allowed two attempts to convince independent bodies of the soundness of his case.[119]

In New Zealand, similar pressures led to the commissioning of G S Orr to report on the state of administrative justice in the Dominion.[120] Many of the concerns which had driven the recommendations of the Franks Committee were found to exist in New Zealand, including the feeling that public confidence in the administrative system suffered by reason of its sense of 'closedness'. As is well-known, the New Zealand reforms involved the creation of an Ombudsman[121] (the first such officer in the British Commonwealth, and actually created before the Orr Report) and an Administrative Division of the Supreme Court.[122]

Of special interest are the comments of the New Zealand Minister for Justice when the Bill to create the Administrative Division of the Supreme Court was being introduced. Like the remarks of the various speakers at the Commonwealth and Empire Law Conference, they reflected very much a common lawyer's view of administration. He said that the goal of the legislation was the 'restoration' of the Court to its proper position at the apex of the system of adjudication. Under the new arrangements, he said, decisions would be given by 'judges of high status who can command a degree of confidence in the parties and in the community generally'.[123]

In Canada, in 1967 the government of Ontario appointed a Royal Commission into Civil Rights. Known popularly as the McRuer Commission, it was named after its chairman, the Hon J C McRuer, a former Chief Justice of the High Court of Ontario. Unlike the Reports of the Franks Committee and the Orr Commission in New Zealand, the McRuer Report[124] did not lead directly to any substantial legislative initiatives. But what

---

[119] *Supra* n 115, paragraphs 104-105. The Franks Committee's report eventually gave rise to the *Tribunals and Enquiries Act 1958*. On the Franks Committee and its aftermath, see Wade and Forsyth, *supra* n 72, chapter 23.

[120] See Orr, *Report on Administrative Justice in New Zealand* (1964).

[121] *Parliamentary Commissioner (Ombudsman) Act 1962*.

[122] *Judicature Amendment Act 1968*.

[123] Quoted in the *Report of the Commonwealth Administrative Review Committee* (the Kerr Committee Report), 1971 Parl Paper No 144, para 159.

[124] *Report of the Royal Commission Inquiry into Civil Rights* (1968).

makes it interesting is that it led to what was probably the final blast from the Anglo-Canadian scholars of the 1930s.

In 1968, John Willis published a short article in the *University of Toronto Law Journal*, in which he attacked not only the report, but also the premises on which the McRuer Commission was based.[125] In fact, Willis did find some things to praise about the Commission's work (notably, its research[126]). But for the most part, the piece was classic 1930s hyperbole. He said that he wrote his piece 'in a mood of irritated dissent'. His aim was to:

> show cause against treating the report as if it were the Ten Commandments, engraved on tablets of stone and brought down by Moses himself from Mount Sinai – which is how the Toronto *Globe and Mail*, opposition members in the Ontario legislature and, to my own personal knowledge, many lawyers are treating it.[127]

Willis went on to express great concern over the Report's legalistic orientation. McRuer and his fellow commissioners had, in Willis's view, completely missed the lessons of the past thirty or forty years. As for the Commission's recommendations concerning procedural safeguards, Willis said that this would:

> inevitably reintroduce into 'non-court' deciding authorities the 'court' atmosphere that they were created to avoid – where following the prescribed ritual is more important than getting at the merits, and strings of procedural objections are regularly made for no other purpose than to give the lawyer who loses on the merits a second string to his bow in the court of review.[128]

In Australia, of course, a massive-scale project of statutory reform of Commonwealth administrative law began with the appointment of the Administrative Review Committee – the Kerr Committee, after its chairman, Mr Justice (later, Sir John) Kerr – in 1968. The Kerr Committee's brief was in some respects broader than that of the Franks Committee. Roughly stated, it was given authority to make

---

[125] 'The McRuer Report: Lawyers' Values and Civil Servants' Values', 18 *UTLJ* 351.

[126] *Ibid.*

[127] *Ibid.*

[128] *Id*, at 358.

recommendations concerning both judicial and merit review of all Commonwealth administrative decision-making.[129]

The Committee recommended both the creation of an administrative review tribunal (which was eventually to come to fruition as the Administrative Appeals Tribunal[130]) and the introduction of a legislative code to simplify judicial review.[131] In light of what was to develop in the case law in the 1970s and 80s (which will be discussed in chapters five to seven), it is interesting to note that apart from Kerr, the Committee also included A F Mason QC – then the Commonwealth Solicitor-General.[132]

For immediate purposes, however, there are two aspects of the Kerr Committee Report which deserve special attention. The first is that, like the recommendations of the Franks Committee and the McRuer Committee (and of the Donoughmore Committee before them), the Kerr Committee's recommendations were largely premised on common lawyers' values. As the Kerr Committee itself said, 'although administrative efficiency is a dominant objective of the administrative process, nevertheless that achievement of that objective should be consistent with the attainment of justice to the individual'.[133]

The second thing of interest is the place the Committee accorded to natural justice in the administrative scheme of things. The Committee noted that the right to a fair hearing was centuries-old,[134] and it placed the denial of natural justice first among the proposed grounds of judicial review.[135] But what the Kerr Committee did *not* do – and this distinguished it from the Franks Committee – was to offer a doctrinal justification for natural justice.

---

[129] For essays commenting on the statutory reforms as a whole, see R Creyke and J McMillan, *The Kerr Vision of Administrative Law*, *supra* n 109. For actual detail of the reform process, including the work of the subsequent Bland and Ellicott Committees, see R Creyke and J McMillan, *The Making of Commonwealth Administrative Law* (1996).

[130] *Administrative Appeals Tribunal Act 1975* (Cth).

[131] Which eventually became enshrined as the *Administrative Decisions (Judicial Review) Act 1977* (Cth). The Kerr Committee's Report is reproduced in R Creyke and J McMillan, *The Making of Commonwealth Administrative Law*, *supra* n 129.

[132] Other members of the Committee were Professor Harry Whitmore, the Dean of Law at the Australian National University, and R J Ellicott QC, who became Commonwealth Solicitor-General and joined the Committee after Sir Anthony Mason's appointment to the bench.

[133] *Supra* n 123, para 12.

[134] Para 39.

[135] Para 258.

The Franks Committee (like the Orr Report) said that procedural fairness was essential to the maintenance of public confidence in the administrative system. The Kerr Committee merely referred to the doctrine's anciency. The section of the Report dealing with natural justice only described the elements of the duty, and made the point of its antiquity. The failure of Australian law to theorise the duty of procedural fairness has already been adverted to. As will be discussed in more depth in chapter seven, this has perhaps been the chief continuing deficiency in the Australian approach to natural justice.

The Emergence of an Australian Administrative Law Scholarship

For today's Australian administrative lawyers, one of the most happy offshoots of all of this activity in the 1960s (apart, that is, from making provision for more litigation) was that it begat an indigenous administrative law scholarship. In chapter two, the comparative dearth of Australian writing on administrative law in the inter-War period – at least as contrasted with England and Canada – was discussed. As disappointing as it may have been in result, the one positive thing that the decision in *Testro Bros v Tait* did was to engender an outpouring of writing, both on natural justice, and on other topics related to administrative law. Much of this, not surprisingly, was critical of the High Court. In the 1966 edition of *Principles of Australian Administrative Law*, for example, Benjafield and Whitmore wrote of *Testro Bros v Tait* that it was 'difficult to avoid the impression that the court is treating each case on an *ad hoc* basis without attempting to develop a coherent body of law as to the circumstances in which the rules of natural justice will be implied, and as to the content to those rules'.[136]

This was a real turning point. There had always been writings about specific aspects of administrative law – most notably, of course, the Commonwealth Court of Conciliation and Arbitration[137] – but as for

---

[136] At 154.

[137] See, *eg*, H Moore, 'Living Wage in the Australian Arbitration Court' (1912) 12 *J Comp Leg* (2nd series) 202, J Brown, 'Judicial Regulation of Wages for Women' (1919) 28 *Yale LJ* 236, J Brown, 'Judicial Settlement of Industrial Disputes' (1924) 2 *Camb L J* 51, F A A Russell, 'The Commonwealth *Conciliation and Arbitration Act, 1928*' (1928) 2 *ALJ* 147, F A A Russell, 'The Clash of Commonwealth Arbitration and State Courts' (1930) 4 *ALJ* 110, G W C Ross, 'Constitutional History of Industrial Arbitration in Australia' (1945) 30 *Minn L Rev* 1, L L Jones, 'Industrial Arbitration in Australia' (1945) 8 *Mod L Rev* 63.

matters of general jurisprudential theory, one of the very few pieces written prior to the early 1960s was an article published in the *Australian Law Journal* in 1930 entitled 'Administrative Legislation in the Commonwealth' by Professor Kenneth Bailey (as he then was).[138] Another was Mr Justice Evatt's 'The Judiciary and Administrative Law in Australia',[139] which was discussed in chapter three.

Apart from these two pieces, one sees in the *Index to Legal Periodicals* only a very occasional reference to administrative law in Australia until 1963 or so.[140] But then, the publication rate underwent a dramatic acceleration.[141] As for treatises, it was not until 1962 that the first Australian work of any substance was published[142] – and even then, the book was criticised on the basis that its content was excessively English.[143] But by the mid-1960s, there was a veritable explosion of academic commentary on the field as a whole. This new Australian literature was to provide the intellectual infrastructure for the developments to come.

The New Property and Natural Justice

The pragmatically-founded judgment of Barwick CJ in *Banks v Transport Regulation Board (Victoria)* meshed very well both with the theory underlying Charles Reich's 'new property' analysis, and the holding in *Ridge v Baldwin*. By indicating a willingness to accord some form of procedural protection to interests created by what I have been describing as the 'new' legislation, the courts saw themselves as filling a gap. In this

---

[138] 4 *ALJ* 7.

[139] (1937) 15 *Can Bar Rev* 247.

[140] *Eg*, T P Fry, 'Australian Disregard of the Doctrine of the Separation of Powers' (1933) 5 *Rocky Mtn L Rev* 221. Others were discussed in chapter 3.

[141] See, *eg*, H Whitmore, 'Australian Administrative Law – a study in inertia' (1963)) 36 *ALJ* 255, D G Benjafield and H Whitmore, 'The House of Lords and Natural Justice' (1963) 37 *ALJ* 140, G Nash, 'Judicial Function and Inspectors Appointed Under the Companies Act' (1964) 38 *ALJ* 111, Anon, 'Case Comment ' (1964) 2 *Adel L Rev* 252, R A Sunbey, 'Case Comment: *Testro Bros v Tait*' (1964) 4 *MULR* 413 and K I Seggie, 'Jurisdictional Error in Administrative Law' (1965) 5 *Syd L Rev* 89.

[142] Friedmann and Benjafield, *Principles of Australian Administrative Law*, and Brett, *Cases and Materials in Constitutional and Administrative Law*. The first edition of *Principles of Australian Administrative Law*, written by Friedmann alone, was published in 1950, but it was a mere hundred and twelve pages in length and there are very few Australian cases mentioned.

[143] L Zines, 'Book Review' (1964) 1 *Fed L Rev* 172.

respect, they were reflecting a general shift in public opinion about the relative values of collective efficiency and individual autonomy which was, among other things, reflecting itself both in scholarship and legislative initiative.

At the risk of generalisation, the gloss had begun to come off the move to greater bureaucracy. The new property cases were, in this sense, part of a continuum. In all of the periods considered thus far, developments in administrative law had centred on trying to find for the courts an appropriate supervisory role amidst the changed environment of governance. The hands-off dicta in *Board of Education v Rice* and *Local Government Board v Arlidge*; the confusing construction of 'superaddition' in *R v Electricity Commissioners*; the fear of a new despotism; the tussle between the courts and the Anglo-Canadian scholars over the *Housing Act* cases; the seeming capitulation of the courts during the 'twilight' phase of natural justice – all of these reflected stages in the evolving political debate over the appropriate limits of judicial involvement in the control of the bureaucracy.

The decision of the House of Lords in *Ridge v Baldwin* represented a significant breakthrough in broadening natural justice's penumbra. While the case can actually be parsed (and, if Lord Reid is to be taken on his face, *should* be parsed[144]) quite narrowly, the decision came to symbolise a willingness upon the part of the courts finally to accept the existence of the administrative state, but yet to open their minds to new ways of thinking about the control of abuse of governmental power. In subjecting a plethora of new types of decision-making processes to the requirements of natural justice, their Lordships threw the doctrine of natural justice a lifeline, rescuing it from Professor Wade's pessimistically termed 'twilight' phase. This lifeline was picked up by the High Court in *Banks*, and as the following chapters will show, to date the High Court has not let it go.

[144] See [1964] AC, at 64-65, 79.

5 The Legitimate Expectation

For much of its life, natural justice's bounds were relatively certain. As was discussed in chapter one, in the days before significant involvement of central authority in day-to-day local government, natural justice was in the main an obligation that attached to the work of inferior judicial officers. Then, through much of the twentieth century, it was thought that natural justice was only required where, in establishing a decision-making framework, the legislature had indicated in some way that the decision-maker was to conduct him or herself in a judge-like fashion.

What linked the olden days with the first decades of the twentieth century was the implicit belief that the obligation to observe natural justice depended upon the decision-maker's functional identity. But *Ridge v Baldwin* and *Banks* again raised the explicit question of public law principle. Both of these were cases cast very much in the common law tradition of pragmatism, in which theoretical niceties are left for *ex post facto* rationalisation.[1]

When Barwick CJ held in *Banks* that a licence could be viewed as 'property' for natural justice purposes, he cast open the Pandora's box of other non-proprietary interests. Charles Reich had convincingly argued that it was wrong to consider what might generically be referred to as welfare benefits as mere 'largesse' which could be withdrawn by the state at will.[2] But simply to try to lump *all* aspects of the welfare state together under the rubric of common law property rights would plainly be both overinclusive and underspecific.[3] Furthermore, only by risking a new form of sematicism could many of the types of *choses* created by the new legislation be treated as property.

---

[1] In his 1987 Hamlyn Lectures (published under the title, *Pragmatism and Theory in English Law*), Professor Atiyah offered as his premise what he termed a 'fairly uncontroversial suggestion', namely that 'English lawyers are not only more inclined to be pragmatic and somewhat hostile to the theoretical approach, but positively glory in this preference' (at 3).

[2] See chapter 4.

[3] On this point, see also P Craig, 'Legitimate Expectations: A Conceptual Analysis' (1992) 108 *LQR* 79, at 97-98.

Moreover, the thrust of the welfare state was in significant part precisely *to move away from* a model of society in which the exclusionary rights associated with proprietary dominion were the chief determinant of wealth, and hence personality. So the question of legal principle remained: if natural justice was not to attach to all interests enjoyed of the state, to which ones was it to attach? *Ridge v Baldwin* and *Banks* bequeathed to administrative law a valuable new spirit of openness, but they provided only a very limited assistance in dealing with the underlying question of public law principle that the new legislation raised.

The Legitimate Expectation

In the main, the courts' chosen vehicle for fleshing out the project begun in *Ridge v Baldwin* and *Banks* has been the so-called 'legitimate expectation' that Lord Denning had introduced into the legal vocabulary in *Schmidt v Secretary of State for Home Affairs*,[4] and its partner cases that were discussed in the last chapter. The aim of this chapter is to explore the way in which the High Court has made use of the legitimate expectation in its development of the contemporary doctrine of natural justice. As suggested in the Introduction, this chapter marks the broad shift from an historical consideration of natural justice to a contemporary one.

When considering the legitimate expectation cases, it is important to note at the outset that it is impossible to define the idea of legitimate expectations in anything but rough terms, for it is at base a rough, reactionary concept. As Dawson J once put it, '[t]he phrase was never a term of art and was meant merely to indicate that to deal administratively with something not amounting to an actual right might nevertheless require the adoption of a fair procedure'.[5] The essence of the idea was once described by McHugh J in the following way:

> Just as the common law has traditionally given a person a right to be heard ... so the common law now gives a person the right to be heard before the exercise of a statutory power prejudices some right, interest, privilege or

---

[4] [1969] 2 Ch 149. See chapter 4.

[5] *Attorney-General (New South Wales) v Quin* (1990) 170 CLR 1, at 54.

benefit which that person can legitimately expect to obtain or enjoy in the future.[6]

Stated like this – at its most simple level of formulation – the concept seems merely to represent another form of the notion of 'fairness writ large and juridically', to borrow once more the words of Lord Morris.[7] It is, moreover, exactly the same sort of sentiment which underlies the whole of the doctrine of natural justice: the state has the power to extinguish proprietary interests, but the courts have said that the interests of common fairness require a prior hearing before this can take place.

The basis of legitimate expectations is the same – an instinctive and intuitive judicial revulsion against an assertion of overweening power by the state. As to judicial instinct being its theoretical root, Lord Denning, who is credited with having coined the expression, has admitted as much. He has said that he is 'sure it came out of my own head and not from any continental or other source'.[8] But lack of theoretical sophistication notwithstanding, since the mid-1970s, the concept of legitimate expectations has come to be the hook on which the High Court has sought to hang a general duty of fairness on government.

The Doctrine of Legitimate Expectations in Australia

The doctrine of legitimate expectations emerged in Australia in much the same way that it did in England – as a manifestation of judicial reflex in the face of obvious unfairness. Appropriately enough, in light of the prominence that migration cases were to come to occupy in the development of the doctrine, the first discussion of legitimate expectations in the High Court was in a deportation case. *Salemi v MacKellar (No 2)*[9] dealt with a question which was to become quite familiar to anyone

---

[6] *Haoucher v Minister for Immigration and Ethnic Affairs* (1990) 169 CLR 648, at 680. In *Salemi v MacKellar (No 2)* (1977) 137 CLR 396, at 438, Stephen J said that the legitimate expectation 'stems ... from the same fertile source as has nourished the concept that those who possess rights and interests shall not ... be deprived of them by the exercise of an arbitrary discretion'.

[7] In *Furnell v Whangerei High Schools Board* [1973] AC 660, at 679.

[8] In a letter to Christopher Forsyth, quoted in C Forsyth, 'The Provenance and Protection of Legitimate Expectations' (1988) 47 *Camb LJ* 238, at 241.

[9] (1977) 137 CLR 396.

interested in natural justice in Australia, *viz* the rights of illegal aliens *vis-à-vis* the issuance of deportation orders.

Salemi was an Italian citizen who had entered Australia on a temporary entry permit. The permit was once renewed but, thereafter, upon its expiry, he became a 'prohibited immigrant' under the provisions of the *Migration Act 1958* (Cth), and formally liable to be deported. What complicated matters, however, was that the Minister for Immigration had issued several press releases regarding an 'amnesty', by which prohibited immigrants who came forward within a certain time frame, and who satisfied certain health and character criteria, would be permitted lawfully to remain in Australia. Salemi fit within the criteria, but when he presented himself in accordance with the instructions set out in the press releases, a deportation order was nonetheless made against him. Not surprisingly, he sought an injunction to prevent the deportation, and a declaration that in the circumstances, he had been denied natural justice.

In *Salemi v MacKellar (No 2)*, Stephen J emerged as the advocate for the legal recognition of expectations – and to take up the rhetorical role played by Lord Denning in the English cases discussed in the last chapter. He would have held that in the circumstances, there was an expectation created by the amnesty announcement, which should have given rise to an obligation on the part of the Minister to observe natural justice before making the deportation order. After discussing Lord Denning's judgments, he said:

> When the discretionary grant of a licence, permit or the like carries with it a reasonable expectation of, although no legal right to, renewal or non-revocation, summarily to disappoint that expectation is unfair; hence the requirement that the expectant person should first be heard ...[10]

Stephen J was of the view that the amnesty announcement amounted to the very same sort of express assurance that had existed in *Liverpool Taxis* (though in point of fact *Salemi v MacKellar* was more akin to a conventional case of estoppel, in that there was a real detrimental reliance). As he put it:

> Any fair reading of the news releases leads to the inference that that assurance was given so as to induce this very expectation in the minds of

[10] 137 CLR, at 439. See also *Attorney-General (Hong Kong) v Ng Yuen Shiu* [1983] 2 AC 629, at 636, where 'reasonable expectation' was the preferred expression.

> prohibited immigrants such as the plaintiff, so that they might come forward and reveal to the authorities their whereabouts and the details of their continued presence in Australia ... They were invited to rely upon the Minister's statement ...[11]

Accordingly,

> If the Minister is now to depart from the terms of the assurance which he gave he will be free to do so, as was the Council [in the *Liverpool Taxis Case*]. But, as Roskill LJ there observed, while it was there for the Council to make up its own mind as to what policy it wished to follow, it was not at liberty, having given an undertaking as to policy intentions, to depart therefrom except 'after due and proper consideration of the representations of all those interested'.[12]

In contrast to Stephen J, Barwick CJ and Gibbs and Aikin JJ did not find on the facts that a legitimate expectation could exist. Rather, they held that the proper interpretation of the relevant provisions of the *Migration Act* was such that the Minister was to have an unfettered discretion in determining whether or not to deport prohibited immigrants. A policy statement such as the amnesty announcement in question could not as a matter of law affect the breadth of the Minister's discretion. In his judgment, though, Barwick CJ also expressed his views on the English legitimate expectation cases. After referring to Lord Denning's use of the expression in *Schmidt*, he said:

> I am bound to say that I appreciate its literary quality better than I perceive its precise meaning and the perimeter of application. But, no matter how far the phrase may have been intended to reach, at its centre is the concept of legality, that is to say, it is a lawful expectation which is in mind. I cannot attribute any other meaning in the language of a lawyer to the word 'legitimate' than a meaning which expresses the concept of entitlement or recognition by law. So understood, the expression probably adds little, if anything, to the concept of a 'right'.[13]

---

[11] *Ibid.*
[12] 137 CLR, at 440.
[13] 137 CLR, at 404.

The first case in which the doctrine was actually applied in the High Court was *Heatley v Tasmanian Racing and Gaming Commission*,[14] decided two months after *Salemi v MacKellar (No 2)*. This case involved a so-called 'warning off notice' given by the Tasmanian Racing and Gaming Commission to Heatley, a punter, which forbad him from entering any racecourse in Tasmania. The Commission could issue such notices by virtue of sub-section 39(3) of the Tasmanian *Racing and Gaming Act 1952*. Sub-section 39(8) of the Act made it an offence to violate a warning off notice. No prior warning was given of the notice, and Heatley was not given a chance to address the assertions upon which the notice was based.

The High Court[15] held that in the circumstances, Heatley had had a legitimate expectation, which entitled him to a hearing prior to the issuance of the notice. He had not shown any interest in the doctrine in *Salemi v MacKellar (No 2)*, but it was Aickin J who offered the first authoritative exposition of the Australian version of the legitimate expectation. He noted that while an ordinary member of the public has no *right* to enter a race meeting, he almost certainly has an expectation that upon payment of the requisite admission charge, he will be able to do so.[16]

Moreover, once a member of the public had been granted permission to enter the racecourse, he had a right 'as against all the world other than the owner [of the course] to continue upon the premises and remain there in accordance with whatever the terms may be of the licence originally granted to him'.[17] This was, he said, a case in which considerations of fairness demanded that a hearing be given. Since the Act gave the Commission the right to destroy both the right to remain in a racecourse, 'as well as to destroy the expectation that they will on future occasions be granted the like right',[18]

> [f]airness requires that the person affected should, save in an emergency, be given notice by the Commission of its intention to issue a warning-off notice and of the grounds for that proposed action and should be afforded an opportunity to make representations to the Commission on his own behalf, which it must consider before taking action.[19]

---

[14] (1977) 137 CLR 487.

[15] Stephen, Mason, Murphy and Aickin JJ, Barwick CJ dissenting.

[16] 137 CLR, at 507.

[17] *Ibid.*

[18] 137 CLR, at 509.

[19] 137 CLR, at 516. In a similar vein, Murphy J said:

What is significant here is that what gave rise in Aickin J's mind to the expectation was simple social custom. What the Court was concerned with, he said, was 'an expectation on the part of members of the public that they will continue to receive the customary permission to go on to racecourses upon payment of a stated fee to a racecourse owner'.[20] In Stephen J's opinion in *Salemi v MacKellar*, the legitimising factor of the expectation had been its reasonableness. In Aickin J's view in *Heatley*, it was simple commonness. This is interesting in that (as will be seen) it became an issue in later cases whether the test for the existence of a legitimate expectation was a subjective or an objective one. On the facts in *Heatley*, the Court was easily able – almost on the basis of taking judicial notice – to impute a subjective expectation to the entire public.[21]

Aickin J's judgment was criticised at the time as representing an inappropriate extension of the principle expounded in the English cases. Vivienne Bath, for example, argued that in the English cases, the affected party had had an actual relationship with an organ of government which gave rise to the expectation that the government would act in a certain way.[22] In *Heatley*, there was no such relationship. Similarly, Peter Cane criticised the judgment because it seemed to mistake the source of the expectations. He noted that the real effect of the decision in *Heatley* was to enforce as against the state rights created by private contract between two parties.[23]

When thought of this way, the holding does seem a little surprising. It is one thing to say that if the state creates an expectation, it should be estopped from destroying it without notice. But it is quite another to say that the state can as a matter of law be required to accord natural justice because two private individuals had *inter se* engaged in a particular course of conduct which allowed expectations to develop in their minds. Moreover, Aickin J's reasoning had left a potential gap in coverage. His

---

> The exercise of the power will probably have an adverse effect on the person and his reputation and possibly his livelihood. It will seriously alter his legal position ... The strong presumption is that the legislature did not intend to authorise the Commission (in exercising its power of warning-off) to depart from the standards of official behaviour towards individuals which are basic to every civilised society (137 CLR, at 495).

[20] 137 CLR, at 509.

[21] See also *Forbes v New South Wales Trotting Club Ltd* (1979) 143 CLR 242.

[22] 'Case Note: *Heatley v Tasmanian Racing and Gaming Commission*' (1978) 9 *Fed L Rev* 504, at 508.

[23] 'Natural Justice and Legitimate Expectations' (1980) 54 *ALJ* 546, at 547.

view could not cover the case of someone who had not yet been permitted entry to the racecourse. As Cane went on to argue, on Aickin J's analysis '[t]he absurd result would be that the Commission could prohibit the plaintiff from entering without complying with natural justice, but not from remaining'.[24]

Yet these sorts of issues did not directly arise in the next judgment of the High Court to consider the place of expectations in Australian administrative law, *FAI Insurances Ltd v Winneke*, decided in 1982.[25] The case involved an application by FAI Insurances Ltd for a renewal of its licence to provide workers' compensation insurance in Victoria, which had been turned down by the Victorian Governor in Council. The High Court held that in the circumstances, the State had an obligation to provide FAI with a summary of the points on which the refusal was based, and an opportunity to respond to them.[26]

FAI had carried on the business of providing workers' compensation insurance in Victoria for twenty years. Provision of workers' compensation benefits was not its main line but, in the words of Mason J, it was 'nevertheless important in enabling the company to offer a comprehensive insurance service'.[27] In 1979, the state Minister of Labour had advised all workers' compensation insurers that henceforth, renewal of licences would be dependent upon them being able to demonstrate compliance with various criteria which were intended to reveal the companies' financial health. With respect to FAI in particular, the Minister had noted that he felt that its level of investment in related companies was higher than desirable.

When FAI applied for the renewal of its licence for the calendar year 1981, it specifically addressed the criteria noted in the Minister's 1979 letter, though it disputed the lawfulness of the Minister making use of some of them as a basis for determining fitness for renewal. The company also explicitly requested that if the Minister considered that the renewal of the licence was in danger, it be given the opportunity to make further submissions on the points of concern. Despite this, the Minister recommended to the Governor in Council, without notice to FAI, that

---

[24] *Ibid.*

[25] 151 CLR 342.

[26] The fact that the decision not to renew was made by the Governor in Council raised the complicating questions of whether the decision was unreviewable *per se*, and if not, how exactly natural justice could be applied to the proceedings of the Executive Council. These will be discussed in more detail in chapter 6.

[27] 151 CLR, at 357.

FAI's licence not be renewed, on the basis of what might broadly be characterised as concerns about undercapitalisation. FAI again requested particulars of the Minister's concerns and the opportunity to respond to them, but no response to this was forthcoming. Instead, the decision was taken by the Governor in Council not to renew the licence.

The full bench of the High Court found that in the circumstances, FAI had been treated unfairly, and was entitled to a declaration that the decision not to renew was void.[28] It was open to the Court to decide the case on the basis of the so-called 'club' or 'licensing' cases, in which the courts had held that a right to natural justice attached to any move to deprive a person of their livelihood.[29] But instead, their Honours chose to expand on the themes expounded by Aickin J in *Heatley*, and to formulate the holding in broad, inclusive terms. The Court's aim was clearly to unify divergent strands of thought on the basis of the common thread of expectations.[30]

Aickin J reiterated his views in *Heatley*: while noting that *stricto sensu*, licence renewal amounts at law to the issuance of a new licence,[31] the fact that FAI reasonably *expected* to be able to carry on created an obligation on the part of the State government to accord natural justice. Similarly, Wilson J said that the nature of FAI's investment in the insurance business gave rise to a legitimate expectation that a renewal of

[28] Murphy J dissenting. Murphy J's distinctive approach to administrative law issues will be discussed below, in chapter 6.

[29] On these generally, see D C Hodgson, 'The Current Status of the Legitimate Expectation in Administrative Law' (1984) 14 *MULR* 686. See also Lord Reid's speech in *Ridge v Baldwin* [1964] AC 40, at 66-71.

[30] This was also the situation in *Attorney-General (Hong Kong) v Ng Yuen Shiu* [1983] 2 AC 629. *Ng Yuen Shiu* stands as the English equivalent (though in fact, it was a Hong Kong case) of *FAI Insurances*, to the extent that it signified that the concept of legitimate expectations had been accepted in English public law. There, the Judicial Committee of the Privy Council held that a representation made by a Hong Kong government official about the manner in which illegal migrants from Macau were to be treated created a right to natural justice if the government intended not to comply with the statement. To get a complete picture on the contemporary English law, however, *Ng Yuen Shiu* ought to be read with *O'Reilly v Mackman* [1983] 2 AC 237, in which Lord Diplock referred (*albeit* in *obiter*) to legitimate expectations. In *Ng Yuen Shiu*, the Privy Council quoted Lord Diplock's speech in *O'Reilly v Mackman*, and wove it together with *Schmidt* and Lord Denning's other legitimate expectation cases. For a summary view of the place of legitimate expectations in English law, see *Council of Civil Service Unions v Minister for the Civil Service* ('the *GCHQ* case') [1985] AC 374, and *Re Westminster County Council* [1986] AC 668, at 692 (*per* Lord Bridge).

[31] 151 CLR, at 378 (citing *Gerraty v McGavin* (1914) 18 CLR 152, at 163-164).

its licence would not be withheld.[32] Mason J spoke of the 'starting point', being 'that an applicant for renewal of a licence generally has a legitimate expectation that his licence will be renewed when the statutory power is entrusted to a statutory authority'.[33] And Gibbs CJ said that:

> [i]t would not be fair to deprive a company of the ability to carry on its business without revealing the reason for doing so, and, if the reason is one related to some alleged misconduct or deficiency in the conduct of the company's affairs, without allowing the company a full and fair opportunity of placing before the authority making the decision its case against the existence of the alleged misconduct or deficiency.[34]

Kioa v West and the Entrenchment of Legitimate Expectations in Australian Law

The case which, more than any other, signalled that the concept of legitimate expectations had 'arrived' in Australia was the High Court's decision in 1985 in *Kioa v West*[35] – even though the discussion of the concept was only in *obiter*. Indeed, *Kioa v West* has come to emblematise the present-day approach to procedural fairness in Australia in a broad sense, and it is probably now the most frequently-cited natural justice authority in the Australian courts.

Kioa v West concerned the plight of a Tongan family which did not wish to return to Tonga after the expiration of their temporary visas. Mr Kioa had come to Australia initially on a student visa, to undertake a short course. His wife and child joined him shortly afterwards. Following completion of his studies, Kioa decided to take some leave here, and he

---

[32] 151 CLR, at 395.

[33] 151 CLR, at 362. On this reasoning, Mason J would presumably not have found a legitimate expectation to have existed in *Breen*.

[34] 151 CLR, at 348. See also Stephen J, 151 CLR, at 351, and Brennan J, 151 CLR, at 412-413.

[35] 159 CLR 550. For some of the early Australian writing on legitimate expectations, see M Sornarajah, 'Natural Justice, Fairness and Administrative Functions' (1977) 5 *U Tas L Rev* 268, Bath, *supra* n 22, Cane, *supra* n 23, Hodgson, *supra* 29, G Johnson, 'Natural Justice and Legitimate Expectations in Australia' (1984) 15 *Fed L Rev* 39, M Allars, 'Fairness: Writ Large or Small' (1987) 11 *Syd L Rev* 306, and P Tate, 'The Coherence of 'Legitimate Expectations' and the Foundations of Natural Justice' (1988) 14 *Mon U L Rev* 15. See also J Hlophe, 'Legitimate Expectations and Natural Justice: English, Australian and South African Law' (1987) 104 *SALJ* 165.

applied for an extension of his visa. For reasons which are not clear from the record, the application for extension did not end up being dealt with by the Immigration Department. But in the meantime, Kioa formed the intention to remain in Australia permanently, and he took up employment.

In July of 1983, Kioa was apprehended at his place of work, and a deportation order was made against him. As part of the process leading up to the making of the deportation order, the submission of the Immigration Department spoke of Kioa's 'active involvement with other persons who are seeking to circumvent Australia's immigration laws'.[36] While this was not referred to as one of the reasons for the deportation order, Kioa alleged (*inter alia*) that the principles of natural justice entitled him to be given the opportunity to rebut this allegation. The question for the High Court on this point, therefore, was whether natural justice applied to decisions to deport – the very same thing that had been in issue in *Salemi v MacKellar (No 2)* and which had been reiterated in a subsequent case.[37]

In holding in *Kioa v West* that natural justice *was* required,[38] the Court noted that since the earlier decisions, significant legislative amendments had taken place, which no longer supported a conclusion that the Minister was to have an unfettered discretion in the making of decisions to deport. But in the course of reaching this conclusion, several of the judges proffered things in *dicta* which indicate that by 1985, the concept of legitimate expectations had become firmly entrenched in Australian public law.

---

[36] See 159 CLR, at 557.

[37] *R v MacKellar, Ex parte Ratu* (1977) 137 CLR 461.

[38] Also of interest in this case is that at least two of the majority found that the reputational interest was the trigger for the duty to accord natural justice. Mason J, for example, was clearly impressed by the fact that it had been alleged that Mr Kioa had been involved with other illegal migrants. His Honour said: 'As [this allegation] was extremely prejudicial, the appellants should have had the opportunity of replying to it' (159 CLR, at 582). On the question of reputation as a 'protectable' interest, he said that the reference to 'right or interest' in the context of his formulation of the trigger for natural justice 'must be understood as relating to personal liability, status, preservation of livelihood and reputation, as well as to proprietary rights and interests' (159 CLR, at 588). See, also, Wilson J, 159 CLR, at 602-603. For a contrast in terminology, see *Bateman's Bay Local Aboriginal Land Council v The Aboriginal Community Benefit Fund Pty Limited* (1998) 155 ALR 684, n 146, where Gaudron, Gummow and Kirby JJ used 'legal right' to include legitimate expectations. Reputation, it may be worthwhile to note, was recognised by the High Court as an interest deserving of legal protection from the Court's foundation: see *Clough v Leahy* (1904) 2 CLR 139, at 157.

Mason J, for example, described it as 'a fundamental rule of the common law doctrine of natural justice'.[39] He said that 'generally speaking, when an order is to be made which will deprive a person of some right or interest *or the legitimate expectation of a benefit*, he is entitled to know the case sought to be made against him and to be given an opportunity of replying to it'.[40] For his part, Gibbs CJ said that he preferred the expression 'reasonable expectation', which had also been used by Stephen J in *Salemi v MacKellar*.[41] While he concluded that natural justice was not required in the circumstances, he, too, found that the existence of created expectations could in principle give rise to an obligation to observe natural justice.

The only contrary voice on this point was Brennan J's. He acknowledged that the law had evolved to the point where it protected, in a procedural sense, matters which did not correspond with traditional common law property rights.[42] Indeed, in this respect, Brennan J seemed to be willing to go further than any of the other judges. In his estimation, natural justice was presumed to be required in any situation where the exercise of 'a power is apt to affect the interests of an individual in a way that is substantially different from the way in which it is apt to affect the interests of the public at large'.[43] But he also thought that the existence or not of a subjective expectation as to a benefit ought to be irrelevant in determining whether the rules of natural justice should govern the exercise of a power.

This is because in his Honour's view, the obligation to accord natural justice arose as a matter of presumed legislative intent. He felt that the obligation for a decision-maker to be fair procedurally was to be

---

[39] 159 CLR, at 582.

[40] *Ibid* (emphasis added). He also said:

> The law has now developed to a point where it may be accepted that there is a common law duty to act fairly, in the sense of according procedural fairness, in the making of administrative decisions which affect rights, interests and legitimate expectations, subject only to the clear manifestation of a contrary statutory intention (159 CLR, at 584).

[41] See *supra*, at 222. In *Haoucher v Minister for Immigration and Ethnic Affairs* (1990) 169 CLR 648, at 653, Deane J also said that this was a better expression. Lord Diplock, too, suggested that 'reasonable expectation' was a preferred term (see the *GCHQ Case* [1985] AC, at 408) and the Privy Council used it in *Ng Yuen Shiu* (see [1983] 2 AC, at 636).

[42] 159 CLR, at 616.

[43] 159 CLR, at 619.

determined through the process of statutory interpretation, not psychological introspection:

> [T]he expectation of an individual whose interests may be affected by an exercise of a power is not relevant to the construction of the statute which creates the power. The construction to be placed on the statute cannot depend on whether an individual has an expectation that the power will be exercised in his favour or that he will be consulted and given an opportunity to put a case before the power will be exercised against him. It is not the state of mind of an individual but the interest which an exercise of power is apt to affect that is relevant to the construction of a statute.[44]

As will be discussed in chapter seven, Brennan J's approach makes sense when it is read with his assertion of the doctrinal basis for the application of natural justice. For the moment, it is sufficient to observe that of the various members of the High Court since *Banks*, it is Brennan J who has been most consistent in holding that the obligation to accord natural justice arises as a result of presumed parliamentary intent. To foreshadow for a moment the focus of chapter seven, other justices – notably Mason CJ and Deane J in the recent cases – have expressed the view that the source of natural justice obligations is the common law, rather than legislation.

The question adverted to by Brennan J in *obiter* in *Kioa* – the extent to which the individual's actual expectations matter – was raised four-square in the High Court's next encounter with a legitimate expectation case, *South Australia v O'Shea*.[45] Unfortunately, the Court did nothing to clear up the confusion on the issue. In *O'Shea*, the Court held that a legitimate expectation, which will attract natural justice, must be distinguished from a 'mere hope', which does not. But their Honours did not offer a principled basis on which to make the distinction between expectations that are legitimate, and hopes which lack legitimacy. Moreover, in holding that O'Shea did not have a 'legitimate' expectation, it imputed to him understandings and appreciations that almost certainly he did not have.

O'Shea was a sexual offender, who had in 1977 been convicted of certain paedophilic offences. As he had been convicted of similar offences in 1962 and 1967, he was sentenced to detention at Her Majesty's

---

[44] 159 CLR, at 617-618. See also Wilson J, 159 CLR, at 602-603.
[45] (1987) 163 CLR 378.

pleasure, by virtue of sub-section 77a(3) of the *Criminal Law Consolidation Act 1935* (SA). Nevertheless, in 1980, the Governor in Council, acting on a recommendation of the Parole Board, released O'Shea on licence. O'Shea subsequently breached one of the conditions of his licence and he was reincarcerated. In 1983, he was again released on licence, but in 1985, when it was found out that he was planning to operate a camp for young children under a false name, he was once more taken into custody.

Despite this, the Parole Board *again* recommended that O'Shea be released on licence. The recommendation was made after a hearing, which O'Shea was permitted to attend, with counsel, and at which he had been permitted to make representations. This time, however, the Governor[46] refused to act on the recommendation. O'Shea sought judicial review of the Governor's decision, claiming that he had a legitimate expectation that the Parole Board's recommendation would be acted upon, and that he was therefore entitled to a hearing before the Governor in Council.

The relevant provisions of the *Criminal Law Consolidation Act* vested in the Governor a discretion to release a preventative detainee if he was satisfied 'on the recommendation of the Parole Board, that [the detainee] is fit to be at liberty'.[47] Deane J dissenting, the Court[48] held that this was not sufficient to give rise to an expectation of release in O'Shea that would trigger the obligation to provide him with the opportunity to make representations to the Governor in Council.

In the view of Mason CJ (as he had become in 1987), the crucial factor was that O'Shea had been given a full opportunity to make submissions before the Parole Board: 'The hearing before the recommending body provides a sufficient opportunity for a party to present his case so that the decision-making process, viewed in its entirety, entails procedural fairness.'[49] It was only if the Governor had based his decision on something new – something on which O'Shea had not had the chance to comment – that natural justice might have been required.[50] In this case, the thing which turned the tide against O'Shea's third release on

[46] Which, in South Australia, means the Governor in Council: *Acts Interpretation Act 1915* (SA), s 23.
[47] Clause 77(c)(3)(b)(i).
[48] Mason CJ, Wilson, Brennan, Deane and Toohey JJ.
[49] 163 CLR, at 389.
[50] *Ibid.* See also on this point, *Calvin v Carr* [1980] AC 547 (PC, NSW).

licence was a consideration of the public interest, which, in the Chief Justice's view, was the Governor in Council's special province. But, he said, O'Shea had not been inhibited in any way from making submissions with respect to it before the Parole Board.

In a joint judgment, Wilson and Toohey JJ arrived at the same result. In their opinion, the relevant provisions of the *Criminal Law Consolidation Act* evidenced a 'strong concern to protect the community' from sexual offenders.[51] But Wilson and Toohey JJ differed from the Chief Justice in characterising the proceedings before the Parole Board. In Mason CJ's view, as has been noted, the hearing before the Board had given O'Shea a chance to make representations on all matters in issue, including questions of the public interest. That was why 'viewed in its entirety', the decision-making process could be said to have been in accordance with the requirements of natural justice. In the eyes of Wilson and Toohey JJ, though, the two stages of the process were quite distinct and served different purposes. The object of the proceedings before the Parole Board was to make an assessment of individual fact – whether O'Shea was fit to be released – based, *inter alia*, on expert evidence. But this alone was not enough to settle the issue: 'Clearly, the legislature believes that, without more, the recommendations of the Board may not offer sufficient protection to the community.'[52]

The Governor in Council's involvement was intended to address this. He was to make an assessment based, not on O'Shea's individual characteristics, but on the collective good. Accordingly, the decision-making criteria used by the Governor were quite different. This being so, having received natural justice before the Parole Board, all that O'Shea had was a 'hope' of release, which, 'of itself, is not sufficient to ground an expectation that will attract legal consequences'.[53] Their Honours continued:

> So far as the concept of legitimate expectation is concerned, Mr O'Shea must be taken to know that the Act committed to the Governor, with the advice and consent of the Executive Council, the responsibility for determining where the public interest lay. He would also know that the reservations expressed in the medical reports and implied in the stringent conditions recommended by the Board would be likely to give the Governor and the

---

[51] 163 CLR, at 396.
[52] 163 CLR, at 401.
[53] 163 CLR, at 402.

> members of the Executive Council cause for anxious consideration as to whether to release Mr O'Shea. The nature of the decision that they were required to make was such that participation by Mr O'Shea was inappropriate.[54]

Brennan J, in contrast, reiterated the line he had taken in *Kioa v West*; that O'Shea's subjectively held expectations were irrelevant to the question of whether a hearing before the Governor in Council was required. In his view, the broad discretion conferred upon the Governor by the *Criminal Law Consolidation Act* was sufficient to counter any claim that natural justice was required.[55] For his part, Deane J would have found that in the circumstances, a legitimate expectation *did* exist.[56] However one defines the concept of expectations, Deane J said,

> a person who has been deprived of his liberty on medical grounds has a 'legitimate expectation' of being released on licence once the stage is reached where the appropriate specialist statutory tribunal, acting on independent medical advice and after full enquiry, has concluded and recommended that he be so released.[57]

This was consistent with the view he had taken in *Kioa v West*.[58]

Haoucher v Minister for Immigration and Ethnic Affairs and *Attorney-General (New South Wales) v Quin*

The High Court's next significant discussion of legitimate expectations came in two judgments which were delivered on the same day in June of 1990. The first of the pair was *Haoucher v Minister for Immigration and Ethnic Affairs*.[59] It dealt with the question of deportation, and the facts in issue were reminiscent of *Salemi v MacKellar (No 2)*, in that the case turned upon the impact of a statement of Ministerial policy upon the right

---

[54] *Ibid.*

[55] 163 CLR, at 410-411.

[56] 163 CLR, at 417.

[57] *Ibid.*

[58] For the story of O'Shea's subsequent dealings with the legal system (including a summary history of his many encounters with the law), see *O'Shea v DPP* (1998) 71 SASR 109. See also *R v O'Shea* (unreported., Sup Ct South Australia, 13 November 1996).

[59] 169 CLR 648.

to deport. The second was *Attorney-General (New South Wales) v Quin*,[60] which involved the question of the justiciability of an expectation of appointment to judicial office. In the former, the Court found that a legitimate expectation existed. In the latter it did not. What connects the two, apart from their date, is the relationship drawn by the judges between expectations of substantive outcome, and resultant rights to procedure.

Haoucher arose because of a provision in the *Migration Act*, which allowed one to seek merit review of deportation orders in the Administrative Appeals Tribunal. Section 66E of the Act gave the AAT the power either to affirm a decision to deport, or to remit the matter to the Minister for reconsideration 'in accordance with any recommendations of the Tribunal'. Haoucher was a citizen of Lebanon, who, in 1985, was convicted of being in possession of cannabis resin with an intent to sell or supply it to others, for which he was sentenced to a period of imprisonment of three years.[61] Prior to this, in 1980, he had been convicted of assault on one of his brothers, and sentenced to imprisonment for three months. At the same time, he had also been convicted of disorderly conduct. At the time, he was warned by the Department of Immigration and Ethnic Affairs that a failure to maintain good behaviour could result in deportation. Nevertheless, in 1982, he was again convicted of disorderly conduct and of using a false name. In 1983, he was convicted of causing damage to property.

Pursuant to the then s 12 of the *Migration Act*, the Minister was empowered to order the deportation of non-citizens who had been in Australia for less than ten years, and who had been sentenced to periods of imprisonment for more than one year. The Minister had, however, adopted a Criminal Deportation Policy which provided, *inter alia*, that ordinarily the Government would only order the deportation of non-citizens who had committed 'serious offences'. With respect to drug-connected matters, the Policy offered as examples of serious offences: '[t]he production, importation, distribution, trafficking or commercial dealing in heroin or other "hard" addictive drugs'. As for non-'hard' drugs (such as the possession of cannabis resin), the policy said that 'involvement in other illicit drugs on a significantly large scale' would also be considered a serious offence. The policy also stated that in normal cases, the Minister would defer to decisions made by the AAT on review.[62]

---

[60] 170 CLR 1.

[61] The facts are summarised in the judgment of Dawson J, 169 CLR, at 656-657.

[62] The relevant portion of the policy stated:

In this case, the AAT had recommended that the Minister's deportation order against Haoucher be revoked, on the basis that Haoucher's involvement in the trafficking of the cannabis was not 'on a significantly large scale'.[63] It also concluded that in the circumstances, the risk of recidivism was low, that Haoucher's ties with Lebanon were not especially strong, and that the benefit to Australia from his deportation would be outweighed by the harm caused to his family – most of whom lived in Australia – were he to be forcibly removed.[64]

Despite this, the Minister rejected the AAT's recommendation and affirmed the deportation order. In his statement of reasons, he said that while he accepted the findings of fact made by the AAT, he did not accept the AAT's 'characterisation' of them, or 'the weight to be given to them in the exercise of my discretion'. In particular, the Minister said that he thought the offence *was* a serious one, and that in light of Haoucher's past criminal record, the risk of recidivism was serious. He also thought that the AAT had overstated the burden that would be placed upon Haoucher's family were he to be deported. Therefore, said the Minister, 'exceptional circumstances existed which justified departing from the recommendation of [the AAT]'.[65]

In his application for judicial review, Haoucher argued that the terms of the Criminal Deportation Policy had created a legitimate expectation that the Minister would comply with the AAT's recommendation, and that if he proposed to depart from the recommendation, the Minister was first obliged to provide him with a hearing. By a three to two majority,[66] the High Court agreed with Haoucher. But what is most interesting is to compare the different approaches taken by the judges to the legitimacy of Haoucher's expectation that he be able to remain in Australia. For what the judgments show is that among the judges, there seem to have been really very different notions of the idea of 'legitimate' expectations.

It is the policy of the Australian Government that recommendations of the Administrative Appeals Tribunal should be overturned by the Minister only in exceptional circumstances and only when strong evidence can be produced to justify its decision. Furthermore, it is the policy of the Government that, when the Minister decides to deport a person contrary to a recommendation of the Tribunal, the Minister will table in the parliament at the first opportunity a statement of his/her reasons for doing so (see 169 CLR, at 657).

[63] 169 CLR, at 657.

[64] *Ibid.*

[65] 169 CLR, at 658.

[66] Deane, Toohey and McHugh JJ, Dawson and Gaudron JJ, dissenting.

In her dissent, Gaudron J for the most part adopted the sort of approach taken by Mason CJ in *O'Shea*, namely that the question was whether 'viewed in its entirety' the decision-making process could be said to be fair.[67] In her opinion, all that had happened here was that the Minister had taken a different view of the evidence placed before the AAT. Haoucher could not be said to have been denied the opportunity fairly to present his case, when all that happened at the Ministerial stage was a different weighing up of facts found in a process in which he *had* been fully involved. In her view, she said,

> a decision which results from a difference between the final decision-maker and the recommending body as to the evaluation of precisely the same body of facts is not one which will ordinarily be viewed as involving a breach of the rules of natural justice merely because no opportunity was given to put a case that the facts should be evaluated in the same way as they were by the recommending body. That is because, at least ordinarily, it may be said that 'the decision-making process, viewed in its entirety, entails procedural fairness'.[68]

Her Honour arrived at this conclusion after having considered the fact that the *Migration Act* provided for a two-step decision-making process, in which the first step was merely recommendatory. This fact – that the first step was a recommendation, rather than a decision *per se* – 'contemplates that the final decision may differ from the recommendation'.[69] It also 'necessarily imports a degree of freedom of choice or discretion in the evaluation of the facts as found by the recommending body'.[70]

Dawson J approached the matter in a similar way. Stated crudely, Haoucher had in his view had the chance to say all before the AAT, and a further hearing before the Minister could serve no constructive purpose: 'In this case, it is not suggested that there is any new material which could be placed before the Minister to lead him to a contrary conclusion ... Any

---

[67] In fact, credit for this approach perhaps should go to Barwick CJ. Though it was not referred to by Mason CJ in *O'Shea*, in *Brettingham-Moore v St Leonards Municipality* (1969) 121 CLR 509, at 521, Barwick CJ said it was 'in relation to the carrying out of the whole process prescribed by the statute that the question as to the requirements of natural justice is to be considered'.

[68] 169 CLR, at 674 (quoting *South Australia v O'Shea*, *per* Mason CJ).

[69] 169 CLR, at 673.

[70] *Ibid*.

further hearing would result only in the repetition of those matters before the Minister.'[71] This was not, he said, a case like *FAI v Winneke*, where there had been no hearing in the first place.[72] Dawson J also said that it was misleading to speak of a legitimate expectation of procedural protection: 'To speak, as the cases often do, of the legitimate expectation of procedural fairness generally is ... to confuse the interest which is the basis of the requirement with the requirement itself.'[73] 'It adds nothing', he concluded, 'to say that there was a legitimate expectation, engendered by the promise or practice that a certain procedure would be followed.'[74]

For his part, Deane J predictably found that in the circumstances a legitimate expectation did exist. Intriguingly, though, he seemed to be of the opinion that what gave rise to the legitimate expectation was the fact that Haoucher had gone to the trouble of seeking review before the AAT, and that there, he had carried the day. The Deportation Policy, in his view, had little to do with it. '[T]here is much to be said for the view', he said,

> that where a person has made the effort and incurred the expense involved in persuading the Tribunal to make findings and recommendations in his or her favour, after a full hearing on the merits in proceedings in which the Minister has been fully heard as an active opposing party, there will arise a new and distinct legitimate or reasonable expectation that the Minister will accept the findings and abide by the recommendations of that Tribunal. If that be so, *then quite apart from the context provided by published government policy*, the Minister was under an obligation to observe procedural fairness in determining whether the deportation order ... should stand.[75]

Toohey J's contribution to the debate came in the form of an assertion, which, significantly, was later on to be picked up by some of his colleagues in *Minister for Immigration and Ethnic Affairs v Teoh*,[76] that in order for a legitimate expectation to be founded, there need not actually have been any subjective expectation at all.

---

[71] 169 CLR, at 663.
[72] *Ibid.*
[73] 169 CLR, at 659.
[74] 169 CLR, at 660.
[75] 169 CLR, at 654 (emphasis added). Deane J also said in this case that he thought that natural justice applied presumptively to all government decision-making (169 CLR, at 653). This extraordinary assertion will be discussed in chapter 7).
[76] (1995) 183 CLR 273. See *infra*, at 259.

Drawing upon Brennan J's view that whether natural justice is required is a matter of statutory construction, he said that while a pattern of governmental conduct could give rise to a legitimate expectation that the pattern would continue, this was not the only type of legitimate expectation case. In other cases, the '[l]egitimate expectation does not depend upon the knowledge and state of mind of the individual concerned'.[77] What Toohey J had in mind in this regard were cases in which the duty to observe natural justice arose as a result of legislative intent, whether express or implied, but the passage is of tremendous interest, for as will be seen, his views on the place of actual expectations came to assume some prominence.[78]

Attorney-General (New South Wales) v Quin stemmed from the reorganisation of the New South Wales inferior courts in the mid-1980s.[79] At the time, all but one of the one hundred and one stipendiary magistrates sought appointment to the new Local Court, which had succeeded the old Court of Petty Sessions. Of the hundred would-be reappointees, ninety five were successful. What led to the litigation was the fact that in 1983, after the *Local Courts Act* was passed, but before it came into force, the stipendiary magistrates were given to expect by the Chairman of the Bench of Stipendiary Magistrates that they would be automatically appointed to the new court.[80] But before the new appointments were made, the Attorney-General formed the view, arrived at following substantial consultation, that five out of the hundred (including Quin) were not fit for reappointment.

In a proceeding in the New South Wales courts, *Macrae v Attorney-General (NSW)*,[81] it was held that Quin and the other non-reappointed stipendiary magistrates had been denied natural justice, as during the course of the reappointment process, the Attorney-General had taken into

---

[77] 169 CLR, at 670.

[78] For his part, McHugh J held, as he had in *O'Shea*, that a legitimate expectation had to be distinguished from a 'mere hope' (169 CLR, at 682), but he found that in these circumstances, a legitimate expectation had in fact been engendered by the Deportation Policy (169 CLR, at 683).

[79] Whereby the *Justices Act 1902* (NSW) was repealed and replaced by the *Local Courts Act 1982* (NSW). The scheme for the reorganisation was such that the stipendiary magistracies ceased to exist when the *Local Courts Act* came into force, on January 1, 1985. The *Local Courts Act* contained a saving provision, however, whereby former magistrates who were not reappointed were to be given appointments in the state Public Service, at a protected rate of pay.

[80] See 170 CLR, at 8.

[81] (1987) 9 NSWLR 268.

account adverse comments on Quin and his colleagues, on which they had not had the opportunity to comment. A declaration was issued, remitting the matter back to the Attorney-General for reconsideration according to law. Significantly, in light of what Dawson J was later to say in *Haoucher* about it being misleading to speak of a legitimate expectation of procedure,[82] the New South Wales Court of Appeal had found that Quin and the others had had a legitimate expectation, not of appointment to the new Court, but of procedural fairness in the appointments process.

The problem, however, was that by the time the *Macrae* case had wended its way through the superior courts, the new Local Court was in operation. By the time *Macrae* had ended, all of the initial appointments to the Local Court had been made, and some additional vacancies had already been filled. The Attorney-General therefore proposed to treat Quin's application (for by this time, he was the only one of the five non-reappointees left who was still pursuing his claim to reappointment to the magistracy) along with other applications for appointment as Magistrates.

In other words, rather than succeeding to the new Court virtually automatically, as had most of his colleagues in the old stipendiary magistracy, he would have to compete for a position with other candidates, and be judged according to merit. It sounds odd to say that the basis of a lawsuit is that a person was complaining of having to be judged according to his or her merits, but from Quin's perspective, had it not been for the Attorney-General's initial denial of natural justice, he would have had a *de facto* claim upon a judicial appointment. The complication was that in the *Macrae* case, the New South Wales Court of Appeal had described Quin's legitimate expectation as one to *procedure*, not as to substantive outcome.

In the New South Wales courts, Quin succeeded in obtaining a declaration to the effect that in order to comply with the Court of Appeal's original declaration in *Macrae*, the Attorney-General was to treat Quin's application on its own merits, and not in comparison with any others.[83] But the High Court[84] took a different view. In Mason CJ's opinion, Quin's claim was defeated on two bases. First, he noted that in fact, Quin's expectation was of an appointment to the new Court, and that this was on the basis of the representation made by the Chairman of the Bench of Stipendiary Magistrates. But a representation could not, said the Chief Justice, act so as to fetter the lawfully-conferred discretion upon the

---

[82] See *supra*, at 243.

[83] Unreported, 23 December 1988.

[84] Mason CJ, Brennan and Dawson JJ, Deane and Toohey JJ dissenting.

Crown: 'The Executive cannot by representation or promise disable itself from, or hinder itself in, performing a statutory duty or exercising a statutory discretion to be performed or exercised in the public interest ...'[85]

In this case, Mason CJ interpreted section 12 of the *Local Courts Act*, which provided that the Governor may 'appoint any qualified person to be a Magistrate', as conferring upon the Crown such a discretion. It was therefore free, he said, for the Attorney-General to adopt and change policies for the appointment of judges to the Local Courts. Whatever expectation Quin may have had, it could not operate to frustrate the discretion given by Parliament to the Crown with respect to the judicial appointments process.

In addition, Mason CJ thought that Quin was barred from the relief he sought on the basis that a legitimate expectation could not confer a right to substantive outcome. As his Honour noted, while the expectation which grounds the authority of the court to intervene may be substantively-oriented, the right conferred by the expectation is to procedural fairness.[86] In contrast to Dawson J in *Haoucher*, he said that legitimate expectations *may* be of procedural entitlement (as the New South Wales Court of Appeal had concluded in *Macrae*), but this cannot be dispositive of the content of the resulting entitlement to natural justice: 'The procedural right which forms the subject-matter of the legitimate expectation will not necessarily be the same as the procedure which procedural fairness ... will demand.'[87]

It was with this latter aspect of Mason CJ's analysis that Dawson J had trouble in *Quin*. While he concurred with the Chief Justice in the result (and in particular, on the question of Quin effectively urging the High Court to countenance a fettering of discretion), he returned to his theme in *Haoucher* that an expectation as to procedure could not be deemed 'legitimate', in the sense of conferring an entitlement to natural justice. He reiterated his view that the whole notion of legitimate expectations was to provide some means of protection of interests which fall short of rights.[88] Whether fair procedure is required depends not on whether the party in question expects that it will be provided, but on

[85] 170 CLR, at 17.
[86] 170 CLR, at 21.
[87] *Ibid.*
[88] 170 CLR, at 54.

whether 'the circumstances call for fair procedure'.[89] In Dawson J's view, it was almost trite – and possibly tantamount to opening the floodgates – to speak of a 'legitimate expectation' of procedure.[90]

Brennan J was *ad idem* with Mason CJ and Dawson J on the fettering question. In his view, the power to appoint to public office must, in the absence of statutory provisions to the contrary, 'be at large if its exercise is to answer the purpose for which it is conferred, namely, to advance the interests of the public'.[91] But he also took the opportunity to offer his views, which by now were becoming familiar, on the subject of legitimate expectations generally. To answer the question posed to the Court by Quin's argument, he said:

> The question can be put quite starkly: when an administrative power is conferred by the legislature on the executive and its lawful exercise is apt to disappoint the expectations of an individual, what is the jurisdiction of the courts to protect that individual's legitimate expectations against adverse exercises of the power? I have no doubt that that answer is: none.[92]

Deane and Toohey JJ, dissenting, would have found that the nature of Quin's expectation did entitle him to the relief he sought, *viz* to have his application for appointment considered on its own, and not as against other applications. In Deane J's opinion, this case was like *FAI v*

---

[89] 170 CLR, at 55. He also asserted that insofar as it recognised the possibility of a legitimate expectation of procedure, which in turn was the source of a *right* to procedure, the judgment of the Privy Council in *Ng Yuen Shiu* was wrong. See 170 CLR, at 56-57.

[90] He said:

> No doubt people expect fairness in their dealings with those who make decisions affecting their interests, but it is to my mind quite artificial to say that this is the reason why, if the expectation is legitimate in the sense of well-founded, the law imposes a duty to observe procedural fairness. Such a duty arises, if at all, because the circumstances call for a fair procedure and it adds nothing to say that they also are such as to lead to a legitimate expectation that a fair procedure will be adopted (170 CLR, at 55).

[91] 170 CLR, at 33.

[92] 170 CLR, at 35. This was because, in his Honour's view, to hold otherwise would be tantamount to substituting merit review for judicial review:

> Judicial review provides no remedies to protect interests, falling short of enforceable rights, which are apt to be affected by the lawful exercise of executive or administrative power. If it were otherwise, the courts would be asserting a jurisdiction, in protection of individual interests, to override the law by which a power to affect those interests is conferred upon the repository (*ibid*) (*Cf* Forsyth, *supra* n 8, at 240-241).

Winneke, where an expectation as to an entitlement – there, the renewal of a licence, here, the reappointment to curial office – gave rise to procedural rights.[93] Toohey J was slightly differently focused in his reasoning. He thought the case raised issues of judicial independence. The initial procedure adopted by the Attorney-General, of allowing a *de facto* claim upon reappointments by the Stipendiary Magistrates, reflected recognition of 'the security of tenure that is essential to the independence of the judiciary'.[94] Moreover, it created a legitimate expectation that Quin and the others would be reappointed, provided they were not found to be unfit for office. Since the assertion of Quin's unfitness had flowed from unfair procedures, it followed logically that Quin had the right to have his fitness assessed according to *fair* procedures.

Annetts v McCann and *Ainsworth v Criminal Justice Commission*

The next case in which the High Court visited the question of individual expectations giving rise to procedural rights was *Annetts v McCann*,[95] decided later in the same year as *Haoucher* and *Quin*. *Annetts v McCann* arose out of the tragic (and, at the time, newsworthy) death of two young jackaroos in the desert of Western Australia. After news of the deaths came to light, rumours began to circulate, alleging possible wrongdoing. The two youths had died of thirst, but one of the two had also been shot in the head, and it was uncertain whether he had taken his own life, or whether his friend had shot him.[96] McCann was a Coroner, conducting an inquest into the deaths. Pursuant to section 24 of the Western Australian *Coroners Act 1920,* McCann gave the parents of the deceased youths standing to appear at the Inquiry.

The rights conferred by section 24 upon people who had been given standing included the right to examine and cross-examine witnesses. Apart from that, the Coroner had exclusive discretion to determine the circumstances under which people would be heard.[97] Nevertheless, the

---

[93] 170 CLR, at 46-47.

[94] 170 CLR, at 67.

[95] (1990) 170 CLR 596.

[96] See the judgment of Toohey J, 170 CLR, at 619.

[97] Section 7 of the Act vested the Coroner with 'all the power, authority and jurisdiction which belong to the office of a Coroner in England', except to the extent to which the Act varied this. The position in England apparently is that no person may address a Coroner except with the Coroner's leave. See [1990] WAR, at 163-165.

Annetts claimed that natural justice required that they be given the right also to make submissions to McCann, which he refused. The Annetts thereupon applied to the Supreme Court of Western Australia for a writ of mandamus, to direct McCann to allow them to appear.

The Full Court refused the application, holding that under the *Coroners Act*, the Coroner had a discretion whether or not to hear submissions, and that the Annetts could not, therefore, claim a denial of natural justice.[98] The High Court[99] allowed an appeal from this decision, holding that in the circumstances, the Annetts had a legitimate expectation, which gave them the right to make submissions concerning possible findings as to their son's involvement in the shooting of his mate.

While the Court split in the end result, all of the justices agreed that a right to make submissions of one form or another existed on the facts at hand. In a joint judgment, Mason CJ and Deane and McHugh JJ said that the case was an easy one. It could, they said,

> now be taken as settled that, when a statute confers power upon a public official to destroy, defeat or prejudice a person's rights, interests or legitimate expectations, the rules of natural justice regulate the exercise of that power unless they are excluded by plain words of necessary intendment.[100]

Here, it was obvious that the work of McCann could affect the interests of the Annetts. This was so for two reasons. In light of the wording of sub-section 24(1) of the *Coroners Act* – 'any person who, in the opinion of the coroner, has a sufficient interest in the subject or result of the inquest ...' – the fact that McCann had given the Annetts standing served as evidence of the fact that they had an interest in the proceedings.[101] The interest they represented, the majority concluded, was 'the protection of the reputation of their deceased son'.[102] But the conferral of standing also, in the eyes of the majority, gave rise to a legitimate expectation: it created 'a legitimate expectation that the Coroner would not make any finding adverse to the interests which they represent without giving them the opportunity to be heard in opposition to that finding'.[103]

---

[98] *Annetts v McCann* [1990] WAR 161.

[99] Mason CJ, Deane, and McHugh JJ, Brennan and Toohey JJ dissenting.

[100] 170 CLR, at 598 (internal citations omitted).

[101] 170 CLR, at 599.

[102] *Ibid.*

[103] *Ibid.*

This latter conclusion is significant. The *Coroners Act* did not itself give rise to the legitimate expectation. It merely gave the Coroner the right to give standing to 'any person who, in the opinion of the coroner, has a sufficient interest'. The factor which legitimised the Annetts' desire to be heard was the action of Coroner McCann. This is interesting, for it is difficult to discern any pattern in the High Court's holdings on this point. In some of the cases: *Salemi v MacKellar (No 2)*, *O'Shea* and *Quin*, it was held that actions of governmental officials could not counter a decision by parliament to confer a discretion upon the decision-maker. But in others: *FAI v Winneke*, *Haoucher* and, now, *Annetts v McCann*, it was held that it could.

The only contentious question in the eyes of the Chief Justice and Deane and McHugh JJ was whether the *Coroners Act* made plain an intention to exclude the rules of natural justice. Of course, their conclusion was that it did not. But the way in which they reasoned to their conclusion cannot help but raise eyebrows. The majority noted that in 1920, when the Act was passed, it 'simply would not have occurred to anyone in the legal profession that the common law rules of natural justice applied to an inquiry whose findings could not alter legal rights or obligations'.[104] Accordingly, there was nothing which would suggest that the West Australian parliament would have intended to *exclude* them! As a matter of simple logical deduction, this is, of course, compelling enough. But as a matter of legal reasoning, it rings quite disingenuous.

In his judgment, Toohey J approached the case in more or less the same way as the majority. While he was in favour of dismissing the appeal, he expressed the view that McCann ought to have been required to provide the parents with the opportunity to make submissions on any proposed finding which would reflect adversely on the character of the younger Annetts.

In Toohey J's view, any finding by the Coroner which suggested criminality in the young Annetts' conduct would have affected the interests of the parents: 'The relationship of parent and child and the emotional consequences for the family of such a finding demand that such an opportunity [*ie.* to make submissions] be afforded.'[105] This, too, seems compelling when viewed in one way. But when viewed in another way, one wonders about the *legitimising* factor of the expectation in Toohey J's opinion. Could it have been the emotion that generally attends coronial

---

[104] 170 CLR, at 600.

[105] 170 CLR, at 620.

proceedings? Or the emotional effect of any finding by Coroner McCann which would have cast their son's character in a bad light?

Whatever the case, Brennan J took a similar view. If and when McCann arrived at the stage of making adverse findings against the character or reputation of young Annetts, then he should afford the elder Annetts the right to make submissions.[106] But he reached this view by a very different route from the other judges. In keeping with the approach to legitimate expectations he enunciated in *Kioa*, *Haoucher* and *Quin*, he said that the views or expectations of the Annetts themselves were irrelevant to the issue of whether natural justice was required. The only key to answering that question was an examination of the provisions of the *Coroners Act*: 'The only sound foundation for judicial review is, in my opinion, the statute which creates and confers the power, construed to include any terms supplied by the common law.'[107]

Ainsworth v Criminal Justice Commission,[108] the next case in the line, involved a report made by the Queensland Criminal Justice Commission ('CJC') into areas of potential difficulty which could follow from a proposal by the Queensland government to introduce poker machines into the state. The statutory scheme provided that the CJC's report would be filed with the state Parliamentary Criminal Justice Committee,[109] and the government's stated intention was to conduct a series of public hearings after receiving the report.

In the report, which received wide publicity, the CJC made disparaging comments about both Leonard Hastings Ainsworth, and Ainsworth Nominees Pty Ltd, a manufacturer and distributor of poker machines of which Mr Ainsworth was the managing director and principal. The CJC also recommended that Ainsworth Nominees not be permitted to participate in the poker machine industry in Queensland. In reaching this view, however, the CJC at no time made enquiries of either Ainsworth or Ainsworth Nominees Pty Ltd, or put to them the substance of the allegations which had been made against them and which formed the basis for the disparaging comments as well as the recommendation.

Ainsworth and Ainsworth Nominees (together, 'the Ainsworths') sought a declaration from the Supreme Court of Queensland that they had been denied natural justice. The Supreme Court denied the application, on

[106] 170 CLR, at 612.
[107] 170 CLR, at 606.
[108] (1992) 175 CLR 564.
[109] *Criminal Justice Act 1989* (Qld), para 2.18(1)(a).

the basis of the High Court's holding in *Testro Brothers v Tait*[110] that investigations which did not have the effect of prejudicing legal rights did not attract natural justice.[111] In the High Court, the Ainsworths argued both that the legislation in question – the Queensland *Criminal Justice Act 1989* – *did* require the observance of natural justice, and that the common law had moved on since *Testro Brothers v Tait* was decided in 1963.

The High Court[112] agreed with the Ainsworths. On the first argument, the majority held in a joint judgment that a provision of the *Criminal Justice Act* which required the CJC to 'act independently, impartially, fairly and in the public interest' in 'all proceedings'[113] was sufficient to attract a requirement to observe natural justice.[114] On the second argument, the majority was of the view that the law *had* moved on since *Testro Bros v Tait*:

> As the law has progressed since that case, the only question which now arises is whether the report adversely affected a legal right or interest, including an interest falling within the category of legitimate expectation, such that the [CJC] was required to proceed in a manner that was fair to the appellants.[115]

As said, Brennan J raised his voice in protest at this. He reiterated his by now commonplace view that the obligation to observe natural justice arose as a consequence of parliamentary intent.[116] But he then proceeded to engage in the same stretch of imputed legislative intent that he had in

---

[110] (1963) 109 CLR 353. For more on this case, see chapter 3.

[111] See 175 CLR, at 572.

[112] Mason CJ, Brennan Dawson, Toohey and Gaudron JJ.

[113] Para 3.21(2)(a).

[114] Taken in context, the majority said, the provision provided evidence of a parliamentary intent that the work of the CJC be consistent with the requirements of procedural fairness:

> [A] body established for the purposes and with powers and functions of the kind conferred on the Commission [*ie* the CJC] and its organisational units is one whose powers would ordinarily be construed as subject to an implied general requirement of procedural fairness, save to the extent of clear contrary provision. That is because it is improbable that, though it did not say so, the legislature would intend that a body of that kind should act unfairly (175 CLR, at 574-575).

See, also 175 CLR, at 576:

> [T]he nature of the Commission and its functions and responsibilities are such that a supplementary duty of fairness is necessarily to be implied in those areas involving its functions and responsibilities which are not covered by the [statutory] duty of fairness.

[115] 175 CLR, at 577.

[116] 175 CLR, at 584-585.

Annetts v McCann. In *Ainsworth* he said that there was an interpretive presumption that an obligation to observe natural justice accompanied 'a statutory function the exercise of which is apt to affect the reputation of an individual'.[117]

Both Brennan J and the majority agreed that reputation was a protected interest in the circumstances.[118] Where they differed was the starting point for the enquiry. Brennan J began by asking whether the *Criminal Justice Act* ought properly to be interpreted so that natural justice applied. The other judges, in contrast, said that natural justice would apply here as an 'implied general requirement' of the common law. The starting point was that natural justice applied because the common law dictated that this was the case. The interpretive question for them was whether the *Criminal Justice Act* should be interpreted so as to *exclude* natural justice.

Their analytical approach, in other words, was the inverse of Brennan J's. As will be argued in chapter seven, this difference masks an abstruse clash in view, not only about the legal foundation for judicial review in Australian administrative law, but also about the relative positions of the legislative and judicial branches of government within the Australian constitutional framework.

The *Teoh* Case

The High Court's most controversial discussion of the notion of legitimate expectations was in its 1995 judgment in *Minister for Immigration and Ethnic Affairs v Teoh*.[119] Few, if any, of the High Court's administrative law pronouncements have attracted as much attention as *Teoh*.[120] For the

[117] 175 CLR, at 591. For more on Brennan J's view on reputation as a protected interest, see *NCSC v News Corporation* (1984) 156 CLR 296, at 326. See also *Johns v Australian Securities Commission* (1993) 178 CLR 408.

[118] It is interesting to contrast the judgments in *Ainsworth* with that of Stephen J in *R v Collins, Ex parte ACTU-Solo Enterprises Pty Ltd* (1976) 8 ALR 691. There he held – *à la Testro Bros v Tait* – that a writ of certiorari would not issue against a report of a Royal Commission, where the report did not affect the rights of the report's subject, or 'subject [them] to a new hazard' (8 ALR, at 699). One wonders why reputation was not considered a 'new hazard' in *R v Collins*.

[119] *Minister of State for Immigration and Ethnic Affairs v Ah Hin Teoh* 183 CLR 273.

[120] A small sample of the torrent – and breadth – of commentary which followed the judgment in *Teoh* includes: the Hon A Nicholson, 'Address to the Children First! Forum', Melbourne 1995, National Children's Youth Law Centre, 'High Court Breathes New Life

most part, reflection on the Court's administrative law work remains the province of the academic lawyer, rather than the journalist. But *Teoh* was different. It attracted a notice that stretched far beyond the compass of those ordinarily interested in the doctrine of natural justice.

In part, one supposes, this reflects the fact that today, the work of the High Court generally attracts greater attention than it did in years past. Another reason for *Teoh's* high profile, undoubtedly, is the fact that the case concerned children's rights. Yet a third reason surely must be the essence of the holding itself. For the essence of the holding was that the simple ratification of a treaty could give rise to enforceable legal interests. Despite its protestations to the contrary, the Court was clearly introducing a significant change to the law. And in doing this, the Court was clearly altering the way in which the *rule* of law had traditionally been understood to operate in Australia.

In *Teoh*, the High Court held that the ratification by the executive of a treaty gave rise to a legitimate expectation that executive decision-making processes would be in conformity with it, and that if the executive intended to deviate from the terms of a ratified treaty, it first had to provide an affected person with an opportunity to argue against the deviation.

Specifically, the Court held that Article 3(1) of the *International Convention on the Rights of the Child* (to which Australia is a party), which provides that '[i]n all actions concerning children ... the best interests of the child shall be a primary consideration', created a legitimate expectation that the Minister for Immigration and Ethnic Affairs would take the best interests of any affected children into account as a primary consideration when deciding whether to issue a deportation order against a

---

into CROC' (1995) 3 *Rights NOW!* 2, M Allars, 'One Small Step for Legal Doctrine, One Giant Leap Towards Integrity in Government: *Teoh's* Case and the Internationalisation of Administrative Law' (1995) 17 *Syd L Rev* 204, R Snell, '*Kioa* to *Teoh*' (1995) 20 *Alternative L J* 136, A Twomey, '*Minister for Immigration and Ethnic Affairs v Teoh*' (1995) 23 *Fed L Rev* 348, H Burmester, 'The *Teoh* Decision – A Perspective From the Government Service' (1995) 5 *AIAL Forum* 6, J McMillan, '*Teoh* and Invalidity in Administrative Law' (1995) 5 *AIAL Forum* 10, K Walker, 'Treaties and the Internationalisation of Administrative Law', in C Saunders (ed) *Courts of Final Jurisdiction: The Mason Court in Australia* (1996), N Williams, 'Legitimate Expectations – Beyond *Teoh*', in L Pearson (ed) *Administrative Law: Setting the Pace or Being Left Behind?* (1997), S Sheridan, 'Legitimate Expectation: Where Does the Law Now Lie?', in J McMillan (ed), *Administrative Law Under the Coalition Government* (1997). See also J McMillan and N Williams, 'Administrative Law and Human Rights', in D Kinley (ed) *Human Rights in Australian Law* (1998), at 83-88.

parent. If the Minister proposed *not* to take the best interests of the children into account as a primary consideration, he or she first had to provide the prospective deportee parent with a hearing regarding the departure from the Convention's provisions.

As Mason CJ and Deane J acknowledged in their joint judgment,[121] until *Teoh* it was well established that the provisions of an international treaty to which Australia is a party did not form part of Australian law until they had been incorporated into municipal law by a valid act of parliament.[122] That was as a consequence of the constitutional system of separation of powers. It is trite that for Australia, the principle of separation of powers lies at the heart of the rule of law.

In *Teoh*, however, the High Court held that the ratification *could* give rise to domestic legal consequences, quite independently of parliamentary inaction. This was rather different from the position it had taken in 1982, in *Simsek v MacPhee*. There, the Court had held that a claim that natural justice was required as a result of Australia's accession to treaties had to fail. Since the treaties did not form part of domestic law, they could not give rise to a legitimate expectation.[123] In *Teoh*, however, a majority of the High Court took a different view.

The facts in *Teoh* were straight-forward. In May of 1988, Ah Hin Teoh, a Malaysian national, arrived in Australia. He came to care for the three children of his dead brother, all of whom were Australian citizens. He married his brother's widow – who was the mother of the children – and he became the *de facto* parent for them. In addition, Mr Teoh and the new Mrs Teoh had three children of their own. The problem was that Mrs Teoh was a heroin addict, and Mr Teoh was caught trying to import heroin into Australia for her use. He was sentenced to six years' imprisonment.

---

[121] 183 CLR, at 286-287.

[122] In *A-G Canada v A-G Ontario* [1937] AC 326 at 347, the principle was stated in the following way:

> Within the British Empire there is a well-established rule that the making of a treaty is an executive act, while the performance of its obligations, if they entail alteration of the existing domestic law, required legislative action. Unlike some other countries, the stipulations of a treaty duly ratified do not within the Empire, by virtue of the treaty alone, have the force of law.

See also *Chow Hung Ching v R* (1948) 77 CLR 449, *Bradley v The Commonwealth* (1973) 128 CLR 557, *Simsek v MacPhee* (1982) 148 CLR 636, *Koowarta v Bjelke-Petersen* (1982) 153 CLR 168, *Kioa v West* (1985) 159 CLR 550, *Dietrich v R* (1992) 177 CLR 292, and *J H Rayner (Mincing Lane) Ltd v Department of Trade and Industry* [1990] 2 AC 418.

[123] 148 CLR, at 644.

As a result of this, Mr Teoh's application for permanent residency was refused on the basis that he was not of good character. Teoh appealed this to the Immigration Review Panel ('IRP'), but his appeal was dismissed. His visitor's permit having expired, a Deportation Order was then made against Teoh – even though the IRP recognised that the deportation of Teoh would cause extreme hardship to Mrs Teoh and the children. Teoh sought review of the deportation order in the Federal Court under the *Administrative Decisions (Judicial Review) Act*. His claim was that he had been denied procedural fairness in the deportation decision-making process. At the initial stage, however, the claim was a vague one – there was no reference to the Convention on the Rights of the Child.[124]

At first instance in the Federal Court, he was unsuccessful. French J denied his application. But on appeal, the Full Court found in his favour.[125] The Minister then appealed to the High Court. In the High Court, four separate judgments were delivered: a joint judgment by Mason CJ and Deane J, a concurrence by Toohey J, a judgment concurring in result (but for quite different reasons) by Gaudron J, and a dissent by McHugh J.

Mason CJ and Deane J said that they accepted the basic legal tenet that the mere ratification of treaties did not transform them into enforceable domestic law.[126] But, they held, ratification did mean *something*. They were unwilling to think of ratification 'as a merely platitudinous or ineffectual act'.[127] Instead, they held that ratification ought to be characterised as 'a positive statement by the executive government of this country to the world and to the Australian people that the executive government and its agencies will act in accordance with the convention'.[128] In light of this, they held that in the absence of any move by the government to displace the expectation, the act of ratification was sufficient to found a legitimate expectation that administrative decision-

---

[124] See the judgment of Toohey J, 183 CLR, at 295, 298. Counsel for Teoh has told me that the argument about the Convention was only formulated on the morning of the appeal to the Full Court of the Federal Court. Up to that point, the intention was to base the case upon the *parens patriae* jurisdiction of the courts. The Convention only came into counsel's ken when it was mentioned in passing to him on the morning of the appeal by (ironically) a friend who was employed in the Government Solicitor's office.

[125] (1994) 49 FCR 409, per Black CJ, Lee and Carr JJ.

[126] 183 CLR, at 286-287.

[127] 183 CLR, at 291. See, also, 183 CLR, at 302 (*per* Toohey J).

[128] 183 CLR, at 291.

makers will act in conformity with the provisions of the treaties to which the Government has bound us.

Applying that principle to the facts at hand, the majority found that even though the IRP had commented on the problems that the children would face as a result of the deportation of Mr Teoh, the majority found that the good character requirement had not been regarded as *the* primary consideration. But what was most interesting about this holding was that the Chief Justice and Deane and Toohey JJ were prepared to find the legitimate expectation to exist even though Mr Teoh had no knowledge whatsoever of the Convention or its contents. As Toohey J put it:

> the matter is to be assessed ... in terms of *what expectation might reasonably be engendered* ... A subjective test is particularly inappropriate when the legitimate expectation is said to derive from something as general as the ratification of the Convention.[129]

The approach taken by Gaudron J is interesting in a different respect. Unlike her other colleagues who found for Mr Teoh, Gaudron J did not base her reasons on natural justice rights stemming from the Convention or its terms. In her Honour's view, this was not so much a case involving rights stemming from *treaties*, as it was a case of rights stemming from the common law. As she said,

> citizenship carries with it a common law right ... to have a child's best interests taken into account, at least as a primary consideration, in all discretionary decisions ... which directly affect the child's individual welfare.[130]

In other words, Gaudron J looked at the significance of the treaty's contents in reverse to the way in which the majority had looked at it: she said that the treaty merely gave written expression to this 'fundamental human right'. She left open, though, the question of what would happen in a case where the contents of the convention were 'not in harmony with community values and expectations'.[131]

---

[129] 183 CLR, at 301 (emphasis added). *Cf R v Home Secretary, Ex parte Khan* [1984] 1 WLR 1337. There, the Court of Appeal held that natural justice was required only where the British government was purporting to rely on a policy which had not been explained to the applicant.

[130] 183 CLR, at 304.

[131] 183 CLR, at 305.

McHugh J – who, as will have been noted, had thus far been one of the active proponents of the idea of legitimate expectations – dissented strenuously from the reasoning of his colleagues, and in places, his judgment came close to displaying that testiness which one usually associates with dissents in the Supreme Court of the United States.

Simply put, McHugh J was of the view that ratification of the treaty did not give rise to any legitimate expectation at all. Accordingly, it was not a document that the decision-maker was bound to consider in deciding whether or not Mr Teoh should be deported. He thought that since Mr Teoh had no knowledge of the treaty, and had not been given any undertakings that it would apply, it would be 'strange, almost comic', to have to tell him that the Convention would not be applied.[132]

As for the characterisation of the act of ratification, in contrast to the majority McHugh J said that it amounted solely to a statement to the international community – a statement, moreover, that Australia *intends* to fulfil its obligations. It was not a representation that Australia would be in compliance with the treaty's provisions forthwith upon signature.[133]

His Honour also said that even if he were wrong, and that ratification could in the abstract give rise to a legitimate expectation, there were in this case clear policy guidelines which would have displaced the expectation. Finally, he said that apart from anything else, this was not an action concerning children. Even if it did have some sort of status in Australian law, the Convention would not be applicable on these facts. The decision to deport Teoh would have consequences for the children, to be sure, but it was an action concerning deportation of an undesirable alien. He said that if the majority's interpretation were to hold, then *anything* which touched upon children – sentencing of criminals, a decision to put someone in bankruptcy – would have to comply with the treaty.[134]

---

[132] 183 CLR, at 314.

[133] As an aside, in *Simsek v MacPhee*, Stephen J referred to a different impact upon our relations with other nations that emphasis on treaties by the courts could have:

> It may be observed in passing that to seek to apply anything like the full content of the maxim *audi alteram partem* to cases before the Committee, which may have to consider a wide range of confidential information about conditions overseas and whose conclusions might, if made public, affect good relations with other countries, might well stultify its operations and would not serve the best interests of applicants whose cases come before it (148 CLR, at 644).

[134] Though despite McHugh J's pessimistic prognosis, McMillan and Williams have noted that there has been 'a limited appearance of *Teoh* in litigation' (*supra* n 120, at 88, n 133).

Legitimate Expectations and the New High Court

The High Court's most recent judgment involving the question of legitimate expectations came in October of 1998, in *Sanders v Snell*.[135] What makes this case especially interesting is that it was the first of the cases heard by the 'new' Court. Only Gaudron J was left of the judges who heard the major legitimate expectation cases of the 1980s and early 1990s. *Sanders v Snell* did not involve the question of a lack of expectation, so the status of *Teoh* itself cannot be commented on, but the judgments did indicate a sensitivity to the criticism about the legitimate expectation cases that McHugh J had offered in *Teoh*. Nevertheless, the case suggests that the law as established in the 1980s and 1990s cases will continue to be the yardstick against which the obligation to accord natural justice will be determined.

Sanders v Snell involved the question of the lawfulness of the termination of the employment of the Executive Officer of the Norfolk Island Tourist Bureau by one of the Ministers in the Norfolk Island Government. In fact, for the most part the judgment concerns the torts of inducing breach of contract and misfeasance in public office. The facts were that the Executive Officer had a contract of employment with the Norfolk Island Tourist Bureau which provided that the contract could be terminated either on the misconduct of the Executive Officer, or with two months' notice. Section 15 of the *Norfolk Island Government Tourist Bureau Act 1980* (NI), however, provided that the Minister could give the Tourist Bureau binding directions 'as to the conduct of the business or affairs of the Bureau'.

For reasons which were not exactly clear from the record (but which clearly involved some personal mistrust), the Minister gave directions to the Bureau to sack the Executive Officer. When the Bureau refused, the Minister dissolved the Bureau and appointed a new one which proceeded to carry out the directions. Significantly, one of the reasons that the original Bureau refused to act was that the chairman was of the view that the Minister should first have given the Executive Officer a hearing. The

---

Cases in which *Teoh* has been considered by the Federal Court include *Browne v Minister for Immigration and Multicultural Affairs* [1998] FCA 566 (29 May 1998), *Lam v Minister for Immigration and Multicultural Affairs* [1998] FCA 154 (4 March 1998), *Vaitaiki v Minister for Immigration and Ethnic Affairs* (1998) 150 ALD 608, and *Department of Immigration and Ethnic Affairs v Ram* (1996) 41 ALD 517.

[135] (1998) 157 ALR 491.

Bureau's letter of refusal said that 'it would seem contrary to natural justice to do such a thing without giving the Executive Officer an opportunity to hear what he is accused of, and to give his side of the story'.[136] The evidence was that another member of the government had also advised the Minister that natural justice was required, but the Minister was steadfast in his desire to get rid of the Executive Officer.

The Full Court of the Federal Court held that in the circumstances, the Minister was among other things liable to the Executive Officer for the tort of misfeasance in public office.[137] The High Court held that no evidence had been led which would have supported this conclusion and it remitted the matter back to the trial judge. But for present purposes, what is of interest is what the Court had to say about the natural justice aspects of the case.

The majority[138] accepted that the tort of misfeasance in public office could extend to acts that are invalid for want of procedural fairness.[139] The question, therefore, was whether natural justice extended to the Minister's making of the direction to the Tourist Bureau. The majority said that it did. This was, they said, a 'livelihood' case – just like *Banks v Transport Regulation Board* and *FAI Insurances v Winneke*. In a small place like Norfolk Island, there were, moreover, reputational aspects which would accompany a sacking. But their Honours said that in the circumstances, the Executive Officer also had a legitimate expectation:

> In this case [the Executive Officer] had an expectation that his contract of employment would continue until the members of the Bureau resolved (for whatever reason) to give notice of its termination or [misconduct had been established]. The direction that [the Minister] sought to give to the Bureau would defeat that expectation.[140]

Therefore, the Court held that the power to give directions under the *Norfolk Island Government Tourist Bureau Act* was 'a power that should

[136] See 157 ALR, at 499.
[137] (1997) 73 FCR 569 (rev'g in part Beaumont J, at first instance).
[138] Gleeson CJ, Gaudron, Kirby and Hayne JJ, Callinan J dissenting.
[139] 157 ALR, at 502. Though *cf* Brennan J in *Northern Territory v Mengel* (1995) 185 CLR 307, at 356-357, holding that not all actions that breach the requirements of natural justice constitute misfeasance in public office (referred to, 157 ALR, at 505-506).
[140] 157 ALR, at 504.

be read as requiring the giving of procedural fairness to those whose rights or legitimate expectations are affected by its exercise'.[141]

The Legitimate Expectation and Australian Public Law

So what is one to make of these cases – of the line now stretching more than twenty years, from *Heatley* in 1976, to *Sanders v Snell* in 1998? The picture that emerges from them is a mixed one; one of tremendous dynamism and change, yet of constancy at the same time. The change is obvious enough: the obligation to observe natural justice now extends far further than it ever has before – possibly even, as Deane and McHugh JJ have suggested, presumptively to *all* governmental decision-making.[142] So insofar as we are contrasting the formulation of the doctrine of natural justice as it is understood in Australia today with that as it was understood up until the 1970s, it is clear that the landscape has been completely re-cast. No longer is the obligation to observe natural justice focused on the identity or the function of the decision-maker. The question is now one of effect: whether a governmental decision has the effect of interfering with 'rights, interests or legitimate expectations'.[143]

But, perhaps paradoxically, the constancy lies in the same thing which has been responsible for the doctrine's broadening: its formulation. The sort of effect-based trigger for natural justice that came to be enunciated by the High Court in the legitimate expectation cases is the same as the trigger in the older cases, when it was said that a decision which affected property rights was deemed to be judicial in character. In chapter four, the extent to which in the 1950s natural justice in this country remained in an un-theorised state was discussed. The picture that emerges from the 1970s, 1980s and 1990s cases is, in a theoretical sense, much the same – one of a doctrine that is in many respects essentially reactionary in form. The High Court has come to phrase the trigger for natural justice so broadly that, without some limitation, it is dramatically overinclusive. The problem is that the limitation: legitimate expectations *v*

---

[141] 157 ALR, at 505. Callinan J took quite a different view. He did not think that there was anything in the Minister's conduct to give rise to an expectation on the part of the Executive Officer that he would receive a hearing (157 ALR, at 508).

[142] See *Haoucher* 169 CLR, at 653 (*per* Deane J) and *Teoh* 183 CLR, at 311 (*per* McHugh J).

[143] This formulation is an often-used one. It was first cast by Mason J in *Kioa* (see 159 CLR, at 584).

'mere hopes', has been phrased in a way that is incapable of precision in application.

In fact, the legitimate expectation cases throw up a series of theoretical issues. One is the seeming inconsistency in application of the enunciated test. Consider, for instance, the decision in *O'Shea.* To apply the criteria used in previous cases, the Governor of South Australia had by his past conduct – having granted release in all the previous instances upon receiving a recommendation from the Parole Board – engendered an expectation of release that was no less solid in its foundation than that which was found to have existed in *FAI Insurances v Winneke*. And unlike in *Haoucher*, the asserted basis for the legitimacy of the expectation in *O'Shea* was not merely a government policy but an Act of Parliament.

Now, common sense would suggest, as the majority said, that the ultimate decision to release in cases of this nature must of course also depend upon an assessment of the public interest. The public interest would always, one intuitively would assume, be deemed to be a relevant consideration concerning decisions to release. This was the knowledge imputed to O'Shea by Wilson and Toohey JJ. As they said, a person in O'Shea's shoes 'must be taken to know that the Act committed to the Governor, with the advice and consent of the Executive Council, the responsibility for determining where the public interest lay'.[144]

But the critical point is that the Act did not say this. The statutory provision in question, sub-section 77a(3) of the *Criminal Law Consolidation Act*, made no reference whatever to the Governor's decision being based on the public interest. On the contrary, the expressed criterion was purely individualistic: an offender's fitness to be at liberty. And as for an imputation of legislative intent, the past practice within the government in these instances would seem to militate against it.

Similar criticisms can be made of Mason CJ's assertion that 'viewed in its entirety' one could conclude that O'Shea had been accorded natural justice. Essential to this claim was the observation that he had had the chance before the Parole Board to make representations regarding the public interest. The record was unclear on this (which, presumably, ought to have raised an evidentiary concern), but if Wilson and Toohey JJ were right in saying that the activities of the Governor in Council fulfilled a different role from those of the Parole Board, then the Chief Justice's claim loses much of its persuasiveness. The point is that if it is read

[144] 163 CLR, at 402.

according to the Court's previously stated terms of the notion of legitimate expectations, one cannot help but be left with the feeling that the concept is one of extreme malleability according to the judicial view of the relative equities of the case at bar.

In a like way, one has difficulties squaring Mason CJ's approach in *Quin* with his approach in *FAI Insurances v Winneke*, a case with which, as Deane J noted,[145] it bore much similarity. There is no reason of principle, for instance, why the Victorian Governor's discretion to issue licences to sell insurance ought to have been any more limited than the discretion of the Governor of New South Wales to appoint magistrates. Moreover, in *FAI Insurances v Winneke* there had been at best been an expectation engendered by conduct. In *Quin*, the expectation had been engendered by an actual representation by someone in a position of authority.

The only way to reconcile the two judgments is to distinguish them either on the basis of subject-matter, or on the basis of relative deservedness of the two claimants. As to the former, one could alternatively say that licencing cases were different (which would have been correct in law[146]) or that judicial appointments cases were different (or, perhaps it would be more accurate to say, exceptional).

As to the latter, one could without raising many eyebrows say that Quin – like O'Shea before him – was not someone whose plight reeked of injustice. A claim like Quin's – that he had a right to judicial office without his fitness being considered on the merits – would strike many people as absurd. Nor (because of its sheer novelty) was it the sort of claim that raised the spectre of rampant bureaucratic malevolence.

There is also much to be critical of in the judgments in *Haoucher*. The analysis of Gaudron and Dawson JJ, in particular, seems curious when one considers it in a broader systemic light. Both judges were of the view that in the circumstances, the requirements of natural justice had been satisfied by the hearing before the AAT. But to arrive at this conclusion, they had to discount the value *per se* of an opportunity to speak.

Yet, on any reading of the basis for natural justice, the opportunity provided by a hearing must have some intrinsic value: to ensure that the decision-maker has had the advantage of the fullest possible argument on the pros and cons of the proposed decision and to make the affected person feel that he or she has had their day in court. And while one understands

---

[145] See his judgment in *Quin*, 170 CLR, at 46-47.

[146] See *supra* n 29, and accompanying text.

the corresponding systemic value in decisional closure at some point, it reads jarringly to hear judges trained in the common law tradition of oral advocacy suggest that hearings can only serve a fact-finding purpose, and that the opportunity to convince a decision-maker through argument is of no real value.

At the same time, and notwithstanding his constancy in theme, Brennan J's reasoning in these cases also revealed some inconsistency. In both *Kioa v West* and *Quin*, Brennan J held that legitimate expectations could be relevant insofar as the *content* of natural justice was concerned, but not so as to act as a trigger for the duty. But then, confusingly, he suggested that the trigger for natural justice ought to be allied with standing.[147] This approach contains within it two problems: first, it surely has the equation backwards. To say that if one has standing to challenge a decision, then natural justice is presumed to have been required in the course of making that decision, is to place the remedy before the right. Standing ought to follow natural justice, not the other way around.

Secondly, the law of standing is a creature of the common law, not the parliament.[148] So, insofar as Brennan J was of the view that the obligation to observe natural justice stems from a judicial assessment of parliamentary intent, then it is puzzling that the yardstick could be the common law of standing. *Locus standi* is very much related to effect. So, too, is the matter of the content of natural justice. If one says that the content of natural justice is variable, one is making a statement about the relative deservedness of entitlements. When we say that the context of one decision is such that natural justice demands a formal hearing, but that the context of another only requires some sort of an opportunity to make written submissions, we are acknowledging a hierarchy of interests measured according to effect.

But this undercuts Brennan J's doctrinal premise, namely that the obligation to accord natural justice is determined by reference to parliament's wishes rather than a citizen's individual predicament. What is important, according to Brennan J's conception, is what parliament either explicitly or impliedly had to say about the decision-making process. As he was to say, 'the law governing the extent and exercise of a

---

[147] 170 CLR, at 40-41. See, also, on this *O'Reilly v Mackman* [1983] 2 AC 237, at 275 (*per* Lord Diplock) and Forsyth, *supra* n 8, at 258-259.

[148] For more on the law of standing as it was understood at the time of these cases, see M Allars, 'Standing: The Role and Evolution of the Test' (1991) 20 *Fed L Rev* 83, especially at 97-101.

power exists independently of the circumstances which evoke its exercise'.[149]

This was, he said, a matter of simple practical necessity: 'a repository of power must know what the law requires for the valid exercise of the power before attempting its exercise'.[150] But when, as in *Kioa* and *Quin*, he also said that the content of natural justice is variable, or that legitimate expectations could have a bearing on the doctrine's content, he was acknowledging that the impact on the individual *is* important. And integral to an assessment of the impact of a decision on an individual must be some view as to the individual's subjective feelings about the decision. By allowing that standing ought to drive the determination of what decision-making procedures were required (which was effectively what he was saying), Brennan J was laying his thesis on a shaky foundation.

The decision in *Teoh* raises its own set of theoretical concerns. The most obvious, of course, is that which attracted most of McHugh J's ire – the holding that one need not have any real expectation at all to be deemed to have had a legitimate expectation in law. As a matter of simple linguistics, the suggestion seems a *non sequitur*. Moreover, it also seems contrary to the position that Mason CJ had taken in *Quin*. There, Mason CJ referred to the suggestion by the Privy Council in *Ng Yuen Shiu* that legitimate expectations are intended to further a governmental duty of good administration.[151] True as this might be, he said, 'the content of [the duty of good administration] is still defined by reference to the claimant's legitimate expectation. In the absence of such an expectation, there is no corresponding duty to accord fairness.'[152]

Yet, having said all of this, the significance of the holdings in these cases cannot be denied. They make it clear that the doctrine of natural justice is a vibrant one in Australia today. The focus of the next chapter will be to examine another aspect of this vibrancy: the means by which the doctrine's compass has been extended to cover the activities of governmental actors who for much of our legal history, were assumed to be not amenable either to the imposition of natural justice requirements, or to judicial review more generally.

---

[149] *Annetts v McCann* (1990) 170 CLR 596, at 604.

[150] *Ibid.*

[151] See [1983] 2 AC, at 638.

[152] 170 CLR, at 20-21.

6 Judicial Review and the Crown

Alongside the expansion of the scope of natural justice through the use of the legitimate expectation, one of the most interesting developments in Australian public law in the 1980s was the assertion by the High Court of a general right to engage in review of decisions made by the Crown itself, as distinct from decisions made by the Crown's servants. But this was not an Australian development alone. In a series of cases decided within a few years of one another, the High Court of Australia, the House of Lords and the Supreme Court of Canada were all driven to the same conclusion: that as a matter of logic, the Queen as Sovereign should be no more immune from judicial review than should be those who administer the state on her behalf.

Yet what makes this development so especially striking in the Australian context is not so much the coincidence of logic, as the boldness with which the assertion came to be made. For the fact is that the way in which the scope of reviewability is now stated makes it clear that in Australia, there are now few, if any, governmental decisions which can be said to be non-reviewable *per se*.[1] It also makes it clear that the courts will also reserve the right to impose general standards of fairness upon the Crown as it goes about its business.[2] The aim of this chapter is to explore these cases, and to place them alongside the legitimate expectation cases

---

[1] Emphasis here is placed on '*per se*'. Statutory codes for review often exclude categories of cases. The *Administrative Decisions (Judicial Review) Act 1977* (Cth), for example, formally excludes from statutory review decisions of the Governor-General (sub-s 3(1)).

[2] It should be stated that defining 'the Crown' is something not without difficulty – especially in the case of what were once termed the Dominions. For the purposes of this work, the Crown is taken to include the Queen herself, together with her Privy Counsellors, as well as her representatives, together with their Executive or Privy Counsellors. For more on the question of the definition of the Crown in this context, see H V Evatt, *The King and His Dominion Governors* (1936), A B Keith, *The King and the Imperial Crown* (1936), E Forsey, *The Royal Power of Dissolution of Parliament in the British Commonwealth* (1943), J B Harper, 'The Crown as the Source of Legal Powers in Australia' (1938) 1 *Res Jud* 310, and 8(2) *Halsbury's Laws of England* (4th ed.), 'Constitutional Law and Human Rights', paragraphs 351-354.

discussed in the last chapter. What emerges is a picture of a judiciary which is sceptical about the ability of the political process to exercise any self-control over abuse of procedure and which, as a consequence, has been continuing to expand its own role in imposing procedural obligations on the government.

Law, Politics, and the Limitations on Judicial Authority

At the outset, it is worthwhile to acknowledge that it is incorrect to think that the idea of a real Crown immunity, broadly construed, has ever been a feature of public law in the common law system. 'The King can do no wrong', Blackstone famously wrote.[3] The reality is that as a statement of law – even taken historically – this is highly misleading. It was, and remains, the law that the Sovereign may not be sued in her personal capacity.[4] But implicit in the very expression 'public law' is the notion that the courts have the right to pronounce upon the lawfulness of action taken in the Crown's name.[5] As early as the thirteenth century Bracton said that the king had to be under the law for 'it is the law that makes the king'.[6] And, of course, central to Dicey's vision of the rule of law, from which so much of our present-day public law doctrine is assumed to stem, is the notion that *qua* government, the Crown should be subject to the law just as much as any individual citizen.[7]

Moreover, throughout history there have been several celebrated instances in which the courts have adjudicated upon matters going to the heart of the Crown's authority. Importantly, a number of these date from the seventeenth century, during the period leading up to the Constitutional settlement, so can be considered 'foundational' in terms of modern constitutional assumptions.

---

[3] 1 *Comm* 245.

[4] *Warders and Commonality of Sadlers' Case* (1588) 4 Co Rep 54b, 76 ER 1012. See also 12(1) *Halsbury's Laws of England* (4th ed), paragraph 101.

[5] See *Raleigh v Goschen* [1898] 1 Ch 73.

[6] *Ipse autem rex non debet esse sub homine sed sub deo et sub lege, quia lex facit regem* ('The king must not be under man but under God and the law, because it is the law that makes the king') (*De Legibus et Consuetudinibus Angliae* (S Thorne, ed 1968, vol 2, at 32). See also http://bracton.law.cornell.edu/bracton/Common/index.html.

[7] *The Law of the Constitution* (8th ed. 1915), at 189. On the question of Cabinet members being personally liable for their activities, see *Wilkes v Lord Halifax* (1769) 14 St Tr 1406 and *Re M* [1994] 1 AC 377.

The *Case of Prohibitions del Roy*[8] and the *Case of Proclamations*[9] are two of the better known of these cases.[10] In the former, the King's Bench held (or, perhaps to put it more accurately, persuaded the King[11]) that the Crown no longer had a prerogative right to take an active part in the business of curial adjudication. And in the latter, it held that the Crown no longer had the right to create crimes through the prerogative. The right to do so lay solely with parliament. In the course of this holding, Coke CJ said that 'the king hath no prerogative, but that which the law of the land allows him'.[12]

But equally, it is a fact that this royal impleadability was never an open-ended one. The hyperbole and boldness of cases like the *Case of Prohibitions* and the *Case of Proclamations* can in large measure be attributed to the tumult of the times in which they were decided. The courts throughout history have generally displayed a decided reluctance to intrude upon what one might crudely term 'affairs of state'. In his *Commentaries*, Blackstone described the position of the Crown exercising its prerogatives as 'irresistible and absolute'.[13] After the constitutional settlement, and particularly after the idea of cabinet government began to take shape, Blackstone's formulation came to represent a common law code for saying that the courts ought not to question the government of the day on matters of policy or political judgment.

In the Australian setting, Blackstone's admonition was accepted as a constitutional principle from the beginning. In no less than four instances in the first fifty years of the Commonwealth's existence, the High Court indicated an unwillingness to probe into what might broadly be described

---

[8] (1608) 12 Co Rep 63, 77 ER 1342.

[9] (1611) 12 Co Rep 74, 77 ER 1352.

[10] Others, lesser-known, include the *Case of Dispensing Power* (1607) 12 Co Rep 18, 77 ER 1300, the *Case of Customs, Subsidies, and Impositions* (1608) 12 Co Rep 33, 77 ER 1314, the *Case of Pardons* (1610) 12 Co Rep 30, 77 ER 1311, and the *Case of Commendams* (*Colt & Glover v Bishop of Coventry*) (1616) Hob 140, 80 ER 290.

[11] In his report of the case, Coke merely said that the King was 'greatly offended' at Coke's position (77 ER, at 1343), but another witness offered a rather fuller narration of the event. Sir Roger Boswell said that after Coke's statement that the King had no right to involve himself in the proceedings, 'His Majestie fell into that high indignation as the like was never knowne in him, looking and speaking fiercely with bended fist, offering to strike him, etc, which the lord Cooke [*sic*] perceiving fell flatt on all fower' (quoted in Sir W Holdsworth, *A History of English Law* Vol 5 (2nd ed. 1937), at 430-431).

[12] 12 Co Rep, at 76, 77 ER, at 1354.

[13] 1 *Comm* 251.

as 'counsels of the Crown'.[14] As Isaacs and Powers JJ put it in one of these cases, the accepted legal position was that it was 'not open to impute *mala fides* with respect to the issue of a royal proclamation, which is the act of the King himself or his representatives'.[15]

The reasons for this reluctance are ones not difficult to appreciate. The courts suffer from a number of distinct instrumental disadvantages when it comes to assessing affairs of state. For one thing, even though it happens frequently that former politicians are appointed to judicial office (though this today is not as common in the High Court as it once was), in institutional terms, the courts lack political expertise. Their decisions often have political ramifications – of that there can be no doubt – but in arriving at their decisions judges employ legal rather than political reasoning. Of course, to put it this way is to invite criticism about attempting to draw a line between 'law' and 'policy'. It is conceded that no such line can be drawn – most public law cases *do* have political ramifications. But it must equally be conceded that at a basic level, judges and politicians employ different evaluative criteria in their work.

Related to this is the fact that almost always, judges will be at a significant disadvantage when it comes to having enough information at hand to properly evaluate decisions involving governmental policy. Rules of evidence, it will be remembered, are designed to keep information *away* from courts. So the practical ability of judges to grapple with policy-laden affairs of state is doubly-hampered by their institutional isolation from other parts of government. Though this isolation has been viewed as a principle of foundational law only since the constitutional settlement, it in fact has its roots in the very beginning of the common law system, when a corps of full-time professional judges, functionally separate from the King's other advisors, came to exist.[16] In modern Australian terms, of

---

[14] *Duncan v Theodore* (1917) 25 CLR 510, *James v Cowan* (1930) 43 CLR 386, *Victoria Stevedoring and General Contracting Co Pty Ltd v Dignan* ('*Dignan's Case*') (1931) 46 CLR 73, and *Australian Communist Party v The Commonwealth* (1951) 83 CLR 1. The expression 'counsels of the Crown' is taken from the judgment of Dixon J in the latter case (83 CLR, at 179).

[15] *Duncan v Theodore* 25 CLR, at 525-526.

[16] On the foundation of the judiciary, see, generally, J H Baker, *An Introduction to English Legal History* (3rd ed. 1990), chapters 2 and 3, S F C Milsom, *The Historical Foundations of the Common Law* (2nd ed. 1981), chapter 1, T F T Plucknett, *A Concise History of the Common Law* (5th ed. 1956), chapter 2, Sir V Windeyer, *Lectures on Legal History* (2nd ed. rev, 1957), and Sir W Holdsworth, *A History of English Law*, Vol 1, chapter 3 (7th ed. 1956).

course, this structural disability has been formally entrenched in Chapter III of the Constitution, and given life by various decisions of the High Court.[17]

A third disadvantage suffered by the courts with respect to passing judgment on affairs of state is of rather more recent origin. That is a *systemic* concern – the concern that the courts do not enjoy any sort of popular mandate for their work. To put it in contemporary terms, the courts suffer from a 'democratic deficit'. This has only been really a consideration since the reform movements of the nineteenth century. But since then, the notion of popular sovereignty has emerged as another foundational element of the political order.[18] Indeed, in the eyes of many nowadays, the notion of an electoral mandate has become perhaps the most critical determinative of political authority of all.[19] Most of the criticism that one hears of the courts today in Australia has at base this view. In particular, the claims that one often heard in the early 1990s, after judgments like *Mabo*[20] and *Wik*[21] and the *Political Free Speech*[22] cases

---

[17] Especially, the *Boilermakers' Case* (*A-G Commonwealth v R* [1957] AC 288, aff'g *R v Kirby, Ex parte Boilermakers' Society of Australia* (1956) 94 CLR 254) and *Brandy v Human Rights and Equal Opportunities Commission* (1995) 183 CLR 245. See also *R v Spicer, Ex parte Australian Builders Labourers' Federation* (1957) 100 CLR 227, at 289, 310. For a scholarly discussion of the separation of powers in Australia, see F Wheeler, 'The Separation of Federal Judicial Power: A Purposive Analysis' (unpublished PhD thesis, ANU, 1999).

[18] This view – that government in Australia represents an act of agency on behalf of the sovereign people – is one that was enunciated several times by the High Court in the 1980s and 1990s. In *Australian Capital Television v The Commonwealth* (1992) 177 CLR 106, at 137, for example, Mason CJ said:

> The very concept of representative government and representative democracy signifies government by the people through their representatives. Translated into constitutional terms, it denotes that the sovereign power which resides in the people is exercised on their behalf by their representatives.

See also *R v Duncan, Ex parte Australian Iron and Steel Pty Ltd* (1983) 158 CLR 535, at 589 (*per* Deane J), *University of Wollongong v Metwally* (1984) 158 CLR 447, at 477 (*per* Deane J), *Leeth v Commonwealth* (1992) 174 CLR 455, at 484 (*per* Deane and Toohey JJ), *Nationwide News Pty Ltd v Wills* (1992) 177 CLR 1, at 72 (*per* Deane and Toohey JJ) and *Theophonous v Herald and Weekly Times Ltd* (1994) 182 CLR 104, at 180 (*per* Deane J). Also see J Williams, 'The Protection of Rights Under the Australian Constitution: A Republican Analysis' (unpublished ANU PhD thesis, 1997), chapter 10.

[19] Witness, for example, the terms of the debate over the republic in Australia and reform of the House of Lords in the United Kingdom. In both cases, there is a sizeable view that whatever ultimately may take the place of the current institution, it must enjoy some form of electoral sanction.

[20] *Mabo v Queensland (No 2)* (1992) 175 CLR 1.

– that the High Court was overstepping its bounds by 'making law'[23] – only make sense if one subscribes to the view that the authority to effect social change must stem from prior approval by the electorate.

Even in the eyes of those who may not subscribe to the vulgar sort of criticism of the judiciary that one heard sometimes voiced in Australia in the early 1990s, the relationship between electoral mandate and policy formation is now so unconsciously entrenched that today, the expression 'rule of law' has unconsciously become a *de facto* synonym for populist democracy. The older notion of the rule of law equating with the systemisation or regularisation of state power is now often forgotten.[24] Indeed, many people would undoubtedly be horrified to learn that when Bagehot wrote the first edition of *The English Constitution*,[25] the franchise was held by only about a third of the adult population in England![26]

The Separation of Powers and the Tension in Administrative Law

Taken together, these structural disabilities constitute a substantive basis for the doctrine of the separation of powers. Just as politicians are not thought to have the opportunity for deliberative repose that judges do, or their freedom from the tyranny of the ballot box, and hence are not deemed institutionally appropriate to sit in judgment in courts of law, so are courts thought in principle to be institutionally incompetent to sit in day-to-day government. As Sir Anthony Mason once put it, 'courts are ill-equipped to review policy'.[27] In this respect, the expression 'separation of powers' need not be merely a theoretical formula for safeguarding liberty through checks and balances. It can also represent a practical formulation for the division of governmental labour.

---

[21] *Wik Peoples v Queensland* (1996) 187 CLR 1.

[22] *Australian Capital Television v Commonwealth* (1992) 177 CLR 106, *Nationwide News Pty Ltd v Wills* (1992) 177 CLR 1, *Lange v Australian Broadcasting Commission* (1997) 189 CLR 520.

[23] See, *eg*, the references of Sir Anthony Mason in 'The Importance of Judicial Review of Administrative Action as a Safeguard of Individual Rights' (1994) 1 *AJHR* 1, at 10.

[24] On this older meaning in the Australian context, see I Holloway, 'Sir Francis Forbes and the Earliest Australian Public Law Cases' (unpublished, 1998).

[25] (1867).

[26] W R Cornish and G de N Clark, *Law and Society in England 1750-1950* (1989), at 82.

[27] 'The Importance of Judicial Review of Administrative Action as a Safeguard of Individual Rights', *supra* n 23, at 10.

But juxtaposed against this statement of constitutional principle *cum* formula for task allocation, is the deeply-felt sense of duty held by most judges – which in fact long pre-dates both Dicey and the constitutional settlement – to do justice in individual cases. It is fashionable in some circles to attribute to the judiciary an ignorance of the concerns of the non-white, non-middle class world. Yet, however apt this may or may not be with respect to particular judges, there is within the judiciary as an entity an institutional sensitivity to individual injustice which is rooted in a common law tradition stretching back several centuries. It is this, more than anything, which gives rise to tension in the field of administrative law. On one hand, governments today are organised in such a way that the frequent exercise of discretion is not only a good thing, but a necessary thing. On the other, the common law courts hold a deep institutional suspicion of arbitrariness – and arbitrariness is but a small, subjectively-viewed, step from the exercise of broad discretion.

The theory of administrative law, of course, is that judges are not concerned with the justness of individual decisions. As Lord Brightman once put it, '[j]udicial review is concerned, not with the decision, but with the decision-making process'.[28] But to state it this way is to take a view of judicial office that is blinded from reality. Lord Denning once captured the reality (in characteristically colourful terms) when he said that 'the judgments of Her Majesty's judges are the judgements of the Queen herself'. Speaking of the coronation oath, in which the Sovereign vows that she will 'cause law and justice, in mercy, to be executed', he said that judges must accordingly, 'execute, not law alone, but "law and justice": and they must do so "in mercy"'.[29]

Now, Lord Denning may have been given to a rhetorical flourish which few judges today would feel comfortable emulating, but he encapsulated well the sense of social responsibility that many members of the judiciary feel attaches to their office. The point is that when an individual comes before a court and can show that he or she has suffered some sort of ill-treatment at the hands of another, there are few judges who will not feel some compulsion to try to provide some redress. As T R S Allan has reminded us, equity is as important an element of the common law system as formal legality.[30] The question, therefore, is where the political process should end and the legal process should begin. At what

---

[28] *Chief Constable of North Wales Police v Evans* [1982] 1 WLR 1155, at 1173.

[29] *Gems in Ermine* (1964), at 14.

[30] See *Law, Liberty and Justice* (1993), at 28-32.

stage ought the judges – with their built-in institutional *naïevité* and their democratic deficit – to feel justified in engaging in critical oversight of the development and implementation of value choices by the political branches of government.

This is, of course, the basic question of administrative law *realpolitik*. In principle, of course, judges should *never* feel comfortable in this task. At least no judge who subscribes to the theory of supremacy of parliament should feel comfortable in this task. Lord Greene, for example, was being faithful to a Diceyan view of the constitution when he said that '[t]he judiciary is not concerned with policy. It is not for the judiciary to decide what is in the public interest. These are the tasks of the legislature which is put there for the purpose.'[31] But the first lesson of administrative law must be that, the constitutional principle of supremacy of parliament is at best honoured in the breach. Given the modern style of legislative drafting, in which the tendency is to vest administrative decision-makers with broad discretion, administrative law would be a *niche* field – much like admiralty or ecclesiastical law, perhaps – if the courts really did acknowledge parliamentary commands as being statements of paramount law. That it is not – that, as the Law Institute of Victoria once put it, administrative law has been the Australian legal profession's 'sunrise industry'[32] – is proof positive of the fact that the courts are not always loyal to legislative text.

Natural justice cases provide us with a better vantage point than most with which to view the tensions at play in administrative law. That is because even though judgments in them are phrased, as in all administrative law cases, in terms of lawfulness and *vires* and lack of authority to dictate substantive outcome, the doctrine of natural justice is, as we have seen in the preceding chapters, concerned *by its very essence* with judicial perceptions of fairness, equity and substantive deservedness.

Natural justice is, in other words, concerned with exactly the same sorts of things of which Lord Denning spoke so romantically in his description of the judicial function. So the critical question is, where does politics end and law begin? At what point in the decisional spectrum do the courts assume a right to dictate procedural obligations to administrators?

---

[31] 'Law and Progress', 13th Haldane Memorial Lecture (1944), at 11.

[32] 'Seminar in Print, Administrative Law: The Profession's Sunrise Industry?' (1984) 58 *Law Inst J* 78.

Functional Identity, Diceyism and Judicial Review

As has been discussed, it seemed at one time that the dividing line between justiciable and non-justiciable cases could be drawn by reference to the functional identity of the actor. If the decision-maker in question was chosen by parliament to be a Minister, or a public servant, or a tribunal, then judicial review was available.[33] This was in keeping with the Diceyist views both that no person was above the law, and that the Queen in Parliament was supreme in stating the law.

Judicial review in these cases would be carried out under the guise of an (unstated) direction by parliament to the courts to police the bounds of jurisdiction, so as to ensure that no member of the executive usurped authority that had not been given to him. On this view, judicial review – and, consequently, the supervising judiciary – had a modest role in the constitutional scheme of things. Judicial review was not itself a free-standing principle of public law, but was rather a corollary of other free-standing principles: parliamentary supremacy and the separation of powers. The trigger for judicial intervention was the violation of one of these.[34]

On the other hand, if decision-making authority was vested in the Sovereign herself, or in the Governor-General or in the Cabinet, it was taken as an indication that the subject-matter of the decision-making process was not appropriate for review in non-political fora. If parliament had chosen to vest decision-making authority in the Sovereign or the Cabinet, this could be taken as a parliamentary signal that the decisions were truly 'political' and should be immune from judicial review. As John Willis succinctly put it, 'the form is the Minister, the substance is the

---

[33] See, eg, *Arthur Yates & Co Pty Ltd v Vegetable Seeds Committee* (1945) 72 CLR 37, *Television Corporation v The Commonwealth* (1963) 109 CLR 59 and *Murphyores Inc Pty Ltd v Commonwealth* (1976) 136 CLR 1. See also *Padfield v Minister for Agriculture, Food and Fisheries* [1968] AC 997, *Secretary of State for Education and Science v Tameside Metropolitan Borough Council* [1977] AC 1014, *R v Criminal Injuries Compensation Board, Ex parte Lain* [1967] 2 QB 864, *Congreve v Home Office* [1976] 1 QB 629, *Laker Airways v Department of Transport* [1977] 1 QB 643.

[34] In Australia, this of course has a formal constitutional dimension. See *Bank of New South Wales v Commonwealth* (1948) 76 CLR 1, at 363 (*per* Dixon J). See, also, *R v Coldham, Ex parte Australian Workers' Union* (1983) 153 CLR 415 and *O'Toole v Charles David Pty Ltd* (1991) 171 CLR 232.

civil service; the form is the Governor in Council, the substance is the cabinet.'[35]

Murphy J was making the same point when he said that '[w]hen parliament authorises the [Governor in Council] to make a decision it is because parliament considers the decision warrants a political determination'.[36] A Canadian judge once described it similarly: the vesting of decision-making authority in the Crown itself shows 'the judgment of parliament that this is an area inordinately sensitive to changing public policies and hence it has been reserved for the final application of such a policy by the executive branch of government'.[37]

At the same time, if the decision-making authority in issue derived not from legislation but from the royal prerogative then (Sir Edward Coke's views in the *Case of Proclamations* notwithstanding) the jurisdictional basis for judicial review was not thought to be secure. In part, this was because in the limited form in which it has existed since the constitutional settlement, the prerogative reeks of policy judgment, something which the courts have seldom felt comfortable openly to question. It was in this latter sense that Isaacs and Powers JJ said in *Duncan v Theodore* that it was not open to impute *mala fides* with respect to the issue of royal proclamations, which they described as 'the act of the King himself or his representatives'.[38] And it was in the same vein that the Privy Council once said that '[t]hose who are responsible for the national security must be the sole judges of what the national security requires'.[39]

But there always were limitations to this 'determination by identification' rule. It was clear, for instance, that it did not apply to insulate governmental action before it actually reached the Crown.[40] Similarly, it has been long-held that the courts have the right to review subordinate legislation for *vires*, notwithstanding that it had been made by

---

[35] 'Case Comment' (1951) 29 *Can Bar Rev* 296, at 301.

[36] *FAI Insurances Ltd v Winneke* (1982) 151 CLR 342, at 374. See also *Namatjira v Raabe* (1959) 100 CLR 664, at 669.

[37] *Attorney-General of Canada v Inuit Tapirisat of Canada* [1980] 2 SCR 735, at 756 (*per* Estey J).

[38] 23 CLR, at 525-526. See also *R v Arndel* (1906) 3 CLR 557, at 572 (*per* Griffiths CJ).

[39] *The Zamora* [1916] 2 AC 77, at 107.

[40] In *Brettingham-Moore v St Leonards Municipality* (1969) 121 CLR 509, the High Court held that in principle, a hearing could be compelled in the process of gathering information for the purpose of preparing a report for the Governor, which he would use as the basis of an exercise of discretion.

the Governor in Council.[41] Judicial review could also take place, the Privy Council once said, if bad faith could be shown on the part of the Crown in making a regulation.[42]

In *Attorney-General v De Keyser's Royal Hotel*, the House of Lords held that the courts could properly enquire whether a prerogative, in fact, existed.[43] In New Zealand, the courts have phrased the right of review of Crown action *very* broadly. Not only do they have the right to examine the correctness of any legal determination made by the Governor-General of New Zealand, but they can 'always inquire, in any case, whether the Governor-General (or the Minister as the case may be) could reasonably have formed any opinion, on law or on fact, which is set up as the foundation of [a] regulation'.[44] Likewise, the Ontario Court of Appeal once held that when the Governor in Council was exercising a statutory power, 'such a statutory power can be validly exercised only by complying with statutory provisions which are, by law, conditions precedent to the exercise of the power'.[45]

This sort of scepticism about mere identity as an insulating cloak was also apparent in cases like *Sankey v Whitlam*[46] and *Conway v Rimmer*.[47] As Gibbs CJ said in *Sankey v Whitlam*, '[i]t is in all cases the duty of the court, and not the privilege of the executive government to decide whether a document will be produced or may be withheld'.[48] But when the courts indicated a willingness to reserve their right to judge claims of secrecy

---

[41] See, *eg*, *Young v Tockassie* (1905) 2 CLR 470, *Bishop v MacFarlane* (1909) 9 CLR 370, *Commonwealth v Progress Advertising and Press Agency Co* (1910) 10 CLR 457, *Broadcasting Company of Australia v Commonwealth* (1935) 52 CLR 52 and *Shanahan v Scott* (1957) 96 CLR 245.

[42] *Attorney-General (Canada) v Hallett and Carey Ltd* [1952] AC 427, at 444.

[43] [1920] AC 508 (though their Lordships then said that if the prerogative were shown to exist, that would be the end of the matter).

[44] *Reade v Smith* [1959] NZLR 996, at 1000.

[45] *Border Cities Press Club v Attorney-General for Ontario* [1953] 1 DLR 404, at 412 (*per* Pickup CJO). See, also, *Re Davisville Investment Co Ltd and City of Toronto* (1977) 15 OR (2[d]) 553 (CA) and *Re Doctors Hospital and Minister of Health* (1976) 68 DLR (3[d]) 220 (Ont HC). See also *Padfield v Minister of Agriculture, Food and Fisheries* [1968] AC 997.

[46] (1978) 142 CLR 1.

[47] [1968] AC 910. Though see also the earlier case of *Robinson v South Australia (No 2)* [1931] AC 704, in which the Privy Council indicated a willingness to look behind a claim of public interest privilege.

[48] 142 CLR, at 38.

made by the Crown,[49] it was but a small step to an assertion of a more general right of review. For that matter, *Banks v Transport Regulation Board*[50] was itself a case in which the interests of the Governor came into play. It was only with some curial footwork that Barwick CJ was able to characterise the case as a reviewable one. There, the decision to revoke Banks's taxi licence had been affirmed by the Governor in Council. The Chief Justice's approach was to say that since the initial decision to revoke was void for being *ultra vires*, the affirmation by the Crown could have had no legal effect.[51]

In truth, though, the real change came in the 1980s, as the High Court was working its way through the legitimate expectation cases that were discussed in the last chapter, many of which involved decision-making at the highest levels of government.[52] In the legitimate expectation cases, the High Court came to the view that it did not matter who the decision-maker was in determining whether natural justice applied to the decision-making process. What mattered was that the decision-maker was acting to affect the 'rights, interests or legitimate expectations' of an individual, as an individual. If that was the case, then the courts would ordinarily impose an obligation to observe natural justice.

Ex necessitate, the Court found itself compelled to broaden the reach of natural justice to cover decision-making processes by governmental actors who hitherto had been presumptively immune from judicial review. But this, of course, immediately gave rise to a further question: on what the basis, in lieu of identity, were law and politics to be distinguished?

Natural Justice or Procedural Fairness?

In considering the developments of the late 1970s and 1980s, it is worthwhile to dwell for the moment on the more general observation that there has in recent years been a shift in not just the scope of natural justice,

---

[49] *Cf Duncan v Cammell, Laird & Co* [1942] AC 624. More generally on the question of Crown privilege, see Sir W Wade and C Forsyth, *Administrative Law* (7th ed. 1994), at 846-851.

[50] (1968) 119 CLR 222. For a discussion of this case, see chapter 4.

[51] See 119 CLR, at 240-242.

[52] *Eg*, *FAI Insurances v Winneke* (Victorian Governor in Council), *South Australia v O'Shea* (South Australian Governor in Council), *A-G (NSW) v Quin* (Attorney-General of New South Wales), *Kioa v West*, *Haoucher v Minister for Immigration*, *Teoh v Minister for Immigration and Ethnic Affairs* (Commonwealth Cabinet Minister).

but also in its focus. As will be seen, this has been an essential part of its expansion to encompass the Crown.

Before the 1960s, the concern of natural justice was almost exclusively with the protection of formal legal or proprietary rights. But since *Ridge v Baldwin* and *Banks*, the courts have steadily worked to extend natural justice to attach to a whole range of non-proprietary interests. In chapter four, these were referred to as the 'new property', but many of them were really quite different in kind from property rights as these are understood in the common law. This could not help but have had a significant effect on the way in which judges viewed natural justice cases.

Peter Cane once argued that the real effect of the recognition of expectations as a source of procedural obligations was that natural justice would come to be concerned more with human rights than with legal rights.[53] This is an intriguing point, and it will be returned to in Chapter Eight. For now, though, it is perhaps more accurate to say that before the 1960s, natural justice cases were in many respects akin to disputes over rights *in rem*. But with the 'new property' cases, and even more so with the legitimate expectation cases, the focal point of disputes over natural justice was increasingly no longer things tangible. Rather, the focus became the status of the individual affected by the governmental action. Natural justice cases became actions more fully *in personam*. It was this shift – from a concern about the deprivation of property to a concern about relative status of citizen *v* state – that had the consequence of acting as a liberating influence on the courts.

One of the ways in which this shift in focus became apparent was in an alteration in the terminology used by the courts to describe these cases. Instead of speaking about natural justice, with all of the accumulated historical nuances that that carried with it,[54] judges began to speak instead of 'procedural fairness', and of a simple 'duty to act fairly'. Thus far, I have been using the expressions natural justice and procedural fairness more-or-less interchangeably. But it is appropriate at this stage to look at them more closely, to see whether in fact they mean the same thing.

Re H K[55] is the case which is generally considered to have introduced the notion of simple administrative 'fairness' in this sense. The case dealt with the question of whether someone who was being refused entry into

[53] 'Natural Justice and Legitimate Expectations' (1980) 54 *ALJ* 546, at 547-548.
[54] See the Introduction.
[55] [1967] 2 QB 617.

the United Kingdom had any right to natural justice. Lord Parker CJ said that:

> even if an immigration officer is not [acting] in a judicial or quasi-judicial capacity, he must at any rate give the immigrant an opportunity of satisfying him of the matters in the [legislation] and for that purpose let the immigrant know what his immediate impression is so that the immigrant can disabuse him. That is not, as I see it, a question of acting or being required to act judicially, but of being required to act fairly.[56]

His Lordship then continued:

> Good administration and an honest *bona fide* decision, as it seems to me, require not merely impartiality, nor merely bringing one's mind to bear on the problem, but of acting fairly; and to the limited extent that the circumstances of any particular case allow, and within the legislative framework under which the administrator is working, only to that extent do the so-called rules of natural justice apply, which in a case such as this is merely a duty to act fairly.[57]

Two things strike one about Lord Parker's judgment in this case. First, he made specific reference to the link between fairness and the principles of good administration. This echoed the point that had been made by Hamilton LJ in the Court of Appeal in *Local Government Board v Arlidge*.[58] Secondly, Lord Parker was ambiguous in his use of the two expressions 'the so-called rules of natural justice' and 'being required to act fairly'. Taken grammatically, these passages seem to say that the two were synonyms, and that the right to disabuse the immigration officer was what natural justice required in the circumstances. This was the view later taken by Lord Morris in *Furnell v Whangerei Schools Board*, when he said that '[n]atural justice is but fairness writ large and juridically. It has been described as fair play in action.'[59]

Yet other judges seemed to feel that Lord Parker was suggesting something different; that natural justice was something which applied to a judicial or quasi-judicial actor, whereas procedural fairness was something

---

[56] [1967] 2 QB, at 630.

[57] *Ibid.*

[58] [1914] 1 KB 160, at 203-204.

[59] [1973] AC 660, at 679. See also *Bushell v Environment Secretary* [1981] AC 75, at 95 (*per* Lord Diplock).

which applied to everyone else.[60] In *Bates v Lord Hailsham*, for example, Megarry J said: 'in the sphere of the so-called quasi-judicial the rules of natural justice run, and ... in the administrative or executive field there is a general duty of fairness'.[61] Similarly, Lord Pearson once said that while the obligation to observe natural justice only applied to judicial or quasi-judicial tribunals, as regards entities entrusted with administrative or executive functions, 'Parliament is not to be presumed to act unfairly', and 'the courts may in suitable cases (perhaps always) imply an obligation to act with fairness'.[62]

In *Dunlop v Woollahra Municipal Council*,[63] Wooten J of the Supreme Court of New South Wales indicated agreement with Lord Pearson's view,[64] and said that natural justice should be preserved 'with its traditional content', as 'a concept applicable to a certain class of function – the traditional class containing virtually all judicial functions and many administrative functions to which it is appropriate'.[65] Other governmental functions, in contrast, should be 'treated as subject to an implied condition that [they] be fairly exercised'.[66] Laskin CJ, in the Supreme Court of Canada, once expressed much the same opinion.[67] Moreover, the oft-quoted statement of Lord Loreburn LC in *Board of Education v Rice* – that 'everybody who decides anything' has a duty to 'fairly listen to both sides'[68] – was thought to support such a position.

For a time, there was a flurry of academic writing on the supposed differences between natural justice and procedural fairness.[69] In an

---

[60] See P Craig, *Administrative Law* (3rd ed. 1994), at 289-292.

[61] [1972] 1 WLR 1373, at 1378 (though *cf* his seeming views to the contrary in *McInnes v Onslow-Fane* [1978] 1 WLR 1520).

[62] *Pearlberg v Varty* [1972] 1 WLR 534, at 547.

[63] [1975] 2 NSWLR 446.

[64] [1975] 2 NSWLR, at 472.

[65] [1975] 2 NSWLR, at 470-471.

[66] [1975] 2 NSWLR, at 471.

[67] *Nicholson v Haldimand-Norfolk Regional Board of Commissioners of Police* [1979] 1 SCR 311, at 324-328.

[68] [1911] AC 179, at 182. This case is discussed in depth in chapter 2.

[69] See, *eg*, J F Northey, 'Pedantic or Semantic' [1974] *NZLJ* 133, J F Northey, 'The Aftermath of the *Furnell* Decision' (1974) 6 *NZU L Rev* 59, D J Mullan, 'Fairness: The New Natural Justice' (1975) 25 *UTLJ* 281, G D S Taylor, 'Natural Justice – the Modern Synthesis' (1975) 1 *Mon U L Rev* 258, G D S Taylor, 'Fairness and Natural Justice' (1977) 3 *Mon U L Rev* 191, M Loughlin, 'Procedural Fairness: A Study of the Crisis in Administrative Law Theory' (1978) 28 *UTLJ* 215, D J Mullan, 'Natural Justice and Fairness – Substantive as well as Procedural Standards for the Review of Administrative Decision-Making?' (1982) 27 *McGill LJ* 250.

important piece which came towards the tail end of it, Margaret Allars argued that the idea of a simple duty of procedural fairness – which she saw in the High Court's judgment in *Kioa v West* – held the key to breathing real life back into the notion of procedural protection. She noted that in the United Kingdom, 'the fluidity of the fairness principle [had] provided an opportunity for judges to recognise that in some circumstances practices followed and obligations incurred by administrators have a normative effect with legal consequences'.[70]

Allars was quite correct to draw the link between the low-threshold idea of procedural fairness and the legitimate expectation cases. But the fluidity of which she wrote, and which was discussed in the last chapter, has been responsible as well for a general blurring of the demarcation between judicial (or quasi-judicial) and non-judicial decision-making that the distinction between natural justice and procedural fairness was thought to indicate.

In fact, what has happened in Australia is that procedural fairness and natural justice *have* become synonyms. In *Forbes v New South Wales Trotting Club Ltd*, for example, Murphy J drew on American terminology and said that '[n]atural justice and fairness are different ways of expressing the concept or facets of the concept of due process'.[71] In *Twist v Randwick Municipal Council*, Mason J also used the two as synonyms,[72] and in *Salemi v MacKellar (No 2),* Gibbs J denied that the two expressions represented different concepts. 'Some judgments', he said, 'suggest that the duty to act fairly arises from a principle separate from, although analogous to, the principles of natural justice, but I would prefer to regard the duty to act fairly as simply flowing from the duty to observe the principles of natural justice.'[73] The point is that with the trigger for the duty now being expressed so broadly – to include any infringement of an 'interest or legitimate expectation' – there is no longer a need for a separate duty to attach to non-judicial actors. This, of course, was a critical element in extending the reach of natural justice to include the Crown.[74]

[70] 'Fairness: Writ Large or Small?' (1987) 11 *Syd L Rev* 306, at 309.

[71] (1979) 143 CLR 242, at 276.

[72] (1976) 136 CLR 106, at 112.

[73] (1977) 137 CLR 396, at 418 (internal citations omitted). On Gibbs J's statements in this case, see Allars, 'Fairness: Writ Large or Small?', *supra* n 70, at 310.

[74] Though there were some who pressed for the distinction to be maintained. See, *eg*, J F Northey, *The Basis of Judicial Review in Administrative Law* (1981), at 7.

The New Respondents

In 1969, Peter Hogg published in the *Australian Law Journal* an influential article entitled 'Judicial Review of Action by the Crown Representative'.[75] In it, he argued that to cast Crown immunity broadly to cover decisions made by the Governor in Council was antithetical to the rule of law. He said that it was:

> inconsistent with that fundamental characteristic of our constitution which Dicey described as the second element of the rule of law. This is the notion that no official, however eminent, has any powers other than those conferred upon him by statute or the prerogative; and no official act, however formal, is valid unless it is authorised by statute or the prerogative.[76]

Hogg's argument eventually came to be cited with approval by Sir Harry Gibbs,[77] but the first of what one might perhaps call the 'new respondent' cases which applied Hogg's reasoning (though without citation) was actually a Canadian one (which also came later to be relied on by the High Court). This was the 1980 decision of the Supreme Court of Canada, in *Attorney-General (Canada) v Inuit Tapirisat of Canada*.[78] The case involved the question of whether natural justice applied to the process of setting long-distance telephone rates. The Inuit Tapirisat was a group which represented certain aboriginal Canadians. It claimed that it had been denied natural justice when the Governor-General of Canada in Council denied its request for a hearing to argue that a telephone rate increase was not warranted.

Inuit Tapirisat dealt only with the exercise of statutory power by the Crown, but on that point, the Canadian judges had no doubt that Dicey's prescription about legal equality between the citizen and the government was applicable: '[T]he essence of the principle of law here operating', said Estey J for the majority, 'is simply that in the exercise of a statutory power the Governor in Council, like any other person or group of persons, must keep within the law as laid down by parliament or the legislature. Failure to do so will call into action the supervising function of the superior court ....'[79]

---

[75] 43 *ALJ* 215.

[76] *Id*, at 220.

[77] *R v Toohey, Ex parte Northern Land Council* (1981) 151 CLR 170, at 192.

[78] [1980] 2 SCR 735.

[79] [1980] 2 SCR, at 752.

This same question was visited in Australia a year later in *R v Toohey, Ex parte Northern Land Council*.[80] Though not a natural justice case, *R v Toohey* laid the jurisdictional groundwork for *FAI Insurances v Winneke*, and thus occupies an important place in the natural justice story. *R v Toohey* involved the *Aboriginal Land Rights (Northern Territory) Act 1975* (Cth), which gave the Minister for Aboriginal Affairs the power to establish land trusts, and to recommend to the Governor-General that Crown lands should be conveyed to these trusts to be held for the benefit of Aboriginal groups which could establish traditional ownership rights over the lands.[81] Recognising the potential complexity of such issues, the scheme provided for by the Act was that a Land Commissioner was first to investigate claims made by Aboriginal groups, and then to file a report with the Minister for Aboriginal Affairs in which he was to outline his findings of fact, and to indicate whether or not he recommended that a land grant be made.[82]

The starting point for *R v Toohey* was a claim made under the *Aboriginal Land Rights Act* for a large tract of wasteland on the Cox Peninsula, in the Northern Territory. The Cox Peninsula is separated from the city of Darwin by only about three and a half miles by sea but, as Gibbs CJ noted in his judgment, by road the peninsula was really quite remote.[83] Nevertheless, after it was learned that a land claim was to be made, Town Planning Regulations were made by the Northern Territory Government which effectively annexed to Darwin parcels of land in and around the Cox Peninsula. This, of course, would have made the land no longer 'unalienated' and, hence, non-grantable to Aborigines. The annexed tracts amounted to approximately 1,680 square miles.[84] This was extraordinary (and clearly suspicious) since Darwin's population was only 50,000, and its pre-annexure size was 55 square miles.[85] By the annexation, Darwin's size would have increased by approximately three thousand per cent! The clear inference drawn from the circumstances, of course, was that the Northern Territory Government was simply attempting to forestall the vesting of title to any land near Darwin in Aboriginal hands.[86]

---

[80] (1981) 151 CLR 170.

[81] Sub-s 11(1).

[82] Para 50(1)(a).

[83] See 151 CLR, at 175.

[84] 4,350 square kilometres.

[85] 142 square kilometres.

[86] When reading this case, it is interesting to look at the *Darwin Regional Land Use Structure Plan 1990*, drawn up when the litigation over the land claim on the Cox

The litigation in the High Court actually involved a *mandamus* application – to compel the Honourable John Toohey, later Toohey J of the High Court, but then a judge of the Federal Court and the Northern Land Commissioner, to issue a discovery order against the Northern Territory government. Toohey J thought that he did not have the right to compel discovery, in light of the fact that the decision in question – the decision to make the annexing regulation – was one of the Territorial Administrator (who, for the purposes of the litigation, was assumed to be 'the Crown'[87]). The precise legal issue to be decided by the High Court was set out by Stephen J: 'does it make any difference in law that the relevant power was one exercised not by a Minister of the Crown but by the representative of the Crown on the advice of his Ministers?'[88] In a word, the Court held that it did not.

In the view of Gibbs CJ, the case was one involving power conferred by statute, not one of Crown authority generally. In light of this, he concluded in much the same terms as had Estey J in *Inuit Tapirisat* and Hogg in his article: 'It seems fundamental to the rule of law that the Crown has no more power than any subordinate official to enlarge by its own act the scope of a power that has been conferred on it by the Parliament ...'[89] In his approach, the question was one of the *vires* of the regulations: '[I]f the Crown in Council makes a regulation which appears on its face to be made for a purpose that was not authorised by the statute under which it purports to be made, the regulation will be invalid.'[90]

Mason J took a somewhat broader view. Unlike the Chief Justice, he did not restrict his comments to the exercise of discretion under statute, though he noted that it is generally much easier to review statutory

---

Peninsula was still on-going. The Plan suggests that the reason that the Cox Peninsula needed to be annexed to Darwin was to cope with land demands when the population of Darwin reached one million (p 40), an extraordinary thing when one considers that at the time, the population was less than 75,000. As to the urgency of defeating the aboriginal land claim, the Plan said:

> If granted, the effect of the claim would be transform this large publicly owned land asset into private (Aboriginal Freehold) land, the availability of which for urban use would be doubtful at best, as the unique title established by Commonwealth law denies even the Territory Government any powers of acquisition (*Ibid*).

[87] On this, see also *Namatjira v Raabe* (1959) 100 CLR 664, at 669 (discussed in chapter 3), where the High Court described the Administrator as 'the head of the government' of the Northern Territory.

[88] 151 CLR, at 204.

[89] 151 CLR, at 187.

[90] 151 CLR, at 192.

discretions than discretions exercised under the prerogative.[91] But after reviewing the authorities, he concluded that the old rule, stated in terms like those used by Blackstone, or by Isaacs and Powers JJ in *Duncan v Theodore*, could no longer be sustained: '[I]t is at least arguable', he said, 'whether [Crown immunity] should now apply to acts affecting the rights of the citizen which, though undertaken in the name of the Sovereign, are in reality decisions of the executive government.'[92]

Instead of a blanket immunity determined by reference to the identity of the decision-maker, Mason J proposed that the test for reviewability should be one based on judicial competence to undertake the review. Though offered in *obiter*, this was in many ways the most significant part of the judgment. He explicitly acknowledged the concerns about the appropriateness of curial second-guessing of policy-based governmental action, but he said that '[t]he purpose of preventing unnecessary judicial interference is better achieved, and achieved with greater fairness to the citizen, by denying review in those cases in which the particular exercise of power is not susceptible of the review sought'.[93]

Mason J acknowledged that a power being 'not susceptible of review' was more often likely to be the case if it was based on the prerogative than on statute. That was for a variety of reasons. Statutory discretion, he said,

> very often affects the right of citizens; there may be a duty to exercise the discretion in one way or another; the discretion may be precisely limited in scope; it may be conferred for a specific or ascertainable purpose; and it will be exercisable by reference to criteria or considerations express or implied.[94]

'The prerogative powers', he continued, 'lack some or all of these characteristics. Moreover, they are in some instances by reason of their very nature not susceptible of judicial review.'[95]

In another part of his judgment, Mason J said that the sorts of cases in which the courts had refused to review the exercise of the prerogative were ones in which 'the prerogative power in question was not, owing to its nature and subject matter, open to challenge for the reason put forward'.[96] Presumably what his Honour was referring to in these passages were cases

[91] 151 CLR, at 219.
[92] 151 CLR, at 220.
[93] 151 CLR, at 222.
[94] 151 CLR, at 219.
[95] *Ibid*.
[96] 151 CLR, at 220.

involving what were referred to earlier as 'affairs of state' – cases involving the exercise of pure political judgement or the formulation of governmental policy. In this respect, most people would have an intuitive sense of the sorts of instances which Mason J had in mind. Speaking extrajudicially, he once said:

> although [decisions] are no longer immune from review simply because they are decisions made in the exercise of prerogative power, their nature may be such that they are not susceptible of review. Decisions affecting national security, foreign affairs, to prosecute or not to prosecute and the grant of pardons to convicted people come to mind.[97]

Indeed, it is difficult to imagine, for instance, a court reviewing Prime Minister Menzies' declaration in September 1939 that Australia was at war with Germany, even though the fact that he did not seek the prior approval of the Australian parliament has since given rise to some controversy about the constitutional appropriateness of Menzies' action.[98] Likewise, it is difficult to imagine a court ever reviewing a decision, say, to award or not to award the Order of Australia. But having said this, the fact is that apart from the 'obvious' cases, the Mason test is really quite difficult to articulate. How *does* one determine whether an exercise of a power is 'susceptible of judicial review'? To refer to Mason J's list of factors which tend to make it easier to review statutory discretion than prerogative discretion, it is often the case – regardless of the source of the power – that an exercise of governmental discretion will affect the rights of citizens. And if we use the new trigger for natural justice, the exercise of discretion will *almost always* affect someone's 'interests and legitimate expectations'. Furthermore, it is seldom, if ever, that a discretion is completely untrammelled or its exercise unconnected with criteria or 'considerations express or implied'.[99]

Moreover, one frankly wonders just how obvious the 'obvious' cases will always be. In both England and New Zealand, for example, the courts

---

[97] 'The Importance of Judicial Review of Administrative Action as a Safeguard of Individual Rights', *supra* n 23, at 8. See also *Barton v R* (1980) 147 CLR 75 (holding that the decision of the Attorney-General to exercise the prerogative power to lay an indictment was not reviewable).

[98] Mason J actually spoke to this example. He said that 'the refusal of the courts to review the exercise of the royal prerogatives relating to war and the armed services is based on the view that they are not, by reason of their character and their subject matter, susceptible of judicial review' (151 CLR, at 219-220). See also *Chandler v DPP* [1962] 3 All ER 142.

[99] See, *eg*, the comments of Kitto J, *infra* at 237.

have reviewed refusals to grant pardons.[100] And in *Coutts v The Commonwealth*, Mason ACJ and Deane J would have applied the rules of natural justice to a decision by the Governor-General to dismiss an officer from the RAAF on the basis of medical unfitness. In Mason ACJ's view, there were on the facts sufficient decisional criteria to make the decision justiciable.[101] Similarly, in *Heddon v Evans,* McCardie J suggested that it was open to the courts to allow an action for malicious abuse of military authority.[102]

More dramatically, in *Operation Dismantle v The Queen*, the Supreme Court of Canada indicated that it was even willing to review a decision by the Canadian Cabinet to permit the United States to carry out tests of cruise missiles in the Canadian north.[103] In response to an assertion by the Government of Canada that such a decision was not (to use Mason J's language) by reason of its character and subject matter susceptible of judicial review, Wilson J, speaking for the entire Court on this point, said that she was not moved by an argument that certain issues 'involve moral and political considerations which it is not within the province of courts to assess'.[104] She said that 'however unsuited courts may be for the task, they are called upon all the time to decide questions of principle and policy'.[105]

Now, in *Operation Dismantle* the Supreme Court was in fact dealing with a constitutional issue, which to an extent placed it in a different position from a court sitting in administrative judicial review in Australia. But the fact remains that the Canadian judges did feel that the issue before them was 'susceptible of review'. The courts may in the end choose to defer to the political judgement of the government (as, indeed, the Supreme Court of Canada did). But as to the basic question, a case like *Operation Dismantle* shows that there can be no automatic immunity from review, no matter what the issue.[106] That is because, as Mason J phrased the test, the question is one

---

[100] *R v Home Secretary, Ex parte Bentley* ('the *Bentley Case*') [1994] QB 349 and *Burt v Governor-General* [1992] 3 NZLR 672.

[101] (1985) 157 CLR 91. The majority reached the opposite conclusion, and Mason ACJ said that in his view, natural justice would not be applicable in the case of a decision to dismiss taken solely on a discretionary basis. For a critical commentary on the case, see A O'Neil, 'Case Comment' (1986) 10 *Fed L Rev* 212.

[102] (1919) 35 TLR 642.

[103] [1985] 1 SCR 441. As an aside, the reason that the Canadian north was an attractive testing-ground was that it resembled the terrain of the northern Soviet Union, over which the missiles would have to travel in the event of hostilities.

[104] [1985] 1 SCR, at 465.

[105] [1985] 1 SCR, at 465-466.

[106] See, also, Allars, *supra* n 73, at 322.

of judicial competence to undertake the review, which can only be determined by the judges themselves.

Natural Justice and the Crown

The next step – the imposition of an actual duty to observe natural justice on the Crown and its advisors – was accomplished by a series of cases decided between 1982 and 1986. The first of the series was *FAI Insurances Ltd v Winneke*,[107] which was discussed at length in the last chapter. As will be remembered, the case involved an application by FAI Insurances Ltd for a renewal of its licence to provide workers' compensation insurance in Victoria. The application was turned down by the Victorian Governor in Council, and the High Court held that in the circumstances, the State had an obligation to provide FAI with a summary of the points on which the refusal was based, and an opportunity to respond to them.

The point, though, that the decision not to renew was made not by a bureaucrat, but by the Governor in Council raised the complicating questions of whether the decision was unreviewable *per se* and, if not, exactly how natural justice could be applied to the proceedings of the Executive Council. In fact, the evidence in the case was that it was a practice of long-standing in Victoria (and other Australian jurisdictions) to assign responsibility for ordinary administrative decisions to the Governor in Council. Moreover, there was old colonial-era precedent to the effect that when he was exercising statutory authority, as he was in this case, the Governor was obliged to grant hearings.[108] But the High Court was not content to let the matter rest on localised nineteenth century jurisprudence. Instead, it preferred to offer a modern basis for its conclusion. As Sir Anthony has said, '[t]he decision broke new ground in that the Court decided for the first time that the fact that a statutory power is vested in the Governor in Council does not mean that it is beyond review'.[109]

Murphy J – who was the only former cabinet member among the Court, it is interesting to note – dissented. In *R v Toohey*, Murphy J had

[107] (1982) 151 CLR 342.

[108] See *Roebuck v Borough of Geelong West* (1876) 2 VLR(L) 189, *Shire of Kowree v Shire of Lowan* (1897) 19 ALT 153. See also *Smith v R* (1878) 3 App Cas 614 (PC, Qld).

[109] The Importance of Judicial Review of Administrative Action as a Safeguard of Individual Rights', *supra* n 23, at 8.

found himself in an awkward position. On one hand, his plain instinct was to defer to the executive – a view he made plain in his administrative law judgments.[110] But on the other, his anti-monarchical prejudices led him to shy away from expressing his views as to justiciability in terms of the immunity of the Crown. His solution in *R v Toohey* was to say that it was simply not open for the courts to question the purpose for which legislative power was being used.[111] In *FAI Insurances*, he reiterated this position. In his view, judicial review should not have been available in the circumstances, for what was at issue was a political decision. There was no jurisprudential basis for review in this case except *R v Toohey*, whose premises he continued to reject. But this, he said, did not mean that natural justice or a duty of fairness did not attach to the decision-making process. It did. But in the context fairness involved 'political standards enforceable by the political process'.[112]

Gibbs CJ, in contrast, based his judgment on the presumption that natural justice would obviously normally apply to a licensing case, and that there was no evidence of a parliamentary intention to exclude it: 'It would not be right to impute to the legislature an intention to confer an arbitrary or unfettered power to refuse to renew an approval, having regard to the consequences that such a refusal might entail.'[113] In other words, the Chief Justice began by taking an effects-based approach to the issue. Only then did he consider the matter of the decision-maker's identity. In this regard, he noted that the Governor here was neither acting personally nor exercising the royal prerogative. Rather, he was acting on ministerial advice. In the circumstances, therefore, '[i]t would be to confuse form with substance to hold that the rules of natural justice are excluded simply because the power is technically confided in the Governor in Council'.[114]

Of the other judges, Stephen J was closest in approach to Gibbs CJ. His judgment is especially useful in that he reviewed the history of executive decision-making arrangements in Victoria.[115] He made the point that in colonial Australia, when legislative drafting habits were being formed, Governors really did govern.[116] The legislative convention which

[110] See *infra*.
[111] 151 CLR, at 228-231.
[112] 151 CLR, at 374.
[113] 151 CLR, at 349.
[114] *Ibid*.
[115] 151 CLR, at 353-355.
[116] See 151 CLR, at 353, where Stephen J discussed the historical reasons for this. He quoted Geoffrey Sawer as saying that in colonial Australia, the Executive Councils

had grown up here was one of vesting formal decision-making power in the Crown. In the United Kingdom, the actual day-to-day involvement of the Sovereign in the business of government had been steadily decreasing since the rise of cabinet government in the late eighteenth century. So when the British administrative state came to appear, the idea of a departmental minister, in theory responsible to parliament, was implanted in the consciousness of the legislative draftsman. In Australia, the history was different. The legislative pattern here was to devolve administrative decision-making power to the Crown. But drafting conventions aside, in the modern era in both countries the *real* decision-maker was the responsible minister. So, like the Chief Justice, Stephen J based his opinion on the importance of not mistaking form for substance.

Mason J's conclusion proceeded from the same premises as the Chief Justice's and Stephen J's, *viz*, that the effective decision-maker here was not Sir Henry Winneke, the Governor, but rather J H Ramsey MLA, the Minister for Labour and Industry. But, as had been the case in *R v Toohey*, it was Mason J who took the broadest sweep in his statement of the law. In his view, 'the fundamental issue' was whether the Governor in Council could as a matter of legal principle be bound to observe the rules of natural justice.[117]

Mason J noted that the Victorian legislature had not directed its mind to the question. Possibly, he said, this was 'because it thought that [natural justice] had no application to the Governor in Council'.[118] One would have thought that this ought to have ended the matter, but in Mason J's view, it did not. On the contrary, the legislature's silence left the question still open. This was, it will be remembered, much the same view he was later to take in *Annetts v McCann*, the case involving the question of whether natural justice applied under the Western Australian *Coroners Act 1920*.[119]

In *FAI Insurances v Winneke*, as in *Annetts v McCann*, Mason J's answer to the fundamental issue was in the affirmative. The statute in question, the Victorian *Workers' Compensation Act*, purported to confer a completely unfettered discretion upon the Governor to decide whether or

'resembled the Tudor rather than the Victorian Privy Council' ('Councils, Ministers and Cabinets in Australia' [1956] *Pub Law* 110, at 111). The different practice in England and other of the self-governing colonies was described in C K Allen, *Law and Orders* (1945), at 45, and A B Keith, *The King and the Imperial Crown* (1936), at 60-61.

[117] 151 CLR, at 359.

[118] 151 CLR, at 362.

[119] See chapter 5.

not licences should be issued. Mason J noted that cases in the past had regarded this as an indication that natural justice was not to apply.[120] But, he said, there was a convention that in exercising his discretion, the Governor was obliged to follow advice. This was, indeed, only a convention and not a principle of judicially-enforceable law, but it was enough in Mason J's opinion to give the Minister a close enough link with the Governor's action to make natural justice applicable to the decision-making process as a whole:

> [T]he nature of the relationship between the Governor and the Executive Council supplies no reason for denying the availability of judicial review for *ultra vires* ... once as a matter of construction of a statute the conclusion is reached that the discretion given to the Governor in Council is limited, whether in scope or purpose or by reference to criteria or otherwise.[121]

'Once the true relationship between the Governor and the Executive Council is understood', he continued,

> it becomes apparent that the doctrines of ministerial and collective responsibility provide no objection to the application of the rules of natural justice to the exercise of a discretion by the Governor in Council. As the Governor ultimately acts in accordance with advice tendered to him, the final decision is not a decision for which he has to account. The effective decision is that of the Executive Council and the Ministers who are responsible for that decision to the parliament and to the electorate.[122]

So this was the holding on the threshold issue. Natural justice could in principle apply to the exercise of discretion by the Crown, according to the very same principles by which it applied to the exercise of discretion by Ministers. What that meant as a practical matter was that the obligation to accord natural justice would ordinarily apply to the formulation of the recommendation which was to be put to the Governor in Council.[123] The question that then remained to be answered according to the specific circumstances of the case was whether there was anything

---

[120] He referred, *inter alia*, to *Salemi v MacKellar (No 2)* (1977) 137 CLR 396, at 420, *R v MacKellar, Ex parte Ratu* (1977) 137 CLR 461, *Testro Brothers Ltd v Tait* (1963) 109 CLR 222, and *Franklin v Minister of Town and Country Planning* [1945] AC 87.

[121] 151 CLR, at 365.

[122] 151 CLR, at 365-366.

[123] It was on this basis that Aickin J gave his judgment. See 151 CLR, at 383. For Wilson J's views on the point, see 151 CLR, at 396, 398-399.

which would have indicated that the obligation to observe natural justice should be excluded.

Taking the approach that he had urged in *R v Toohey*, Mason J asked whether decisions made by the Governor in Council were 'intrinsically unsuited' for justiciability. He acknowledged that given the nature of the method by which Governor and Executive Council carried out their proceedings, it was 'less, perhaps much less, likely' that parliament intended that natural justice generally apply.[124] Indeed, as noted, he had earlier suggested that parliament had probably thought that it *would not* apply. But, as he was to restate in *Annetts v McCann*, parliament's intention or lack thereof was not determinative. Given the nature of the particular decision in issue – including its possible ramifications – it was possible in the circumstances, notwithstanding his assessment of parliament's likely *actual* beliefs, to impute to the legislature an intention that the Governor in Council would act in conformity with the principles of natural justice, by giving the applicant an adequate opportunity to present its case before a decision was made not to renew the workers' compensation insurance licence.[125] As to the actual logistics of the duty, he thought that the obligation to receive whatever submissions were made by FAI could have been delegated to a departmental employee.

Tellingly, Mason J said that his conclusion:

> offers some protection to the citizen against the legislative practice of conferring statutory discretions on a Governor in Council instead of the Minister or a statutory officer in the hope of thereby avoiding judicial review, particularly for want of compliance with the rules of natural justice, in circumstances where the legislature does not directly dispense with the duty to accord natural justice.[126]

One would be hard-pressed to imagine a statement that sounds more like an enunciation of a principle of constitutionalism than this. Yet, notwithstanding the general looseness of their language (particularly that of Mason J), the majority judgments in *FAI Insurances v Winneke* reveal a very precise technical problem which stood in the way of a complete opening up of the field. That was that the ordinary public law prerogative remedies do not lie against the Crown. Ordinarily, the writ of certiorari is

---

[124] 151 CLR, at 369.
[125] 151 CLR, at 370.
[126] 151 CLR, at 372.

available to quash a decision that is made contrary to the requirements of natural justice.[127] But by definition, writs of certiorari and mandamus could not be issued against the Sovereign[128] and, as Gibbs CJ said, 'in the absence of express statutory provision, there is no power to make a declaration against the Governor in Council'.[129] The solution in the circumstances was to issue a declaration against the Attorney-General, who could be expected to advise the Governor to act accordingly. Maitland was clearly correct when he suggested that the old thinking about the law of actions could continue to dog us from the grave![130]

But technical finesse aside, the remedial point highlights a deeper concern with principle. Gibbs CJ said that an express statutory authorisation would be necessary before a declaration could be made against the Crown. It is interesting to juxtapose this against Mason J's inquiry as to whether there was evidence of a parliamentary intention to exclude natural justice – for otherwise it would apply. To cast back to his judgment in *R v Toohey*, one wonders why it was not possible to read a lack of direct legal remedy as an indication of non-justiciability. If there is no power to compel the party in question to do anything, could that not be evidence that the actor is inherently unsuited for judicial review?

This question is made even more intriguing when one remembers that in 1978, the Victorian state parliament passed the *Administrative Law Act*. Its stated intention was to clarify the law respecting the prerogative writs. At second reading, the Attorney-General was quite specific in saying that the legislation did not intend to extend the scope of judicial review beyond what existed at the time.[131] Given the pre-existing state of the law, could this not be taken as a tacit indication of legislative wishes that it did not wish the law (on this point, at least) not to be altered?

The position at the Commonwealth level is even more stark. The *Administrative Decisions (Judicial Review) Act 1977* specifically *excludes* decisions of the Governor-General from its coverage. Moreover, the evidence is clear that the legislative view was that it was not desirable to

---

[127] *Stollery v Greyhound Racing Control Board* (1972) 128 CLR 509. See also *Council of Civil Service Unions v Minister for the Civil Service* ('the *GCHQ Case*') [1985] AC 374.
[128] *Chabot v Lord Morpeth* (1844) 15 QB 446. See also Aronson and Dyer, *Judicial Review of Administrative Action* (1996), at 732-733 (on certiorari), 770 (on mandamus).
[129] 151 CLR, at 351.
[130] The famous statement, of course, was: 'The forms of action we have buried, but they still rule us from their graves' (*The Forms of Action at Common Law* (1909), at 2).
[131] Victoria, *Parliamentary Debates*, Legislative Council, 25 October 1978, at 5092 (the Hon H Storey).

have decisions of the Governor-General subject to judicial review.[132] Taking Mason J's point, one wonders why both Acts, but the Commonwealth one in particular, could not be said to provide evidence of legislative signals that decisions of the Crown were not to be reviewable. Now that reference to *Hansard* may freely be made in the process of interpretation,[133] one wonders whether the signals ought not to be seen as even stronger.

Natural Justice and the Exercise of Prerogative Power

The first definite step in extending natural justice obligations to cover the exercise of prerogative, rather than statutory, power was in the House of Lords' decision three years after *FAI*, in the *GCHQ Case*.[134] Significantly, in *GCHQ*, the House of Lords adopted the very same approach to the question of reviewability of Crown decisions as was taken by the High Court in *FAI*.

GCHQ involved a decision by the Minister for the Civil Service (who happened also to be the Prime Minister, Mrs Thatcher) to forbid employees at the British government's secret communication facilities (the Government Communications Headquarters – 'GCHQ') from belonging to trade unions. Between 1979 and 1981, there had been a series of smallish-scale industrial disruptions at the facilities. Most of these had not been to protest working conditions within the GCHQ, but were carried out at the behest of the trade union movement, in demonstration against the Thatcher government's moves to reform industrial relations law.

---

[132] See H Whitmore, 'Administrative Law in the Commonwealth: Some Proposals for Reform' (1972) 5 *Fed L Rev* 7, at 14. Whitmore, who was a member of the Kerr Committee, wrote:

> [The Committee] recognised that technical difficulties prevent effective review of decisions by the Governor-General. It considered that the present law could operate as a 'safety valve' for the Government, and foresaw that Members of Parliament would carefully scrutinise powers conferred on the Governor-General knowing that they would be placed substantially outside the system of review.

See also P Bayne, 'The Court, the Parliament and the Government – Reflections on the Scope of Judicial Review' (1991) 20 *Fed L Rev* 1, at 4.

[133] *Acts Interpretation Act 1901* (Cth), s 15AB, *Interpretation of Legislation Act 1984* (Vic), s 35.

[134] *Council of Civil Service Unions v Minister for the Civil Service* [1985] AC 374.

It became a matter of record in the proceedings that some of the trade union literature expressed particular satisfaction at the success in causing disruption to Britain's defence preparedness through the industrial action taken at GCHQ.[135] The government attempted to obtain a 'no-strike' promise from the union representing GCHQ employees. When it was not forthcoming, the Minister issued her instruction forbidding union membership. While, being Crown servants, the GCHQ employees did not have a contract of employment, the evidence was that prior to this instruction, the government had always negotiated with their union before introducing changes to employment conditions. Accordingly, after the 'no union membership' instruction, the union commenced action, claiming that the Minister had denied it natural justice by not consulting with it prior to issuing her instruction. The union's argument was that in the circumstances, it had a legitimate expectation of prior consultation.

The Minister's decision to forbid union membership was made pursuant to an Order in Council, which gave her the authority to make regulations for 'controlling the conduct of the service'.[136] The Order in Council had itself been issued not pursuant to any statutory authority, but rather by virtue of the royal prerogative, exercised on advice. This led the Crown to argue that the instruction, as a delegated decision made under the prerogative, was unreviewable *per se*.

In the end, all of their Lordships found that in light of the fact that national security was involved, the obligation to observe natural justice was displaced. Lord Roskill stated the rationale in language much like that used by Mason J in *FAI Insurances v Winneke*, when he said that things like 'the making of treaties, the defence of the realm, the prerogative of mercy, the grant of honours, the dissolution of parliament and the appointment of ministers as well as others are not, I think, susceptible to judicial review because their nature and subject matter are such as not to be amenable to the judicial process'.[137] But – also like the High Court in *FAI* – all of the speeches in *GCHQ* indicated a feeling that since natural justice would ordinarily apply in circumstances of this nature, there was no reason that it ought not to apply as a matter of

---

[135] See the speech of Lord Fraser of Tullybelton [1985] AC, at 395.

[136] Art 4(a)(ii).

[137] [1985] AC, at 418. It is interesting to note that while counsel for both parties referred to Australian authority in argument, none was cited in judgment by their Lordships. See [1985] AC, at 355 (L Blom-Cooper QC for the unions) and [1985] AC, at 385 (R Alexander QC for Mrs Thatcher).

principle, even though the source of the Minister's power was the royal prerogative.

Lord Scarman said that he thought it could be 'said with confidence' that if the subject matter of the dispute was justiciable, then it should not matter that the governmental power in question was rooted in the prerogative, rather than legislation.[138] The old limitation was gone, he said, 'overwhelmed by the developing modern law of judicial review'.[139] Similarly, Lord Roskill said that he could not see 'any logical reason' why the source of the governmental power should matter if the effect of the exercise of the power was to harm rights or legitimate expectations.[140] Only Lord Fraser expressed some doubt on this point, because 'to permit such review would run counter to the great weight of authority'.[141] But even he acknowledged that he could see no reason of logic why prerogative power should be treated differently from statutory power for judicial review purposes.[142]

Most sweeping of all, though, was Lord Diplock's pronouncement that he thought that any discussion of the legal nature of the prerogative was 'of little practical assistance'.[143] His view was instead firmly rooted in contemporary pragmatism.[144] Lord Diplock said that he saw 'no reason why simply because a decision-making power is derived from the common law [which is how he described the source of the prerogative] and not a statutory source, it shall *for that reason only* be immune from judicial review'.[145]

---

[138] [1985] AC, at 407.

[139] *Ibid.*

[140] [1985] AC, at 417.

[141] [1985] AC, at 348.

[142] *Ibid.*

[143] [1985] AC, at 409.

[144] He was not, though, as sweeping as had been Lord Denning. In *Laker Airways v Department of Trade* [1977] 2 WLR 234, at 250, Lord Denning had said that the exercise of a power under the prerogative 'can be examined by the courts just as any other discretionary power which is vested in the executive'. In *GCHQ*, Lord Roskill said that stated this way, the principle was 'far too wide' ([1985] AC, at 416). But *cf* D G T Williams, 'The Prerogative and Preventative Justice' (1977) 36 *Camb L J* 201.

[145] [1985] AC, at 410 (original emphasis). Lord Diplock continued with his now-famous summary of the bases for judicial review:

> Judicial review has I think developed to a stage today when without reiterating any analysis of the steps by which the development has come about, one can conveniently classify under three heads the grounds upon which administrative action is subject to control by judicial review [his Lordship then set out his description of the three heads of review as being 'illegality', 'irrationality' and 'procedural impropriety'].

This approach was followed by the Full Court of the Federal Court in *Minister for Arts, Heritage and Environment v Peko-Wallsend Ltd.*[146] This was one of a series of Peko-Wallsend cases, involving mining rights in the Northern Territory.[147] In this instance, Peko-Wallsend and other mining interests were concerned at a government decision to include part of the Kakadu National Park on the World Heritage List. The mining interests had licences to explore and mine on the lands in question, but the listing of the property would have had the effect of rendering mining operations unlawful.

The legal question which arose in this case was whether the Commonwealth Cabinet was obliged to provide a hearing of some sort to Peko-Wallsend before making the listing. The Full Court concluded that the decision to seek listing was not justiciable,[148] but Wilcox and Sheppard JJ both found that there was no reason of principle why natural justice could not attach to the exercise prerogative power, including cabinet proceedings.[149] Only Bowen CJ – who was a former member of the Commonwealth Cabinet – took a different view. He said that '[t]he prospect of Cabinet itself, even by delegation, having to accord a hearing to individuals who may be adversely affected by its decisions, is a daunting one. It could bring the proceedings of Cabinet to a grinding halt.'[150]

The High Court picked up on the question of natural justice attaching to cabinet proceedings in *South Australia v O'Shea.*[151] This was the case, also discussed in the last chapter, involving the decision by the South Australian Cabinet to deny the convicted paedophile O'Shea release from an indefinite term of preventative detention. In the end, the Court held that O'Shea had not been denied natural justice, on the basis that he did not have any legitimate expectation which was deserving of protection. But Mason CJ and Deane J made it clear that in their opinion, the fact that the decision to not release had been made by the Cabinet would not

---

[146] (1987) 15 FCR 274.

[147] See also *Minister for Aboriginal Affairs v Peko-Wallsend* (1986) 162 CLR 24. The history of the litigation was summarised in the judgment of Wilcox J in the Federal Court, 15 FCR, at 274.

[148] See 15 FCR, at 279 (Bowen CJ), 280 (Sheppard J), 308 (Wilcox J).

[149] 15 FCR, at 281 (Sheppard J), 304-308 (Wilcox J). An interesting discussion of this case, written by a fellow Justice of the Federal Court, is in the Hon R S French, 'The Rise and Rise of Judicial Review' (1993) 23 *UWA L Rev* 120, at 135-137.

[150] 15 FCR, at 279.

[151] (1987) 163 CLR 378.

otherwise have been a bar to a finding that natural justice was required. This was the closest that the High Court had come to the boldness of the Supreme Court of Canada in the *Operation Dismantle* case.

Reiterating his view in *FAI Insurances v Winneke*, Mason CJ said that where the decision in question is 'of a kind usually made by a Minister or statutory officer', 'it is not to be supposed that parliament intended to exclude a duty to act fairly by vesting authority to make the decision in the Governor in Council'.[152] Furthermore, in the Chief Justice's view, there was nothing in the nature of the decision which should have signalled to the Court that it ought to have backed off: 'the nature of the decision to be made, the release of the offender or the continuation of his preventative detention, concerned considerations personal to Mr O'Shea rather than issues of general policy'.[153]

As had been the case in *FAI Insurances v Winneke*, there was at play here a local quirk of constitutional law. In South Australia there is a jurisdictionally curious – but for the purposes of the present discussion doctrinally important – feature that all actions taken by the Governor are specifically required by statute to be exercised on advice.[154] And, as was discussed in chapter five, the High Court characterised the Governor in Council/Cabinet stage as one where the focus was on 'the public interest'. In Mason CJ's view, though, as a systemic feature this was not fatal to a claim based on natural justice. Even though the Cabinet *ordinarily* was concerned with affairs of state, this did not preclude it from deliberating on issues of individual autonomy. And when it did, natural justice would apply. As his Honour put it:

> There is a common law duty to act fairly in the making of administrative decisions which affect the rights, interests and legitimate expectations of an individual, subject only to the clear manifestation of a contrary statutory intention. This common law duty is capable of applying to the Governor in Council, there being nothing in the relationship between the Governor and the Executive which inhibits the existence of such a duty.[155]

So much for principle. What of practicality? How could a court effectively police a natural justice requirement in an entity like the Cabinet, whose proceedings were, by plain convention, both secret and

[152] 163 CLR, at 386.
[153] 163 CLR, at 387.
[154] *Acts Interpretation Act 1915* (SA), s 23.
[155] 163 CLR, at 386.

informal.[156] The normal obligations which flow from an obligation to observe natural justice – what the Americans would call 'notice and comment' obligations – are alien to the workings of the Anglo-Australian idea of Cabinet secrecy. But neither was this necessarily fatal in the Chief Justice's eyes. In his opinion, it was not an intrusion into Cabinet's control of its own proceedings for the courts to insist that Cabinet adopt a certain decision-making procedure. There was 'no persuasive reason', he said, 'why the courts should not, in an appropriate case, require as an incident of natural justice ... that there be placed before Cabinet by the responsible Minister the written submissions of the individual affected by the decision to be made or an accurate summary of such submissions'.[157] In what sounded almost like a veiled threat, he continued:

> If at some later stage it were to appear that the parliament was entrusting the Governor in Council with the making of decisions affecting individuals so as to avoid the need to act fairly the court might be compelled to go further, but at this stage such a course is not warranted.[158]

It was with equal candour that Mason CJ spoke of the relationship between matters of policy and fairness of decision-making processes. He rejected the argument that because the factor to be decided by the Cabinet here was the public interest, this rendered the decision-making process non-justiciable. Matters of public policy and individual fairness could operate hand in hand, in his opinion:

> True it is that the courts do not substitute their view of policy for that prescribed by the Executive, but this does not mean that policy issues stand apart from procedural fairness. Although it is unrealistic and impractical to insist upon a person having the opportunity to present submissions on matters of high level general policy, the same considerations do not apply to the impact of policy on the individual and to those aspects of policy which are closely related to the circumstances of the particular case.[159]

---

[156] See *Whitlam v Australian Consolidated Press Ltd* (1985) 73 FLR 414, at 421-422. See also Murphy J's judgment in *FAI Insurances v Winneke*, 151 CLR, at 373-375.

[157] 163 CLR, at 387-388. He went on to say that this 'would in all probability conform to existing practice' (at 388). See also Wilson and Toohey JJ, 163 CLR at 402-403.

[158] 163 CLR, at 388.

[159] 163 CLR, at 389. See generally on this issue F Wheeler, 'Judicial Review of Prerogative Power in Australia: Issues and Prospects' (1992) 14 *Syd L Rev* 432.

Typically of Sir William Deane, in his judgment in *O'Shea*, he cut a wide swathe in his assessment of the range of actors to whom a duty to observe natural justice could attach. 'There was a time', he said, when the identity of the decision-maker would both have excluded an obligation to observe natural justice and have precluded judicial review. But 'that time has now gone in this country':

> If those common law requirements would otherwise apply to require that a person affected by a decision made in the exercise of a statutory power or authority be given an opportunity of being heard, the fact that the decision-making power or authority is entrusted to the Governor in Council will neither automatically deprive the person affected of the right to insist upon that opportunity nor render the decision in question immune from challenge in the courts of the land.[160]

The 'Fiction' of Responsible Government

Implicit in these sorts of statements is the view that the courts represent the only real means of control of the executive; that responsible government is no longer an effective means of controlling abuse of power. There is a paradox in this, of course, insofar as the justification for engaging in judicial review of the Crown involved reference to the Diceyist principle of the legal sovereignty of parliament – the notion, as Gibbs CJ put it in *R v Toohey*, that it is 'fundamental to the rule of law that the Crown has no more power than any subordinate official to enlarge by its own act the scope of a power'.[161] But this notwithstanding, it is apparent that the authority of parliament as a source of control did not command respect amongst the High Court.

This was not always the case. *Board of Education v Rice*, which was discussed in chapter two, represented an overt expression of faith in the principle of responsible government as a means of exerting control over administrative wrong-doing. It so happened that the appeal in *Rice* fitted nicely with the Liberal government's line in the battle that it had been waging with the House of Lords (in its political capacity) over the Lords'

---

[160] *Ibid*, though it should be noted that in *Commonwealth v Northern Land Council* (1993) 176 CLR 604, the High Court held that courts ought to respect the confidentiality of cabinet workings.
[161] 151 CLR, at 187.

right to veto legislation,[162] but such views could be seen in Australia, too. In *Randall v Northcote Corporation*, decided in 1910, for instance, Higgins J said, 'If the ratepayers do not like the mode in which the affairs of the town are administered, their remedy is generally to be sought in the pressure of public opinion at the polling booth'.[163]

It was sometimes said that responsibility for checking executive excess was a task shared by parliament and the courts. In *Johnson and Co v Minister of Health*, for example, Lord Greene MR spoke of the intersection of the concepts of executive responsibility to parliament and judicial review. He said: 'Every Minister has a duty to the King to act fairly, the breach of which is punishable by parliament. But he also has a duty to the law ...'[164] This was quoted with approval by Williams J in the *Communist Party Dissolution Case*.[165]

More recently, in the *Fleet Street Casuals Case*, Lord Diplock said much the same thing. Speaking of the Executive in the plural, he said: 'They are accountable to parliament for what they do so far as regards efficiency and policy, and of that parliament is the only judge; they are responsible to a court of justice for the lawfulness of what they do, and of that the court is the only judge.'[166]

Of the two duties, the former – the duty to the legislature – was thought in principle to provide the more effective avenue for control. That is because the power of the legislative assembly to check executive overzealousness was thought to be unlimited. As a British cabinet member once put it: 'I am the servant of the House of Commons; every action I take, every decision I come to ... can be brought up and discussed here.'[167] It was for this same reason that as recently as 1966, Prime Minister Holt was expressing doubt about the need for an Ombudsman in Australia – it was

---

[162] Which, of course, the Lords lost. The *Parliament Act 1911* removed the Lords' absolute veto. For a wonderfully written account of this whole episode, and of the changes to the working constitution that it wrought, see G Dangerfield, *The Strange Death of Liberal England* (1935).

[163] 11 CLR 100, at 120.

[164] [1947] 2 All ER 395, at 399.

[165] *Australian Communist Party v Commonwealth* (1951) 83 CLR 1, at 221-222.

[166] *Inland Revenue Commissioner v National Federation of Self-Employed and Small Businesses Ltd* [1982] AC 617, at 644.

[167] Quoted in Sir C T Carr, *Concerning English Administrative Law* (1941), at 13.

Holt's view that parliament could exercise sufficient scrutiny over the government and government officials.[168]

Yet, concerns about the weakness of responsible government are not new. As long ago as 1915, Dicey was bemoaning the decline of parliament as a means of control over the Cabinet.[169] In 1903, Harrison Moore was moved to write of 'a change in the working of our constitutional forces',[170] which meant that legislation was 'no longer devised by a body distinct from and jealous of the Executive, but [rather] expresses to a very great extent the views of the Executive as to the public needs'.[171]

In the 1950s, Devlin J expressed concern extrajudicially that 'while members can still make themselves felt on questions of principle, the detail of the legislation – and it is the detail that the citizen finds most worrying – is almost entirely the work of the ministries'.[172] Likewise, at the Commonwealth and Empire Law Conference in Sydney in 1965, Billy Sneddon, as Commonwealth Attorney-General, expressed some doubt about the effectiveness of ministerial responsibility, especially in light of the strength of the modern party system.[173]

This point was also made by Sir William Wade in his Hamlyn Lectures. He said that ministerial responsibility perhaps at one time did act as a working mechanism of restraint, '[b]ut this comforting proposition became less and less tenable as the party system grew in efficiency and in

---

[168] Noted in 'Administrative Tribunals', *Current Affairs Bulletin*, 24 April 1967, at 171. This was also a view which was apparently held by Prime Minister McMahon. See R Creyke and J McMillan, 'Administrative Law Assumptions ... Then and Now', in Creyke and McMillan (eds), *The Kerr Vision of Administrative Law* (1998) 1, at 3.

[169] In 'Development of Administrative Law in England' (1915) 31 *LQR* 148, at 152, he wrote that the reference by Lord Loreburn LC to responsible government in *Local Government Board v Arlidge* was 'somewhat unfortunate':

> It is calculated to promote the belief that such ministerial responsibility is a real check upon the action of a Minister or a Cabinet ... But any man who will look plain facts in the face will see in a moment that ministerial censure not in fact by parliament nor even by the House of Commons, but by the party majority who keep the Government in office is a very feeble guarantee indeed against action which evades the authority of the law courts.

[170] 'The Enforcement of Administrative Law' 1 *Comm L Rev* 13, at 14.

[171] *Ibid.*

[172] 'Public Policy and the Executive' [1956] *Cur Leg Prob* 1, at 14.

[173] 'Ministerial Responsibility in Modern Parliamentary Government', in *Proceedings of the Third Commonwealth and Empire Law Conference* (1966) 1, at 6, 8-10. See also the *Report of the Commonwealth Administrative Review Committee* ('the Kerr Committee Report'), 1971 Parl Paper No 144, chapter 15.

rigidity and as it became obvious that parliament had become the obedient instrument of the government of the day'.[174]

More recently, though, there have been statements from the High Court which suggest that there is an active judicial perception in Australia that the parliamentary horse has gone lame. In *R v Toohey*, both Gibbs CJ and Mason J indicated that they were less than convinced that responsible government provides much protection against anything in Australia today. Gibbs CJ said that 'under modern conditions of responsible government parliament could not always be relied on to check excesses of power by the Crown or its ministers'.[175]

Mason J said that he wanted to add to his reasons for judgment 'the comment that the doctrine of ministerial responsibility is not in itself an adequate safeguard for the citizen whose rights are affected'.[176] He said that this was 'now generally accepted and its acceptance underlies the comprehensive system of judicial review of administrative action which prevails in Australia'.[177]

Even Sir Gerard Brennan, who, as noted, has been steadfast in linking judicial review to legislative intent, was once moved to say that 'as the wind of political expediency now chills parliament's willingness to impose checks on the Executive and the Executive now has a large measure of control over legislation, the courts alone retain their original function of standing between government and the governed'.[178]

---

[174] *Constitutional Fundamentals* (1980), at 41.

[175] 151 CLR, at 192.

[176] 151 CLR, at 222. His Honour quoted this passage in his piece, 'The Importance of Judicial Review', *supra* n 23, at 1.

[177] *Ibid.*

[178] 'Courts, Democracy and the Law' (1991) 65 *ALJ* 32, at 35. There was even an element of this view in *Sanders v Snell* (1998) 157 ALR 491, the High Court's recent encounter with the doctrine of legitimate expectations, which was discussed in chapter 5. The Court did not touch upon the question of responsible government directly, but the reasoning of the judgments implicitly indicates a lack of faith in the ability of political processes to act as any sort of a brake upon unlawfulness. The reason that the majority in the case held that the matter had to be remitted back to the trial judge is that they found that there was no evidence of knowledge on the Minister's part of the unlawfulness of his conduct. The majority concluded that the warning by another Cabinet Minister that natural justice was required before the direction to sack the Executive Officer of the Bureau could be implemented was to be taken in a lay sense, and not to amount to actual advice of the Minister's legal position. They did not say so, but it was surely implicit in the majority view that political advice could not be presumed to amount to legal control.

Lionel Murphy, Sir Gerard Brennan and the Policy of Deference to Politics

These views aside, of the members of the Court in the late 1970s and 1980s, it was only Sir Gerard Brennan and Lionel Murphy who prominently expressed any willingness to defer to parliament's prerogative to control the executive. In *Minister for Aboriginal Affairs v Peko-Wallsend*, for example, Brennan J said that a Ministerial action could only be deemed justiciable if the Minister was alleged to have failed to comply with a statutory obligation that attended the decision-making process. It was then that a question of lawfulness arose. Otherwise, the matter was one of political responsibility:

> [If] the Minister's decision may be founded on policy for which the Minister is responsible to the parliament, the court does not review decisions affecting the interests of contending parties on the ground that no weight or insufficient weight has been given to evidence or information favouring one party.[179]

This was, of course, the point made by Murphy J in *FAI Insurances v Winneke*. Brennan J was not suggesting that the Minister had the right to be unfair in his proceedings. Rather, he was saying that the avenue of enforcement of whatever duty of fairness that existed was not the courts but the political process. In *FAI Insurances*, it will be remembered, Murphy J said the same thing. He would have held that the decision not to renew the insurance licence was not justiciable, but he thought that a duty to observe the principles of natural justice could still exist. His view of the non-justiciability of the issue 'did not mean that standards of good faith, fair dealing, natural justice and propriety are not applicable'.[180] They were, he said, 'but they are political standards enforceable by the political process, sometimes very effectively and sometimes ineffectively'.[181]

In a similar vein, in *R v Toohey*, Murphy J had said that 'whether or not parliament provides a regular procedure for its control of delegated legislation, it retains control'.[182] This point was picked up by Sheppard J of the Federal Court in *Minister for Arts, Heritage and Environment v*

---

[179] (1986) 162 CLR 24, at 64. See also his comments in *A-G (NSW) v Quin* (1990) 170 CLR, at 35-36.

[180] 151 CLR, at 374.

[181] *Ibid.*

[182] 151 CLR, at 229.

Peko-Wallsend. He said that he wanted to 'emphasise that the question is not whether the Cabinet is bound to act according to law; it is whether its decisions are amenable to the jurisdiction of the Court'.[183] This notion – of a duty of procedural fairness existing, but being enforceable through non-judicial means – had actually been enunciated in the High Court as early as 1926,[184] but apart from the lone voices of Lionel Murphy and Sir Gerard Brennan (and Mr Justice Sheppard), it has been lost in the modern era.[185]

Lionel Murphy in fact had one of the more eclectic approaches to natural justice among High Court judges in recent times. In cases like *R v Toohey* and *FAI Insurances v Winneke*, he was prepared to urge that the courts adopt a very deferential view of what constituted a fair decision-making process *vis-à-vis* the Executive. Yet, in other contexts, he was prepared to go much further than any of his colleagues in extending the compass of procedural fairness. In *Forbes v New South Wales Trotting Club Ltd*, for instance, he suggested that any attempt to exclude natural justice through contract would be invalid as being contrary to public policy.[186]

In *Heatley v Tasmanian Racing and Gaming Commission*, he said that there was a presumption of statutory interpretation against a government 'depart[ing] from the standards of official behaviour towards individuals which are basic to every civil society'.[187] He also once said that any broad-based assertion of private power (which he saw as including the operation of 'public halls, restaurants, theatres [and] racecourses'[188]) which 'affects members of the public to a significant

---

[183] 15 FCR, at 281.

[184] See *Moreau v Federal Commissioner of Taxation* 39 CLR 65, at 68 (*per* Isaacs J). See also Isaacs J's judgment in *Boucaut Bay Co Ltd v The Commonwealth* (1927) 40 CLR 98, at 105.

[185] The extent to which the notion of the executive's chief responsibility as being to parliament has similarly been eroded in England is typified by *R v Secretary of State for the Environment, Ex parte Brent LBC* [1982] QB 593, in which a minister was held to have failed to observe natural justice in refusing to meet with a local government delegation which wanted to protest against a policy decision to reduce a grant, even though the policy had been both fully debated in parliament and fully explained to the local authorities. See also *R v Secretary of State for Transport, Ex parte Greater London Council* [1986] QB 556. More generally, see Wade and Forsyth, *supra* n 49, at 551-553.

[186] (1987) 143 CLR 242, at 274.

[187] (1977) 137 CLR 487, at 495.

[188] *Forbes*, 143 CLR, at 274. Historically, Murphy J may not have been that far off the mark in his assessment of the way in which law regulated power. Paul Craig has written of the means by which the old common law imposed a general duty of reasonableness on those who wielded monopolistic power. See, 'Constitutions, Property and Regulation'

degree' should be deemed to amount to an exercise of public power. He continued:

> Such public power must be exercised *bona fide*, for the purposes for which it is conferred and with due regard to the persons affected by its exercise. This generally requires that where such power is exercised against an individual, due process or natural justice must be observed.[189]

The Limits of Discretion and the Widening of Judicial Review

When they are contrasted with sentiments like those expressed by Justices Brennan, Murphy and Sheppard, and the general tenor of the deferential judgments of the 1950s and before, the reach of the majority judgments in the 1980s cases seems striking. If Sir Anthony Mason was accurate in delimiting the range of subjects which are not 'susceptible of review', when he said that they included 'decisions affecting national security, foreign affairs, to prosecute or not to prosecute and the grant of pardons to convicted people',[190] this represents a profound extension of the reach of natural justice. Yet, considered in an historical light, the widening was only to be expected. All of the ingredients for the breaking down of the barriers to curial scrutiny of political decision-making processes had been in existence for some time.

Most critically in this respect, it is one of the basic truths of public law that the courts have seldom if ever taken discretion-conferring or state of mind provisions at face value.[191] The courts have always been willing to read limits into legislative enactments which on their surface contain no limits at all. As long ago as 1599, the Common Pleas said that a statutory

---

[1991] *Pub Law* 538. As to Murphy's views on individual rights generally, see the essays in M Coper and G Williams (eds), *Justice Lionel Murphy: Influential or Merely Prescient?* (1997).

[189] 143 CLR, at 275.

[190] 'The Importance of Judicial Review of Administrative Action as a Safeguard of Individual Rights', *supra* n 23, at 8. See also *Barton v R* (1980) 147 CLR 75 (holding that the decision of the Attorney-General to exercise the prerogative power to lay an indictment was not reviewable).

[191] Cases of wartime exigency being a possible exception. See, *eg*, *Liversidge v Anderson* [1942] AC 206 and *R v Halliday, Ex parte Zadig* [1917] AC 260. Even then, there have been instances of the courts refusing to allow the Executive a free rein in the exercise of discretionary power. See, *eg*, *R v Connell, Ex parte Hetton Bellbird Collieries* (1944) 69 CLR 407.

provision which allowed royal servants to 'do according to their discretions' had to be interpreted in such a way that the actions 'be limited and bound with the rule of reason and law'.[192] Even in the case that most administrative lawyers would now prefer to forget, *Nakkuda Ali v Jayaratne*, the Privy Council said that a 'state of mind' provision 'must be intended to serve in some sense as a condition limiting the exercise of an otherwise absolute power'.[193]

It followed from this that some means of external control was necessary. If we accept that there can be no such thing under the rule of law as completely unfettered discretion (for such a thing could not amount to 'law'), then some form of external arbiter is required. Otherwise, their Lordships said in *Nakkuda Ali*, the universally imputed legislative intent that the discretion be limited would be frustrated: 'if the question whether the [condition precedent for the exercise of power] is to be conclusively decided by the man who wields the power, the value of the intended restraint is in effect nothing'.[194] In the Australian setting, this point was perhaps best summed up by Kitto J, when he said:

> It is a general principle of law ... that a discretion allowed by statute to the holder of an office is intended to be exercised according to the rules of reason and justice, not according to private opinion; according to law, and not humour, and within those limits within which an honest man, competent to discharge the duties of his office, ought to confine himself. The courts, while claiming no authority in themselves to dictate the decisions that ought to be made in the exercise of such a discretion in a given case, are yet in duty bound to declare invalid a purported exercise of the discretion when the proper limits have not been observed.[195]

The way in which Kitto J phrased the judicial responsibility in cases involving executive discretion is significant. In many respects it was reminiscent of the way in which Lord Denning described the judicial role generally, as quoted at the outset of this chapter. To return to first principles, in judicial review cases the courts are supposed only to be

---

[192] *Rooke's Case* 5 Co Rep 99b, at 100a, 77 ER 209, at 210. The Court continued: 'For discretion is a science or understanding to discern between shadows and substance, between equity and colourable glosses and pretences, and not to do according to their wills and private affections ...' (*ibid*).
[193] [1951] AC 66, at 77.
[194] [1951] AC, at 77.
[195] *R v Anderson, Ex parte Ipec-Air Pty Ltd* (1965) 113 CLR 177, at 189.

concerned with the lawfulness of administrative decisions, and not their propriety. Yet it is the logical consequence of the application of one of the fundamental tenets of our constitutional system – that it falls to the judicial branch to determine questions of legality – that has been responsible for the expansion of natural justice to include in the appropriate circumstances the work of the Crown.

If we accept the premise that the principle of legality is a feature of the constitution, then it follows that the courts must have the right to determine whether the government – whether it is acting through the Sovereign or one of her ministers, or whether it is proceeding under statute or by virtue of the prerogative – is obeying the law.[196] But, as with any other case involving the exercise of discretion, lawfulness will depend upon the reasonableness of the outcome and the fairness of the process.

It is for this reason that it has proven largely impossible to draw a firm dividing line between the bounds of judicial review and the province of merit review. Even under the older position, as set out in cases like *Attorney-General v De Keyser's Royal Hotel*,[197] whereby the courts claimed to reserve only the right to determine whether a prerogative existed, the seeds had been sown for what amounted to substantive review of the Crown's actions. 'The power to interpret is the power to destroy', Sir Otto Kahn-Freund said.[198] It is no less true that implicit in the power to determine whether a prerogative exists is the power to determine its scope, including whether, for it to be lawfully exercised, legal notions of procedural fairness are required.

So to speak of 'non-justiciability' in this area is plainly nonsensical. The potential justiciability of *all* government action follows from the very first principles of our constitutional structure. This was nicely illustrated by the judgment of the House of Lords in the *Fleet Street Casuals Case*.[199] This involved an attempt by a federation representing a group of small businesses to challenge a decision by the taxation authorities to 'cut a deal' with a group of people employed casually in the newspaper industry

---

[196] It was in this context, for example, that in *R v Criminal Injuries Compensation Board, Ex parte Lain* [1967] 2 QB 864, at 881, Lord Parker CJ said that if the decisions of a tribunal created under the prerogative were to have any lawful effect, then they themselves had to comply with the law.

[197] *Supra* n 43.

[198] 'The Impact of Constitutions on Labour Law' (1976) 35 *Camb LJ* 240, at 244 (paraphrasing Marshall CJ in *McCulloch v Maryland* (1819) 17 US (4 Wheat) 316).

[199] *Inland Revenue Commissioner v National Federation of Self-Employed and Small Businesses Ltd* [1982] AC 617.

– in the days when the Fleet Street print unions were still strong. A group of small businesspeople was outraged at what it perceived to be special treatment afforded to trade union interests, and it sought to challenge the action.

The House of Lords held that the federation was not sufficiently connected to the matters to have standing. But it also held that standing was not something that should be decided at the outset. In certain cases, the Lords held, whether or not there is the necessary sufficiency of interest in the matters complained of can only be determined after an evidentiary hearing.[200]

The significant point in this for present purposes was their Lordships' implicit acknowledgment of the contingent nature of our legal system. For us, law is circumstance-dependent. Any statement of law must have a factual sub-stratum. A judge invited to review a decision by the executive must engage in a fact-finding exercise at one level or another before deciding whether he or she has the authority to overturn it. In some cases, this fact-finding exercise may consist simply of statements on affidavit, but the truth is that one simply cannot say that the actions of the Crown are not reviewable *per se*.

The real question, therefore, is what *stance* the courts will take with respect to actions of the government – whether by the Crown itself or by a Crown servant or agent – which strike the court as being unfair or unjust. To restate the trite principle, the correctness or preferability of an administrative decision is meant to be no concern of the courts. This was the point made so forcefully by Murphy J in *FAI Insurances v Winneke* and *R v Toohey*, but it is also something that the whole High Court has felt need to reiterate in recent years. In *Wu Shan Liang*, for example, the majority quoted with approval a statement by Brennan J that '[t]he duty and jurisdiction of the court to review administrative action do not go beyond the declaration and enforcing of the law which determines the limits and governs the exercise of the repository's power'.[201]

Yet the recent natural justice cases stand in testament to the High Court's willingness to ignore its own admonition when faced with cases of patent unfairness. This is where there has been a real change in judicial attitude. In older cases – of which *Duncan v Theodore* was an example –

---

[200] See Lord Wilberforce [1982] AC, at 630, Lord Diplock [1982] AC, at 643-644.

[201] *Minister for Immigration and Ethnic Affairs v Wu Shan Liang* (1996) 185 CLR 259, at 272 (quoting *A-G (NSW) v Quin* (1990) 170 CLR 1, at 35-36). See also *GCHQ* [1985] AC, at 414-415.

the courts were prepared to assume a deferential stance, not only to the ultimate value judgements made by political actors, but also to the political dynamics by which the value judgements were made. Even where the Privy Council acknowledged that if bad faith could be shown the making of a regulation could in principle be challenged, it was clear that their Lordships were inclined to take a deferential stance both to the necessity of the regulation and to the political process by which it came about.[202] The attitude shown in cases like *R v Toohey*, *FAI Insurances v Winneke* and *South Australia v O'Shea* was really quite different. And to return to the subject of the last chapter, to speak of the legal protection of expectations is necessarily to place substance at the forefront of the judicial review process.

That reflects the difference between cases involving legal rights and ones involving expectations. In the former, the law has made a prior determination of entitlement. But in the latter, the court must evaluate the worthiness of the expected outcome, so as to determine whether it amounts to a legitimate expectation or to a 'mere hope'. So even if the courts do not see themselves as substituting their own preferred outcomes for those of the executive, the fact that they are weighing the substantive determinations made by the executive against what the citizenry *expected* the government to do, means that almost always, the reasons for judgment will have a substantive impact on any subsequently-made decision.

This, then, takes us back to the base question: at what stage will a representative of government – whether the Queen herself or one of her servants – be said to have gone from acting irresponsible to acting unlawfully? A review of the cases suggests that the answer to this is becoming less certain. At one time, the answer was predicated on identity – just as was the duty to observe natural justice generally. But in the 1980s, the High Court (together with the House of Lords and the Supreme Court of Canada) abolished identity as the criterion for justiciability. In its stead came the more pragmatic, yet more malleable, question of whether a given power is not 'susceptible of review'.

In chapters four and five, the question was raised in different contexts as to the jurisprudential basis by which the High Court had extended the reach of natural justice in the way it had. In chapters two and three, it was suggested that the doctrine of natural justice had suffered in Australia by not

---

[202] *Attorney-General (Canada) v Hallett and Carey Ltd* [1952] AC 427. The case concerned the issuance of an Order in Council which had the effect of expropriating a stock of barley grain owned by Hallett and Carey Ltd. See *supra* n 42.

having been exposed to the sort of close academic scrutiny that it had in England and Canada in the first half of the century. The way in which the High Court has approached the issue of the reviewability of the Crown places both of these things in the scholar's eye. The cases examined in this chapter make clear that the High Court's approach to the question of procedural fairness is a pragmatic one; a 'rolling up of shirtsleeves and getting down to business' sort of fairness.[203] But given the questions of legitimacy, competency and constitutional propriety that go along with judicial review, they make more pressing than ever the question of the juridical basis by which the duty to observe natural justice is said to arise in the first place.

[203] In *Bushell v Environment Secretary* [1981] AC 75, at 95, Lord Diplock said :

> What is fair procedure is to be judged not in light of constitutional functions as to the relationship between the minister and the other servants of the Crown who serve in the government department of which he is the head, but in light of the practical realities as to the way in which administrative decisions involving forming judgments based on technical considerations are reached ...

7 The Jurisdictional Basis for the Duty of Fairness

It will have become apparent by now that in recent times, the High Court has been comparatively unrestrained in its imposition of procedural requirements on governmental decision-makers. Since its judgment of thirty years ago in *Banks v Transport Regulation Board*,[1] the Court has spread the obligation to treat individuals fairly to a range of governmental activity that would have been quite inconceivable to earlier generations. As noted earlier, Aronson and Dyer have described administrative law as a project of the 'civilising' of government discretion.[2] In a lecture given in 1989, to commemorate the tenth anniversary of the statutory reforms to Commonwealth administrative law,[3] Sir Gerard Brennan used similar language. He said:

> After ten years it may not be possible to say that this society is fairer, or more egalitarian, or more compassionate than it was before. But it is possible to say that this society is one which now accords to the individual an opportunity to meet on more equal terms with the institutions of the state ... The interests of individuals are more fully acknowledged, and the repositories of power are constrained to treat the individual both fairly and according to law.[4]

Compassion as a Public Law Virtue?

As a point of judicial disposition, many people would be inclined to approve of Sir Gerard's sentiments. As statements of positive law, the

---

[1] (1968) 119 CLR 222.

[2] M Aronson and B Dyer, *Judicial Review of Administrative Action* (1996), at 124.

[3] For details of this, see chapter 4.

[4] 'Reflections' (1989) 58 *Canberra Bulletin Pub Admin* 32, at 33 (quoted in J McMillan and N Williams, 'Administrative Law and Human Rights', in D Kinley (ed) *Human Rights in Australian Law* (1988) 63, at 70).

High Court's decisions on natural justice in the 1980s and 1990s can, one supposes, commend themselves to the reasonable compassionate observer. To state it in the terms used by Aronson and Dyer, the exercise of governmental discretion in Australia *has* become civilised – at least to a much greater degree than formerly was the case. It is no longer imaginable, for example, that a taxi driver could have his licence withdrawn, only to be told by a stern looking judge (like, say, Lord Goddard) that he had no rights in his livelihood at all, or that parents whose child dies in tragic circumstances (like Mr and Mrs Annetts) would be denied the full opportunity to speak at a coronial inquest.

In terms of an ideal of public service conduct, this might all be to society's ultimate good. As the Federal Court once admonished us, it is in our national interest to be seen as a civilised and compassionate nation.[5] But to the legal scholar, consideration of the doctrine of natural justice cannot stop at compassion. The scholar must also be concerned with the means by which changes to public law are carried out, and the extent to which this conforms to accepted bases for legal change.

It is basic to our constitutional system, though often overlooked, that the rule of law applies to the courts as much as to the political branches. As the editors of *de Smith* have said, 'the standards applied by the courts in judicial review must ultimately be justified by constitutional principles, which govern the proper exercise of public power in any democracy.'[6] The judiciary, like the legislature and the executive, must be able to demonstrate the lawful basis for its actions. Curial arbitrariness or faithlessness to principle should be just as offensive as executive arbitrariness. Indeed, it is salutary to remember that the length of the Chancellor's foot was a public concern long before any fear of a 'headless

---

[5] *Chaudhury v Minister for Immigration* (1994) 49 FCR 84, at 87-88. This has been a repeated theme in the Federal Court. See, *eg*, Smithers J in *Ates v Minister of State for Immigration and Ethnic Affairs* (1983) 67 FLR 449, at 455-456 (decisions need to be taken 'by reference to a liberal and even compassionate outlook appropriate to a free and confident nation and conscious of its reputation as such') and Burchett J in *Fuduche v Minister for Immigration, Local Government and Ethnic Affairs* (1993) 45 FCR 515, at 527 (the *Immigration Act* requires 'a broad and generous construction ... in furtherance of the good name of Australia that its humanity demands'). See also J McMillan and N Williams, 'Administrative Law and Human Rights', in D Kinley (ed) *Human Rights in Australian Law* (1998), *supra* n 4 , at 75-76.

[6] S A de Smith, H Woolf and J Jowell, *Judicial Review of Administrative Action* (5th ed. 1995), at 14.

fourth branch of government'.[7] It was in precisely that spirit that Sir Owen Dixon sought to warn of the conscious judicial innovator, who 'is bound under the doctrine of precedents by no authority except the error he committed yesterday'.[8]

The Legitimate Bases for Legal Change

Judicial positivism is, without reference to any supporting basis for its legitimacy, little more than an expression of individual curial prejudice. To use Sir Owen Dixon's words once more, an activist judge who grounds legal change in his or her own view of the need for change, 'wrests the law to his authority',[9] which is antithetical to any principled notion of the rule of law. As Lord Devlin once cautioned, mere enthusiasm for change is not a judicial virtue.[10]

In the common law system, there are only three bases for establishing lawfulness. Judicial innovation, therefore, must be grounded in one of the three: legislative enactment, common law principle, or successful revolution.[11] Accordingly, since genuine legal revolution is so rare, in almost all cases it will fall for a judge-made innovation in the law to legitimise itself by reference to a legislative command (including formal constitutional amendment), or the yardstick of common law principle.

For the reasons touched upon in chapter six, the concern about legitimacy is particularly acute in matters of political and social controversy, as is the case with so many administrative law disputes. Jeremy Waldron once wrote that although '[i]t is said that hard cases make bad law one of our tasks in jurisprudence is to consider the justification of

---

[7] An expression used by the American Bar Association's Committee on Administrative Management. It described administrative agencies as a 'headless "fourth branch" of the government containing a haphazard deposit of irresponsible agencies and uncoordinated powers' (*Report of the Committee with Studies of Administrative Management in the Federal Government* (1937), at 39). See also *FTC v Ruberoid Co* (1952) 343 US 470, at 487, where Jackson J spoke of a 'veritable fourth branch'. See further P Strauss, 'The Place of Agencies in Government: Separation of Powers and the Fourth Branch' (1984) 84 *Colum L Rev* 573.

[8] 'Concerning Judicial Method', in *Jesting Pilate* (1965) 152, at 159.

[9] *Id*, at 158.

[10] 'Judges and Lawmakers' (1976) 36 *Mod L Rev* 1, at 5.

[11] See *State (Pakistan) v Dosso* PLD [1958] SC 533, *Uganda v Commissioners of Prisons* [1966] EA 540. See also D W Greig, *International Law* (1976), at 149-151 and I Brownlie, *Principles of International Law* (4th ed. 1990), at 92-95.

legal institutions'.[12] 'If this enterprise is to be conducted in a spirit of argument rather than ideology', he continued, 'then hard cases – indeed *the hardest cases* – must be our primary point of reference.'[13] Taking this observation in the present context, for the modern High Court approach to natural justice to amount to a satisfactory part of the body of administrative law, the cases must accord with something more than mere populist approval.

The decision of the High Court in *Teoh*[14] provides an illustration in point of the pertinence of Waldron's admonition. It becomes immediately clear from any reading of the majority judgments what the desired outcome was. But much less clear is the legal justification for this outcome.

In their analysis of the legitimate expectation cases, of which *Teoh* represents the high water mark, Aronson and Dyer grouped the holdings into three categories. First, they said, were the cases where there had been an actual expectation which had arisen out of positive government statement – cases such as *Haoucher*[15] and *Liverpool Taxis*.[16] Secondly were the cases where, despite the non-existence of a positive statement by the government, circumstance had given rise to what they termed a 'likely' expectation. Cases in this group included *FAI Insurances v Winneke*[17] and *Annetts v McCann*.[18] Thirdly, though, were cases like *Teoh* and *Ainsworth v Criminal Justice Commission*,[19] where there was neither a real expectation nor a likelihood of one. Aronson and Dyer described these as cases of *prescriptive* expectation.[20]

In *Teoh*, as will be remembered, the High Court held that regardless of Mr Teoh's ignorance of Australia's treaty obligations, and quite apart from the fact that the treaty in question was debarred by constitutional principle from having force in domestic law, a legitimate expectation could be said to have existed that the Immigration officials would take the

---

[12] 'Property, Justification and Need' (1993) 6 *Can J Law and Jurisp* 185.

[13] *Ibid* (original emphasis).

[14] (1995) 183 CLR 273. For a discussion of these cases, see chapter 4 and 5.

[15] *Haoucher v Minister for Immigration and Ethnic Affairs* (1990) 169 CLR 648.

[16] *R v Liverpool Corporation, Ex parte Taxi Fleet* [1972] 2 QB 299.

[17] (1982) 151 CLR 342.

[18] (1990) 170 CLR 596.

[19] (1992) 175 CLR 564.

[20] *Supra* n 2, at 417 (relying in part on the classifications used in P Finn and K Smith, 'The Citizen, the Government and 'Reasonable Expectations' (1992) 66 *ALJ* 139, at 141-142).

interests of the Teoh children into account as a 'primary consideration' before deciding whether or not to deport Teoh.

It is possible to mount a legal justification for the result, by imputing the requisite expectation to parliament rather than to Teoh. But this the majority did not do. Instead, they simply asserted that people in Mr Teoh's shoes *ought* to be able to hold such expectations. That was implicit in the holding that the test for legitimate expectations was to be an objective rather than a subjective one.[21] Yet, their Honours did not ground this assertion in any theory of the constitution. On this basis, the judgments in *Teoh* must surely fail the challenges proffered by Jeremy Waldron and Sir Owen Dixon. No disrespect is meant to the High Court if one says that *Teoh* smacks of result-oriented jurisprudence, or that their Honours sought in *Teoh* to (in Sir Owen Dixon's words) wrest the law to their authority.

The point is that underlying our feelings as lawyers about individual outcomes must be the serious questions of the legitimacy of the High Court's recent changes to the law. The result in *Teoh* may indeed have been the best one in the circumstances (at least looked at from the standpoints of Teoh and his family, or those who are in favour of children's rights, or international lawyers). But the legal precedent which was the result of the High Court's holding insists upon the jurisprudential question. By what right can the courts prescribe to the government that they must accord domestic legal status to documents which do not form part of domestic law? In a similar way, the Crown cases discussed in the last chapter clearly invite the observer to ask by what right a court can impose procedural obligations upon the workings of the Cabinet. In both cases, the question is: by reference to what principle of legal legitimacy can the High Court show that its extension of the law has a legal foundation?

Pragmatism, Legitimacy and the Changing Constitution

In fact, questions of the legitimacy of judicial review have been at the forefront of administrative law since at least the seventeenth century. In 1616, for example, King James I issued an order forbidding judicial interference with the work of the Sewer Commissioners. In terms which

---

[21] See also Aronson and Dyer, *id*, at 418-419.

have a modern ring (if a quaint cast), the order spoke of, among other things, the need for 'speedy and sudden execution' of the Commissioners' orders, and the inappropriateness of the 'direct frustration and overthrow of the authority of the Commissioners' by the judges.[22]

The answer to the legitimacy question in the early days was, in keeping with common law tradition, a pragmatic one: the courts engaged in review, and first the King, and later Parliament, acceded to it. It was thus that Lord Reid felt that he could justify the doctrine of natural justice on the basis that 'for a long time the courts have, without objection from parliament supplemented procedure laid down in legislation where they have found that to be necessary for this purpose'.[23]

The various battles over privative clauses, which have been carried on right to the present day, also make the point. In chapter three, Billy Hughes's description of the interplay between parliament and the High Court as a 'miserable battledore and shuttlecock business' was noted. At some stage in the badminton game, parliament will simply give up, and acknowledge (however begrudgingly) that the courts can effectively never be completely excluded from review. But this alone does not answer the question of juridical principle. However much we might admire the spirit inherent in such interchanges, unless it is accompanied by a statement of justifying constitutional principle, judicial doggedness in circumventing privative clauses lends itself to a charge of wresting the law to the judges' authority.

For the most part, however, the lack of a juridical certainty associated with natural justice has not really been much of a problem until this century. This was so for three reasons. First, before the advent of what I have been calling the 'new' legislation, natural justice had a relatively limited scope. There were cases involving the protection of the quasi-proprietary rights we have in our reputations.[24] And it was of course accepted all along that natural justice applied to the workings of the actual courts of law.[25] Apart from that, however, natural justice was concerned in

---

[22] Quoted in L L Jaffe and E G Henderson, 'Judicial Review and the Rule of Law: Historical Origins' (1956) 72 *LQR* 345, at 353-354.

[23] *Wiseman v Borneman* [1971] AC 297, at 308. As an aside, it is interesting to note that even eight years after *Ridge v Baldwin*, Lord Reid continued to use the old language of functional classification.

[24] *Eg*, *Wood v Woad* (1874) LR 9 Ex 190.

[25] See, *eg*, *Cameron v Cole* (1943) 68 CLR 571, at 589, in which Rich J said:

> It is a fundamental principle of natural justice, applicable to all courts whether superior or inferior, that a person against whom a claim or charge is made must be

the main with the protection of legal proprietary rights against encroachment by the government.

On this, the notion of private property was so sacrosanct in the English legal tradition that in reality, the right to sit in judicial review of property-encroaching cases could be said to have been a principle of constitutional law. *Of course* it was seen to be a 'rule of universal application', 'founded upon the plainest principles of justice', as Willes J put it in *Cooper v Wandsworth Board of Works*,[26] that a man had to be heard before his rights in property could be destroyed. One would be hard-pressed to imagine the Common Pleas having said anything else.

It was in a similar way that in *Local Government Board v Arlidge*, Lord Parmoor could say that in his view, it did not matter whether the proceedings before the Board were classified as judicial or not in order for natural justice to apply. The mere fact that the order was one which affected Arlidge's property rights was enough to oblige the Board to act 'in a judicial spirit, in accordance with the principles of substantial justice'.[27] The important thing, though, is that however broadly the doctrine of natural justice may have been described in the old cases, the actual penumbra of the law was limited by the narrow range of disputes that were seen to raise justiciable issues.

Secondly, it is a fact that for the greater part of its history, the common law has eschewed matters of fine constitutional principle. The common law tradition, possibly in contrast to the continental tradition, is one of stolid pragmatism.[28] But with the onset of the 'new' legislation, unstated assumptions about the appropriateness of curial muscle-flexing came first under strain and then under direct challenge. As discussed in chapter six, once the universal franchise came to be a feature of our parliamentary system, the imperative to justify the overt exercise of political power by reference to a democratic mandate became a pressing one. In the seventeenth century, it was possible to have a series of constitutional clashes amongst Crown, judiciary and parliament in which the opinions of ordinary Englishmen and women were for the most part irrelevant. This simply could not be the case today. Cynicism about

---

given a reasonable opportunity of appearing and presenting his case. If this principle be not observed, the person affected is entitled *ex debito justiciae*, to have any determination which affects him set aside.

[26] (1863) 14 CB(NS) 180 at 190, 143 ER 414, at 418.

[27] [1915] AC 120, at 142.

[28] See, chapter 5, n 1.

media manipulation aside, every political office-holder today – including the judge – is acutely aware of the authority of the opinion-poll.

Thirdly, by the mid-nineteenth century, it could no longer be assumed with confidence that parliaments actually wished to respect individual property rights. To return to *Cooper v Wandsworth Board of Works* and *Municipal Council of Sydney v Harris*,[29] both cases arose in the context of a pretty clearly-stated parliamentary intent to interfere with the traditional rights of private land-owners. Furthermore, many of the new cases dealt with things other than property rights in the strict sense. And even those cases which did involve land oftentimes could not be pigeon-holed into the category of 'state encroachment on holder in fee' case. New types of rights and interests – often previously unknown to the common law – were at issue. *Gillen v Laffer*[30] provides an illustration of this.

The point is that judges may have conservative inclinations, but they are generally not conscious *saboteurs*. During the period in which the new legislation was still new, judges on the whole were aware of the bureaucratic revolution going on all around them – of that, the controversy over *The New Despotism* and the *Housing Act* cases can leave no doubt. They may not have liked it but they were all, at least by the early part of this century, schooled in Dicey and the Whiggish rhetoric of the Glorious Revolution. Unlike the judges of Coke's day, parliamentary supremacy was as integral a provision of their constitution as the sanctity of property rights. As a former Chief Justice of Canada once said:

> We may well feel that judicial supremacy is the highest of all values under a democratic regime of law, and a value to which even the legislature should pay tribute. But we have not enshrined it in any fundamental constitutional law or in our political system. On the contrary, the cardinal principle of our system of representative government, inherited from Great Britain, has been the supremacy of the legislature.[31]

So in searching for ways in which to respond to these sorts of new cases – cases in which parliament was exercising its supreme power in ways unfamiliar to the common law – the courts came to seek refuge in

---

[29] See chapter 2.

[30] (1925) 37 CLR 210.

[31] B Laskin, 'Certiorari to Labour Boards: The Apparent Futility of Privative Clauses' (1952) 30 *Can Bar Rev* 986, at 990 (quoted by Sir Gerard Brennan, in 'The Purpose and Scope of Judicial Review', in M Taggart (ed), *Judicial Review of Administrative Action in the 1980s: Problems and Prospects* (1986) 18, at 26).

the Diceyan formulation of the rule of law. Dicey's rule of law has as its central creed that the executive government is subject to the ordinary law as much as any individual.[32] Judicial review of executive action, therefore, came to be styled as an act of implied agency. Being no longer able to rely solely upon the authority of common law antiquity to justify review (even though it was an antiquity which in fact pre-dated the constitutional settlement), as the legal issues with which they were now dealing were not ones rooted in antiquity, the courts resorted to the other doctrinal justification for legal action – the legislative command. The courts were to be parliament's policemen, ensuring that the executive did not overstep its lawful boundaries. The understood foundation for judicial review, in other words, was the notion of *ultra vires*.

The *Ultra Vires* Principle and Judicial Review

Sir William Wade and Christopher Forsyth have been probably the two most staunch defenders in recent times of the *ultra vires* principle. They have described it as the 'central principle' of administrative law.[33] Without it, they argue, judicial review loses its legitimacy: 'Every administrative act is either *intra vires* or *ultra vires*; and the court can condemn it only if it is *ultra vires*'.[34] From a Diceyist perspective, this is entirely proper. As Christopher Forsyth has written, 'the prime role of [the *ultra vires* principle] is to provide the necessary constitutional underpinning for the greater part ... of judicial review'.[35] He said that '[n]o one is so innocent as to suppose that judicial creativity does not form the grounds of judicial review; but by adhering to the doctrine of *ultra vires* the judiciary shows that it adheres to its proper constitutional position ...'[36] Spigelman CJ recently put it similarly: in justifying judicial review by reference to the *ultra vires* principle, 'the sovereignty of parliament,

---

[32] *The Law of the Constitution* (8th ed. 1915), at 189.
[33] Sir W Wade and C Forsyth, *Administrative Law* (7th ed. 1994), at 41.
[34] *Id*, at 44. For an Australian comment on this point of view, see Aronson and Dyer, *supra* n 2, at 110-115.
[35] 'Of Fig Leaves and Fairy Tales: The *Ultra Vires* Principle, the Sovereignty of Parliament and Judicial Review' (1996) 55 *Camb LJ* 122.
[36] *Id*, at 136.

understood in the sense of a parliamentary monopoly of public power, is affirmed'.[37]

Administrative law, under this view, can largely be characterised as an exercise in statutory interpretation. Taking this in the context of natural justice, such a characterisation does not pose a problem when a statute lays down express conditions for the exercise of power. But what of the case where an Act is silent on an issue which nonetheless offends common law values? The solution is a trick of judicial *legerdemain*. As Wade and Forsyth put it:

> It is presumed that Parliament did not intend to authorise abuses, and that certain safeguards against abuse must be implied in the Act. These are matters of general principle, embodied in the rules of law which govern the interpretation of statutes. Parliament is not expected to incorporate them expressly in every Act that is passed. They may be taken for granted as part of the implied conditions to which every Act is subject and which the courts extract by reading between the lines, or (it may be truer to say) insert by writing between the lines. These implied conditions are to be taken as part and parcel of the Act, just as much as express conditions. Any violation of them, therefore, renders the offending action *ultra vires*.[38]

de Smith, the other of the classic English texts on judicial review, expresses a similar view. After describing the sovereignty of parliament and the rule of law as twin constitutional principles which govern the exercise of public power in a democracy,[39] the editors say:

> The apparent inconsistency between the rule of law and Parliamentary supremacy may be resolved by the courts making the presumption that Parliament intended its legislation to conform to the rule of law as a constitutional principle ... Parliament, when enacting legislation, is presumed to intend that the future implementation and enforcement of its legislation should conform with the fundamental principles of the constitution as elucidated in standards set by the common law.[40]

---

[37] The Hon J J Spigelman, 'Foundations of Administrative Law: Toward General Principles of Institutional Law' (1999) 58 *A J Pub Admin* 3, at 4.
[38] *Supra* n 33, at 42.
[39] *Supra* n 6.
[40] *Id*, at 16.

For present purposes, Lord Guest once described this process of presumption in the context of inferring the existence of a duty to observe natural justice:

> [T]he courts will imply into the statutory provision a rule that the principles of natural justice should be applied. The implication will be made on the basis that parliament is not to be presumed to take away parties' rights without giving them an opportunity of being heard in their interest. In other words, parliament is not to be presumed to act unfairly.[41]

It is clear that approaches such as these can require the courts regularly to turn a Nelsonian eye to what would seem to be perfectly clear statements of legislative intent. While not a natural justice case, the decision of the House of Lords in *Anisminic*[42] provides a wonderful illustration of this technique – which Wade and Forsyth describe as a 'necessary artificiality'[43] – in action. There, the British Parliament had made it quite clear that it wished the determinations of the Foreign Compensation Commission to be immune from judicial review. Nothing could be plainer from a statutory provision which said that '[t]he determination by the Commission of any application made to them under this Act shall not be called in question in any court of law'.[44] Nevertheless, their Lordships were able to read this provision as still permitting review for legal error.[45]

Anisminic is an important case not only for the legal rule that it established, but also for the fact that it illustrated one of the basic truths of public law in the Anglo-Commonwealth tradition. That is that many judges will, if moved to do so by what they perceive to be circumstances of individual hardship, proceed contrary to the actual wishes of parliament. But the method used by the House of Lords in *Anisminic* was

---

[41] *Wiseman v Borneman*, [1971] AC 297, at 310. See also Jacobs J in *Salemi v MacKellar (No 2)* (1977) 136 CLR 396, at 451.

[42] *Anisminic v Foreign Compensation Commission* [1969] 2 AC 147.

[43] *Supra* n 33, at 43.

[44] *Foreign Compensation Act 1950*, sub-s 4(4). Though it would have been improper for their Lordships (in their judicial capacity) to refer to it at the time, a review of *Hansard* makes it clear that the government's intention was to insulate the Foreign Compensation Commission from all legal challenge. In second reading in the Lords, Lord Jowitt LC said that the intention was to allow the FCC to 'decide, and decide finally' how the money in the foreign compensation pot was to be divided up (*Parliamentary Debates*, House of Lords, 27 June 1950).

[45] On *Anisminic*, see Wade and Forsyth, *supra* n 33, at 734-740.

not to deny the constitutional stricture of the supremacy of parliament. Rather, it was to impute to parliament an intention not to deny the citizen access to the courts – though on the actual facts of the case, the contrary view, if anything, was the warranted one. As Sir William Wade himself acknowledged in an analysis of *Anisminic*: 'The intention of Parliament was clear ... In refusing to enforce it, the court was applying a presumption which may override even their constitutional obedience ... This is tantamount to saying that judicial review is a constitutional fundamental which even the sovereign Parliament cannot abolish.'[46]

Professor Wade's frankness illustrates the great weakness of the *ultra vires*/statutory interpretation conception of judicial review. It leaves itself open to charges of intellectual dishonesty – which, for a doctrine of law, is a serious enough charge. But, as Christopher Forsyth has reminded us, its countervailing saving is that it does not do violence to constitutional principle. In the same way that the general introduction of legal fictions saved English land law from collapse, so, too, can 'necessary artificialities' preserve judicial review from necessarily fatal charges of constitutional illegitimacy.

In fact, the statutory interpretation approach was the basis adopted for the imposition of natural justice requirements in new legislation cases for some time. In some of the earlier 'new legislation' cases in the High Court, the *ultra vires* principle was clearly conceived of as the foundation for the imposition of the doctrine of natural justice. In *Municipal Council of Sydney v Harris*, for example, Isaacs J was of this opinion. In his view, it will be remembered, natural justice was applicable because in cases involving interference with property rights, it was 'plain on ordinary principles of construction that the persons affected must have some opportunity to be heard in their own defence'.[47]

Similarly, in *Gillen v Laffer*, Higgins J said that the question was whether *audi alteram partem* was 'tacitly implied' in the provision in issue.[48] This, he said, 'depend[ed] on the construction of the particular Act'.[49] He quoted the passage in *Maxwell on Statutes* which said that in 'giving judicial powers to affect prejudicially the rights of person or

---

[46] *Id*, at 737. See also H W R Wade, *Constitutional Fundamentals* (1980), at 66. For an example of a most strident (and generally extraordinary) criticism of Professor Wade for taking the view that he does on this point, see H M Seervai, *Constitutional Law of India – A Critical Commentary* (4th ed. 1993), at x-xiv, and Postscript to chapter XVI.

[47] (1912) 14 CLR 1, at 14.

[48] (1925) 37 CLR 210, at 225.

[49] 37 CLR, at 227.

property, a statute is understood as silently implying, when it does not expressly provide [the *audi alteram partem* principle]'.[50] Two years later, in *Boucaut Bay Co Ltd v The Commonwealth*, Starke J said that whether a Minister had to provide a hearing to someone whose contract to provide a coastal shipping service in the Northern Territory was to be cancelled turned upon the 'true meaning' of the agreement between the Commonwealth and the contractor.[51]

Even in some old-fashioned property cases from the period, there were hints of the courts using the interpretive approach to determine whether natural justice was required. *De Verteuil v Knaggs*[52] was an example of this. The case involved a property right that most people today would find abhorrent – the rights to property in indentured labourers. The Governor of Trinidad had made an order that a plantation owner have his indentured servants removed from him, on the basis that they were suffering ill-treatment. The Governor made his order pursuant to a local Ordinance, which allowed him to act if he thought it necessary 'on sufficient ground shown to his satisfaction'.[53] In deciding that a hearing was required before such an order could be validly made, the Privy Council found that it was an 'obvious implication' in the legislative scheme.[54]

The *Ultra Vires* Doctrine and Natural Justice in the Modern High Court

The references to *ultra vires* in the judgments of Isaacs and Higgins JJ in the 1920s have already been discussed. But the *ultra vires* approach to natural justice continued to receive a forceful espousal in the High Court into the 1970s.[55] In 1976, in *Twist v Randwick Municipal Council*, Barwick CJ spoke of the duty to observe natural justice in somewhat open-ended terms.[56] Similarly, in *Banks v Transport Regulation Board*, his

[50] 37 CLR, at 225 (quoting *Maxwell* (6th ed. 1920), at 638).

[51] (1927) 40 CLR 98, at 102.

[52] [1918] AC 557 (PC).

[53] *Immigration Ordinance No 161*, s 203.

[54] [1918] AC, at 560.

[55] This was also the position in Canada. See *Attorney-General of Canada v Inuit Tapirisat of Canada* [1980] 2 SCR 735, at 755 (discussed in chapter 6). See also *Alliance des Professeurs Catholiques de Montreal v Labour Relations Board* [1953] 2 SCR 140.

[56] 136 CLR 106, at 109-110.

judgment had been equivocal on the issue of the precise jurisdictional basis for judicial review. But in *Salemi v MacKellar (No 2)*, in 1977, Barwick CJ made clear his view as to the proper source of an obligation to accord procedural fairness. His was a decidedly 'Wade-ish' view of the issue:

> The relevant principles [concerning the duty to observe natural justice] are both fundamental and, in my opinion, fairly well settled. The courts have no power of amendment of an Act of Parliament. They may interpret its language and, perhaps, in doing so, at times reach a result which the Parliament may not have contemplated but which, by the terms it has employed, the Parliament has effected ...
>
> The courts in construing a statute may make express what is implicit in it. Thus they may decide that the statute requires those whom it vests with a power of decision affecting the rights and property of others to adopt procedures which, in the opinion of the courts, are necessary to ensure natural justice. Those procedures are various and stem from the particular statutory situations with which the courts have to deal ... [Fairness] is what is required of a repository of power when on the proper construction of the statute that power is qualified by the need to accord natural justice. *But the basic question is whether the statutory power is so qualified. Whether it is to be so qualified is a matter for the Parliament ... [I]t is fundamental that what the courts do in qualifying the powers is no more than to construe the statute.*[57]

To conceive of the issue otherwise, in the Chief Justice's view, could lead to negative constitutional – and social – consequences. He echoed the views of Sir Owen Dixon, his predecessor as Chief Justice, when he said that '[i]t is most important ... that the courts do not transgress the line dividing the judicial from the legislative function. To do so is to weaken both functions which ought for the health of society to retain their mutual independence.'[58]

In the same case, Jacobs J made a slightly different observation: 'The legislature', he said, 'is assumed by the courts to be aware of the principles of natural justice which are a part of the common law. The application of those principles depends on the circumstances of the case.'[59]

---

[57] (1977) 137 CLR 396, at 400-401 (emphasis added).
[58] 137 CLR, at 401-402.
[59] 137 CLR, at 451.

As noted, Wade and Forsyth, *de Smith* and Lord Reid have also made the same point. But Jacobs J acknowledged the Quixotic reality of the courts' quest for parliamentary intent in natural justice cases:

> I recognise that the search for legislative intention can be described as somewhat artificial. What the courts do in the absence of express legislative intention is to ensure that power, whether it be judicial or quasi-judicial or executive, be exercised fairly, weighing the interests of the individual and the interests of society as a whole.[60]

The view taken by Sir Garfield Barwick leads one to think of he and Lionel Murphy as substantively ill-matched bedfellows on the question of parliamentary sovereignty, but by far the most continuingly vocal advocate in the High Court for the *ultra vires* approach to natural justice has been Sir Gerard Brennan. As was foreshadowed in chapter five, in the legitimate expectation cases in particular Brennan J indicated concern with the way in which his colleagues were expounding the basis of the doctrine of natural justice. Yet, his preoccupation went to the basis for judicial review generally. As Sir Anthony Mason has put it, Sir Gerard's 'perception of the limitation of the judicial role stemmed, in part, from his view of the relationship between the three arms of government.'[61]

Sir Anthony attributed this to Brennan's shared view of the nature of judicial power with Sir Owen Dixon: 'It could be said that the separation of powers, at least the separation of the judicial power, was central to his thinking, as indeed was Sir Owen Dixon's notion of judicial method.'[62] Perhaps the most overt indication of Brennan J's views in this respect was seen in his judgment in 1993, in *Walton v Gardiner*. Referring to the sixth edition of Wade[63] (curiously, one of the few instances in which Professor Wade's work has actually been cited on this point in the High Court), Brennan J said:

> Where a statute confers a jurisdiction or power, [the court] must construe the statute in order to exercise its supervisory jurisdiction. If the statute, either expressly or by implication, limits the power or prescribes rules governing its exercise, the Court enforces the limitation or the observance of the rules in

---

[60] *Ibid.*

[61] 'Judicial Review: The Contribution of Sir Gerard Brennan', paper presented at the Public Law Conference, Canberra, 6 November 1998.

[62] *Ibid.*

[63] (1988), at 42.

> obedience to the intention of the legislature. That legislative supremacy is the justification for judicial supervision is clear enough when the limitation or the rules are expressed; it is no less the justification for judicial supervision when a limitation or governing rule is implied.[64]

On the doctrine of natural justice more narrowly, it is interesting to examine the changing tone of Brennan J's assertions about jurisdictional basis in the legitimate expectation cases of the 1980s. In *FAI Insurances v Winneke*, for example, he was relatively gentle:

> [T]he rules of natural justice describe collectively the kinds of procedural conditions implied by the common law in statutes which confer powers but which do not express, or do not express exhaustively, the procedures to be observed in exercising the powers conferred.[65]

And:

> The construing of a statute with a view to determining whether the principles of natural justice are to be applied requires more than mere exegesis of the statutory text; the common law attributes to the statute an operation which accords as closely as may be with the requirements of justice.[66]

Three years later, in *Kioa v West*, the chiding became just a little bit more pointed:

> The supremacy of Parliament, a doctrine deeply embedded in our constitutional law and congruent with our democratic conditions, requires the courts to declare the validity or invalidity of executive action ... in accordance with criteria expressed or implied by statute. There is no jurisdiction to declare a purported exercise of statutory power invalid for failure to comply with procedural requirements other than those expressly or impliedly prescribed by statute.[67]

By the end of the decade, in *Annetts v McCann*, he was downright insistent:

---

[64] 177 CLR 378, at 408.
[65] (1982) 151 CLR 342, at 407.
[66] 151 CLR, at 409.
[67] (1985) 159 CLR 550, at 611.

> The relevant law must be found in the statutory provisions which create the power and confer it on the repository, though the terms of the statute may be expanded by the implication of conditions supplied by the common law ... This is the foundation and scope of the principles of natural justice. The common law confers no jurisdiction to review the exercise of power by a repository when the power has been exercised or is to be exercised in conformity with the statute which creates and confers the power.[68]

A series of problems come to mind with Brennan J's enunciation of the statutory interpretation/*ultra vires* basis for natural justice. First, he left unanswered the question of natural justice applying to the royal prerogative, something which he actually acknowledged himself.[69] Wade and Forsyth, the two leading academic proponents of the *ultra vires* approach, recognised this as well, saying that 'prerogative power is as capable of abuse as is any other power, and that the law can sometimes find means of controlling it'.[70] The point is that the Brennan analysis leaves a gap in coverage.

Secondly, and perhaps more critically, there is a gap of logic in Brennan J's reasoning with respect to the *scope* of natural justice. This was an issue adverted to earlier, in chapter five. As will be recalled, Brennan J held that legitimate expectations could be relevant insofar as the *content* of natural justice was concerned, but not so as to act as a trigger for the duty. But he also suggested that the trigger for natural justice ought to be allied with the test for standing – which is a creature of the common law, and which is determined according to standards measured according to subjective effect. As suggested in chapter five, to apply Brennan's proffered test is to undercut his thesis about the constitutional foundation of judicial review.

The feeling of perplexion with Brennan J's reasoning on this point increases when one considers his judgment in *Annetts v McCann*. On one hand, he continued to display a greater overt faithfulness to the constitutional premise of parliamentary sovereignty than his colleagues.

---

[68] (1990) 170 CLR 596, at 604.

[69] See *Kioa*, 159 CLR, at 611. See also his piece 'The Purpose and Scope of Judicial Review', *supra* n 31. On the question of review of the prerogative in Australia generally, see F Wheeler, 'Judicial Review of Prerogative Power in Australia: Issues and Prospects' (1992) 14 *Syd L Rev* 432.

[70] *Supra* n 35, at 384 (referring, *inter alia*, to *GCHQ*). In *Constitutional Fundamentals* (1980), Professor Wade said that he thought the expression 'prerogative' was often used too widely, and that if it was properly understood, there would be less controversy over the scope of reviewability of non-statutory power. See especially at 41-48.

But his reference in *Annetts v McCann* to 'terms supplied by the common law'[71] sits ill with this view of the constitution. It of course bears a conspicuous resemblance to the suggestion by Byles J in *Cooper v Wandsworth Board of Works* that the common law could 'supply the omission of the legislature'.[72] Indeed, in *Annetts v McCann*, as in *Attorney-General (NSW) v Quin*, the magisterial appointment case, when it came to actual result, Brennan J based his conclusion on the way in which the *common law* acts to protect reputational interests.[73] Yet, when, in the next legitimate expectation case, *Ainsworth v Criminal Justice Commission*,[74] the High Court reiterated that the common law could give rise to an independent obligation to be 'fair' quite apart from any statutory requirements to the same effect, Brennan's was a voice once more heard in protest.[75]

Thirdly, the *ultra vires* approach is, as noted earlier, arguably intellectually dishonest. Though the curial slight of hand involved in cases like *Anisminic* has in recent years been reiterated by the House of Lords as the source of judicial review power,[76] the *ultra vires* principle as enunciated by Wade and Forsyth has been subjected to strident criticism, both from the academy and from members of the judiciary.[77] Lord Justice Laws, for example, has said that it is a pure fiction to ascribe modern-day principles of judicial review like the protection of legitimate expectations to the intention of the legislature. He said that concepts like these:

---

[71] (1990) 170 CLR 596, at 606.

[72] (1863) 14 CB(NS) 180, at 194, 143 ER 414, at 420. For more on this case, see chapter 1.

[73] 170 CLR, at 608-609 (referring to *NCSC v News Corporation Limited* (1984) 156 CLR 296, *Mahon v Air New Zealand* [1984] AC 808, and *In re Pergamon Press* [1971] Ch 388). Brennan J described the idea that natural justice applies to protect reputational interests as a 'general principle', which is applicable 'unless the statute relating to the performance of the Coroner's functions excludes its application' (170 CLR, at 609).

[74] (1992) 175 CLR 564.

[75] (1992) 175 CLR 564, at 584-585.

[76] *Boddington v British Transport Police* [1998] 2 WLR 639 and *R v Lord President of the Privy Council, Ex parte Page* [1993] AC 682. See also C Forsyth, 'Collateral Challenge and the Foundations of Judicial Review: Orthodoxy Vindicated and Procedural Exclusivity Rejected' [1998] *Pub L* 364.

[77] See, *eg*, P Craig, '*Ultra* Vires and the Foundations of Judicial Review' (1998) 57 *Camb LJ* 63, Sir J Laws, 'Law and Democracy' [1995] *Pub L* 72, Lord Woolf, '*Droit Public* – English Style' [1995] *Pub L* 57, P Craig, *Administrative Law* (3rd ed. 1994), at 12-17, Sir J Laws, 'Illegality: The Problem of Jurisdiction', in M Supperstone and J Goudie (eds), *Judicial Review* (1992), at 67, D Oliver, 'Is the *Ultra Vires* Rule the Basis of Judicial Review?' [1987] *Pub L* 543.

> [w]hich represent much of the bedrock of modern administrative law, were suddenly interwoven into the legislature's intentions in the 1960s and 70s and onward, in which period they have been articulated and enforced by the courts. They owe neither their existence nor their acceptance to the will of the legislature. They have nothing to do with the intention of Parliament, save as a fig leaf to cover their true origins. We do not need the fig leaf any more.[78]

Fourthly, and perhaps most critically of all, is the fact that in the right sort of case, Brennan J could be moved to ignore his own admonitions. He could find himself drawn away from principle by the press of individual circumstance. Such was the case in *J v Lieschke*.[79] The case involved a proceeding under the *Child Welfare Act 1939* (NSW), to have five infant children removed from the custody of their mother, on the basis that they were suffering from neglect. It was apparently the practice in these sorts of proceedings in New South Wales that parents were ordinarily not given full standing.[80] This naturally offended Brennan J's sense of justice. But in arriving at his conclusion that the children's mother ought to have had the right to standing in the proceedings, he made statements which had a most *un*Brennan-like mien to them.

Rather than referring to Wade, or to one of his own previous decisions, or even to the principled exposition of the basis for the doctrine of natural justice by Barwick CJ in *Salemi v MacKellar*, Brennan J instead relied on Barwick CJ's much more open-ended view in *Twist v Randwick Municipal Council*, and on Dixon CJ's judgment in *Commissioner of Police v Tanos*.[81] Indeed, there was no mention whatever in his judgment in *Lieschke* of the necessity of engaging in statutory interpretation in order to find *ultra vires* action on the part of the governmental actor. Instead, he seemed to suggest that natural justice applied to the facts at hand as a matter of common law. 'The general principle which governs this case', he said,

> is clearly established. It is stated by Barwick CJ in *Twist v Randwick Municipal Council* in these terms:

[78] 'Law and Democracy', *supra* n 77, at 79.
[79] (1987) 162 CLR 447.
[80] See 162 CLR, at 454-455.
[81] (1958) 98 CLR 383. See chapter 3.

> The common law rule that a statutory authority having power to affect the rights of a person is bound to hear him before exercising the power is both fundamental and universal ... But the legislature may displace the rule and provide for the exercise of such a power without any opportunity being afforded the affected person to oppose its exercise. However, if that is the legislative intention it must be made unambiguously clear.
>
> The principle governs the proceedings of administrative agencies and, *a fortiori*, the proceedings of the established courts: see per Dixon CJ and Webb J in *Commissioner of Police v Tanos*.[82]

Given the doggedness of his position on natural justice in the legitimate expectation cases, this seems an extraordinary passage to read.[83]

The Common Law as the Preferred Source of Natural Justice Obligations

Of the judges who have eschewed a need to base the right to natural justice on legislative intent, Sir Anthony Mason has probably been the most forthright, though he found consistently good company in Sir Harry Gibbs, Sir William Deane and Sir Daryl Dawson. The first of Sir Anthony's judgments to be considered for present purposes was that in *Twist*. In fact, *Twist* was in many ways an easy case, for it involved an old-fashioned, 'power to demolish unsightly building' statute.[84] The only issue was whether a right to a *de novo* appeal of a demolition order obviated the necessity of according natural justice at first instance. Not surprisingly given the context, Mason J (as he then was) said that

---

[82] 162 CLR, at 456 (quoting *Twist*, 136 CLR, at 109-110, and *Tanos*, 98 CLR, at 396).

[83] Though see also his judgment in *NCSC v News Corp Ltd* (1984) 156 CLR 296, at 326, where he said:

> If a statute were enacted to authorise an administrative agency to publish matter reflecting adversely upon the reputation of a person after an inquiry into that person's conduct, the statute might be expected to specify the procedural protection which the agency would be required to accord to that person. When the limits of a statutory function are ascertained the interests which are apt to be affected by the performance of the function can be identified. Then it is possible for a court to say – in the absence of express statutory provision – what has to be done to be fair to those whose interests are apt to be affected by the performance of the function.

[84] The *Local Government Act 1919* (NSW).

normally, 'it could not be doubted that an intended exercise of the power would attract the rules of natural justice or the duty of fairness'.[85]

In a similar vein, Gibbs J denied that in the circumstances it was necessary to find a statutory 'hook' on which to base an obligation to impose natural justice requirements: 'when the power which is being exercised is a statutory one, it is not necessary to be able to find in the words of the statute itself a duty to hear the party affected or otherwise to act judicially'.[86] Rather, the right to procedural fairness depended on the particular situation: '[t]he question whether the principles of natural justice must be applied, and if so what those principles require, depends on the circumstances of each case'.[87] This, of course, stood in marked contrast to the view of Barwick CJ, who, as noted, thought that whether natural justice applied depended on the intent of the legislature, and hence demanded a 'universal' opinion.[88]

Yet, the real exposition of a doctrine of natural justice free from dependence on interpretive presumptions was to come through Sir Anthony Mason's judgments in the major legitimate expectation cases of the 1980s and 1990s. Indeed, for the most part, Brennan J's reiteration of the Wade/Forsyth view must be read in the context of a reaction against the judgments of his brother Mason in these cases. In *FAI Insurances v Winneke*, for example, Mason J said:

> The fundamental rule is that a statutory authority having power to affect the rights of a person is bound to hear him before exercising the power. The application of the rule is not limited to cases where the exercise of the power affects rights in the strict sense. It extends to the exercise of a power which affects an interest or a privilege or which deprives a person of a 'legitimate expectation', to borrow the expression of Lord Denning MR ... in circumstances where it would not be fair to deprive him of that expectation without a hearing.

---

[85] 136 CLR, at 112.

[86] 137 CLR, at 419.

[87] *Ibid.* See, also, *Bread Manufacturers of New South Wales v Evans* (1981) 180 CLR 404, at 415. Gibbs CJ's view was reminiscent of that once expressed by Lord Wilberforce. In *Wiseman v Borneman* [1971] AC 297, at 317, he said he was 'not satisfied' with an approach that relied upon legislative intent: 'It is necessary to look at the procedure in its setting and ask the question whether it operates unfairly ... to a point where the courts must supply the legislative omission.'

[88] 137 CLR, at 401.

> Natural justice in its application to decisions affecting the grant, refusal, renewal and revocation of licences has been beset with complexities. Some of these abstract complexities have been banished from the stage or at least relegated to the wings ... *It is now authoritatively established that the exercise of a power revoking a licence will attract the rules of natural justice, certainly when the revocation results in the loss of a right to earn a livelihood or to carry on a financially rewarding activity.*[89]

This passage is interesting for its sheer sweep – it represents an illustration of one of Sir Anthony Mason's attempts to codify the common law.[90]

The majority judgments three years later, in *Kioa v West*, show something of the curious non-collegiate way in which the High Court of Australia tends to conduct its business. In his judgment, Gibbs CJ relied upon Mason J's judgment in *FAI Insurances v Winneke* as the basis for applying the doctrine of natural justice.[91] Mason J, in contrast, referred only in passing to *FAI*. Instead, he reiterated (and refined) his views:

> It is a fundamental rule of the common law doctrine of natural justice expressed in traditional terms that, generally speaking, when an order is to be made which will deprive a person of some right or interest or the legitimate expectation of a benefit, he is entitled to know the case sought to be made against him and to be given an opportunity of replying to it. The reference to 'right or interest' in this formulation must be understood as relating to personal liberty, status, preservation of livelihood and reputation, as well as to proprietary rights and interests.[92]

He said that the law had:

> now developed to a point where it may be accepted that there is a common law duty to act fairly, in the sense of according procedural fairness, in the making of administrative decisions which affect rights, interests and legitimate expectations, subject only to the clear manifestation of a contrary statutory intention.[93]

---

89 151 CLR, at 360 (internal citations omitted) (emphasis added).
90 See also in this respect his judgment in *Minister for Aboriginal Affairs v Peko-Wallsend* (1986) 162 CLR 24.
91 See 159 CLR, at 563.
92 159 CLR, at 582.
93 159 CLR, at 584.

In *Annetts v McCann*, Mason CJ (as he now was) joined with Deane J and McHugh J in offering the following view of the doctrine's scope:

> It can now be taken as settled that, when a statute confers power upon a public official to destroy, defeat or prejudice a person's rights, interests or legitimate expectations, the rules of natural justice regulate the exercise of that power unless they are excluded by plain words of necessary intendment.[94]

Relying on the judgment of Dixon CJ and Webb J in *Tanos*, the three judges continued:

> [A]n intention on the part of the legislature to exclude the rules of natural justice was not to be assumed nor spelled out from 'indirect references, uncertain references or equivocal considerations'. Nor is such an intention to be inferred from the presence in the statute of rights which are commensurate with some of the rules of natural justice.[95]

Annetts v McCann, it will be remembered, was the case in which the High Court bizarrely found that there was no legislative intent to exclude natural justice on the basis that West Australian parliament in 1920 would not have thought that natural justice would apply to coronial proceedings. *Quod voluit non dixit*: parliament could not be said to have intended that it be excluded. More importantly from a doctrinal point of view, though, this case made it clear just how far Australian law had shifted from the *ultra vires* position. Rather than requiring a legislative indication that natural justice was to apply (even if the indication was implied by the common law), what instead was required was a legislative indication – and not by implication, but by 'clear manifestation' – that it was not to apply.[96]

In *Haoucher v Minister for Immigration and Ethnic Affairs*,[97] Deane J went even further, and suggested that natural justice ought, as a legal presumption, to apply to *all* government decision-making. He said that the law seemed to him:

---

[94] 170 CLR, at 598.

[95] *Ibid.*

[96] Similarly, in *Municipal Council of Sydney v Harris*, 14 CLR, at 11, Barton J held that the obligation to observe natural justice was one which was presumptively implied in 'interference with property' cases. Where a statute is silent on the matter of a hearing right, he said 'the courts will not assume that the legislature intended to prohibit it, unless such intention can be gathered from the statute by clear implication'.

[97] 169 CLR 648.

> to be moving towards a conceptually more satisfying position where common law requirements of procedural fairness will, in the absence of a clear contrary legislative intent, be recognised as applying generally to governmental executive decision-making.[98]

In *Teoh*, McHugh J indicated his agreement with this and said that 'the rational development of this branch of the law requires acceptance of the view that the rules of procedural fairness are presumptively applicable to administrative and similar decisions made by public tribunals and officials'.[99] It is doubtful that expressed in such direct terms, these statements accurately reflect the state of the law in Australia.[100] But their usefulness lies in the fact that they throw down the gauntlet with respect to the legitimacy issue. Indeed, the issue is almost neat in its symmetry. In *Banks*, the High Court began the liberalisation of the doctrine of natural justice, but, as discussed in chapter six, Barwick CJ glossed over the jurisprudential issues. In *Teoh*, the Court carried the project through to its ultimate point – a natural justice-triggering legitimate expectation being found to exist when there was no expectation at all. But (as discussed in chapter five), in doing so, it made plain just how shaky the project's doctrinal underpinnings had become. In *Haoucher*, Sir William Deane said that he thought that this shift was much more 'conceptually satisfying', but with respect to his Honour, he did not attempt to explain why this was the case.

One might well agree that in terms of *outcome*, a presumptive application of the rules of natural justice to all government decision-making (though presumably Deane and Toohey JJ must only have had in mind government decision-making which affects people on an individual basis) is more satisfying than one which allows bureaucrats a shield to be unfair. But according to what principles of constitutional law can this approach be more satisfying? On what juridical basis is an approach like this legitimate? To be sure, it has the pragmatic advantage that it does not suffer from the gap in coverage that Brennan J's did. As has been seen, all of the other High Court judges from this period except Murphy J, and

---

[98] 169 CLR, at 653.

[99] *Minister for Immigration and Ethnic Affairs v Teoh* (1995) 183 CLR 273, at 311.

[100] For John McMillan's criticisms of this view, see 'Developments Under the ADJR Act: The Grounds of Review' (1991) 20 *Fed L Rev* 50, at 70-74. See also Wilcox J in *Minister for Arts, Heritage and Environment v Peko-Wallsend Ltd* (1987) 15 FCR 274, at 306: 'the law has not yet reached the stage of applying the obligation of natural justice to every decision which disadvantages individuals.'

perhaps Gibbs CJ, considered power exercised under the prerogative as reviewable in principle as power exercised under statute.[101] But for Justices Deane and McHugh (and, implicitly, Mason CJ) to have left their claim unexplained in terms of underlying principle is to leave it as little more than a vulgar, if compassionate, assertion of legal positivism.[102]

Legislated Decision-Making Procedures and Common Law Natural Justice

One possible means of justifying this approach in accordance with commonly accepted constitutional principles is to read a legislative non-reaction to the cases as amounting to a tacit approval of the extension of the reach of natural justice – in effect, to make use of Wade's and Forsyth's (and Jacob J's[103]) point that parliament is presumed to legislate in light of the common law. As has been noted, in *Wiseman v Borneman*, Lord Reid made comments which could arguably lend themselves to such a view:

> Natural justice requires that the procedure before any tribunal which is acting judicially shall be fair in all the circumstances ... For a long time the courts have, *without objection from parliament* supplemented procedure laid down in legislation where they have found that to be necessary for this purpose.[104]

But this, then, raises the question of how the High Court has reacted to legislative statements as to procedure.[105] This, as will be remembered, had lain at the base of the judgment of the Lord Thankerton's speech in *Franklin v Minister of Town and Country Planning*.[106] He found the inclusion of a statutory decision-making procedure to have had the effect of excluding the common law rules of natural justice. But if the common law, rather than statute, is to be the source of the duty to observe natural justice, then it remained to be determined what the relationship of

[101] In *R v Toohey*, Gibbs CJ made a special point of noting that his views only dealt with the exercise of a statutory power. See 151 CLR, at 186.

[102] Though in fairness to their Honours, it should be pointed out that the Privy Council has indicated similar views. See *Huntley v Attorney-General for Jamaica* [1995] 2 AC 1.

[103] In *Salemi v MacKellar (No 2)*.

[104] [1971] AC 297, at 308 (emphasis added).

[105] See generally Aronson and Dyer, *supra* n 2, at 457-465.

[106] [1948] AC 87. See chapter 3.

legislative statement as to decision-making procedures and natural justice is to be. A related question is as to the effect of a right of appeal on natural justice obligations at first instance.

In *Twist*, Barwick CJ discussed this. He said that the obligation to observe natural justice can be displaced by legislation – either by formally excluding it or by including statutory procedures in lieu. This was a point that the High Court had made earlier, in *Namatjira v Raabe*, when it said that the existence of a right of appeal *de novo* suggested a legislative intent to displace hearing requirements at first instance.[107] In *Twist*, Barwick CJ said that if parliament has 'addressed itself' to the question of decision-making procedures, a court is not entitled to impose additional procedural requirements as a matter of common law: 'the court, being bound by the legislation as much as the citizen, has no warrant to vary the legislative scheme'.[108]

In *Brettingham-Moore v St Leonards Municipality*, he made much the same point. Ordinarily, he said, natural justice would apply to a decision to dissolve a municipal entity. But since the legislation in question (the Tasmanian *Local Government Act 1962-1966*) contained a provision whereby notice of any proposed change to municipal organisation was to be published, and that aggrieved persons had the right to petition the Governor not to accept the proposal,[109] any requirements the common law would attach to the decision-making process were displaced. He said:

> [Section] 15 is a clear indication by the legislature of the nature of the opportunity which it will afford the aggrieved persons to make known their views ... The case is not one in which the legislature is silent as to the right to be heard, so that the common law can fill the void. The legislature has addressed itself to the very question and it is not for the Court to amend the statute by engrafting upon it some provision which the Court might think more consonant with a complete opportunity for an aggrieved person to present his views and to support them by evidentiary material.[110]

It was to this point that Mason CJ and Deane and McHugh JJ were replying in *Annetts v McCann*, when they said that an intention to exclude natural justice was not to be 'inferred from the presence in the statute of

---

[107] (1959) 100 CLR 664, at 668-669.
[108] 136 CLR, at 110.
[109] Section 15.
[110] (1969) 121 CLR 509, at 524. See, also, 522-523.

rights which are commensurate with some of the rules of natural justice'.[111] Yet, there were in the early 1970s a series of cases in which the House of Lords and Privy Council seemed to offer support for the Barwick view.[112] In *Wiseman v Borneman* itself, for example, the House of Lords held that the inclusion of a disputation procedure in taxation legislation[113] displaced the common law requirements of natural justice. As Lord Morris put it, 'it is, I think, a positive consideration that parliament has indicated what it is that the tribunal must do and has set out [what] the tribunal must take into account ...'.[114]

Similarly, in *Pearlberg v Varty* (which also dealt with taxation legislation), Lord Hailsham LC said that the courts 'have no power to amend or supplement the language of a statute merely because on one view of the matter, a subject feels himself entitled to a larger degree of say in the making of a decision than the statute accords him'.[115] In the same case, Viscount Dilhorne said that the decision-making procedure ought not to be 'regarded as anything other than deliberate and, if deliberate, it should be assumed that parliament did not think that the requirements of fairness made it advisable to provide [any additional hearing rights]'.[116]

In *Furnell v Whangerei High Schools Board*, the Privy Council cited with approval the passage from Barwick CJ's judgment in *Brettingham-Moore* quoted above, and found that the absence of a provision giving rights to early notice of complaint, in a statute dealing with the employment of teachers,[117] 'must have been deliberate since the regulations proceed with great particularity to specify when and how

---

[111] 170 CLR, at 598. Curiously, though, their Honours did not actually refer to Barwick CJ's judgment in *Twist*. Instead, they referred to a decision of the New South Wales Court of Appeal (*Baba v Parole Board of New South Wales* (1986) 5 NSWLR 338, at 344-345, 347, 349) as authority for their proposition that a decision by parliament to impose some procedural requirements on the decision-making process was not to be taken as a sign that the legislature was intending to occupy the field, to borrow the expression from constitutional law. See also *J v Lieschke* 162 CLR, at 460-461.

[112] Though, as Aronson and Dyer note (at 476), the argument has been rejected in a number of cases in Australia. See, *eg*, Baba *v Parole Board of New South Wales* (1986) 5 NSWLR 338, *R v Chairman of Parole Board, Ex parte Patterson* (1986) 43 NTR 13 and *Queensland v Litz* [1993] 1 Qd R 343.

[113] The *Finance Act 1960*, ss 28, 29.

[114] [1971] AC, at 310.

[115] [1972] 1 WLR 534, at 540.

[116] [1972] 1 WLR, at 545.

[117] The Secondary and Technical Institute Teachers Disciplinary Regulations 1969, made under the *Education Act 1964* (NZ).

communication should be made to him and when and how he should make response'.[118]

More recently, in *Rees v Crane*, the Privy Council read the decision to enshrine a decision-making procedure in legislation (actually, the Trinidadian Constitution) as being of special significance.[119] *Rees v Crane* involved an attempt by the Chief Justice of Trinidad and Tobago to have a puisne justice – Crane J – of the Supreme Court dismissed. The circumstances of the attempted dismissal reeked of substantive unfairness (Mr Justice Crane had, for instance, been given formal notice of his suspension from judicial duties by a policeman in a public street). Their Lordships said:

> It is clear that [the Trinidadian Constitution] provides a procedure and an exclusive procedure for such suspension and termination and, if judicial independence, mean anything, a judge cannot be suspended nor can his appointment be terminated by others or in other ways.[120]

But it should be observed that this view – at least, as it was expressed by Barwick CJ in *Brettingham-Moore* and *Salemi v MacKellar* – suffers from a significant logical flaw. In *Salemi v MacKellar*, Barwick CJ had nailed his colours to the Wade-ist mast. Yet, in light of his judgments in cases like *Twist* and *Banks*, he must be taken to have had the view that parliament is *presumed* to intend that natural justice be required when property rights or matters of personal livelihood are in issue. But if parliament *actually* indicated a concern for procedural protection, then he would have said that natural justice is excluded! When the Barwick propositions are set out this way, they seem an odd formulation.[121]

---

[118] [1973] AC 660, at 681. Barwick CJ's judgment in *Brettingham-Moore* was quoted with approval at 679.

[119] [1994] 2 AC 173.

[120] [1994] 2 AC, at 187-188. See also the recent decision of the Full Court of the Federal Court in *Eshetu v Minister for Immigration and Multicultural Affairs* (1997) 145 ALR 621, in which Davies and Burchett JJ (Whitlam J dissenting) held that the *Migration Act* grounds for reviewing decisions were intended to substitute for common law grounds, including natural justice. See 145 ALR, at 625 (Davies J), 145 ALR, at 636 (Burchett J).

[121] As an aside, in the second edition (1968), *de Smith* made the point that it was the inclusion of hearing requirements in statutes that contributed to the decline in natural justice:

> Paradoxically, the decline of the *audi alteram partem* principle as an implied common-law requirement of administrative procedure was hastened by its embodiment in statutory forms. Twentieth century statute law has indirectly reflected

Moreover, Barwick CJ's point stands in contradiction of the way in which the superaddition question was treated during the *R v Electricity Commissioners* period. Then, it was taken that the Court of Appeal had said that a parliamentary indication of decision-making procedures could serve as evidence of a duty to act judicially. In other words, it was thought that the inclusion of formal decision-making procedures could be taken as a signal that natural justice *was* to apply. Further, in many contexts to apply the Barwick approach would lead to an absurd result. As Aronson and Dyer have said, for instance, it would be silly to argue that the existence of a right of appeal to the Administrative Appeals Tribunal ought to be taken as evidence of a legislative intent to exclude natural justice at the initial decision-making stage.[122]

Nonetheless, in the abstract, each of the expressed standpoints have some appeal. If natural justice is a right which enjoys some sort of paramount status (the Mason/Deane/McHugh view), then the courts should view any attempt to oust it with the same suspicion that they have traditionally brought to the interpretation of statutes which purport to interfere with common law rights.[123] But if natural justice is merely a requirement of ordinary common law, then it should be open for parliament to signify that it has 'occupied the field', to borrow an expression from constitutional law (the Barwick view). But if it is neither of these things, and is instead merely a right which arises in non-traditional contexts when parliament says that it should, then it is fair to look for some sort of signal that natural justice should be observed, in the form of statutorily-enshrined decision-making procedures (the *Electricity Commissioners* view).

Lord Diplock once attempted to reconcile the various views by drawing a distinction between the doctrinal places of statutory and common law decision-making procedures – the former, he thought, went

---

the disfavour with which the common law viewed administrative claims to be entitled to take direct action against private property without giving notice or the opportunity to be heard (at 146-147).

[122] At 477. See also *Courtney v Peters* (1990) 98 ALR 645, at 654.

[123] See *Coco v R* (1994) 179 CLR 427, at 463 (general words in legislation are 'insufficient to authorise interference with basic immunities which are the foundation of our freedom; to constitute such authorisation express words are required' (Mason CJ, Brennan, Gaudron and McHugh JJ, quoting Lord Browne-Wilkinson in *Wheeler v Leicester City Council* [1985] AC 1054, at 1065). See also *R v Bolton, Ex parte Beane* (1987) 162 CLR 514, at 523, *Bropho v Western Australia* (1990) 171 CLR 1, at 18, *Balog v ICAC* (1990) 169 CLR 625.

to the question of voidness of the decision on the basis of *ultra vires*, the latter went to fairness of the decision-making process.[124] The simple fact, however, is that the Gibbs and Mason-era High Courts have simply ignored either of the latter two views. *Annetts v McCann* is a prime illustration of a case where the Court felt completely free to use the common law to supplement the decision-making procedures determined by the parliament in question. And all of the cases considered thus far show that the superaddition test of the *Electricity Commissioners* period is long-dead in Australia.

The only area in which the question of legislative intent might now be thought to be relevant to the doctrine of natural justice in Australia is with respect to content. In *Kioa v West*, Mason J said that in the case of a decision made under statute, 'the application and content of the doctrine of natural justice or the duty to act fairly depends to a large extent on the construction of the statute'.[125] Similarly, in *Bread Manufacturers of New South Wales v Evans*, Mason and Wilson JJ said in their joint judgment that the 'application of the rules [of natural justice] is flexible, varying in extent from case to case, and falls to be determined in the case of a statutory body exercising statutory powers by reference to the proper construction of the statute'.[126] Taken with the acknowledgment of a legislative power to exclude natural justice (provided, of course, this is done with words of 'necessary intendment'), these passages could be understood as an admission of parliamentary supremacy after all. But this is not, in fact, how they ought to be understood.

The notion of natural justice having a variable, circumstance-dependent, content is an old one. Tucker LJ's statement in *Russell v Duke of Norfolk*, that '[t]he requirements of natural justice must depend on the

---

[124] In *O'Reilly v Mackman* [1983] 2 AC 237, at 276:

> Where the legislation which confers upon a statutory tribunal its decision-making powers also provides expressly for the procedure it shall follow in the course of reaching its decision, it is a question of construction of the relevant legislation ... whether a particular procedural provision is mandatory, so that its non-observance in the process of reaching the decision makes the decision itself a nullity ... But the requirement that a person who is charged with having done something which, if proved to the satisfaction of a statutory tribunal, has consequences that will, or may, affect him adversely, should be given a fair opportunity of hearing what is alleged against him and of presenting its own case, is so fundamental to any civilised legal system that it should be presumed that Parliament intended that a failure to observe it should render null and void any decision reached in breach of this requirement.

[125] 159 CLR, at 584.

[126] 180 CLR, at 432-433.

circumstances of the case, the nature of the inquiry, the rules under which the tribunal is acting, the subject-matter that is being dealt with, and so forth',[127] has been cited with approval several times by the High Court.[128] It is a point of common sense, for 'fairness' is an adjectival noun, and it must be rooted in circumstance if it is to have any meaning. That is why the statements about the 'proper construction of the statute' in *Bread Manufacturers v Evans* and *Kioa* cannot in fact be seen as requiring paramount importance to be paid to parliamentary intent in determining the content of the duty of procedural fairness. Indeed, if we say that the duty to observe natural justice arises by operation of the common law, then it logically cannot follow that its content may be determined by reference to parliamentary intent. Moreover, as we have seen, in those cases in which parliament actually does express an intention with respect to decision-making procedures, the courts will, where deemed necessary, supplement them (as happened, for instance, in *Bread Manufacturers v Evans*).

A Legitimising Basis for Natural Justice?

In fact, the reference to the proper construction of the statute can only mean a reference to the sorts of procedures which can be accommodated within the statutory framework. The courts will of course do their best to avoid frustrating the parliamentary objects in enacting the statute.[129] But the required procedures themselves are, just as is the initial duty to observe natural justice itself, determined by the common law. The point – and it is a political point, really – is that in considering the doctrine of

---

[127] [1949] 1 All ER 109, at 118.

[128] See, *eg*, *South Australia v O'Shea* (1987) 163 CLR 378, at 400, *R v Ludeke, Ex parte Customs Officers' Association of Australia* (1985) 155 CLR 513, at 530, *Kioa v West*, 159 CLR, at 584-585, *NCSC v News Corporation Ltd* (1984) 156 CLR 296, at 311-312, *Salemi v MacKellar* 137 CLR at 444, *R v Commonwealth Conciliation and Arbitration Commission, Ex parte Angliss Group* (1969) 122 CLR 546, at 552-553, *Mobil Oil Australia Pty Ltd v Federal Commissioner of Taxation* (1963) 113 CLR 475, at 504. See, also, *R v Gaming Board for Great Britain, Ex parte Benaim and Khaida* [1970] 2 QB 417 (CA), *Wiseman v Borneman* [1971] AC 297, *Furnell v Whangerei High Schools Board* [1973] AC 660 (PC, NZ), *University of Ceylon v Fernando* [1960] 1 WLR 223 (PC).

[129] See, *eg*, Lord Reid in *Wiseman v Borneman* [1971] AC 297, at 308: 'But before this unusual kind of power is exercised it must be clear that the statutory procedure is insufficient to achieve justice and that to require additional steps will not frustrate the apparent purpose of the legislation.'

natural justice, the High Court considers the interests of the individual before the interests of the state. To return again to the words of Sir Gerard Brennan quoted at the beginning of the chapter: 'The interests of individuals are more fully acknowledged, and the repositories of power are constrained to treat the individual both fairly and according to law.'[130]

This leads us back to the basic question of legitimacy. However we may regard the desirability of this approach as a political matter, by what legitimising basis has the High Court adopted it? A study of the cases can lead only to one conclusion: that the jurisdictional basis for the doctrine of natural justice in Australia today is an over-arching common law. The cases since the 1980s have all but rejected Diceyan premises as the foundation for judicial review. As Sir Anthony Mason has suggested, the view which is supported by the holdings is that 'the law of judicial review is the creation of the common law and that the courts exercise a jurisdiction to ensure that administrative decision-making conforms to the requirements of the law'.[131] In Sir Anthony's opinion, this view is a rather more satisfactory one than a Wade-Forsyth/Brennan view, being both more realistic in terms of explaining present-day cases, and more in accord with legal history.[132]

In both of these respects, Sir Anthony is undoubtedly correct. The fact is that courts *do* regularly rule with an agnosticism to the evidence of parliament's wishes. Moreover, as discussed in chapter one, the law of natural justice (and of judicial review generally) is much older than the law of parliamentary supremacy. But does the latter justify the former? The problem is that in a judicial context, the High Court has not given an express answer to this; it has not enunciated a juridical basis for the present-day approach in natural justice cases that has been examined in these past three chapters. If the points made in this chapter are taken together with the expansion of the compass of natural justice that was discussed in chapters five and six, the picture which emerges is one of a vastly-expanded doctrine of natural justice, but one which is largely bereft of principled underpinnings; a doctrine whose scope and content are to be determined according to the prejudices and assumptions of the individual members of the judiciary. In a country which prides itself on being governed by the rule of law, one wonders whether this can be a satisfying basis for the exercise of judicial power.

---

130 'Reflections', *supra* n 4.

131 *Supra*, at 386.

132 *Ibid.*

8 A Study in Common Law Constitutionalism

One of the things that this study has shown is that considered in terms of coverage or ambit, the doctrine of natural justice in Australia today is in an exceedingly hale, vigorous state. To be sure, there are problems with the doctrine's application – the inconsistency in judicial approach regarding legitimate expectations *v* 'mere hopes', which was discussed in chapter five, is one such problem – but the fact remains that the range of decision-making processes subject to a duty of procedural fairness is much, much wider than it was just thirty or forty years ago. Sir Gerard Brennan was perfectly accurate when he said that society 'now accords to the individual an opportunity to meet on more equal terms with the institutions of the state', and that individual interests 'are more fully acknowledged, and the repositories of power are constrained to treat the individual both fairly and according to law'.[1]

Sir Gerard was, it is true, actually speaking in commemoration of the anniversary of the statutory reforms to Commonwealth administrative law, but it is no less the case that the process by which 'repositories of power' have been 'constrained to treat the individual both fairly and according to law' is attributable to the growth of the common law – and to the shift in attitude towards natural justice in the High Court since the decision in *Banks v Transport Regulation Board* in 1968.[2]

Indeed, this is perhaps the chief observation to be drawn from this work: the extent to which the civilising mission of administrative law has, in recent times, taken place without direct reference to the authority of parliament. The conventional understanding of natural justice as being rooted in the *ultra vires* principle has been discarded by the High Court. As chapter seven has shown, the existence or not of a duty to accord procedural fairness is determined at first instance in Australia today by the common law, rather than by statute. Judicial review legislation may make

[1] 'Reflections' (1989) 58 *Canberra Bulletin Pub Admin* 32, at 33.
[2] 119 CLR 222.

specific reference to a denial of natural justice as a ground of review,[3] but the tenor of the judgments of the High Court in the cases discussed in chapter five – cases like *South Australia v O'Shea*,[4] *Haoucher*,[5] *Annetts v McCann*[6] and *Teoh*[7]– can leave no doubt that the source of procedural rights against the Australian Executive is not parliamentary command, but common law sanction.

Natural Justice as a Constitutional Principle

It is in this sense that the story of natural justice in Australia can be described as a study in common law constitutionalism. Whether we define a constitution as a paramount source of limitation of state power, or as a set of base norms according to which a society is constituted, in the way it has come to be enunciated by the High Court, the doctrine of procedural fairness amounts to a doctrine of constitutional law.

Indeed, various judges of the Court have said as much. When, for example, Mason J spoke in *FAI Insurances v Winneke* of 'offer[ing] some protection to the citizen against the legislative practice of conferring statutory discretion',[8] he was speaking in constitutional terms. When, in *O'Shea*, he suggested that if it were to appear that parliament was attempting to structure decision-making procedures so as to avoid triggering natural justice obligations, 'the Court might be compelled to go further' in expanding the scope of procedural fairness,[9] he was issuing a constitutional warning to the political branches.

Deane J was even more pointed in his description of the common law as a constitutional bulwark. In *O'Shea*, he said that the rules of natural justice 'reflect the minimum standards of basic fairness which the common law requires to be observed in the exercise of governmental ... authority or power'.[10] And when Deane and McHugh JJ suggested in *Haoucher* and *Teoh* that it would be 'conceptually more satisfying' if procedural fairness

---

[3] See, *eg*, *Administrative Decisions (Judicial Review) Act 1977* (Cth), para 5(1)(a).
[4] (1987) 163 CLR 378.
[5] *Haoucher v Minister for Immigration and Ethnic Affairs* (1990) 169 CLR 648.
[6] (1990) 170 CLR 596.
[7] *Minister for Immigration and Ethnic Affairs v Teoh* (1995) 183 CLR 273.
[8] (1982) 151 CLR 342, at 372.
[9] *South Australia v O'Shea* (1987) 163 CLR 378, at 386. See also Sir Anthony's recent paper, 'Reflections on the Development of Australian Administrative Law', in R Creyke and J McMillan (eds), *The Kerr Vision of Australian Administrative Law at the Twenty-Five Year Mark* (1998) 122, at 124.
[10] 163 CLR, at 416.

were to attach 'generally to government executive decision-making',[11] they were both enunciating a vision of constitutional control of the Executive.

It is undoubtedly the existence of an entrenched Constitution that leads people in Australia sometimes to overlook the continuing relevance of the common law constitution. But the fact is that even though there is a written constitutional document, and even though the common law constitution can in principle be amended by ordinary legislation,[12] Dicey's reference to the law of the constitution stemming from the accumulation of judicial decisions in ordinary litigation[13] remains pertinent in Australia. Sir Owen Dixon once offered a salutary reminder of this when he said that Australia's federal structure sometimes led people to mistake the federation's constitutional foundation:

> Federalism means a rigid constitution and a rigid constitution means a written instrument. It is easy to treat the written instrument as the paramount consideration, unmindful of the part played by the general law, notwithstanding that it is the source of the legal conceptions that govern us in determining the effect of the written instrument.[14]

His work is not often cited today, but the influence of W E Hearn, the first Dean of Law in the University of Melbourne,[15] is apparent in the writing of both Dixon and Dicey.[16] In particular, it was Hearn's work which underlay Dicey's encapsulation of the essence of English

---

[11] Deane J in *Haoucher*, 169 CLR, at 653, McHugh J in *Teoh*, 183 CLR, at 311.

[12] Though as to the practical difficulty of this, witness the story of the privative clause. See M Aronson and B Dyer, *Judicial Review of Administrative Action* (1996), chapter 18.

[13] See *The Law of the Constitution* (8th ed. 1915), at 191.

[14] 'The Common Law as an Ultimate Constitutional Foundation' (1957) 31 *ALJ* 240, at 241. Spigelman CJ recently made a similar observation:

> Because we have a written Constitution, the area of constitutional law is generally identified with exegesis of the terminology of the written document. I believe, however, that we have a broader constitution, of which the *Constitution Act 1900* is simply one, perhaps the most significant, component.

'Foundations of Administrative Law: Toward General Principles of Institutional Law' (1999) 59 *A J Pub Admin* 3, at 8.

[15] Hearn (1826-1888) was a graduate of Trinity College, Dublin. He was appointed Professor of History, Literature, Political Economy and Logic at Melbourne in 1854, and in 1874 became Dean of Law. He also sat as a member of the Victorian Legislative Council from 1878 until his death. On the importance of Hearn's legal work, see also H W Arndt, 'The Origins of Dicey's Concept of the "Rule of Law" ' (1957) 31 *ALJ* 117, at 121-123 and Spigelman, *supra* n 14, at 3-4. On his work as an economist, see J A La Nauze, *Political Economy in Australia: Historical Studies* (1949).

[16] For Dixon's discussion of Hearn's thought, see 'The Law and the Constitution' (1935) 51 *LQR* 590, at 593-596.

constitutionalism as being the rule of law. Indeed, Dicey was later to describe Hearn as the person who, more than anyone else, taught him 'of the way in which the labours of lawyers established in early times the elementary principles which form the basis of the constitution'.[17]

In his book, *The Government of England*, Hearn began by writing that 'the English constitution forms part of the common law'.[18] It was this understanding of the essence of constitutionalism that Toohey J was drawing on when he said that what underlies the expression 'rule of law', 'is that there are known principles according to which decisions should be made affecting the relationship between State and citizen on the one hand and citizen and citizen on the other'.[19] and that '[t]he rule of law demands that these principles should be applied, not as a matter of discretion but by their own force'.[20] It was in the same vein that Isaacs J spoke, nearly seventy-five years ago, of a source of judicial authority being 'certain fundamental principles which form the base of the social structure of every British community.'[21] And when, in *South Australia v O'Shea*, Mason CJ made his statement about the Court reserving the right to go further in expanding the compass of natural justice, he was speaking in terms of a similar understanding of the part played by the common law judiciary in setting the bounds of constitutional control.

But it is precisely this understanding of constitutionalism which gives rise to a concern stemming from the High Court's recent natural justice holdings. That is the significance of the assertion that natural justice rights are grounded in the common law, rather than statute. As has been discussed in earlier chapters (particularly chapter seven), the conventional understanding of the basis of natural justice was that it was related to the *ultra vires* principle; that it stemmed from a presumption about parliament's intentions. To take this in Harlow's and Rawlings's terms,[22] the conventional approach to natural justice embodied a theory of the state which has the constitutional principle of parliamentary sovereignty at its heart.

---

[17] Preface to *The Law of the Constitution* (1st ed. 1885), at vi. Dicey was also to say of Hearn:

> He was to be universally recognised among us as one of the most distinguished and ingenious exponents of the mysteries of the English Constitution had it not been for the fact that he made his fame as a professor not in any of the seats of learning in the United Kingdom but in the University of Melbourne (*ibid*).

[18] (1st ed. 1867), at 1.

[19] 'A Government of Laws, and Not of Men?' (1993) 4 *Pub L Rev* 158, at 159.

[20] *Ibid.*

[21] *Ex parte Walsh and Johnson, In re Yates* (1925) 37 CLR 36, at 79.

[22] See Introduction.

There are – as was discussed in chapter seven – allegations of intellectual dishonesty that can be levelled at the sort of interpretive stretching that must take place to keep faith with the *ultra vires* doctrine. But, as Christopher Forsyth has retorted, such an approach at least does not do overt violence to the constitutional arrangements which emerged after the settlement of 1688. Yet, the recent cases in Australia have involved – Barwick CJ and Murphy and Brennan JJ partially excepted in this respect – an explicit rejection of the statutory interpretation approach to natural justice. So what of a doctrine which stems not from presumptions about legislative entitlement, but from the common law? What constitutional theory is involved in this?

In fact, such a view fits nicely with Professor Hearn's theory of the constitution – that it forms part of the common law. This was a point made by Sir Owen Dixon in a paper delivered in 1957.[23] The thesis of Dixon's paper was that in Australia, the common law amounted to 'an anterior law providing the source of juristic authority for our institutions when they came into being'.[24] What Sir Owen meant by this was that all of our constitutional principles derive their status as constitutional principles from recognition as such by the common law. The condition precedent for the enjoyment of constitutional authority is the recognition by the common law of the constitution as an instrument of paramount status. Without such recognition, the constitution would amount to nothing more than a written text.

In other words, Dixon argued that the common law's existence was anterior to the constitution not only in a temporal sense, but also in a juridical or juristic sense. If the written constitution has paramount status, the common law has *ante*-paramount, or *supra*-paramount, status. The rules of the common law were the source of the authority of parliament, and amount to the constitutional antecedent. The notion of parliamentary supremacy could only operate as a constitutional principle because it was recognised as such by the common law. The common law was the constitutional *grundnorm*. As Dixon put it in another piece:

> It is of the essence of Parliamentary supremacy that the Courts of law, once there is put before them an authentic expression of the legislative will, shall give unquestioned effect to it according to what appears its true scope and intent. But it is of the essence of the supremacy of the law that the Courts shall disregard as unauthorised and void the acts of any organ of

---

[23] 'The Common Law as an Ultimate Constitutional Foundation', *supra* n 14.

[24] *Id*, at 240.

Government, whether legislative or administrative, which exceed the limits of the power that organ derives from the law.[25]

It is in this way that the old 'paradigm' English natural justice cases that were discussed in chapter one can properly be said to have amounted to an exercise in constitutional adjudication.[26] If the constitution is understood in the way described by Dixon, then it is perfectly in keeping with juristic principle to speak of the common law as the source of natural justice rights, which the law will employ to delimit the authority of the executive. But in considering Dixon's point, it is critical to realise that the Australian constitutional antecedent was not an Australian common law, but rather *the common law of England*.

The expression 'common law' can of course be understood in a number of senses. For present purposes, it can on one hand refer to the pragmatically-disposed adversarial system of dispute resolution that is employed in most jurisdictions which formerly enjoyed the status of British colony. In this sense, the Australian common law began to differ from the English common law almost as soon as it was deemed to have been received.[27] But when Sir Owen Dixon wrote of the common law as the constitutional antecedent, he was using the expression in a different sense. He used it to refer to what Salmond described as the 'ultimate legal principle'. By this, Salmond was speaking not of a principle of substantive law, but rather of the historical foundation for the legal order:

All rules of law have historical sources. As a matter of fact and history they have their origin somewhere, though we may not know where it is. But not all of them have legal sources. Were this so, it would be necessary for the law to proceed *ad infinitum* in tracing the descent of its principles ... In other words there must be found in every legal system certain ultimate principles,

---

[25] 'The Law and the Constitution', *supra* n 16, at 596.

[26] See T R S Allan, 'The Common Law as Constitution: Fundamental Rights and First Principles', in C Saunders (ed), *Courts of Final Jurisdiction: The Mason Court in Australia* (1996) 146, at 148.

[27] While no study has yet been done of this aspect of his work in New South Wales, when he was Chief Justice of Newfoundland, Sir Francis Forbes regularly used local custom as a source of Newfoundland common law, and it is almost certain that he regularly did it in New South Wales as well. On his use of local custom in Newfoundland, see *Coleman v Kennedy* (1817) 1 NLR 8, *Broom v Williams* (1817) 1 NLR 15, *Ryan v Simms* (1817) 1 NLR 34, and *Heath v Kean* (1820) 1 NLR 193. In *Hayes v Nave* (1821) 1 NLR 259, however, he said that a 'bad custom' would not be applied. On Forbes's influence on the received law in New South Wales, see generally, I Holloway, 'A Fragment on Reception' (1998) 4 *Aust J Leg Hist* 79 and I Holloway, 'Sir Francis Forbes and the Earliest Australian Public Law Cases' (unpublished, 1998).

> from which all others are derived, but which are themselves self-existent. Before there can be any talk of legal sources, there must be already in existence some law which establishes them and gives them their authority.[28]

It is used in this second sense that 'the common law' can be said to enjoy ante-constitutional status in Australia. But the common law in question was the English common law. It was the English common law which was the source of the authority of the parliament at Westminster which, in turn, was the source of the authority of the parliament at Canberra. The significance of this point in the Australian constitutional context was alluded to by Dixon:

> Wherever the common law has gone the theory of the supremacy of the law has necessarily gone with it. But the theory of legislative sovereignty stands in a different position. Its transfer to lands outside Britain was less easy. For the common law, being English law, and not *ius gentium*, did not recognise the sovereignty of a Legislature as an abstract idea, as a quality belonging to a Legislature inherently ... The King in Parliament was established by the English common law as the English Legislature and that and that alone was endowed by the common law with supreme and unlimited legislative power.[29]

In his (at the time, controversial) article, 'A Government of Laws, and Not of Men?', Mr Justice Toohey made a reasoned argument for common law constitutionalism. He said that some principles in society are fundamental, and that 'it is the role of an independent judiciary to give effect to those principles, within the rule of law, as best it can'.[30] He continued: 'although the relationship in our society between the authority of the legislature and the rule of law fluctuates over the course of time, the rule of law is the dominant factor in the relationship'.[31] In the course of his argument, his Honour quoted with evident approval a reference by Harrison Moore to 'the real subordination of government to law'.[32]

There is, however, a problem with this claim in the present-day Australian setting. When Moore was writing in the early part of this

---

[28] See *Jurisprudence* (8th ed. 1930), at 169. For a variation on this construction, see also his *First Principles of Jurisprudence* (1893), at 220-221. See further A Frame, *Salmond: Southern Jurist* (1995), at 64-68, and R T E Latham, *The Law and the Commonwealth* (1949), at 522-523.

[29] 'The Law and the Constitution', *supra* n 16, at 595.

[30] *Supra* n 19, at 174.

[31] *Ibid.*

[32] *Id*, at 164 (quoting Moore, 'Foreword', to R G Menzies, *The Rule of Law During the War* (1917), at 3).

century, he was doing so in the context of the same understanding about the roots of constitutionalism as Dixon CJ. But now, the High Court has come to deny the continued existence of the constitutional antecedent. The Court has on several occasions insisted that the source of legal authority in Australia is no longer the statute law of the Imperial parliament (*viz*, the *Commonwealth of Australia Constitution Act 1900*), but rather the licence of the Australian people. In *Australian Capital Television v The Commonwealth*, for example, Mason CJ said:

> The very concept of representative government and representative democracy signifies government by the people through their representatives. Translated into constitutional terms, it denotes that the sovereign power which resides in the people is exercised on their behalf by their representatives.[33]

In other words, the sovereign source of governmental power is no longer the law (acting as it formerly did through the conduit of Imperial legislation) but 'the Australian people'. Implicit in this sort of assertion must be a denial of the antecedent constitutional status of the common law and, therefore, also the common law's sovereignty and status as an ultimate legal principle. But when read against the backdrop of the natural justice cases, in which the Court has said that the source of natural justice rights is not legislation but the common law, this demands the question: in light of what the High Court asserts to be the new Australian constitutional reality, on what constitutional basis do we ascribe to the common law a power, independent of legislation, to regulate the decision-making processes determined by the peoples' agents? Surely, in any constitutional setting where the people are the sovereign source of governmental power, the doctrine of sovereignty must be grounded in a practice of according primacy to decision-making procedures set out in parliamentarily-enacted legislation. But this runs very counter to the holdings discussed in the last three chapters.

Natural Justice, the Common Law and Constitutional Dissonance

The point is that the recent natural justice cases reveal a contradiction in the High Court's public law discourse. It is inconsistent to speak both of

---

[33] (1992) 177 CLR 106, at 137. See also the authorities cited in chapter 6 and G J Lindell, 'Why Is Australia's Constitution Binding? The Reasons in 1900 and Now, and the Effect of Independence' (1986) 16 *Fed L Rev* 29. It is interesting to see how similar Chief Justice Mason's vision of government was to that of Pember Reeves, the progressive, whose work was discussed in chapter 2.

popular sovereignty, and of the common law as the source of procedural rights against the government. This is because it is antithetical to our conception of the rule of law that the courts can be seen as the agents of the people. McHugh J may or may not have been correct when he asserted that '[t]he courts, as much as the legislatures, are in continuous contact with the concrete needs of the community',[34] but the constitutional principle of judicial independence operates *vis-à-vis* the people as well. The courts can have no constituency, save the common law – using the expression here in the first sense, described earlier. Moreover, unlike the case of parliament and the ballot box, there is no line of formal constitutional connection between the people and the courts through which a principle-agent relationship could be consummated.

Furthermore, while the Australian common law may amount to a reflection of community values (provided, to paraphrase Archibald Cox, that the courts know us better than we know ourselves[35]), it cannot amount to an ultimate legal principle, for the deep historical rootedness of ultimate legal principles is inconsistent with the generationally shifting nature of popular sovereignty. The common law, enforced by unelected judges, can amount to an ultimate legal principle in the English setting because of its anciency – because the English constitution has its roots in the pre-democratic era. Under the old understanding of the Australian constitution, this could be held to be the case here, as well. But if now in Australia, representative democracy is to be the basis for government (as the High Court says it is), then any sort of claim to common law antecedency must, *ipso facto*, be constitutionally offensive. In a state whose constitutional foundation is not based on an ultimate legal principle but upon popular sovereignty, it surely must be constitutionally impermissible to speak of the common law as the source of natural justice rights.

But this leads us back to the juridical point: according to our constitutional design, a fundamental precept of which is the notion of judicial independence, popular sovereignty can only express itself though legislation. This being the case, the existence of natural justice rights can, if juristic principle is not to be violated, only be determined by reference to the *ultra vires* principle. Yet, the High Court has explicitly rejected this as the basis for the modern Australian doctrine of procedural fairness. In chapter six, it was noted that the editors of *de Smith* have said that 'the standards applied by the courts in judicial review must ultimately be

---

[34] 'The Law-making Function of the Judicial Process – Part II' (1988) 62 *ALJ* 116. Many people, of course, would take a different view from his Honour.

[35] *The Role of the Supreme Court in American Government* (1976), at 117.

justified by constitutional principles, which govern the proper exercise of public power in any democracy'.[36] The conclusion to be drawn from a study of the recent natural justice cases in the High Court is that there is a significant dissonance in the Court's thinking about constitutionalism and the rule of law in Australia.

The Purposive Constitution

There is a second juristic concern stemming from the recent natural justice cases – which, from a pragmatic perspective, is possibly more a pressing one. That is the Court's failure to offer any real purposive justification for the imposition of procedural fairness requirements.

There is a school of thought – typified by the writing of Michael Oakeshott[37] – which holds that the existence of legal authority need not have any explicit social purpose in order to justify itself. In his now well-known scheme, Martin Loughlin classified people who conceive of law (and government) in this way as 'normativists'.[38] According to Loughlin's definition, W E Hearn and Sir Owen Dixon offered normative visions of the constitutional order:

> The normativist style in public law is rooted in a belief in the ideal of the separation of powers and in the need to subordinate government to law. This style [of thought] highlights law's adjudicative and control functions and therefore its rule orientation and its conceptual nature. Normativism essentially reflects an ideal of the autonomy of law.[39]

In Loughlin's taxonomy, normativism is contrasted with what he termed 'functionalism'. In contradistinction to the normativist, who believes that the law begets government, the functionalist 'views law as part of the apparatus of government'.[40] The functionalist's focus 'is upon law's regulatory and facilitative functions and therefore is oriented to aims and objectives and adopts an instrumentalist social policy approach. Functionalism reflects an ideal of progressive evolutionary change'.[41] To classify them in Loughlin's terms, the Anglo-Canadian scholars of the

---

[36] S A de Smith, H Woolf and J Jowell, *Judicial Review of Administrative Action* (5th ed. 1995), at 14.
[37] For more on Oakeshott see chapter 4, nn 24 and 25.
[38] M Loughlin, *Public Law and Political Theory* (1992), at 60.
[39] *Ibid.*
[40] *Ibid.*
[41] *Ibid.*

1930s and the Australian progressives discussed in chapter two were ideal type functionalists.

The usefulness of Loughlin's labels for present purposes lies not in their precision (for, as Loughlin himself acknowledged, most public law thought represent an amalgam of functionalism and normativism[42]), but in the fact that they highlight the range of possible difference in constitutional premises. In the 1920s natural justice cases discussed in chapter two, for example, some judges – notably Isaacs and Higgins JJ – showed functionalist sympathies. In the 1940s and 1950s, Sir Owen Dixon showed both functionalist and normativist strains of thought: his judgments in cases like *Browning*,[43] *Hickman*,[44] and *Namatjira v Raabe*,[45] are functionalist in stance, while his academic writing on the constitution stands in illustration of the applicability of normativism to the Australian setting.

Moving to the present-day, it is clear that some of the more recent members of the Court have come to express a vision of the constitution in terms akin to functionalism. They have suggested that the function of the constitution is not simply to place value-neutral limits on state power. Instead, they have said that they view the allocation of power within the constitutional framework in 'purposive' terms. Michael Detmold has spoken of this as the 'new constitutional law'.[46] John Doyle (as he then was) described it as the 'grand design' vision of the Australian constitution.[47] In fact, it would be wrong to claim that, as yet, the shift in judicial thought amounts to a comprehensive (or coherent) theory of constitutionalism,[48] but there is no doubt that the High Court has shifted away from the simple approach of textualism in constitutional interpretation that endured for so long after the decision in the *Engineers' Case*.[49] In *Davis v The Commonwealth*, for example, Brennan J said that the 'end and purpose of the constitution is to sustain the nation'.[50] More

[42] *Id*, at 61.
[43] *Water Conservation and Irrigation Commission (NSW) v Browning* (1947) 74 CLR 492. On these cases, see chapter 3.
[44] *R v Hickman, Ex parte Fox and Clinton* (1945) 70 CLR 598.
[45] *Namatjira v Raabe* (1959) 100 CLR 664.
[46] 'The New Constitutional Law' (1994) 16 *Syd L Rev* 229.
[47] 'Constitutional Law: "At the Eye of the Storm"' (1993) 23 *UWA L Rev* 15, at 20.
[48] See J M Williams, 'The Protection of Rights Under the Australian Constitution: A Republican Analysis' (unpublished PhD thesis, ANU, 1997), at 373-376.
[49] *Amalgamated Society of Engineers v Adelaide Steamship Company Ltd* (1920) 28 CLR 129. On the case and its import, see M Coper and G Williams (eds), *How Many Cheers for Engineers?* (1997).
[50] (1988) 166 CLR 79, at 110.

specifically, Mason CJ has spoken of at least certain provisions of the constitution as being 'designed to enhance national unity and a real sense of national identity'.[51]

Equally importantly for present purposes, some members of the High Court have indicated a view that 'purposivism' applies also to the common law constitution – and, consequently, that the judicial role in defining and applying public law principle is a purposive one. Sir Anthony Mason once described this as the 'dynamic rule' of constitutional evolution.[52] This was, he said in a different setting, part of the High Court's project of bringing into existence 'a distinctive body of Australian law'.[53] An integral part of this project involved judicial innovation, independent of the action or inaction of the legislature. Sir Anthony said that it was 'no longer feasible for courts to decide cases by reference to obsolete or unsound rules which result in injustice and await future reform at the hands of the legislature'.[54] Likewise, McHugh J has said:

> In certain situations, invoking democratic rhetoric to legitimise the refusal to deliver justice is itself undemocratic, particularly when democratic reform is unlikely. When a legislature fails to recognise and address a problem of law reform, the use of democratic rhetoric to deprive the courts of the opportunity to contribute to the development of the law and the doing of justice is highly questionable.[55]

Paul Finn has argued that we must subject judge-made law, and the judicial law-making process, to the same sort of scrutiny as we do statute law and the legislative process.[56] This, then, is the frame of mind in which we ought to evaluate the High Court's treatment of natural justice: as a doctrine of constitutionalism, employed in functionalist, purposive terms.

---

[51] *Street v Queensland Bar Association* (1989) 168 CLR 461, at 485. See also *Leeth v The Commonwealth* (1992) 174 CLR 455.
[52] 'The Role of a Constitutional Court in a Federation' (1986) 16 *Fed L Rev* 1, at 23.
[53] 'Changing the Law in a Changing Society' (1993) 67 *ALJ* 568.
[54] 'The Australian Judiciary in the 1990s' (unpublished address to the Sydney Institute, 15 March 1994). *Cf* his comments on judicial law reform in *State Government Insurance Commission v Trigwell* (1979) 142 CLR 617, at 633.
[55] *Supra* n 34, See also G Craven, 'The Crisis of Constitutional Literalism in Australia' (1992) 30 *Alta L Rev* 492.
[56] 'Of Power and the People: Ends and Methods in Australian Judge-Made Law' (1994) 1 *The Jud Rev* 255, at 263.

Natural Justice as a Purposive Doctrine

In the past, speaking of procedural fairness in 'natural' terms itself acted as a signal of the doctrine's purpose. The terminology of natural rights was a sufficient link with the Enlightenment as to make plain the law's liberal, humanistic goals in imposing a duty of fairness in decision-making procedures. If government tended to view administration (and administrative law) in functional terms, the function of natural justice was to act as a normativistic check – as a reminder of the normativistic limits that our constitutional system, with the English common law as its antecedent, imposed upon popularly-elected governments.

To a certain extent, there has been a paradox at play in the tension that has been felt to exist in natural justice cases between the judiciary and the executive. That is that the curial aspiration for individual fairness, and the competing administrative desire for governmental professionalism and efficiency, stem from the very same values. As was discussed in chapter one, natural justice as we understand the doctrine today was a creature of the Enlightenment. The Enlightenment may have been concerned with progress, but it was what one might call 'mission-oriented' progress. It was all about progress as a means of liberating humanity; of improving the human condition. To paraphrase Harold Laski, it was about recognising that the liberty of the ordinary person was an end in itself.[57]

The paradox lies in the perception of a tension between individual fairness and collective efficiency. The humanistic goals which have driven both the executive and the judiciary have been one and the same. The problem – and this is a legacy of the peculiarly English version of the Enlightenment, which included the constitutional revolution of 1688 – is that the competing players are driven by constitutional design to view human interest from a comparatively narrowly confined perspective. To return to a point made in the Introduction, at the moment that disputes transform themselves from political to legal ones, formal constitutional strictures impose themselves on the decision-making processes – both administrative and legal. The rub in this – as seen from the perspective of the executive – is in the fact that according to our conception of the rule of law, the courts must have the final word. Because of this, the factor which will ultimately determine the scope and reach of natural justice is the legal or social purpose that the High Court sees it fulfilling.

---

[57] 'Liberty in the modern sense is founded on the principle that the ordinary man is recognised as an end in himself and not as a means to the end of the state' (quoted by Sir W Monckton, in 'Liberty and the Common Law' (1942) 20 *Can Bar Rev* 670, at 674).

There are at least five different (though substantially overlapping) contemporary-sounding purposive justifications that might be offered for a legal attentiveness to the fairness of administrative decision-making procedures.[58] One such justification is what Paul Craig and others have described as an '*instrumental*' purpose: 'helping to attain an accurate decision on the substance of the case'.[59] O'Connor J once said that the notion underlying natural justice is that 'by ensuring that the process is fair, the chances that an unbiased decision-maker will make the best decision in the circumstances is [*sic*] maximised'.[60] Lon Fuller described it in slightly different terms, but he was making essentially the same point when he said that '[t]he procedural limitations that surround the adjudicative function are designed to ensure as rational a decision as possible.'[61] Professor Wade explained this notion in terms which are readily comprehensible to the administrative lawyer:

> The whole theory of 'natural justice' is that ministers, though free to decide as they like, will in practice decide properly and responsibly once the facts have been fairly laid before them ... Arbitrary exercise of an administrative power the courts cannot control, for policy is in the last resort arbitrary. But much can be done to prevent an appearance of arbitrariness, and since in practice it is far more likely to be accidental than intentional, a procedure which satisfies 'natural justice' is the best insurance against such accidents.[62]

One of the most compelling arguments for the instrumentalist view in recent years was offered by D J Galligan, in his book *Due Process and Fair Procedures*.[63] Central to Galligan's argument was that one cannot divorce consideration of decision-making procedures from the decisions they are intended to result in. On the very first page, he indicated his broad agreement with Fuller's point:

> In a modern legal system, the range of legal decisions is considerable, but one common feature is that each tries to advance certain ends and goals. Legal decisions are in that sense purposive, and so the main point of procedures is to serve those purposes.

[58] For slightly different characterisations of the justifications, see P P Craig, *Public Law and Democracy in the United Kingdom and the United States of America* (1990), at 176-179, and the Hon J W von Doussa, 'Natural Justice in Federal Administrative Law' (1998) 17 *AIAL Forum* 1, at 2-3.

[59] *Administrative Law* (3rd ed. 1994), at 282.

[60] 'Is There Too Much Natural Justice?' (1994) 1 *AIAL Forum* 82, at 84.

[61] 'Collective Bargaining and the Arbitrator' [1963] *Wisc LJ* 3, at 29.

[62] H R W Wade, 'Quasi-Judicial and its Background' (1949) 10 *Camb LJ* 216, at 229.

[63] (1996).

That is why, in the instrumentalist view, it is impossible to define a given set of decision-making procedures as being fair or unfair in the abstract. The *indicium* of fairness is, to an instrumentalist, a relative one, measured according to the degree to which the urged decision-making process promotes the decision's underlying purpose. In this sense, the instrumentalist view is well-suited to Loughlin's school of functionalism. As Jeffery Jowell once put it, the rules of natural justice attempt 'to promote fidelity to organisational purpose'.[64] This is accomplished, 'both by permitting the persons affected to argue their case and, where a reasoned decision is required, giving, through the process of justification, what Fuller has described as "formal and institutional expression to the influence of reasoned argument in human affairs"'.[65] In other words, the instrumentalist view is premised on the very same thing as the adversary system: that hearing both sides of a dispute leads to 'better' decision-making.

This was part of what Lord Parker CJ had in mind when he asserted that good administration and natural justice were intertwined ends.[66] And it was in this sense that in *Brettingham-Moore v St Leonards Municipality*,[67] the High Court held that in principle, a hearing could be compelled in the process of gathering information for the purpose of preparing a report for the Governor, which he would use as the basis of an exercise of discretion. The High Court did not say so explicitly, but this holding plainly reflected an instrumentalist concern about the Governor's decision-making process. Instrumentalism was also behind Deane J's articulation of the so-called 'probative evidence rule', whereby he held that decision must be based on 'some probative material or logical ground', otherwise it would be deemed tainted for unfairness.[68]

Yet, the instrumentalist should not be thought to be claiming that the observance of natural justice will always lead to *the* correct decision, in a bi-valent sense. For instrumentalists acknowledge that in many cases, there will be no single correct decision. Rather, they argue, 'correctness' is a function of perspective, and the observance of fair decision-making procedures ensures that the perspective of the decision-maker is as broad as

---

[64] 'The Rule of Law Today', in *The Changing Constitution* (3rd ed. 1994), at 68.
[65] *Ibid.*
[66] *Re H K* [1967] 2 QB 617, at 630. See chapter 6.
[67] (1969) 121 CLR 509.
[68] *Australian Broadcasting Tribunal v Bond* (1990) 170 CLR 321, at 366. See also Aronson and Dyer, *supra* n 12, at 388-391.

is legally permissible. To borrow Lord Parker's characterisation again, the object is to ensure that an 'honest *bona fide* decision' is made.[69]

Nevertheless, the instrumentalist justification for natural justice contains some significant limitations. Most troublingly of all, it views the question of fairness from the perspective of the executive government rather than the individual. Considered in light of the High Court's statements about constitutional purpose referred to earlier, this seems a profound defect. On a pure instrumental view, if the Executive can prove that it does not need any additional information to make the sort of decision it intended to make (*ie*, to make the 'correct' decision in the circumstances), then natural justice can be dispensed with, regardless of the degree of unfairness that might be suffered by the individual(s) affected.

There are also some significant practical complications associated with an instrumental view of natural justice. For example, while the instrumentalist view may be borne out in an adversarial hearing before an administrative adjudicator in which matters of fact are in controversy, for many of the types of decision-making processes that present-day members of the executive must engage in, an instrumental claim would not seem to advance the analysis very far. Most critically, it remains generally the case that natural justice does not attach to the making of regulations, or to other governmental activity which can be described as 'legislative' in character.[70] There are compelling logistical reasons for this rule, but if instrumentalism were the justification for the doctrine of natural justice, then one could not unreasonably expect the law to be otherwise – or at least that it should be permissive on the question of rights to involvement in the making of subordinate legislation.

In the case of non-legislative decision-making, instrumentalism presents other problems. In the case of a policy-laden decision which reflects the long-held political views of a governing party, for example, can one say that the existence of the policy amounts to a violation of the bias rule? An instrumentalist would surely be inclined as a matter of logic to hold that it does, at least insofar as the policy could be argued to represent a mind closed to other avenues of action without first having had the benefit of argument from all interested parties.[71] What of what Lon Fuller

---

[69] *Ibid.*

[70] See Aronson and Dyer, supra n 12, at 431-438. See also G Craven, 'Legislative Action by Subordinate Authorities and the Requirements of a Fair Hearing' (1988) 16 *Melb U L Rev* 569.

[71] On this point, see the discussion of *Franklin v Minister of Town Planning* [1948] AC 87 in chapter 3. See also Aronson and Dyer, *supra* n 12, at 439-446.

described as a 'polycentric' decision?[72] Must a decision-maker confer with every affected person on every aspect of the issue which affects them in order to establish the legitimacy of the decision-making process? This does not immediately commend itself as a matter of logic or as a matter of instinct.

An alternate series of approaches to the conceptualisation of natural justice is to view the doctrine from the perspective of the needs of the citizen rather than those of the government – which Craig rather uninspiringly termed the 'non-instrumentalist' justifications.[73] First among these is what might be termed the '*rule of law*' purpose. This holds that attentiveness to fairness in the course of governmental decision-making promotes confidence in the system of governance, which, in turn, promotes civic peace.

The rule of law justification for natural justice reflects a concern for one of the most critical features of our conception of the rule of law, namely that we do not require excessive police presence in society because compliance with the law is for the most part voluntary. This was a point emphasised by Lord Denning. In *The Road to Justice*, he wrote that people 'do not obey the law simply because they are commanded to do so; nor because they are afraid of sanctions or of being punished. They obey the law because they know it is a thing they *ought* to do.'[74]

Likewise, when Hamilton LJ said in *Local Government Board v Arlidge* that 'the more open the procedure is the better ... Time spent in removing a grievance or in avoiding the sense of it, is time well spent, and the Board's officials will, like good judges, amplify their jurisdiction by rooting it in the public confidence',[75] he was viewing the attractiveness of procedural fairness in 'rule of law' terms. The cost of a denial of natural justice seen from the rule of law perspective was summed up nicely by the High Court in *R v Watson, Ex parte Armstrong*. In a joint judgment, Barwick CJ, Gibbs, Stephen and Mason JJ said:

> It is of fundamental importance that the public should have confidence in the administration of justice. If fair-minded people reasonably apprehend or suspect that the tribunal has prejudged the case, they cannot have confidence

---

[72] 'The Forms and Limits of Adjudication' (1978) 92 *Harv L Rev* 353, at 395. See also Aronson and Dyer, *supra* n 12, at 151-161.
[73] See *supra* n 59, at 282.
[74] (1955), at 2. Galligan spoke to this, as well. He said that 'confidence in a process, confidence that the law has been properly applied or a discretion reasonably exercised, depends to a significant degree on confidence in the procedures as means to those outcomes' (*supra* n 63, at 66).
[75] [1914] 1 KB, at 203-204.

in the decision. To repeat the words of Lord Denning MR which have already been cited, 'Justice must be rooted in confidence: and confidence is destroyed when right-minded people go away thinking: The judge was biased.'[76]

Closely related to this is what one might call the '*libertarian*' or '*rhetorical*' justification for natural justice. This finds its home in the sort of language used by Lord Kenyon CJ in the eighteenth century in *R v Gaskin*: that *audi alteram partem* is one of the 'first principles of justice'.[77] The rhetorical justification probably comes closest to enshrining natural justice as a 'pure' principle of constitutionalism. Not surprisingly, this justification for procedural fairness (or 'procedural due process', as it is known there) has featured in the judgments of the Supreme Court of the United States. In one case, for example, Douglas J said: 'It is not without significance that most of the provisions of the Bill of Rights are procedural. It is procedure that spells much of the difference between rule by law and rule by whim or caprice.'[78] Similarly, Frankfurter J once said that '[t]he history of liberty has largely been the history of procedural safeguards'.[79]

A fourth purpose can be termed the '*dignitarian*' purpose. Inherent in this idea is the tailoring of decision-making procedures so as to promote of the dignity of the human condition. The value of fair procedures is measured according to how well they promote the more general goal of social well-being, rather than according to how well they promote 'correct' decisions. According to this view, the preferability of a decision depends not so much on whether it meets some objectively verifiable criterion of 'correctness', but rather on whether it has satisfied our social demand for recognition as autonomous, free-thinking human beings.

In *Ridge v Baldwin*, Lord Evershed offered a dignitarian basis for the imposition of natural justice when he said that natural justice should be required 'in cases where the body concerned can properly be described as administrative – so long as it can be said, in Sir Frederick Pollock's language, that the invocation is required in order to conform to the ultimate principle of fitness with regard to the nature of man as a rational and social being'.[80]

---

76 (1976) 136 CLR 248, at 263.

77 (1799) 8 TR 209, at 210, 101 ER 1349, at 1350. See *supra* chapter 1, at 24.

78 *Joint Anti-Fascist Refugee Commission v McGrath* (1951) 341 US 123, at 179.

79 *Mcnabb v The United States* (1943) 318 US 332, at 347.

80 [1964] AC, at 86.

Dignitarianism was at the heart of much of Sir Isaiah Berlin's writing about freedom,[81] but a powerful present-day champion of the dignitarian view is T R S Allan. Taking a view contrary to both Galligan and Fuller, Allan has specifically disassociated natural justice and instrumentalism:

> A formal or 'instrumentalist' theory of natural justice overlooks its grounding in recognition of the moral status of the person affected by a decision. It is a legitimate expansion of the rule of law, which extends the scope of natural justice from judicial proceedings to a broader range of administrative decisions, because the purposes of granting a fair hearing are not limited to those of the efficient administration of law or policy.[82]

Part of the basis for Allan's dignitarianism is his view of the social contract:

> The interpretation of law as a moral claim to the citizen's allegiance rests in a view of the law's subjects as morally responsible and autonomous persons entitled to respect. The fairness of ... procedures is an essential element in that claim to allegiance.

This view has been echoed by both John Finnis and the American administrative law scholar Jerry Mashaw. Finnis, for example, wrote that 'a principle component of the idea of constitutional government ... is the holding of the rulers to their side of a relationship of reciprocity, in which claims of authority are respected on condition that authority respects the claims of the common good (of which a fundamental component is respect for the equal right of all to respectful consideration)'.[83] Another proponent of the dignitarian view has been Dawn Oliver. In a recent article in *Public Law*, she wrote that 'the requirements of legality, fairness and rationality in judicial review protect applicants from exercises of power that would be adverse to their interests – their security in the status quo, their status in society, their autonomy, dignity and respect'.[84]

A final justification for the imposition of legal procedural requirements upon governmental decision-makers in fact draws heavily upon all of the other non-instrumental values. That is what might be called

---

[81] See chapters 2 and 4.
[82] *Law Liberty and Justice* (1993), at 29.
[83] *Natural Law and Natural Rights* (1980), at 272-273. See also J Mashaw, *Due Process in the Administrative State* (1985), chapter 4.
[84] 'Common Values in Public and Private Law and the Public/Private Divide' [1997] *Pub L* 630, at 631.

the '*participatory*' or the '*republican*' purpose. This view was explored by Allan in a rejoinder to Galligan's book. In Allan's view,

> the value of participation is not merely, or even primarily, instrumental. It is democracy's guarantee of the opportunity for all to play their part in the political process, in exercise of their moral responsibility as equal citizens, which explains the implicit connection between participation and respect.[85]

According to this view, public participation is thought to be a good *per se*, regardless of the merits of the actual decision in question. As one commentator has put it, this view holds that the purpose of procedural requirements associated with administrative decision-making is to 'facilitate the representation of minority interests, while leaving the choice of substantive values to the processes of politics'.[86] It is a view that has had particular association with American constitutional and administrative law. A classic statement of a republican conception of administrative law can be found in Richard Stewart's famous article, 'The Reformation of American Administrative Law', in which he argued that the consequence of the struggle between competing claims of individual autonomy and administrative efficiency had resulted in administrative decision-making procedures becoming a 'surrogate political process to ensure the fair representation of a wide range of affected interests in the process of administrative decision'.[87]

Translating this into the Australian context, one could argue that in a state founded upon a constitutional premise of popular sovereignty, it is axiomatic that the basic human right (beyond, one supposes, access to the necessities of life) is the right to participate in civil society. Indeed, the very notion of representative democracy is predicated upon people exercising their civil rights – it was this view that lay at the base of the 'representative government' cases.[88] The courts may have neither the expertise nor the mandate to pronounce upon affairs of state, but for democracy to be effective, or for the notion of political accountability to have any real meaning, people must be accorded respect as individuals by the government. And that, precisely, is what the doctrine of natural justice

---

[85] 'Procedural Fairness and the Duty of Respect' (1998) 18 *Ox J Leg Stud* 497, at 509.

[86] M Loughlin, 'The Importance of Elsewhere' (1993) 4 *Pub L Rev* 44, at 47. See also P P Craig, *Public Law and Democracy*', *supra* n 58, at 97-116.

[87] (1975) 88 *Harv L Rev* 1667, at 1670. See also generally J H Ely, *Democracy and Distrust: A Theory of Judicial Review* (1980).

[88] *Nationwide News v Wills* (1992) 177 CLR 1, *Australian Capital Television v The Commonwealth* (1992) 177 CLR 106 and *Lange v Australian Broadcasting Commission* (1997) 189 CLR 520.

could be said to be intended to ensure – that our importance as individuals is not overlooked by our agents in the political government. In this view, the doctrine of natural justice is, in republican terms, both the *quid pro quo* for the rule of law and the *sine qua non* for popular sovereignty.

At first glance, the non-instrumentalist purposes seem in their tenor to be more in keeping with the themes that emerged from the cases in the 1980s and early 1990s than instrumentalism. Most particularly, the advantage of the non-instrumentalist justifications is that they view the doctrine of natural justice from the perspective of the citizen, rather than the state. Yet, the non-instrumental justifications plainly have their limits, too. Do we, for instance, tailor what are often expensive and time-consuming decision-making processes to suit the dignitarian demands of the overly sensitive – the sorts of people who in private law would be described as the 'thin-skulled'?

And of the various non-instrumental views, most would seem to suffer from an historical dis-rootedness. It is only fairly recently, for example, that the social contract could be argued to have included terms concerning governmental respect for our dignity, or ones which hold that participation in government is a good thing. For the greater part of our common law history, the social contract has instead been based upon the reciprocal feudal claims of loyalty and protection. In an historical sense, it is only what I have called the 'rule of law' justification that can have any real basis in law, in the sense that it is concerned with the keeping of the Queen's peace – but this seems a defect in that it leads it to resemble the instrumental justification, at least to the extent that the starting point for ascertaining the importance of natural justice is the government's interests (in maintaining public confidence in itself).

The Modern Australian Justification for Natural Justice?

In earlier chapters, it was suggested that the doctrine of natural justice in Australia had suffered, in a comparative sense, from under-theorisation. The continuing accuracy of this observation is borne out by the fact that in the recent cases, the High Court has been somewhat erratic in its reference to the purpose served by natural justice. In an address to the Australian Legal Convention in 1991, Sir Anthony Mason suggested that the High Court had more than one aim in mind in deciding the natural justice cases: 'One is the protection of the rights and interests of the individual against abuse of executive power ... A second object is an insistence on compliance with procedural fairness in administrative decision-making.'[89]

In truth, though, it is difficult in the Australian context to point to any consistent enunciation of either a legal or a social purpose behind the High Court's move to cast the net of procedural fairness as widely as it has. Insofar as Paul Craig was correct in asserting that the nature of procedural fairness can only be understood when considered against the background of political and constitutional theory,[90] this failure to enunciate a purposive grounding for natural justice leaves us with a significant gap in the theoretical framework of our public law.

Let us consider this in the context of the legitimate expectation cases for, as discussed, they have been the driving force behind the evolution of natural justice during the past twenty-odd years. In England, as has been noted, some judges have expressed an instrumental view of natural justice – that the protection of legitimate expectations is intertwined with the principles of good administration. On one reading of the legitimate expectation cases it could be thought that the High Court had the same ends in mind. This is certainly a view which could easily follow from the assertion that natural justice applies presumptively to all governmental decision-making. It would also seem to fit comfortably with the view in *Teoh* that there need be no actual expectation in order for a legitimate expectation to exist. But on the other hand, the actual outcomes of the cases – reflecting as they seem to do a judicial concern about the degree of unfairness in individual treatment – would suggest that something other than simple 'correctness' of decision-making procedures has been in the back of the High Court's mind in developing the concept.

To take just one example, it is not clear from his judgment in *South Australia v O'Shea* (or his *obiter* in *R v Toohey*) whether at base Mason CJ was more concerned with instrumental or non-instrumental justifications for the imposition of natural justice. One way of reading his insistence that in the appropriate case, natural justice could extend to the Cabinet is as reflecting a concern that the effective decision-makers have all of the relevant information before them, so that they might offer the 'correct' advice. Likewise, his judgment in *Attorney-General (New South Wales) v Quin* could be taken to support the view that the 'correctness' of a decision concerning judicial appointment can only be determined by reference to the Executive's assessment of individual fitness for office. But if one reads, say, his judgment in *Kioa v West*, it seems clear that one of the

[89] *Id*, at 573.

[90] *Public Law and Democracy*, *supra* n 58, at 1.

things which moved Sir Anthony to shape the doctrine of legitimate expectations in the way he did was his perception of a need for a means to redress official callousness. In this sense, one gets the impression that a form of dignitarianism has been at play in the Court's mind.

This view is buttressed by the holdings in *Heatley v Tasmanian Racing and Gaming Commission*, *Annetts v McCann* and *Haoucher*. But what, then, of *Teoh*? One supposes that the *result* in *Teoh* could be justified by reference to dignitarian concerns, but the *reasoning* in the majority judgments does not make explicit reference to anything like this. On the contrary, the reasoning in *Teoh* reads almost completely in instrumental terms: that the accession to the Convention on the Rights of the Child has made its contents a relevant consideration to the determination of the 'correctness' of a decision whether or not to deport when the interests of children are involved.

Oddly, given its statements regarding popular sovereignty, the one purpose which does not seem yet to have found any favour in the High Court is administrative republicanism. In some ways, the republican/participatory justification for natural justice fits most easily of all with the Court's asserted constitutional premises. One wonders why the Court has not taken it up.[91] But the fact that it has not been considered by their Honours serves as confirmation of the continued under-theorisation of natural justice in Australia. The inconsistencies in the application of the doctrine of legitimate expectations that were explored at the end of chapter five illustrate the lack of enunciated constitutional purpose behind the modern Australian doctrine of natural justice. To date, the doctrine of legitimate expectations remains a largely inchoate one. At best, one could argue that the purpose behind the judicially-imposed doctrine of procedural fairness seems a shifting one, being recast by the Court, when needed, to serve a series of ends. But however desirable this may be viewed from a pragmatic perspective, the inchoateness of the doctrine masks a significant concern when the doctrine is considered in terms of purposive constitutionalism.

---

[91] Aronson and Dyer have suggested that in light of legislative initiative in this regard, 'the High Court will probably be most reluctant to develop any general common law requirement of consultation' (*supra* n 12, at 456-457).

Natural Justice and 'The New Agenda'[92]

During most of the period covered by this thesis, government – and consequently, administrative law – was in a state of expansion. Now, government is in a period of contraction. As a result, many of the assumptions which have nourished the law of judicial review are under question. The simple truth is, as Robin Creyke and John McMillan put it so bluntly, that 'administrative law has moved on'.[93] As they wrote:

> The issues are no longer how best to control the burgeoning exercise of discretionary power by the state in relation to its citizens ... Today, as government retracts rather than expands, different issues have developed. Administrative law can no longer proceed from the premise that the exercise of functions that are funded by public monies is undertaken by government officials. The trend [is] towards the discharge of public functions by the private sector ...[94]

In chapter two, William Robson's play on Sir Henry Maine, to the effect that society in the middle part of the century was moving from contract to public administration, was referred to. Now, it might be possible to say that we are moving back to contract. The challenge facing administrative law, therefore – if, to re-state another expression, it is to be anything other than a relic of the Lord Hewart era – is to adapt to the new governmental reality, in which the private sector is entrusted with responsibility for carrying out many of the functions of the administration. As Mark Aronson has described it: 'administrative law's goals of accountability and participation are still important, but the way in which the state has restructured both itself and its delivery of goods and services, requires that the tools for achieving those goals might also have to be adapted'.[95]

Though to date, this project of adaptation has not been (as Aronson has discussed[96]) a successful one, success in the project is imperative. The *Housing Act* cases show the problems that can ensue if the law gets too far out of step with day-to-day governance and the reality of the workaday

---

[92] This expression is taken from R Creyke and J McMillan, 'Administrative Law Assumptions ... Then and Now', in R Creyke and J McMillan, *The Kerr Vision of Australian Administrative Law*, *supra* n 9, at 19.
[93] *Id*, at 33.
[94] *Ibid*.
[95] 'A Public Lawyer's Responses to Privatisation and Outsourcing', in M Taggart (ed), *The Province of Administrative Law* (1997) 40, at 70.
[96] See *id*.

constitution. But the difficult part of the project should in fact not be in the creating of judicial responses to change. The cases discussed in the last three chapters show the extent of the Court's ability to re-shape the law to suit what it perceives to be the needs of society.

In this respect, already we are beginning to see judges draw more explicitly on the private law of equity in discussing administrative law. It is not unlikely that in the future, we will see another fusion take place – this time between equitable principle and administrative law. Sir Anthony Mason, for example, has argued that the development of administrative law has 'mirrored the way in which equity has regulated the exercise of fiduciary powers'.[97] And, as noted in chapter six, as long ago as 1979 Mr Justice Murphy was urging that any broad-based assertion of private power which 'affects members of the public to a significant degree' should be deemed to amount to an exercise of public power, and liable to the common law rules of natural justice.[98]

No, the difficult part of the task facing the common law, and the common law courts, is to reconcile the problems of principle that have been adverted to in this Conclusion. The emphasis on market cost that features so predominantly in *today's* 'new administrative law' will focus the mind of the new decision-maker on efficiency – but in a quite different form than that envisaged by the Anglo-Canadian scholars of the 1930s. Now, the emphasis will be on cost-efficiency, rather than mere alacrity and informality. Attempts by the courts to impose additional costs on decision-making processes, without an articulation of the basis therefor, and of the purpose thereof, will be met with resistance. A failure to articulate principle therefore runs the risk of harming the courts' standing and undermining the common law constitution.

At the very outset, it was suggested that administrative law has its roots in our internal ambivalence. Hence the judicial role: to resolve the consequent political tension. The function of natural justice within this framework has been to ensure that the government does not fail to listen to us – that it continues to hear our ambivalence. But for natural justice to do this, it must have a secure grounding in the legal system. This, then, is the High Court's task for the future: to provide a basis for procedural fairness which is not only robust in its definition, but which also accords with the principles of the real constitution. A society governed by the rule of law can demand no less.

---

[97] 'The Place of Equity and Equitable Remedies in the Contemporary Common Law World' (1994) 110 *LQR* 238.

[98] *Forbes v New South Wales Trotting Club Ltd* (1979) 143 CLR 242, at 274-275.

Bibliography

Ackerman, B.A. (1984), *Reconstructing American Law*, Harvard University Press, Cambridge Mass.

Administrative Review Council (1977), *First Annual Report*.

Aldridge, M. (1979), *The British New Towns: A Programme Without a Policy*, Routledge & Kegan Paul, London.

Allan, T.R.S. (1993), *Law, Liberty and Justice*, Clarendon Press, Oxford.

Allan, T.R.S. (1998), 'Procedural Fairness and the Duty of Respect', 18 *Oxford Journal of Legal Studies*, p 497.

Allars, M. (1987), 'Fairness: Writ Large or Small' *Sydney Law Review*, vol. 11, p 306.

Allars, M. (1990), *Introduction to Australian Administratve Law*, Butterworths, Sydney.

Allars, M. (1991), 'Standing: The Role and Evolution of the Test', 20 *Federal Law Review*, p 83.

Allars, M. (1995), 'One Small Step for Legal Doctrine, One Giant Leap Towards Integrity in Government: *Teoh's Case* and the Internationalisation of Administrative Law', *Sydney Law Review*, vol. 17, p 204.

Allars, M. (1997), *Australian Administratve Law: Cases and Materials*, Butterworths, Sydney.

Allen, Sir C.K. (1931), *Bureaucracy Triumphant*, Oxford University Press, London.

Allen, Sir C.K. (1945), *Law and Orders: An Inquiry Into the Nature and Scope of Delegated Legislation and Executive Powers in England*, Stevens and Sons, London.

American Bar Association (1937), *Report of the Committee with Studies of Administrative Management in the Federal Government*.

Amery, The Rt Hon L.S. (1947), *Thoughts on the Constitution*, Oxford University Press, London.

Amos, M. (1934), 'The Interpretation of Statutes', *Cambridge Law Journal*, vol. 5, p 163.

Anderson, Sir J. (1949), *Administrative Technique in the Public Service*, Birkbeck College, London.

Anon, (1930), 'Book Review: *The New Despotism*', *Canadian Bar Review*, vol. 1, p 77.

Anon, (1952), 'Swearing in of Sir Owen Dixon as Chief Justice', *Commonwealth Law Reports*, vol. 85, p xi.

Anon, (1964), 'Case Comment', *Adelaide Law Review*, vol. 2, p 252.

Anon, (1964), 'Retirement of the Chief Justice', *Commonwealth Law Reports*, vol. 110, p *i*.
Anon, (April 1967), 'Administrative Tribunals', *Current Affairs Bulletin*, vol. 24.
Arndt, H.W. (1957), 'The Origins of Dicey's Concept of the "Rule of Law"', *Australian Law Journal*, vol. 31, p 117.
Aronson, M. and Dyer, B. (1996), *Judicial Review of Administrative Action*, LBC Information Services, Sydney.
Aronson, M. and Franklin, N. (1987), *Review of Administrative Action*, Law Book Co., Sydney.
Arthurs, H.W. (1985), *Without the Law: Administrative Justice and Legal Pluralism in Nineteenth-Century England*, University of Toronto Press, Toronto.
Atiyah, P.S. (1979), *The Rise and Fall of Freedom of Contract*, Clarendon Press, Oxford.
Atiyah, P.S. (1987), *Pragmatism and Theory in English Law*, Stevens and Sons, London.
Bagehot, W. (1st ed., 1867), *The English Constitution*, T. Nelson, London.
Bailey, K.H. (1930), 'Administrative Legislation in the Commonwealth', *Australian Law Journal*, vol. 4, p 7.
Baker, J.H. (3rd ed., 1990), *An Introduction to English Legal History*, Butterworths, London.
Baldwin, R. and Horne, D. (1986), 'Expectations in a Joyless Landscape', *Modern Law Review*, vol. 49, p 685.
Barwick, The Rt Hon Sir G. (1995), *A Radical Tory: Garfield Barwick's Reflections and Recollections*, Federation Press, Sydney.
Bath, V. (1978), 'Case Note: *Heatley v Tasmanian Racing and Gaming Commission*', *Federal Law Review*, vol. 9, p 504.
Bayles, M.D. (1990), *Procedural Justice: Allocating to Individuals*, Kluwer, Dordrecht.
Bayne, P. (1991), 'Mr Justice Evatt's Theory of Administrative Law: Adjusting State Regulation to the Liberal Theory of the Individual and the State', *Law in Context*, vol. 9, p 1.
Bayne, P. (1991), 'The Court, the Parliament and the Government – Reflections on the Scope of Judicial Review', *Federal Law Review*, vol. 20, p 1.
Bayne, P. (1993), 'The Common Law Basis of Judicial Review', *Australian Law Journal*, vol. 67, p 781.
Beecroft, E.A. (1931), 'Courts of Specialized Jurisdiction in Australia', *University of Pennsylvania Law Review*, vol. 79, p 1021.
Benjafield, D.G. and Whitmore, H. (1963), 'The House of Lords and Natural Justice', *Australian Law Journal*, vol. 37, p 140.
Benjafield, D.J. and Whitmore, H. (3rd ed., 1966), *Australian Administrative Law*, Law Book Co, Sydney.
Bennett, J.M. (1974), *A History of the Supreme Court of New South Wales*, Law Book Co, Sydney.

Bennett, J.M. (1980), *Keystone of the Federal Arch: A Historical Memoir of the High Court of Australia to 1980*, Australian Government Publishing Service, Canberra.

Berlin, Sir Isaiah (Spring 1950), 'Political Ideas in the Twentieth Century', *Foreign Affairs.*

Berlin, Sir Isaiah (1969), *Four Essays on Liberty*, Oxford University Press, London.

Beveridge, The Rt Hon Lord W.H. (1953), *Power and Influence*, Hodder and Stoughton, London.

Blackshield, A.R. and Williams, G. (2nd ed., 1998), *Australian Constitutional Law and Theory: Commentary and Materials*, Federation Press, Sydney.

Blackstone, Sir W. (5th ed., 1773), *Commentaries on the Laws of England*, Clarendon Press, Oxford.

Blom-Cooper, L. and Drewry, G. (1972), *Final Appeal: A Study of the House of Lords in its Judicial Capacity*, Clarendon Press, Oxford.

Borrie, W.D. (1994), *The European Peopling of Australasia: A Demographic History 1788-1988*, Australian National University, Canberra.

Bracton, H. de (1250; 1968 ed.), *De Legibus et Consuetudinibus Angliae* (Thorne, S. trans. and ed.), Selden Society, London.

Bradley, A.W. [1964], 'A Failure of Justice and Defect of Police: A Commentary on *Ridge v Baldwin*', *Cambridge Law Journal*, p 83.

Brennan, The Hon Sir G. (1989), 'Reflections', *Canberra Bulletin of Public Administration*, vol. 58, p 32.

Brennan, The Hon Sir G. (1991), 'Courts, Democracy and the Law', *Australian Law Journal*, vol. 65, p 32.

Brett, P. (1962) (2nd ed, 1967 with Hogg, P.), *Cases and Materials on Constitutional and Administrative Law*, Butterworths, Sydney.

Brown, R.D. (1955), *The Battle of Crichel Down*, Bodley Head, London.

Brown, W. Jethro (1899), 'The Hare System in Tasmania', *Law Quarterly Review*, vol. 15, p 51.

Brown, W. Jethro (1899), *The New Democracy: A Political Study*, London, MacMillan, London.

Brown, W. Jethro (1906), *The Austinian Theory of Law*, John Murray, London.

Brown, W. Jethro (1912), *The Underlying Principles of Modern Legislation*, John Murray, London.

Brown, W. Jethro (1914), *The Prevention and Control of Monopolies*, John Murray, London.

Brown, W. Jethro (1919), 'Judicial Regulation of Wages for Women', *Yale Law Journal*, vol. 28, p 236.

Brown, W. Jethro (1921), 'The Separation of Powers in British Jurisdictions', *Yale Law Journal*, vol. 31, p 24.

Brown, W. Jethro (1924), 'Judicial Settlement of Industrial Disputes', *Cambridge Law Journal*, vol. 2, p 51.

Brownlie, I. (4th ed., 1990), *Principles of International Law*, Clarendon Press, Oxford.

Burmester, H. (1995), 'The *Teoh* Decision – A Perspective from the Government Service', *Australian Institute of Administrative Law Forum*, vol. 5, p 6.
Cane, P. (1980), 'Natural Justice and Legitimate Expectations', *Australian Law Journal*, vol. 54, p 546.
Cane, P. (2nd ed., 1992 and 3rd ed., 1996), *An Introduction to Administrative Law*, Clarendon Press, Oxford.
Cardozo, The Hon Benjamin (1921), *The Nature of the Judicial Process*, Yale University Press, New Haven.
Carr, Sir C.T. (1941), *Concerning English Administrative Law*, Columbia University Press, New York.
Castles, A.C. (1973-1976), 'The Judiciary and Political Questions: The First Australian Experience, 1824-1825', *Adelaide Law Review*, vol. 5, p 294.
Castles, A.C. (1982), *An Australian Legal History*, Law Book Co., Sydney.
Chester, Sir N. (1981), *The English Administrative System, 1780-1870*, Oxford University Press, London.
Childers, E., *The Riddle of the Sands*, London, Smith Elder, 1903.
Clapson, M. (1998), *Invincible Green Suburbs, Brave New Towns: Social Change and Urban Dispersal in Postwar England*, Manchester University Press, Manchester.
Clark, M. (Vol., VI, 1987), *A History of Australia*, Melbourne University Press, Australia.
Cohen, E. (1965), *The Growth of the British Civil Service 1780-1939*, F Cass, London.
Coke, Sir E. (1641; 1979 ed.), *Institutes of the Laws of England* (Backowitz, D.S. and Thorne, S.E., eds), Garland Publishing, New York.
Commonwealth of Australia, *Parliamentary Debates*, House of Representatives.
Commonwealth of Australia, Senate Select Committee on Standing Committees 1929-30, *Evidence.*
Coper, M. (1987), *Encounters With the Australian Constitution*, CCH Australia, Sydney.
Coper, M. and Williams, G. (eds) (1997), *How Many Cheers for Engineers?*, Federation Press, Sydney.
Coper, M. and Williams, G. (eds) (1997), *Justice Lionel Murphy: Influential or Merely Prescient?*, Federation Press, Sydney.
Cornish, W.R. and Clark, G. de N. (1989), *Law and Society in England 1750–1950*, Sweet and Maxwell, London.
Corry, J.A. (1935), 'Administrative Law and the Interpretation of Statutes', *University of Toronto Law Journal*, vol. 1, p 286.
Cosgrove, R.A. (1980), *The Rule of Law: Albert Venn Dicey, Victorian Jurist*, McMillan, London.
Cox, A. (1976), *The Role of the Supreme Court in American Goverment*, Oxford University Press, London.
Cozens-Hardy, The Rt Hon Lord (4 May 1911), 'Encroachment of the Executive: The Master of the Rolls on a Modern Danger'.

Craig, P.P. (1990), *Public Law and Democracy in the United Kingdom and the United States of America*, Clarendon Press, Oxford.

Craig, P.P. (1991), 'Constitutions, Property and Regulation', *Public Law*, p 538.

Craig, P.P. (1992), 'Legitimate Expectations: A Conceptual Analysis', *Law Quarterly Review*, vol. 108, p 79.

Craig, P.P. (3rd ed., 1994), *Administrative Law*, Sweet & Maxwell, London.

Craig, P.P. (1998), '*Ultra Vires* and the Foundations of Judicial Review', *Cambridge Law Journal*, vol. 57, p 63.

Cranston, R. (1987), *Law, Government and Public Policy*, Oxford University Press, Melbourne.

Craven, G. (1988), 'Legislative Action by Subordinate Authorities and the Requirements of a Fair Hearing', *Melbourne University Law Review*, vol. 16, p 569.

Craven, G. (1992), 'The Crisis of Constitutional Literalism in Australia', *Alberta Law Review*, vol. 30, p 492.

Creyke, R. (1997), 'Restricting Judicial Review', *Australian Institute of Administrative Law Forum*, vol. 15, p 22.

Creyke, R. and McMillan, J. (eds) (1996), *The Making of Commonwealth Administrative Law: The Kerr, Bland and Ellicott Committee Reports*, Centre for International and Public Law, Canberra.

Creyke, R. and McMillan, J. (eds) (1998), *The Kerr Vision of Australian Administrative Law at the Twenty-Five Year Mark*, Centre for International and Public Law, Canberra.

Crisp, L.F. (4th ed., 1978), *Australian National Government*, Longman Cheshire, Melbourne.

Cullity, M. (1967), 'Book Review', *Federal Law Review*, vol. 2, p 306.

Currey, C.H. (1968), *Sir Francis Forbes: the first Chief Justice of the Supreme Court of New South Wales*, Angus & Robertson, Sydney.

Dangerfield, G. (1935), *The Strange Death of Liberal England*, Constable, London.

Davison, G., Hirst J. and MacIntye, S. (eds) (1998), *The Oxford Companion to Australian History*, Oxford University Press, Melbourne.

Dawson, The Hon Sir D. and Nicholls, M. (1986), 'Sir Owen Dixon and Judicial Method', *Melbourne University Law Review*, vol. 15, p 543.

de Beccaria, il Marchese, *Dei Delitti e della Pene* (English trans), (3rd ed. 1770), F. Newbery, London.

de Smith, S.A. (1948), 'The Limits of Judicial Review: Statutory Discretions and the Doctrine of *Ultra Vires*', *Modern Law Review*, vol. 11, p 306.

de Smith, S.A. (1st ed., 1959) (and succeeding editions), *Judicial Review of Administrative Action*, Stevens, London.

de Smith, S.A., Woolf, The Rt Hon Lord and Jowell, J. (5th ed., 1995), *Judicial Review of Administrative Action*, Sweet and Maxwell, London.

Deakin, A. (1944), *The Federal Story*, Melbourne University Press.

Denning, The Rt Hon Lord (1951), 'The Spirit of the British Constitution', *Canadian Bar Review*, vol. 29, p 1180.

Denning, The Rt Hon Lord (1955), *The Road to Justice*, Stevens, London.

Denning, The Rt Hon Lord (1964), *Gems in Ermine*, The English Association, London.

Detmold, M.J. (1994), 'The New Constitutional Law', *Sydney Law Review*, vol. 16, p 229.

Devlin, The Rt Hon Lord [1956], 'Public Policy and the Executive', *Current Legal Problems*, p 1.

Devlin, The Rt Hon Lord (1976), 'Judges and Lawmakers', *Modern Law Review*, vol. 36, p 1.

Dicey, A.V. (1st ed., 1885) (also 8th ed., 1915), *The Law of the Constitution*, MacMillan & Co, London.

Dicey, A.V. (2nd ed., 1914), *Law and Public Opinion in the Nineteenth Century*, MacMillan & Co, London.

Dicey, A.V. (1915), 'The Development of Administrative Law in England', *Law Quarterly Review*, vol. 31, p 148.

Dixon, M. (1987), 'Delegation, Agency and the Alter Ego Rule', *Sydney Law Review*, vol. 11, p 326.

Dixon, The Rt Hon Sir Owen (1935), 'The Law and the Constitution', *Law Quarterly Review*, vol. 51, p 590.

Dixon, The Rt Hon Sir Owen (1957), 'The Common Law as an Ultimate Constitutional Foundation', *Australian Law Journal*, vol. 31, p 240.

Dixon, The Rt Hon Sir Owen (1965), *Jesting Pilate*, Law Book Company, Melbourne.

Douglas, R. and Jones, M. (2nd ed., 1996), *Administrative Law: Commentary and Materials*, Federation Press, Sydney.

Doyle, J.J. (1993), 'Constitutional Law: "At the Eye of the Storm"', *University of Western Australia Law Review*, vol. 23, p 15.

Dworkin, R. (1978), *Taking Rights Seriously*, Duckworth, London.

Edley, C.R.F. Jr. (1990), *Administrative Law: Rethinking Judicial Control of Bureaucracy*, Yale University Press, New Haven.

Eggleston, Sir F. (1932), *State Socialism in Victoria*, King, London.

Eggleston, Sir F. (1941), *Search For a Social Philosophy*, Melbourne University Press.

Eggleston, Sir F. (1952), *Reflections of an Australian Liberal*, Australian National University, Canberra.

Eggleston, Sir F. (unpublished MS at author's death), 'A Theory of Social Integration'.

Ely, J.H. (1980), *Democracy and Distrust: A Theory of Judicial Review*, Harvard University Press, Cambridge.

Evatt, The Hon Dr. H.V. (1936), *The King and His Dominion Governors: A Study of the Reserve Powers of the Crown in Great Britain and the Dominions*, Oxford University Press, London.

Evatt, The Hon Dr. H.V., 'The Judiciary and Administrative Law in Australia', *Canadian Bar Review*, vol. 15, p 247.

Farris, J.W. de B. (1938), 'Justice of the Courts', *Canadian Bar Review*, vol. 16, p 509.

Finkelman, J. (1935), 'Separation of Powers: A Study in Administrative Law', *University of Toronto Law Journal*, vol. 1, p 313.

Finn, P.D. (1987), *Law and Government in Colonial Australia*, Oxford University Press, Melbourne.

Finn, P.D. (1994), 'Of Power and the People: Ends and Methods in Australian Judge-Made Law', *The Judicial Review*, vol. 1, p 255.

Finn, P.D. and Smith, K. (1992), 'The Citizen, the Government and "Reasonable Expectations"', *Australian Law Journal*, vol. 66, p 139.

Finnis, J. (1980), *Natural Law and Natural Rights*, Clarendon Press, Oxford.

Flick, G.A. (2nd ed., 1984), *Natural Justice: Principles and Practical Application*, Butterworths, Sydney.

Forsey, The Hon E. (1943), *The Royal Power of Dissolution of Parliament in the British Commonwealth*, Oxford University Press, Toronto.

Forsyth, C.F. (1988), 'The Provenance and Protection of Legitimate Expectations', *Cambridge Law Journal*, vol. 47, p 238.

Forsyth, C.F. (1996), 'Of Fig Leaves and Fairy Tales: The *Ultra Vires* Principle, the Sovereignty of Parliament and Judicial Review', *Cambridge Law Journal*, vol. 55, p 122.

Forsyth, C.F. [1998], 'Collateral Challenge and the Foundations of Judicial Review: Orthodoxy Vindicated and Procedural Exclusivity Rejected', *Public Law*, p 364.

Frame, A. (1995), *Salmond: Southern Jurist*, Victoria University Press, Wellington.

Frankfurter, F. (1936), 'Foreword: Courts and Administrative Law – The Experience of English Housing Legislation', *Harvard Law Review*, vol. 49, p 426.

Frankfurter, F. (1938), 'Foreword', *Yale Law Journal*, vol. 47, p 1.

Franks, Sir O. (1947), *Central Planning and Control in War and Peace*, London School of Economics and Political Science, London.

French, The Hon R.S. (1993), 'The Rise and Rise of Judicial Review', *University of Western Australia Law Review*, vol. 23, p 120.

Friedmann, W. (1948), *The Planned State and the Rule of Law*, Melbourne University Press.

Friedmann, W. (1950), 'The Interpretation of Statutes in Modern British Law', *Vanderbilt Law Review*, vol. 3, p 544.

Friedmann, W. (1950), *Principles of Australian Administrative Law*, Melbourne University Press.

Friedmann, W. (1951), 'Judges, Politics and the Law', *Canadian Bar Review*, vol. 29, p 811.

Friedmann, W. and Benjafield, D.G. (2nd ed., 1962), *Principles of Australian Administrative Law*, Law Book Co, Sydney.

Fry, T.P. (1933), 'Australian Disregard of the Doctrine of the Separation of Powers', *Rocky Mountain Law Review*, vol. 5, p 221.

Fry, T.P. (1946), *Australian Courts and Administrative Tribunals*, University of Queensland, Brisbane.

Full Employment in a Free Society ('the Beveridge Report'), (1944), Allen & Unwin, London.

Fuller, L. [1963], 'Collective Bargaining and the Arbitrator', *Wisconsin Law Journal*, p 3.

Fuller, L. (1978), 'The Forms and Limits of Adjudication', *Harvard Law Review*, vol. 92, p 353.

Galligan, B. (1987), *Politics of the High Court*, University of Queensland Press, St. Lucia.

Galligan, D.J. (1996), *Due Process and Fair Procedures*, Clarendon Press, Oxford.

Gellhorn, W., Byse, C., Strauss P.L., Rakoff, T. and Schotland, R.A. (8th ed., 1987), *Administrative Law: Cases and Comments*, Foundation Press, New York.

Gilbert, M. (2nd ed., 1993), *The Dent Atlas of British History*, J M Dent, London.

Goodhart, A.L. (1964), '*Ridge v Baldwin*: Administration and Natural Justice', *Law Quarterly Review*, vol. 80, p 105.

Gordon, D.M. (1929), 'Relation of Facts to Jurisdiction', *Law Quarterly Review*, vol. 45, p 459.

Gordon, D.M. (1931), 'Observance of Law as a Condition of Jurisdiction', *Law Quarterly Review*, vol. 47, p 386; 557.

Gordon, D.M. (1933), 'Administrative Tribunals and the Courts', *Law Quarterly Review*, vol. 49, p 94; 419.

Greaves, H.R.G. (1947), *The Civil Service in the Changing State: A Survey of Civil Service Reform and the Implications of a Planned Economy on Public Administration in England*, G G Harrap, London.

Green, T.H. (1898), *Essays, Moral, Political and Literary*, Longmans, London.

Green, T.H. (1921), *Lectures on the Principles of Political Obligation*, Longmans, London.

Greene, The Rt Hon Lord (1944), 'Law and Progress', the 13th Haldane Memorial Lecture.

Greig, D.W. (1976), *International Law*, Butterworths, London.

Griffith, J.A.G. (ed.) (1976), *From Policy to Administration: Essays in Honour of William A Robson*, Allen & Unwin, London.

Griffith, J.A.G. (1978), 'Administrative Law and the Judges', Pritt Memorial Lecture.

Hailsham, The Rt Hon Lord (1990), *A Sparrow's Flight*, Collins, London.

Halsbury's Laws of Australia.

Halsbury's Laws of England.

Hancock, W.K. (1st ed., 1930), *Australia*, E Benn, London.

Harlow, C. and Rawlings, R. (1984), *Law and Administration*, Weidenfeld and Nicolson, London.

Harper, J.B. (1938), 'The Crown as the Source of Legal Powers in Australia', *Res Judicata*, vol. 1, p 310.

Hart, H.L.A. (1982), *Essays on Bentham*, Clarendon Press, Oxford.
Hayek, F.A. (1944), *The Road to Serfdom*, Routledge, London.
Hayek, F.A. (1948), *Individualism and Economic Order*, Routledge and Kegan Paul, London.
Hayek, F.A. (1960), *The Constitution of Liberty*, Routledge and Kegan Paul, London.
Hayek, F.A. (1973-1979), *Law, Legislation and Liberty: A New Statement of the Liberal Principles of Justice and Political Economy*, Routledge and Kegan Paul, London.
Hearn, W.E. (2nd ed., 1886), *The Government of England: Its Structure and Development*, Longmans Green, London.
Henderson, E.G. (1963), *The Foundations of English Administrative Law*, Harvard University Press, Cambridge Mass.
Hewart, The Rt Hon Baron (1929), *The New Despotism*, E Benn, London.
Hewart, The Rt Hon Baron (1930), *Essays and Observations*, Caswell, London.
Hewart, The Rt Hon Baron (1937), *Not Without Prejudice*, Hutchinson, London.
Higgins, H.B. (1922), *A New Province for Law and Order*, Worker's Educational Association of New South Wales, Sydney.
Himmelfarb, G. (1994), *The De-Moralization of Society: From Victorian Virtues to Modern Values*, Knopf, New York.
Hlophe, J. (1987), 'Legitimate Expectations and Natural Justice: English, Australian and South African Law', *South African Law Journal*, vol. 104, p 165.
Hobhouse, L.T. (1904), *Democracy and Reaction*, T Fischer Unwin, London.
Hobhouse, L.T. (1911), *Liberalism*, Oxford University Press, London.
Hobhouse, L.T. (1922), *The Elements of Social Justice*, Allen & Unwin, London.
Hodgson, D.C. (1984), 'The Current Status of the Legitimate Expectation in Administrative Law', *Melbourne University Law Review*, vol. 14, p 686.
Hogg, P.W. (1969), 'Judicial Review of Action by the Crown Representative', *Australian Law Journal*, vol. 43, p 215.
Hogg, P.W. (3rd ed., 1992), *The Constitutional Law of Canada*, Toronto, Carswell, Toronto.
Hohfeld, W.N. (1913), 'Some Fundamental Legal Conceptions as Applied in Judicial Reasoning', *Yale Law Journal*, vol. 23, p 16.
Holdsworth, Sir W.S. (17 vols., 1937-1957), *A History of English Law*, Methuen, London.
Holloway, I. (1993), 'A Sacred Right: Judicial Review of Administrative Action as a Cultural Phenomenon', *Manitoba Law Review*, vol. 22, p 28.
Holloway, I. (1998), 'A Fragment on Reception', *Australian Journal of Legal History*, vol. 4, p 79.
Holloway, I. (unpublished, 1998), 'Sir Francis Forbes and the Earliest Australian Public Law Cases'.
Holmes, J.D. (1937), 'An Australian View of the Hours of Labour Case', *Canadian Bar Review*, vol. 15, p 495.
Holmes, O.W. Jr. (1881), *The Common Law*, Little, Brown & Co., Boston.

Ignatieff, M. (1998), *Isaiah Berlin: A Life*, Chatto & Windus, London.
Jackson, R. (1959), *The Chief: The Biography of Gordon Hewart, Lord Chief Justice of England*, G.G. Harrap, London.
Jacobs, J.M. (1996), *The Republican Crown: Lawyers and the Making of the State in Twentieth Century Britain*, Dartmouth Press, Aldershot.
Jaffe, L.L. and Henderson, E.G. (1956), 'Judicial Review and the Rule of Law: Historical Origins', *Law Quarterly Review*, vol. 72, p 345.
Jennings, Sir I. (1931), *Principles of Local Government Law*, University of London Press, London.
Jennings, Sir I. (1933), *The Law and the Constitution*, University of London Press, London.
Jennings, Sir I. (1935), 'In Praise of Dicey', *Public Administration*, vol. 13, p 123.
Jennings, Sir I. (1936), 'Courts and Administrative Law – The Experience of English Housing Legislation', *Harvard Law Review*, vol. 49, p 426.
Johnson, G. (1984), 'Natural Justice and Legitimate Expectations in Australia' *Federal Law Review*, vol. 15, p 39.
Johnson, W. (1943), 'The Lawyer and Administrative Boards', *Revue du Barreau*, vol. 3, p 233.
Johnson, W. (1944), 'The Rule of Law Under an Expanding Bureaucracy', *Canadian Bar Review*, vol. 22, p 380.
Jones, D.P. and de Villars, A.S. (2nd ed., 1994) *Principles of Administrative Law*, Carswell, Toronto.
Jones, L.L. (1945), 'Industrial Arbitration in Australia' *Modern Law Review*, vol. 8, p 63.
Joseph, P.A. (1993), *Constitutional and Administrative Law in New Zealand*, Law Book Co, Sydney.
Jowell, J. and Oliver D. (eds) (3rd ed., 1994), *The Changing Constitution*, Oxford University Press, London.
Kahn-Freund, Sir O. (1976), 'The Impact of Constitutions on Labour Law', *Cambridge Law Journal*, vol. 35, p 240.
Keeton, G.W., 'The Twilight of the Common Law', *The Nineteenth Century and After*, April 1949, p 230.
Keeton, G.W. [1955], 'Natural Justice in English Law', *Current Legal Problems*, p 24.
Keith, A.B. (1936), *The King and the Imperial Crown: The Powers and Duties of His Majesty*, Longmans, London.
Kennedy, W.P.M. (1934), 'Aspects of Administrative Law in Canada', *Juridical Review*, vol. 46, p 203.
Kercher, B. (1995), *An Unruly Child: A History of Law in Australia*, Allen & Unwin, Sydney.
Kercher, B. (1996), *Debt, Seduction and Other Disasters*, Federation Press, Sydney.
Kinley, D. (ed.) (1998), *Human Rights in Australian Law*, Federation Press, Sydney.

La Nauze, J.A. (1949), *Political Economy in Australia: Historical Studies*, Melbourne University Press, Melbourne.

La Nauze, J.A. (1965), *Alfred Deakin: A Biography*, Melbourne University Press.

La Nauze, J.A. (ed.) (1968), *Federated Australia*, Melbourne University Press.

Landis, J.M. (1st ed., 1938), *The Administrative Process*, Yale University Press, New Haven.

Laski, H.J. (1925), *A Grammar of Politics*, Allen & Unwin, London.

Laski, H.J. (1940), *Where Do We Go From Here? An Essay in Interpretation*, Penguin, London.

Laski, H.J. (1951), *Reflections on the Constitution*, Manchester University Press, Manchester.

Laskin, B. (1952), 'Certiorari to Labour Boards: The Apparent Futility of Privative Clauses', *Canadian Bar Review*, vol. 30, p 986.

Latham, R.T.E. (1949), *The Law and the Commonwealth*, Oxford University Press, London.

Law Institute of Victoria (1984), 'Seminar in Print, Administrative Law: The Profession's Sunrise Industry?', *Law Institute Journal*, vol. 58, p 784.

Laws, The Rt Hon Sir J. [1995], 'Law and Democracy', *Public Law*, p 72.

Lieberman, D. (1989), *The Province of Legislation Determined: Legal Theory in Eighteenth Century Britain*, Cambridge University Press.

Lindell, G.J. (1986), 'Why Is Australia's Constitution Binding? The Reasons in 1900 and Now, and the Effect of Independence', *Federal Law Review*, vol. 16, p 29.

Lindell, G.J. (ed.) (1994), *Future Directions in Australian Constitutional Law*, Federation Press, Sydney.

Lloyd, The Rt Hon Lord (1991), *The Idea of Law*, Penguin, London.

Loughlin, M. (1978), 'Procedural Fairness: A Study of the Crisis in Administrative Law Theory', *University of Toronto Law Journal*, vol. 28, p 215.

Loughlin, M. (1992), *Public Law and Political Theory*, Clarendon Press, Oxford.

Loughlin, M. (1993), 'The Importance of Elsewhere', *Public Law Review*, vol. 4, p 44.

Macassey, Sir L. (1922), 'Law-making by Government Departments', *Journal of Comparative Legislation and International Law*, vol. 5, p 73.

MacDermott, The Rt Hon Lord (1957), *Protection From Power Under English Law*, Stevens & Sons, London.

MacDonald, R.A. (1980), 'Judicial Review and Procedural Fairness in Administrative Law', *McGill Law Journal*, vol. 25, p 520, *McGill Law Journal*, vol. 26, p 1.

Maine, Sir H. (1888), *International Law*, J. Murray, London.

Maitland, F.W. (1909), *The Forms of Action at Common Law*, Cambridge University Press.

Manetta, N.A., 'The Implication of the Principle *Audi Alteram Partem* in Administrative Law' (unpublished PhD thesis, University of Cambridge, 1991).

Manning, C.A.W. (ed.) (8th ed., 1930), *Salmond on Jurisprudence*, Sweet & Maxwell, London.

Marriot, Sir J. (July 1928), 'Law and Liberty', *The Fortnightly Review.*

Marshall, H.H. (1959), *Natural Justice*, Sweet & Maxwell, London.

Mashaw, J.L. (1985), *Due Process in the Administrative State*, Yale University Press, New Haven.

Mason, The Hon Sir A. (1986), 'The Role of a Constitutional Court in a Federation', *Federal Law Review*, vol. 16, p 1.

Mason, The Hon Sir A. (1993), 'Changing the Law in a Changing Society', *Australian Law Journal*, vol. 67, p 568.

Mason, The Hon Sir A. (1994), 'The Importance of Judicial Review of Administrative Action as a Safeguard of Human Rights', *Australian Journal of Human Rights*, vol. 1, p 1.

Mason, The Hon Sir A. (1994), 'The Place of Equity and Equitable Remedies in the Contemporary Common Law World', *Law Quarterly Review*, vol. 110, p 238.

Mason, The Hon Sir A. (unpublished address to the Sydney Institute, 15 March 1994), 'The Australian Judiciary in the 1990s'.

Mason, The Hon Sir A. (paper presented at the Public Law Conference, Canberra, 6 November 1998), 'Judicial Review: The Contribution of Sir Gerard Brennan'.

McCoubrey, H. and White, N.D. (1993), *Textbook on Jurisprudence*, Blackstone Press, London.

McHugh, The Hon M. (1988), 'The Law-making Function of the Judicial Process', *Australian Law Journal*, vol. 62, p 15; 116.

McMillan, J. (1991), 'Developments Under the ADJR Act: Grounds of Review', *Federal Law Review*, vol. 20, p 50.

McMillan, J. (1995), '*Teoh* and Invalidity in Administrative Law', *Australian Institute of Administrative Law Forum*, vol. 5, p 10.

McMillan, J. (1996), 'Recent Themes in Judicial Review of Federal Executive Action', *Federal Law Review*, vol. 24, p 347.

McMillan, J. (ed.) (1997), *Administrative Law Under the Coalition Government*, Australian Institute of Administrative Law, Sydney.

McMillan, J. (1998), *Administrative Law Under the Coalition Government*, Australian Institute of Administrative Law, Sydney.

Melbourne, A.C.V. (1934, 2nd ed., 1963), *Early Constitutional Development in Australia*, University of Queensland Press, Brisbane.

Menhennitt, C.I. (1935), 'Administrative Tribunals in Victoria', *Res Judicata*, vol. 1, p 28.

Menzies, R.G., (1917), *The Rule of Law During the War*, University of Melbourne.

Mill, J.S. (1st ed., 1848), *Principles of Political Economy With Some of Their Applications to Social Philosophy*, Charles C. Little & James Brown, Boston.

Milsom, S.F.C. (2nd ed., 1981), *The Historical Foundations of the Common Law*, Butterworths, London.

Milsom, S.F.C. (1985), *Studies in the History of the Common Law*, Hambledon Press, London.

Monckton, Sir W. (1942), 'Liberty and the Common Law', *Canadian Bar Review*, vol. 20, p 670.

Moore, Sir W.H. (1903), 'The Enforcement of Administrative Law', *Commonwealth Law Review*, vol. 1, p 13.

Moore, Sir W.H. (1912), 'Living Wage in the Australian Arbitration Court', *Journal of Comparative Legislation*, vol. 12 (2nd ser), p 202.

Mullan, D.J. (1975), 'Fairness: The New Natural Justice', *University of Toronto Law Journal*, vol. 25, p 281.

Mullan, D.J. (1982), 'Natural Justice and Fairness – Substantive as well as Procedural Standards for the Review of Administrative Decision-Making?', *McGill Law Journal*, vol. 27, p 250.

Mulock, Sir W. (1934), 'Address of the Chief Justice of Ontario', *Canadian Bar Review*, vol. 12, p 32.

Murdoch, W. (1923), *Alfred Deakin: A Sketch*, Constable, London.

Nash, G. (1964), 'Judicial Function and Inspectors Appointed Under the Companies Act', *Australian Law Journal*, vol. 38, p 111.

National Children's Youth Law Centre (1995), 'High Court Breathes New Life into CROC', *Rights NOW!*, vol. 3, p 2.

Nettheim, G. (1967), 'The Privy Council, Natural Justice and Certiorari', *Federal Law Review*, vol. 2, p 215.

New South Wales, *Parliamentary Debates*, Legislative Assembly.

Nicholson, The Hon A., 'Address to the Children First! Forum', Melbourne, 1995.

Northern Territory Department of Lands and Housing, *Darwin Regional Land Use Structure Plan 1990.*

Northey, J.F. (1974), 'The Aftermath of the *Furnell* Decision', *New Zealand Universities Law Review*, vol. 6, p 59.

Northey, J.F. [1974], 'Pedantic or Semantic', *New Zealand Law Journal*, p 133.

Northey, J.F. (1981), *The Basis of Judicial Review in Administrative Law*, University of Auckland.

O'Connor, The Hon D. (1994), 'Is There Too Much Natural Justice?', *Australian Institute of Administrative Law Forum*, vol. 1, p 82.

O'Neil, A. (1986), 'Case Comment: *Coutts v The Commonwealth*', *Federal Law Review*, vol. 10, p 212.

Oakeshott, M. (1975), *On Human Conduct*, Clarendon Press, Oxford.

Oakeshott, M. (1975), *Hobbes on Civil Association*, Basil Blackwell, Oxford.

Oakeshott, M. (1983), *On History and Other Essays*, Basil Blackwell, Oxford.

O'Halpin, E. (1989) *Head of the Civil Service: A Study of Warren Fisher*, Routlidge, London.

Oliver, D. [1987], 'Is the *Ultra Vires* Rule the Basis of Judicial Review?', *Public Law*, p 543.

Oliver, D. [1997], 'Common Values in Public and Private Law and the Public/Private Divide', *Public Law*, p 630.

Orr, G.S., *Report on Administrative Justice in New Zealand*, Wellington, Government Printer, 1964.

Osmond, W. (1985), *Frederic Eggleston: An Intellectual in Australian Politics*, Allen & Unwin, Sydney.

Parker, The Rt Hon Lord (1959), 'Recent Developments in the Supervisory Powers of the Courts Over Inferior Tribunals'.

Parkinson, P. (1994), *Tradition and Change in Australian Law*, Law Book Co, Sydney.

Parliamentary Debates, House of Commons.

Parliamentary Debates, House of Lords.

Parris, H. (1969), *Constitutional Bureaucracy: The Development of British Central Administration Since the Eighteenth Century*, Allen & Unwin, London.

Pearson, L. (ed.) (1997), *Administrative Law: Setting the Pace or Being Left Behind?*, Australian Institute of Administrative Law, Sydney.

Percy, Lord E. (1934), *Government in Transition*, Methuen, London.

Phillips, P.D. and Wood, G.L. (eds) (1928), *The Peopling of Australia*, Melbourne University Press.

Phillipson, C. (1923), *Three Criminal Law Reformers: Beccaria, Bentham, Romilly*, Dent, London.

Plucknett, T.F.T. (5th ed., 1956), T F T, *A Concise History of the Common Law*, Butterworths, London.

Podhoretz, N. (February 1999), 'A Dissent on Isaiah Berlin', *Commentary Online*, www.commentarymagazine.com.

Pollock, The Rt Hon Sir F. (1915), 'Note', *Law Quarterly Review*, vol. 31, p 153.

Pollock, The Rt Hon Sir F. (1929), *A First Book of Jurisprudence*, McMillan and Co, London.

Port, F.J. (1929), *Administrative Law*, Longmans Green, London.

Porter, The Rt Hon Lord [1949], 'English Practice and Procedure – More Particularly in Criminal Matters', *Current Legal Problems*, p 13.

Portus, G.V. (ed.) (1933), *Studies in the Australian Constitution*, Angus and Robertson, Sydney.

Pound, R. (1937), 'Fashions in Juristic Theory', Presidential Address to the Holdsworth Club, University of Birmingham.

Pound, R. (1942), *Administrative Law: Its Growth, Procedure and Significance*, University of Pittsburgh Press.

Proceedings of the Third Commonwealth and Empire Law Conference, Sydney, Law Book Co, 1965.

Public inquiry ordered by the Minister of Agriculture into the disposal of land at Crichel Down ('the Report of the Crichel Down Inquiry'), 1954 Cmd 9176.

Pue, W.W. (1995), *Law School: The Story of Legal Education in British Columbia*, University of British Columbia, Vancouver.

Rabin, R. (1990), 'Reflections on the New Property', *University of San Francisco Law Review*, p 273.

Reeves, W.P. (1902), *State Experiments in Australia and New Zealand*, Richards, London.

Reich, C. (1964), 'The New Property', *Yale Law Journal*, vol. 73, p 733.

Reich, C. (1965), 'Individual Rights and Social Welfare: The Emerging Legal Issues', *Yale Law Journal*, vol. 74, p 1245.

Reich, C. (1967), 'Law of the Planned Society', *Yale Law Journal*, vol. 75, p 1227.

Reid, The Rt Hon Lord (1972), 'The Judge as Law Maker', *Journal of the Society of Public Teachers of Law*, vol. 12, p 22.

Report of the Committee on Administrative Tribunals and Enquiries ('the Franks Committee Report'), 1957 Cmd 218.

Report of the Committee on Ministers' Powers ('the Donoughmore Committee Report'), 1932 Cmnd 4060.

Report of the Commonwealth Administrative Review Committee ('the Kerr Committee Report'), 1971 Parl Paper No 144.

Report of the Royal Commission Inquiry Into Civil Rights ('The McRuer Report'), Toronto, The Queen's Printer, 1968.

Richardson, G. and Gunn, H. (eds.), *Administrative Law and Government Action: The Courts and Alternative Mechanisms of Review*, Clarendon Press, Oxford.

Rickard, J. (1984), *H B Higgins, The Rebel as Judge*, Allen & Unwin, Sydney.

Roach, K. (1989), 'The Administrative Law Scholarship of D M Gordon', *McGill Law Journal*, vol. 34, p 1.

Robson, W. (1932), 'The Report of the Committee on Ministers' Powers', *Political Quarterly*, vol. 3, p 351.

Robson, W. [1979], 'Justice and Administrative Law Reconsidered', *Current Legal Problems*, p 107.

Robson, W.A. (1st ed., 1928, and 2nd ed., 1947), *Justice and Administrative Law*, Stevens, London.

Robson, W.A. (1948), *Public Administration Today*, Stevens, London.

Rodman, J.R. (ed.) (1964), *The Political Theory of T H Green*, Appleton-Century-Crofts, New York.

Roe, O.M. (1977), 'Jethro Brown: The First Teacher of Law and History in the University of Tasmania', *University of Tasmania Law Review*, vol. 5, p 209.

Roe, O.M. (1984), *Nine Australian Progressives*, University of Queensland Press, St. Lucia.

Ross, G.W.C. (1945), 'Constitutional History of Industrial Arbitration in Australia', *Minnesota Law Review*, vol. 30, p 1.

Russell, F.A.A. (1928), 'The Commonwealth *Conciliation and Arbitration Act, 1928*', *Australian Law Journal*, vol. 2, p 147.

Russell, F.A.A. (1930), 'The Clash of Commonwealth Arbitration and State Courts', *Australian Law Journal*, vol. 4, p 110.

Sackville, R. (1978), 'Property, Rights and Social Security', *University of New South Wales Law Journal*, vol. 2, p 246.

Salmond, The Hon Sir J. (1893), *First Principles of Jurisprudence*, Stevens & Haynes, London.

Sampford, C. and Galligan, D.J. (1986), *Law, Rights and the Welfare State*, Croom Helm, Sydney.

Saunders, C. (ed.) (1996), *Courts of Final Jurisdiction: The Mason Court in Australia*, Federation Press, Sydney.

Sawer, G. [1956], 'Councils, Ministers and Cabinets in Australia', *Public Law*, p 110.

Sawer, G. (1956), *Australian Federal Politics and Law 1901-1929*, Melbourne University Press.

Sawer, G. (1963), *Australian Federal Politics and Law 1929-1949*, Melbourne University Press.

Sawer, G. (1964), *Ombudsmen*, Melbourne University Press.

Schedvin, C.B. (1970), *Australia and the Great Depression*, University Press, Sydney.

Schorske, C. (1998), *Thinking With History: Explorations in the Passage to Modernism*, Princeton University Press.

Schuck, P.H. (1994), *Foundations of Administrative Law*, Oxford University Press, New York.

Schwartz, B. (1987), *Lions Over the Throne: The Judicial Revolution in English Administrative Law*, New York University Press.

Schwartz, B. and Wade, H.W.R. (1972), *Legal Control of Government: Administrative Law in Britain and the United States*, Clarendon Press, Oxford.

Scott, F.R. (1948), 'Administrative Law: 1923-1947', *Canadian Bar Review*, vol. 26, p 268.

Seervai, H.M. (4th ed., 1993), *Constitutional Law of India – A Critical Commentary*, Tripathi, Bombay.

Seggie, K.I. (1965), 'Jurisdictional Error in Administrative Law', *Sydney Law Review*, vol. 5, p 89.

Shapiro, M. (1988), *Who Guards the Guardians: Judicial Control of Administration*, University of Georgia Press, Athens.

Shawcross, The Rt Hon Sir H. (1948), 'The State and the Law', *Modern Law Review*, vol. 11, p 1.

Simpson, A.W.B. [1988], 'Rhetoric, Reality and Regulation 18B', *Denning Law Journal*, p 123.

Simpson, A.W.B. [1989], 'The Judges and the Vigilant State', *Denning Law Journal*, p 145.

Sinclair, K. (1965), *W P Reeves, New Zealand Fabian*, Clarendon Press, Oxford.

Snell, R. (1995), '*Kioa* to *Teoh*', *Alternative Law Journal*, vol. 20, p 136.

Sornarajah, M. (1977), 'Natural Justice, Fairness and Administrative Functions', *University of Tasmania Law Review*, vol. 5, p 268.

Spigelman, The Hon J.J. (1999), 'Foundations of Administrative Law: Toward General Principles of Institutional Law', *Australian Journal of Public Administration*, vol. 58, p 3.

Stephen, The Rt Hon Sir N. (1986), *Sir Owen Dixon: A Celebration*, Melbourne University Press.

Stephenson, M.A. and Ratnapala, S. (eds) (1993), *Mabo: A Judicial Revolution*, University of Queensland Press, St Lucia.

Stevens, R. (1979), *Law and Politics: The House of Lords as a Judicial Body, 1800-1976*, Weidenfeld and Nicolson, London.

Stevens, R. (1993), *The Independence of the Judiciary: The View From the Lord Chancellor's Office*, Clarendon Press, Oxford.

Stewart, R. (1975), 'The Reformation of American Administrative Law', *Harvard Law Review*, vol. 88, p 1667.

Strauss, P. (1984), 'The Place of Agencies in Government: Separation of Powers and the Fourth Branch', *Columbia Law Review*, vol. 84, p 573.

Stubbs, R.St.G. (1951), 'Lord Bennett', *Canadian Bar Review*, vol. 29, p 631.

Sunbey, R. A. (1964), 'Case Comment: *Testro Bros v Tait*', *Melbourne University Law Review*, vol. 4, p 413.

Supperstone, M. and Goudie, J. (eds.) (1992), *Judicial Review*, Butterworths, London.

Sykes, E.I. (1936), 'Book Review', *Res Judicata*, vol. 1, p 56.

Sykes, E.I., Lanham, D.J., Tracey, R.R.S. and Esser, K.W. (4th ed., 1997), *General Principles of Administrative Law*, Butterworths, Sydney.

Taggart, M. (ed.) (1986), *Judicial Review of Administrative Action in the 1980s: Problems and Prospects*, Oxford University Press, Auckland.

Taggart, M. (ed.) (1997), *The Province of Administrative Law*, Hart Publishing, Oxford.

Tate, P. (1988), 'The Coherence of "Legitimate Expectations" and the Foundations of Natural Justice', *Monash University Law Review*, vol. 14, p 15.

Taylor, G.D.S. (1975), 'Natural Justice – the Modern Synthesis', *Monash University Law Review*, vol. 1, p 258.

Taylor, G.D.S. (1977), 'Fairness and Natural Justice', *Monash University Law Review*, vol. 3, p 191.

Tennant, N. (1928), 'Administrative Finality', *Canadian Bar Review*, vol. 6, p 497.

The Laws of Australia.

Toohey, The Hon J. (1993), 'A Government of Laws, and Not of Men?', *Public Law Review*, vol. 4, p 158.

Twomey, A. (1995), '*Minister for Immigration and Ethnic Affairs v Teoh*', *Federal Law Review*, vol. 23, p 348.

Valverde, M. (1991), *The Age of Light, Soap, and Water: Moral Reform in English Canada, 1885-1925*, McLelland & Stewart, Toronto.

Van Caenagem, R.C. (1995), *An Historical Introduction to Western Constitutional Law*, Cambridge University Press.

Victoria, *Parliamentary Debates*, Legislative Assembly.

Victoria, *Parliamentary Debates*, Legislative Council.

von Doussa, The Hon J.W. (1998), 'Natural Justice in Federal Administrative Law', *Australian Institute of Administrative Law Forum*, vol. 17, p 1.

Wade, H.W.R. (1949), 'Quasi-judicial and its Background', *Cambridge Law Journal*, vol. 10, p 216.

Wade, H.W.R. (1951), 'The Twilight of Natural Justice?', *Law Quarterly Review*, vol. 67, p 103.

Wade, H.R.W. (1st ed., 1961 (and succeeding editions)), *Administrative Law*, Clarendon Press, Oxford, 1st ed, 1961.

Wade, H.R.W. (1963), *Towards Administrative Justice*, University of Michigan Press, Ann Arbor.

Wade, H.R.W. (1980), *Constitutional Fundamentals*, Stevens, London.

Wade, Sir H.W.R. and Forsyth C.F. (7th ed. 1994), *Administrative Law*, Clarendon Press, Oxford.

Waldron, J. (1993), 'Property, Justification and Need', *Canadian Journal of Law and Jurisprudence*, vol. 6, p 185.

Walker, D.M. (ed.), *Oxford Companion to Law*, 1980

Webb, S. (1890), *Socialism in England*, Swan-Sonnenschein, London.

Webb, S. & B. (1902), *The Problems of Modern Industry*, Longman Green, London.

Webb, S. & B. (1914), *Industrial Democracy*, Longmans, London.

Webb, S. & B. (1920), *A Constitution for the Socialist Commonwealth of Great Britain*, The Fabian Society, London.

Weber, E., televised lecture entitled 'The Western Culture', 3 May 1992.

Wheeler, F. (1992), 'Judicial Review of Prerogative Power in Australia: Issues and Prospects', *Sydney Law Review*, vol. 14, p 432.

Wheeler, F.D., 'The Separation of Federal Judicial Power: A Purposive Analysis' (unpublished PhD thesis, Australian National University, 1999).

Whitfield, L.A., *Founders of the Law in Australia*, Canberra, The Australian National University, Canberra.

Whitmore, H. (1963), 'Australian Administrative Law – A Study in Inertia', *Australian Law Journal*, vol. 36, p 255.

Whitmore, H. (1972), 'Administrative Law in the Commonwealth: Some Proposals for Reform', *Federal Law Review*, vol. 5, p 7.

Williams, D.G.T. (1977), 'The Prerogative and Preventative Justice', *Cambridge Law Journal*, vol. 36, p 201.

Williams, J.M., 'The Protection of Rights Under the Australian Constitution: A Republican Analysis' (unpublished PhD thesis, Australian National University, 1997).

Willis, J. (1933), *The Parliamentary Powers of English Government Departments*, Harvard University Press, Cambridge Mass.

Willis, J. (1935), 'Three Approaches to Administrative Law: The Judicial, the Conceptual, and the Functional', *University of Toronto Law Journal*, vol. 1, p 53.

Willis, J. (1938), 'Statute Interpretation in a Nutshell' *Canadian Bar Review*, vol. 16, p 1.

Willis, J. (1939), 'Administrative Law and the *British North America Act*', *Harvard Law Review*, vol. 53, p 251.

Willis, J. (1968), 'The McRuer Report: Lawyers' Values and Civil Servants' Values', *University of Toronto Law Journal*, vol. 18, p 351.

Willis, J. (1979), *A History of Dalhousie Law School*, University of Toronto Press, Toronto.

Windeyer, The Rt Hon Sir V. (2nd ed. (rev), 1957), *Lectures on Legal History*, Law Book Co., Sydney.

Wisdom, J. (1964), *Philosophy and Psychoanalysis*, Oxford, Basil Blackwell.

Woolf, The Rt Hon Lord [1995], '*Droit Public* – English Style', *Public Law*, p 57.

Wyatt-Paine, W. (6th ed., 1920), *Maxwell on Interpretation of Statutes*, Sweet & Maxwell, London.

X Y Z (1930), 'Book Review: *The New Despotism*', *Political Quarterly*, vol. 1, 125.

Zines, L. (1964), 'Book Review', *Federal Law Review*, vol. 1, p 172.

Zines, L. (1969), 'Mr Justice Evatt and the Constitution', *Federal Law Review*, vol. 3, p 153.

Zines, L. (1991), *Constitutional Change in the Commonwealth*, Cambridge University Press.

Zines, L. (3rd ed. 1992), *The High Court and the Constitution*, Butterworths, Sydney.

Zines, L. (1996), 'Social Conflict and Constitutional Interpretation', *Monash University Law Review*, vol. 22, p 195.

Index